Mimbres Archaeology at the NAN Ranch Ruin

Mimbres Archaeology at the NAN Ranch Ruin

Harry J. Shafer

UNIVERSITY OF NEW MEXICO PRESS
ALBUQUERQUE

©2003 by the University of New Mexico Press
All rights reserved. Published 2003
Printed in the United States of America.
15 14 13 12 11 10 09   1 2 3 4 5 6 7

First paperbound printing, 2009
Paperbound ISBN: 978-0-8263-4712-1

    Library of Congress Cataloging-in-Publication Data
Shafer, Harry J.
    Mimbres : archaeology at the NAN Ranch Ruin /
        Harry J. Shafer.— 1st ed.
           p. cm.
Includes bibliographical references and index.
      ISBN 0-8263-2204-2 (CLOTH : ALK. PAPER)
1. NAN Ranch Site (N.M.)
2. Mimbres culture.
3. Indians of North America—New Mexico—Mimbres River Valley—Antiquities.
4. Excavations (Archaeology)—New Mexico—Mimbres River Valley.
5. Mimbres River Valley (N.M.)—Antiquities. I. Title.
  E99.M76 S53 2003
  978.9'692—dc21
                2003005011

Book design and type composition by Kathleen Sparkes
Body and display type are Minion family.
Body type set in Minion 10/13.

*To Margaret Ross Hinton
and the Hinton family
and the ancient Mimbreños*

Contents

Preface xiii

Chapter One: The World of the Mimbreños 1

Chapter Two: Mimbres Archaeology 11

Chapter Three: NAN Ruin Pithouse Communities 21

Chapter Four: Pithouse to Pueblo Transition: Late Three Circle Phase 40

Chapter Five: Classic Period Architecture and Space Use 55

Chapter Six: Classic Period Community and Social Organization 88

Chapter Seven: Foods and Subsistence 110

Chapter Eight: Mortuary Customs 135

Chapter Nine: Bioarchaeology of the Mimbres People 163

Chapter Ten: Mimbres Pottery 174

Chapter Eleven: Technologies and Crafts 194

Chapter Twelve: Lost Ancestors or Oracles of Power 210

Appendix I: Pottery Vessels from the NAN Ranch Ruin 224

Appendix II: Appendix Table 1, Pottery Vessel Data 256

Notes 263

References Cited 271

Index 287

List of Figures

PREFACE

P.1 Aerial view of the NAN Ranch Ruin / xiv
P.2 NAN Ranch Ruin site map / xv
P.3 C. B. and Burt Cosgrove, Jr., at the NAN Ranch Ruin in August 1926 / xvi

1.1 Location and extent of the Mimbres regional system / 1
1.2 Ceramic vessels collected by Jesse Fewkes / 2
1.3 View of the middle Mimbres Valley, showing the valley oasis surrounded by a desert landscape / 3
1.4 Clovis point recovered from a Late Pithouse period midden at the NAN Ranch Ruin / 5
1.5 Pottery vessel forms modeled after bottle gourd shapes / 7
1.6 Model of Mimbres population estimates using 0.3 percent annual growth rate / 8
1.7 Locations of large Mimbres towns / 9

2.1 View of the Cosgroves' excavations at the Swarts Ruin / 12
2.2 Regional archaeological cultures in the American Southwest / 13
2.3 Three Circle phase pithouse structure at the Old Town Ruin / 14
2.4 Condition of the NAN Ranch Ruin in June 1978 / 16
2.5 Mimbres River in early summer 1980 / 17
2.6 C. B. and Burt Cosgrove, Jr., and crew at the NAN Ranch Ruin in 1926 / 17

3.1 Schematic profile of a pithouse / 21
3.2 Y-Bar site map, showing visible pit structure depressions and the great kiva / 23
3.3 Reconstructed vessel forms from the Y-Bar site / 24
3.4 Pithouse courtyard cluster at the Old Town Ruin / 26
3.5 Pithouse villages at the NAN Ranch Ruin / 26
3.6 Plan of superimposed pithouse rooms 95, 97, 99, 100, and 105 at the NAN Ranch Ruin / 27
3.7 Georgetown phase room 105 at the NAN Ranch Ruin / 27
3.8 Floor plan of San Francisco phase room 95 at the NAN Ranch Ruin / 29
3.9 Plan map of San Francisco phase room 86 at the NAN Ranch Ruin / 30
3.10 Artifacts associated with burial 127 in room 86 at the NAN Ranch Ruin / 30
3.11 Possible courtyard cluster of Three Circle phase structures beneath the south room block at the NAN Ranch Ruin / 31
3.12 Plan of Three Circle phase room 83 at the NAN Ranch Ruin / 33
3.13 Photo of Three Circle phase room 102 at the NAN Ranch Ruin / 33
3.14 Plan of Three Circle phase great kiva room 52 at the NAN Ranch Ruin / 34
3.15 View of great kiva room 52 after excavation / 34
3.16 Traces of painted lines, possibly a serpent motif, on a plastered wall of great kiva room 52 / 35
3.17 Views of Three Circle phase round pit room 71 at the NAN Ranch Ruin / 36

4.1 Map of Late Three Circle phase village at the NAN Ranch Ruin / 41
4.2 Schematic profiles of a modified pithouse and sunken floor room / 42
4.3 Example of a Late Three Circle phase slab-lined hearth in room 80 at the NAN Ranch Ruin / 44

LIST OF FIGURES / ix

4.4 Suggested detail of ceiling hatchway for Late Three Circle phase room 91 at the NAN Ranch Ruin / 44

4.5 Plan of Late Three Circle/early Classic period room 89 at the NAN Ranch Ruin / 45

4.6 Schematic profile of rooms 102, 104, and 39 at the NAN Ranch Ruin / 46

4.7 Plan of Late Three Circle phase room 104 at the NAN Ranch Ruin, showing floor and subfloor features / 46

4.8 Plan of Late Three Circle phase granary room 51 at the NAN Ranch Ruin / 47

4.9 Late Three Circle/early Classic granary room 76 at the NAN Ranch Ruin, showing slabs beneath adobe floor / 48

4.10 Room 91 at the NAN Ranch Ruin, showing superposition of room 89 / 48

4.11 Plan map of room 91, showing floor and subfloor features / 49

4.12 Ashy deposits in southwest part of room 91, suggesting possible thermal features for steam / 49

4.13 Subfloor cache of a Mimbres redware jar containing 412 amethyst quartz crystals / 50

4.14 "Tlaloc" rock art figure overlooking the valley near the McSherry Ruin / 53

5.1 Excavations in the Classic period ruins of the south room block at the NAN Ranch Ruin / 55

5.2 Adobe mixing pit / 56

5.3 Room 55 south wall at the NAN Ranch Ruin, showing use of Sugarlump rhyolite in construction / 57

5.4 Wall fall from room 25 at the NAN Ranch Ruin / 58

5.5 Room 40 at the NAN Ranch Ruin after excavation, showing interior support posts / 58

5.6 Details of hearth construction in room 12 at the NAN Ranch Ruin / 59

5.7 Hearth and floor vault in room 29 at the NAN Ranch Ruin / 59

5.8 Air vent in the south wall of room 28 at the NAN Ranch Ruin / 62

5.9 Doors at the NAN Ranch Ruin / 63

5.10 Possible ladder rest in room 50 at the NAN Ranch Ruin / 63

5.11 Ceiling hatchway fall in room 47 at the NAN Ranch Ruin / 64

5.12 Corrugated storage jar beneath the floor of room 46 at the NAN Ranch Ruin / 64

5.13 Room 63/23 at the NAN Ranch Ruin, illustrating functional differences in room use through time / 65

5.14 Schematic profile of rooms 75/25 and 35/16 at the NAN Ranch Ruin, showing multiple floors and functional changes through time / 66

5.15 Walled bin in room 25B at the NAN Ranch Ruin / 66

5.16 Room 22 at the NAN Ranch Ruin, illustrating slab-line hearth, floor and wall patches / 67

5.17 Pit with sherds in the floor of room 22 / 67

5.18 Plan of room 22, showing the location of floor and subfloor features / 68

5.19 Floor plan of room 28 at the NAN Ranch Ruin, showing floor and subfloor features / 69

5.20 Hearth, vault, and ladder rest in room 12 at the NAN Ranch Ruin / 70

5.21 Graph showing mean number of burials per hearth type at the NAN Ranch Ruin / 70

5.22 Room 12 floor plan / 71

5.23 Schematic profile, floors above and below room 12 at the NAN Ranch Ruin / 71

5.24 Wall shelves (subfeature 18) in the west wall of room 12 at the NAN Ranch Ruin / 72

5.25 Room 29 floor plan at the NAN Ranch Ruin, showing location of floor features and burials / 73

5.26 East wall niche in room 29 / 73

5.27 Room 42 floor plan at the NAN Ranch Ruin / 74

5.28 Granary rooms 7 and 75A at the NAN Ranch Ruin / 75

5.29 Plan of large communal room 74 at the NAN Ranch Ruin / 77

5.30 Room 58 at the NAN Ranch Ruin, illustrating benches along the west, south, and north walls / 78

5.31 Photos of room 39 at the NAN Ranch Ruin / 78

5.32 Room 39, showing floor and subfloor features / 79

5.33 Ram's horn tenon on the floor of room 39 / 80

5.34 Plan of room 45 at the NAN Ranch Ruin, showing floor features / 81

5.35 Circular structure in the east room block courtyard at the NAN Ranch Ruin / 82

5.36 Profile showing multiple surfaces in the east plaza at the NAN Ranch Ruin / 83

5.37 Concentration of adobe-mixing pits in the east plaza at the NAN Ranch Ruin / 83

5.38 Circular roasting pit beneath room 8 at the NAN Ranch Ruin / 85

6.1 Rooms 92/93 suite at the NAN Ranch Ruin / 90

6.2 Plan of south room block at the NAN Ranch Ruin / 91

6.3 Cluster of Late Three Circle phase rooms beneath the south room block at the NAN Ranch Ruin / 92

6.4 Proposed five-stage construction sequence for the south room block at the NAN Ranch Ruin / 93

6.5 Site plan showing location of rooms at the NAN Ranch Ruin with floor vaults / 99

6.6 NAN Ranch Ruin room suites / 100

6.7 NAN Ranch Ruin room suites / 102

6.8 Plan of rooms 8/9/10 suite at the NAN Ranch Ruin / 104

6.9 Plan buried beneath room suite 9 / 106

6.10 Plan of Delk and NAN 15 ruins / 108

7.1 Check dams in the upper Rio de Arenas watershed / 113

7.2 Mimbres irrigation system in the Rio de Arenas valley / 114

7.3 Main ditch of the Gavilan Canyon rainfall irrigation system / 115

7.4 Map of the Gavilan Canyon rainfall irrigation system / 115

7.5 Photo of gap between the reservoir and main ditch to the Gavilan Canyon rainfall irrigation system / 116

7.6 Map of ditch and reservoir on the NAN Ranch Ruin terrace / 117

7.7 Photo of squash seeds from subfloor cache in room 41 at the NAN Ranch Ruin / 122

7.8 Frequency distributions of Style II and Style III hemispherical bowl volumes at the NAN Ranch Ruin / 125

7.9 Indice graphs showing fluctuating exploitation of jackrabbit, cottontail, artiodactyl, and gophers through time at the NAN Ranch Ruin / 128

7.10 Mimbres scenes depicting subsistence pursuits / 130

7.11 Cutting dates from the NAN Ranch Ruin in relation to rainfall patterns through time / 133

8.1 Early interpretations of Mimbres burial practices / 136

8.2 The Cosgroves' map of the Swarts Ruin, showing relative location of burials / 137

8.3 Worked sherds associated with burial 86 at the NAN Ranch Ruin / 151

8.4 Drawing of unfired Style I jars from burial 86 at the NAN Ranch Ruin / 152

8.5 NAN Ranch Ruin burial 175 cremation pit after excavation / 152

8.6 Plan of cremation cemetery in the east plaza at the NAN Ranch Ruin / 153

8.7 Four views of cremations at the NAN Ranch Ruin, showing variability / 154

8.8 NAN Ranch Ruin burial 170 and mortuary vessel in situ / 155

8.9 Textile impressions on inside of mortuary bowl from NAN Ranch Ruin burial 141 / 156

8.10 Stone cairn over burial 121 in room 41 at the NAN Ranch Ruin / 156

8.11 Stone effigy mortar from cairn above burial 154 and recycled metate with petroglyphs from burial 151 at the NAN Ranch Ruin / 157

8.12 Bird burial beneath the floor of room 82 at the NAN Ranch Ruin / 161

9.1 Examples of occipital lesions on infants from the NAN Ranch Ruin / 170

10.1 Pot-polishing stones, sherd scrapers, and a sherd paint palette from the NAN Ranch Ruin / 175

10.2 Warped Style III bowl with poorly applied paint / 176

10.3 Two views of paint on a Style III bowl smeared with a polishing stone / 176

10.4 Badly warped vessel that is possibly a kiln waster from pit feature 11-13 from the east plaza at the NAN Ranch Ruin / 177

10.5 Neutron activation analysis plots showing distribution of Mimbres Style III Black-on-white clusters and Mimbres Partially Corrugated, Mimbres Fully Corrugated, and Mimbres Style III Black-on-white / 179

10.6 Mimbres Black-on-white stylistic sequence arranged chronologically / 183

10.7 Mimbres plain and textured brownware sequence arranged chronologically / 185

10.8 Trade wares: El Paso Brownwares / 187

10.9 Trade wares: Cibola Whitewares / 187

10.10 Trade wares: Reserve and other smudged wares / 188

10.11 Trade wares: Hohokam and Chihuahua wares / 188

11.1 Projectile chronology at the NAN Ranch Ruin / 197

11.2 Manos and metate / 199

11.3 Cairn over NAN Ranch Ruin burial 88, consisting of a metate and four manos / 200

11.4 Three-quarter grooved greenstone axes / 200

11.5 Tcamahias / 201

11.6 Chipped stone knives / 201

11.7 Tubular stone pipes / 202

11.8 Palettes and quartz crystals / 202

11.9 Bone awls and pins / 203

11.10 Decorated bone awls and pins / 203

11.11 Spatulate tools of modified jackrabbit innominates / 204

11.12 Examples of textiles from the NAN Ranch Ruin / 204

11.13 Examples of jewelry from the NAN Ranch Ruin / 206

12.1 Proposed model of a Classic Mimbres kiva that re-creates their cosmology / 213

Appendix

A.1   Mimbres Redware, Style I, and early Style II Black-on-white / 224

A.2   Mimbres Style II Black-on-white / 225

A.3   Mimbres Style II Black-on-white / 226

A.4   Mimbres Style II Black-on-white / 227

A.5   Mimbres Style II to III, Style II jars and Style II variant / 228

A.6   Mimbres Style II to III and early Style III bowls / 229

A.7   Mimbres early Style III vessels / 230

A.8   Mimbres early Style III vessels / 231

A.9   Mimbres early Style III bowls and seed jars / 232

A.10 Mimbres early and middle Style III vessels / 233

A.11 Mimbres middle Style III vessels / 234

A.12 Mimbres middle Style III vessels / 235

A.13 Mimbres middle Style III vessels / 236

A.14 Mimbres middle and middle-late Style III vessels / 237

A.15 Mimbres middle and middle-late Style III vessels / 238

A.16 Mimbres middle and middle-late Style III vessels / 239

A.17 Mimbres middle-late Style III vessels / 240

A.18 Mimbres middle-late Style III vessels / 241

A.19 Mimbres late Style III / 242

A.20 Mimbres late Style III / 243

A.21 Mimbres late Style III / 244

A.22 Mimbres late Style III, Style III Polychrome and middle-late Style III flare-rim bowls / 245

A.23 Mimbres middle-late Style III flare-rim bowls and effigy jars / 246

A.24 Mimbres effigy vessels, Style III jars, and fully corrugated bowl / 247

A.25 Style III jars, Mimbres Style III white-slipped bowls / 248

A.26 Mimbres Style III white-slipped vessels and Mimbres plain brownware vessels / 249

A.27 Plain, neck-banded, and neck-corrugated vessels / 250

A.28 Three Circle Neck Corrugated pitchers and jars, textured brownware mugs, and Mimbres fully corrugated mugs / 251

A.29 Mimbres Fully Corrugated pitchers and mugs / 252

A.30 Mimbres Fully Corrugated and plain vessels / 253

A.31 Mimbres Partially Corrugated vessels / 254

A.32 Mimbres Partially Corrugated, composite corrugated/plain, and trade vessels / 255

List of Tables

1.1 Chronological scheme for the Mimbres area used in this book / 6

2.1 NAN Ranch Ruin tree-ring dates / 18

2.2 NAN Ranch Ruin archaeomagnetism dates / 19

2.3 NAN Ranch Ruin obsidian hydration dates / 20

3.1 Accelerator mass spectrometer (AMS) dates from great kiva room 52 at the NAN Ranch Ruin / 35

5.1 Room data for all excavated rooms and structures at the NAN Ranch Ruin / 60

6.1 Estimated number of deaths per household in the south room block at the NAN Ranch Ruin / 96

6.2 Projected death rate per generation/house life in the south room block at the NAN Ranch Ruin / 97

6.3 Inferred number of generations for each household in the south room block at the NAN Ranch Ruin / 97

7.1 Radiocarbon dates associated with the NAN Ranch Ruin ditch and reservoir / 118

7.2 Wild and domestic plants identified from the NAN Ranch Ruin and other Mimbres Valley sites / 119

7.3 Faunal remains from the NAN Ranch Ruin / 127

8.1 NAN Ranch Ruin burial data / 141

8.2 Burial type by phase / 146

8.3 Body position (all burials) / 147

8.4 Body orientation by phase / 148

8.5 Distribution of age categories by phase / 148

8.6 Distribution of sexed adults by phase / 149

8.7 Distribution of rock cairns over graves by phase / 149

8.8 Number of vessels per burial by phase / 150

8.9 Animal burials at the NAN Ranch Ruin / 160

9.1 Life tables / 164

9.2 Age and sex distribution of Classic Mimbres phase burials / 165

9.3 Child/women ratios / 167

9.4 Crude mortality rates / 167

9.5 Summary of dental disorders / 171

10.1 Listing of trade wares in the NAN Ranch Ruin collection by type and phase / 189

11.1 Distribution of modified jackrabbit innominates by room / 205

A.1 Pottery vessel data / 256

Preface

The purpose of this book is to present new interpretations about the rise and disappearance of the ancient Mimbres culture that once thrived in southwestern New Mexico from about A.D. 600 to 1140. This new information is based on two decades of extensive excavations and research at the NAN Ranch Ruin, a large Classic Mimbres pueblo site overlying a pithouse village in the Mimbres Valley. Changes that took place throughout the archaeological history trace a fascinating restructuring of Mimbres culture and society. The catalyst, as argued in this book, was the implementation of irrigation agriculture about A.D. 850 to 900. The social restructuring that accompanied the shift in subsistence technology resulted in a number of material changes, including substantive changes in architecture from pithouses to surface pueblos; the establishment of lineage-based residences and lineage cemeteries, and newly expressed ritual activity and symbolic behavior manifested in architecture, mortuary behavior, and decorated ceramics.

The NAN Ranch Ruin investigations have yielded the most comprehensive body of information ever gathered at a single Mimbres site. Synthesizing such an enormous database is a complex and time-consuming undertaking, but the task certainly proved worthwhile. Mimbres culture is no longer seen as just a culture whose architecture was a poor copy of the ancient Anasazi to the north but with pottery that was unrivaled in terms of its painted imagery and design. The Mimbres phenomenon was a regional fluorescence in its own right that drew upon resources and people from neighboring groups in the desert and mountains. Their culture developed out of a hunting and gathering and early agricultural tradition in the northern Mexican deserts and mountain foothills, beginning perhaps as early as 1500 B.C. This early preceramic agricultural tradition thrived for nearly 1,500 years in the desert plains and foothills of southwestern New Mexico before substantive changes occurred that began the Mogollon tradition in about A.D. 200. The Mogollon tradition is a regional cultural pattern that is distinguished from Hohokam and Anasazi regional traditions, based on differences in material culture. The Mimbres culture developed out of the Mogollon tradition.

The NAN Ranch Ruin is a large Mimbres site once composed of at least five clusters of rooms, each containing from two rooms to over 50 (Figures P.1, P.2). Situated on an ancient terrace of the Mimbres River, the surface architecture covers approximately 100 m east-west and 65 m north-south, or some 6,500 sq m. Lying beneath the ruin is a large pithouse village, which was ancestral to the pueblo. The site was named after the ranch cattle brand, NAN, by C. B. Cosgrove, who, with the help of his son, Burt Jr., in 1926[1] was among the first to excavate at the site (Figure P.3). The opportunity to carry out archaeological investigations at the NAN Ranch Ruin came with an invitation from Margaret Hinton and the Hinton family, owners of the Y-Bar NAN ranch. Their intent was for me to conduct scientific archaeological research on the property in conjunction with a Texas A&M University archaeological field school. Margaret was cognizant of the uniquely preserved Mimbres sites on the ranch and of the need for an in-depth archaeological study. She was also aware of the research conducted in the Mimbres Valley in the 1970s by the Mimbres Foundation and realized that similar archaeological research on the ranch might contribute important information to an understanding of Mimbres culture. But she was adamant that students at Texas A&M University and elsewhere participate in the research. The NAN Ranch Ruin was selected for research through a consensus of opinions by Margaret Hinton and the author because it afforded the opportunity for intensive investigations of a large, reasonably well-preserved Classic Mimbres site.

Archaeological method, theory, and technology have

P.1: Aerial view of the NAN Ranch Ruin.

grown immensely since the 1920s, when the last major excavations were conducted at Mimbres pueblo communities. New theoretical and technical tools applied to a careful study of a large Mimbres community promised to carry our understanding of how the Mimbres people organized their households and communities far beyond the knowledge gained from work carried out in the 1920s and 1930s. Research in the Mimbres River Valley in the 1970s by a team directed by Steven LeBlanc from the University of New Mexico Mimbres Foundation[2] laid the systematic groundwork for the NAN Ranch project. The Mimbres Foundation research refined the regional chronology, which had not been revised since Emil Haury's definitive work in the 1930s. But the field had changed significantly by the 1970s, with new approaches to studying the past. The Mimbres Foundation research was conducted in the "new archaeology" or processual paradigm, which emphasized the study of culture process and culture change and provided an excellent interpretive model around which we were able to frame our own research objectives. Our research initially began as a study of Mimbres ecology from the perspective of one large site but certainly grew beyond that. As the quality and diversity of our data accumulated from season to season, our research concerns expanded beyond those issues of technological organization that were central to archaeologists interested in studying culture change. Perhaps most importantly, careful excavations revealed temporal, stratigraphic, and contextual relationships in the material culture not seen before in Mimbres archaeology. All of these important research tools—chronology, technological organization, contextual analysis, exploring the role of symbolism and religion—were incorporated in our NAN Ranch Ruin research.

Excavations of the NAN Ranch Ruin were carried out under the author's direction by students and staff of the Texas A&M University summer archaeological field school from 1978 to 1989 and by Earthwatch volunteers. Other brief investigations were carried out in 1990, 1991, and 1996, with volunteer assistance of graduate students and former staff members. This project has yielded a detailed picture of the history and developmental changes during the span of time the Mimbres occupied this site.[3] We now have a much clearer picture of who the

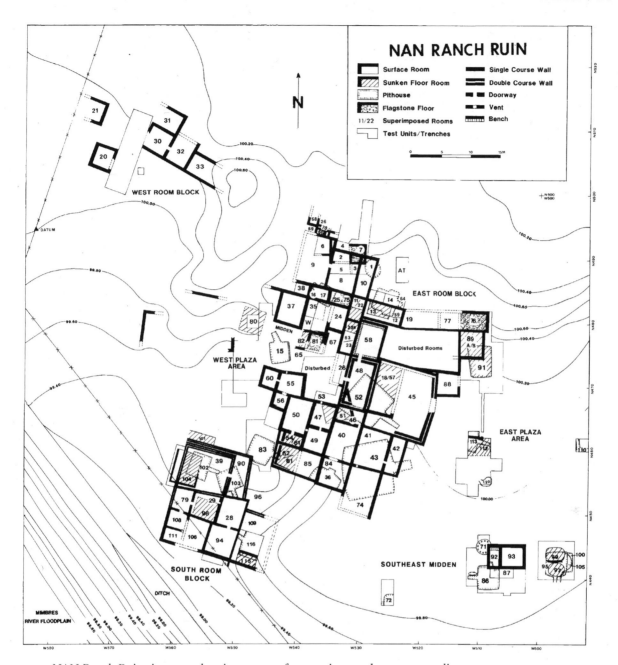

P.2: NAN Ranch Ruin site map, showing extent of excavations and structure outlines.

ancient Mimbreños were in relation to their neighbors to the north and east. The Mimbres Valley was one of the most densely populated areas of the American Southwest at the end of the eleventh century, and I will attempt to explain why this was so. This development flourished for a time, but by A.D. 1140 the valley was largely depopulated and most of the people had moved southward into northern Mexico, while others may have been absorbed into the regional cultures in the Rio Grande Valley. The new interpretations of the Mimbres culture trace the process of development of the NAN Ranch Ruin community from a pithouse village to a large Classic period pueblo settlement and final abandonment. Some of the best information available on the organization and

P.3: C. B. and Burt Cosgrove, Jr., at the NAN Ranch Ruin in August 1926 (photo courtesy of Carolyn O'Bagy Davis).

structure of large Classic period towns is provided by the NAN project findings. New information on the architecture provides insights into how Mimbres society was organized and structured. Changes in architecture, mortuary patterns, and material culture from the pithouse period, through the pithouse-pueblo transition, and into the pueblo period document a restructuring of Mimbres society from a pattern of residential mobility to a pattern of sedentary villages. The architecture was complexly dynamic and shows that the culture changed in relation to organizational changes in the Mimbres' subsistence technologies. Technological changes involved progression from dryland to irrigation farming between A.D. 650 and 1000 and the formation of corporate groups to construct and maintain the irrigation systems. Mimbres society was also becoming more settled during this period, shifting from residentially mobile to fully sedentary villages by the A.D. 900s. Within this milieu of change, social behaviors gave rise to patterning and elaboration in the material world that reached its zenith in the middle Classic Mimbres period, from about A.D. 1050 to 1110. The Mimbres pueblo phenomenon, which began about the mid–A.D. 900s, lasted nearly a century and a half (from about A.D. 950 to 1140). The material expression of social and ideological behaviors is revealed in the architecture, mortuary customs, and painted pottery. The distinctive Mimbres mortuary custom of placing many of the dead beneath floors of seemingly occupied rooms is explained within a context of the social organization, subsistence technology, and beliefs associated with ancestors and the powerful role they played in maintaining universal harmony and bringing rain. These explanations are presented within a framework or model of the Mimbres worldview, which expressed elements of their cosmology through symbolism. The model of Mimbres cosmology is based on the fundamental structure of American Indian beliefs and ethnographic sources, particularly their notion of a layered universe and how the living and dead may have coexisted within that universe.

Organization of the Book

Chapter 1 introduces the reader to the ancient Mimbreños and their world and places them geographically in space as well as in time in the Southwest landscape. Archaeological cultures are defined on the basis of material patterning that occurs at a definable period of time within a specific geographic area or region. Such is the case for the ancient Mimbreños. We know them only through their customs and beliefs as expressed in their material culture and not from the language(s) spoken or their physical characteristics.

The history of archaeological research in the Mimbres Valley is presented in chapter 2. The purpose of presenting a more comprehensive review of the archaeological history is to emphasize two major points: first, that the history of Mimbres research has been in part played out at the NAN Ranch Ruin, and second, that the development and directions of previous research affected the evolving research design in the Texas A&M University excavations at that site.

The story of the Mimbreños as told from the perspective at the NAN Ranch Ruin began with the first occupation at the site in the Late Pithouse period. Chapter 3 presents a description of the earliest pithouse villages in this part of the valley and traces the first 300 years of growth of the NAN community. Foundations for the eventual development of the Classic Mimbres community and society were laid during this period.

In chapter 4, the transition is traced from a community structured around clusters of pithouses of the Three Circle phase, beginning in about A.D. 750, to the first aboveground pueblo-style structures of the Late Three Circle phase, shortly after A.D. 900. Substantive changes in the organization of Mimbres society from families to lineages also occurred in the tenth century A.D. This reorganization may have involved the consolidation of dispersed lineage members into a common residential unit, as suggested by the first appearance of lineage cemeteries. I propose that the implementation of irrigation agriculture was the catalyst for these changes. Other material responses to the socioeconomic reorganization involved the rapid evolution of black-on-white pottery.

The zenith of Mimbres culture was reached in the Classic Mimbres period, from about A.D. 1010 to 1140. Chapter 5 describes Classic period architecture and space use. The dynamic changes seen in the growth and development of the architecture mirror the changes that were taking place in Mimbres culture and society. This chapter describes the organization of residential units and variability in room function and traces evolutionary growth in aggregated architectural units. Indoor space use revolved around habitation rooms or clusters of habitation rooms, corporate kivas, and attached common rooms such as storerooms, granaries, and civic-ceremonial rooms. Examples of each room type are described to illustrate defining features and characteristics of each. Outdoor space included roofs, courtyards, and plazas, indicating the range of activities that took place in these areas outside the dwellings.

In Chapter 6 I examine the patterns of social organization of the NAN community and define four tiers of complexity based on the architecture and internal features of rooms. The first tier is the habitation room, which formed the nuclear or extended family household. The second tier consisted of the extended or corporate household, formed by a cluster of habitation rooms sharing common rooms and space. The third tier was the aggregated room block, formed by clusters of corporate households, and the fourth tier consisted of the community as a whole, with its various corporate households and aggregated room blocks formed around courtyards and plazas. It is necessary to define household composition to understand community organization. A key ingredient in understanding and identifying lineage households was recognizing the subtleties in identifying corporate kivas, the core to lineage households, and lineage cemeteries. The consolidation of families and lineages into compact settlements created large Classic Mimbres communities. I argue that this consolidation was necessary for the organization and maintenance of the irrigation systems and sustained by food surpluses provided by the successful implementation of irrigation agriculture. The importance of maintaining lineal rights to agricultural lands is seen as a factor in the way households were organized and in the placement of lineage cemeteries in restricted areas within the community. The establishment of corporate groups is strongly hinted at by the occurrence of restricted-access corporate kivas in each lineage household and lineage or corporate cemeteries with restricted access.

Foods and subsistence patterns are discussed in chapter 7. The economic patterns of the early Mimbreños and their predecessors were based on hunting, gathering, and supplemental gardening following seasonal mobility. This pattern continued into the second half of the Mimbres sequence, albeit with gardening gradually assuming more economic importance, or until the Three Circle phase, when new agricultural opportunities emerged in the form of new varieties of corn. The subsistence emphasis shifted from a mixed economy of hunting, gathering, and gardening to a more agriculturally based economy that continued throughout the Classic Mimbres period.

The uniquely Mimbres mortuary behavior is presented in chapter 8. A common myth in southwestern lore is that the Mimbres buried the dead beneath the floors of their houses and placed inverted "killed" bowls over the heads. Like most myths, it holds only a grain of truth. Mimbres mortuary behavior was more varied and complex than previous scholars had presumed. Variability in placement of the dead evolved over time from exclusively extramural, or outdoors, to predominately intramural, or indoors. The burial placement and how a person was treated depended on who they were, who they were kin to, and where they died. The greatest variability occurred in the Late Three Circle phase transition and early Classic Mimbres period with the uses of intramural cemeteries, isolated outdoor, or extramural, burials, and a formal cremation cemetery. Additional variability is seen in mortuary accouterments in the presence or absence of mortuary vessels, numbers of mortuary vessels, placement of mortuary vessels, presence or absence of jewelry items, kinds of jewelry items, and presence or absence of rock cairns over the burials.

Basic mortuary data from the NAN Ranch Ruin is presented along with interpretations as to what the patterning may reveal about the structure and organization of Mimbres society.

Chapter 9 describes the bioarchaeology of the NAN Ranch Ruin skeletal population, summarizing the most comprehensive study ever undertaken of a Mimbres skeletal population. The physical characteristics of a population are affected by such factors as genetics, diet and hygiene, social behaviors, and belief systems. The overall success in providing basic health and nutrition to a population may be reflected in the mortality rates, growth and development, osteological studies, and dental evidence. This chapter summarizes the results of demographic, growth and development, dental, and osteological studies that provide information on various aspects of the population as a whole as well as comparisons between residentially segregated populations at the site. The issue of genetic affinity is also addressed in order to trace the ancestry or define the descendants of the NAN Ranch Ruin population.

Certain elements of Mimbres material culture are presented in chapters 10 and 11. Chapter 10 is a holistic discussion of Mimbres pottery. The technology, stylistic evolution, production, and functional roles and contexts of the pottery are all taken into consideration. Early on, Mimbres pottery served such secular roles as cooking, serving, and storage containers. Ritual roles are suggested by the initial appearance of red-slipped wares and later white-slipped wares. As Mimbres society became more complex and the roles served by the pottery more specific, forms and decorations evolved. The issue of production is also addressed in terms of who was making the pottery and where the potters may have lived. Neutron activation analysis has identified patterns in the production and movement of Mimbres pottery across the landscape. These production and distribution patterns provide some interesting insight into the behaviors related to this class of material culture. The most prolific period for the production of Mimbres painted pottery occurred in the last half of the eleventh century A.D., correlating with a time when food surpluses may have been the most abundant.

Chapter 11 highlights other material culture categories, such as stone, bone, textiles, and jewelry. Although the Mimbres are not known for their technologies other than ceramics, these material categories played essential roles in the Mimbres daily lives and social expressions. Stone was crucial to make tools for basic secular tasks, such as milling implements, cutting and piercing tools, and hunting weapons and as building material. The role of certain artifacts, such as grooved stone axes, may have been both highly functional and symbolic. Other items, such as tubular pipes, tcamahias, palettes, and jewelry, served in a variety of special social and ritual contexts. The Mimbres apparently had a rich and colorful fiber industry that produced various kinds of baskets, mats, nets, cordage, and clothing. Only carbonized or poorly preserved fragments and fossil casts of this class of material culture remain. Yet the sample of fiber artifacts from the NAN Ranch Ruin represents the largest extant sample from a Classic Mimbres site and is revealing in the kinds of fiber artifacts and technological traditions present. Shell was used exclusively for jewelry, but bone provided raw material for a variety of implements and ornaments, some used in daily tasks, others obviously items of embellishment.

In Chapter 12 I attempt to explore the meaning of the rich body of symbolism left by the ancient Mimbreños. The physical, social, and symbolic contexts of the expressions are used in an effort to understand their meaning. Why did the Mimbres produce the black-on-white pottery? Why did they place an inverted bowl with a "kill" hole over the head of many of the deceased? Why were some people buried outside the structures? What themes can we infer from the images on the pottery? Does the architecture reflect elements of structure in the Mimbres cosmos? My model for the rise and fall of the Mimbres phenomenon traces the evolution of Mimbres culture and society from families to corporate groups. The process is traced from dispersed groups of mobile gardeners residing seasonally in small pithouse villages in the Early Pithouse period to more sedentary pithouse dwellers growing increasingly dependent on agriculture in the Late Pithouse period. The incorporation of irrigation farming necessitated a full-time commitment to irrigation agriculture in the Late Three Circle phase transition and Classic Mimbres period. This shift in subsistence technology correlated with a restructuring of Mimbres society from a family-oriented subsistence and residence pattern to corporate enterprises structured around irrigation agriculture. The success of this new technology created periods of food surplus that set in motion a series of social and economic processes responsible for the material culture used to identify the Classic period phenomenon. These processes also led to a reorganization of

Mimbres social and residential patterns and the creation of large multiroom block towns. Climate change around the beginning of the twelfth century brought an end to the good times and to the infrastructure that supported the irrigation networks. The collapse of the social institutions that provided the contexts for the production of Classic Mimbres material culture, especially the painted pottery, brought an end to the Classic period. Family groups began to disperse and migrated to various areas of southern New Mexico and northern Mexico in the first decades of the twelfth century.

Acknowledgments

It all started with a phone call. Who would have ever imagined that when I answered the telephone in my office on that day in 1976, I would spend the rest of my career and 25 years of research at a Classic Mimbres site? Margaret Hinton invited me to bring an archaeological field school to the NAN Ranch to conduct archaeological investigations, specifically to investigate the relatively undisturbed NAN Ranch Ruin. Although such serendipity is not that uncommon in the sciences, that phone call changed my life and that of many students, staff, and volunteers who became involved in the project.

The NAN Ranch project and the completion of this book would not have been possible without the help and cooperation of many individuals. Foremost are the landowners: Margaret and Andy Hinton, Virginia Burford, and their families. In addition to their invitation to conduct archaeological investigations on the ranch, Margaret and Andy also graciously provided ranch facilities to the Texas A&M University Archaeological Field School, including buildings for the field kitchen, an office, a study, and a laboratory and housing facilities for the director. They also entertained us royally each Fourth of July, often with a country-and-western band. Field school students camped in the proximity of the ranch headquarters and enjoyed the benefit of the ambiance of the surroundings and swimming pool, even with the spring water temperature of 54 degrees. The people who really watched over our camp and looked after our field needs, however, were ranch foreman Harlie Cox and his wife, Linda. Harlie was always on the spot to backfill the season's excavations and to see that our camp needs and requests were met. At the same time, he managed a large working cattle ranch. We must have been a pain at times, but if we were, Harlie and Linda never revealed it to us. Everyone who participated in the project came to admire them and to appreciate their help and hard work ethic.

Harlie and Linda also invited me and my staff to attend the annual Father's Day Cowbells Association barbecues and socials, where we met and came to know many of the ranch families in the Mimbres area. Foremost among the local people who helped the project in one way or another were Terry and Blackie Oliver, Amanda Johnson, Mr. and Mrs. Forrest Delk, the late John and Mary Alice King, and Clint and Dee Johnson. Their combined knowledge and friendship is deeply appreciated.

Funding of the project came from several sources: the National Geographic Society; Earthwatch; the College of Liberal Arts, Office of University Research, and Scholarly Enhancement Program at Texas A&M University; the Texas Coordinating Board of Higher Education Advance Research Program; and private grants. Field school funding came from the Texas A&M University College of Liberal Arts, the Department of Anthropology, and the Federation of Aggie Mothers Clubs.

A number of colleagues and graduate students have consistently provided invaluable field and laboratory assistance and guidance during the course of the NAN Ranch project. Darrell Creel (1984–87, 1989) directed the NAN Ranch survey and excavations at NAN 15 (Pueblo Vingeroon) and NAN 20 (Gavilan Irrigation project). D. Gentry Steele was a constant confidant throughout the field phases and guided special studies and theses research in human osteology and faunal analysis. Other colleagues involved in the field research include Michael Waters, who supervised the geological studies, and Vaughn Bryant, who guided the ethnobotanical research; W. D. James supervised the neutron activation analyses, and David Carlson provided guidance in statistical studies. Kate Mulle-Wille served as a field codirector for two seasons (1981, 1982).

Graduate students, staff, and volunteers who served as field staff members include Anna J. Taylor (1978–82), Elaine Hughes (1978–82), Diane Young Holliday (1980–85), Marianne Marek (1981–87), Harold Drollinger (1984–87), Jean Christiansen (1979, 1980), Melissa Usrey (1979), Lain Ellis (1982–87, 1989), Karen Gardner (1986–87), Ann Shultz Creel (1981, 1984–85, 1987, 1989), Mollie Creech Meyers (1979–81), John Dockall (1986–87, 1989), Kelly Bedford (1987, 1989), Harold Chandler (1986–87, 1989, 1994), David and JoAnn Jordan (1984–87, 1989,

1994), Donald Jackman (1980, 1981), Jane Rathbun (1981), and Connie Judkins (1994). Undergraduate field assistants were Joe A. Shafer (1986) and Dallas Morris (1986). Others who contributed directly or indirectly to the field success were Brian Shaffer, Suzanne Wilson Patrick, Beth Ham, Damon Burden, and Robin Lyle. Each of these individuals played key roles in achieving project goals, maintaining discipline in the documentation, and sustaining the overall integrity of the research through their dedication.

I am also indebted to the staff at the New Mexico Office of Cultural Affairs, specifically Thomas Merlan, Daniel Reilley, Curtis Schaafsma, and the Cultural Properties Review committee, for providing the necessary permits to conduct archaeological excavations on private property.

The preparation of this book could not have been accomplished without the assistance of my students and colleagues. Most of the graphics were prepared by Jason Barrett, assisted by Damon Burden, Charlotte Donald, and Wayne Smith. Kay Tidemann helped prepare the appendix, provided the photograph for Figure 1.3, and assisted in the preparation of the tables. Dawn Alexander read and commented on earlier drafts of the chapters. Brian Shaffer and Karen Gardner provided the images for Figure 7.10, and Brian also provided images and information for Figures 1.2, 7.9, and 11.10. Diane Holliday provided the prints for Figure 9.1. Permission to use the images for Figure 1.2 was given by the Smithsonian Institution, and Peabody Museum at Harvard University gave permission to use the image for Figure 2.1. LaVerne Herrington, a native of Silver City, assisted in numerous ways, including providing moral support throughout the project and giving her permission to use the illustrations shown in Figures 7.2A and 7.2B from her unpublished dissertation. Charlotte Donald helped prepare the photographic images and burial data. Angie Shafer, Ashley Smallwood, and Victoria Springer assisted in the production of the tables. Holly Meier, Julie Gottshall, and W. D. James provided neutron activation data in the ceramic studies, and David Carlson gave overall support throughout the production of this book. Jerry Brody and Steve Lekson also had a little something to do with the book's publication. Finally, but certainly not the least, was the encouragement provided by my wife, Molly, and my family, Joe, Julie, Chris, Amy, and Jennifer. If I have overlooked anyone who came to my aid at anytime during the course of this project, I apologize, for I have not intended to do so.

CHAPTER ONE

The World of the Mimbreños

Introduction

The ancient Mimbreños lived at the NAN Ranch site along the Mimbres River in southwestern New Mexico from about A.D. 600 to 1140. The Mimbreños are well known in archaeological and art history circles for the naturalistic and geometric designs painted on their pottery. The Mimbres culture holds a certain fascination for those who have an interest in southwestern archaeology due to the artistic legacy of their painted pottery. This decorative style has no equal in the American Southwest: the stylistic images of the pottery symbolize and identify a unique cultural heritage.

Naturalistic images taken from Mimbres pottery have been incorporated into a multitude of modern items from T-shirts, ashtrays, pillows, and jewelry to community logos. Owing to the popularity and fascination of this ancient culture, one cannot enter a souvenir shop in the Southwest without seeing numerous modern items depicting Mimbreño designs and motifs. It is unfair to claim the pottery as the single distinguishing characteristic of these ancient people, however, because the story of why they painted the pottery is far more intriguing. This book is about Mimbres archaeology and presents new interpretations on the rise and fall of this ancient culture. It is not a site report, providing all of the data from our excavations—many more volumes would be needed to do that. I have included site data when necessary to support the interpretations presented, however. The book explores the cultural developments behind the ceramic tradition from the perspective of the NAN Ranch Ruin and how these developments may have affected regional dynamics.

The heartland of the ancient Mimbres culture and regional system was along the Mimbres River, which drains the mountain foothills and desert plains of southwestern New Mexico (Figure 1.1). *Mimbres* derives from

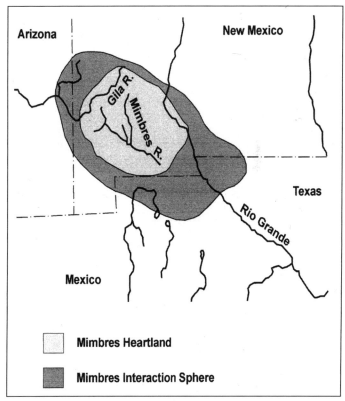

1.1: Location and extent of the Mimbres regional system.

the Spanish word for *willow*, which grow along the river. The Mimbres area extends across the Continental Divide to the upper Gila River, from Red Rock to the West Fork and across the Mimbres Mountains and Black Range to the western slopes of the Rio Grande Valley, from Radium Springs to the Palomas drainage.

The ancient Mimbreños have captivated the attention of archaeologists and art historians since the widespread recognition of their distinctive black-on-white pottery during the early part of this century. Bowls and jars

1.2: Ceramic vessels collected by Jesse Fewkes (photos courtesy of the Smithsonian Institution and Brian S. Shaffer).

painted with black designs on a white or gray background are the most conspicuous artifacts found among the earlier pueblo ruins in the American Southwest. Designs are characteristically geometric patterns, often balancing solid and hachure elements in design patterns repeated two, three, or four times around the vessels. In most respects the Mimbres followed this same pattern, with geometric designs on the interior of bowls and on the exterior of jars, but with one major departure from this mode. The Mimbres often added to the repertoire naturalistic designs of animals, humans, animal/humans, composite animals, and even plants or material items painted in the bottoms of the bowls or imaginatively interwoven in the fabric of geometric designs. Action scenes of daily life or ritual performances add a dimension to the subject matter not found anywhere else in the American Southwest and entice the imaginations of casual viewers of the pottery and scholars alike. The geometric designs are often exquisitely executed and complexly organized. By comparison, the naturalistic designs are done with equal graphic skill but portray simple figures in a distinctive folk style. This graphic expression of the Mimbres symbolic world serves only to heighten the level of intrigue about these people, much as the great Anasazi ruins stimulate the imaginations of tourists and archaeologists.

Local ranchers, military personnel, and townspeople knew of the Mimbres ruins as early as the late nineteenth century. By the end of the century, some were digging among the ruins in search of painted bowls. It soon became common knowledge among the locals that the pottery was usually placed over or near the heads of skeletons buried beneath the floors. To get to the pots, they dug through the overlying rooms. The systematic destruction of Mimbres archaeological sites had begun. One amateur collector, E. D. Osborne of Deming, New Mexico, sent drawings of the pottery to Jesse Fewkes at the Smithsonian Institution in 1913. Captivated by the uniqueness of the naturalistic designs, Fewkes visited Osborne six months later and conducted limited excavations at the Old Town Ruin, in the lower Mimbres River Valley. Fewkes purchased a collection of pottery from Osborne as well and produced the first publication describing the distinctive Mimbres pottery, highlighting the naturalistic Mimbres designs. The fascination with Mimbres imagery was born. Fewkes brought the picturesque Mimbres designs to the attention of the archaeological and museum communities[1] (Figure 1.2), which resulted in several major expeditions to the Mimbres Valley in the 1920s to amass large collections of pottery. Fewkes's purchase from Osborne, however, stimulated the collecting and commercial looting of pots to be sold on the antiquities market, a problem that unfortunately still plagues the region.

The Setting

The picturesque lands once occupied by the ancient Mimbreños in southwestern New Mexico incorporate parts of the Gila Wilderness, Mimbres Mountains, and grasslands of the Deming Plain. The northern part consists of mountainous volcanic uplands ranging from 7,500 to 10,000 ft, which form the Mogollon Plateau. Physiographically the area includes the Colorado Plateau transition to the north and the Basin and Range and Sierra Madre in Mexico to the south. The semiarid region displays considerable topographic relief, with elevation ranges from about 4,000 ft in the Deming Plain to over 10,000 ft in the northern uplands (Figure 1.3). The Continental Divide, Pinos Altos, and Diablo ranges

1.3: View of the middle Mimbres Valley, showing the valley oasis surrounded by a desert landscape (photo courtesy of Kay Tidemann).

separate the two major stream systems in the Mimbres area, the upper Gila and the Mimbres rivers. Both head in the Gila Wilderness, but only the waters of the Gila River, a tributary of the Colorado River, eventually empty into an ocean body, the Gulf of California. The Mimbres River drains into an interior desert bolson or basin south of Deming, New Mexico.

The Mimbres and upper Gila River valleys form the heartland of the Mimbres area. All large Mimbres towns were situated in the Transitional Zone south of the Mogollon Plateau from the mountain foothills to the edge of the upper Chihuahua grasslands, a zone that provided the preconditions for ancient farming: permanent water and a long growing season.[2] The lands between 4,000 and 6,000 ft, from the grasslands of the Chihuahuan Desert to the piñon-juniper parklands, was an optimal environment for agriculture.

The temperature and moisture ranges of the climate provided both opportunities and limitations to the socioeconomic options of the region's ancient inhabitants. Likewise, the distribution of such natural resources as soils, plants, minerals, and especially water provided a kind of circumscription on the location of settlements and material culture composition. Large Mimbres settlements occur only where permanent water could be found, spaced far enough apart in the Mimbres and Gila valleys to provide sufficient lands for irrigation for each settlement and a buffer between settlements for the harvesting of other resources.

The climate in the Mimbres region is semiarid, and both the climate and precipitation vary due to the wide range in elevation and uneven topography.[3] Average temperatures can vary from 60 degrees Fahrenheit in the southern part to 51 degrees in the higher elevations. Rainfall varies equally, from about 10 in in the southern part to 14 in in the mountains. Extremes recorded at Fort Bayard, New Mexico, show a record 37 in in 1905 and a century low of 5 in in 1951.[4] Monsoonal rains from July to early September provide much of the needed moisture, and even then one area may receive significant amounts of rain while only a few miles away, no rain falls. These extreme and unpredictable conditions that area ranchers face today were of equal concern to the ancient Mimbreños.

The Mimbres region is rich in mineral resources, as attested to by the long history of gold, silver, and copper mining. These metals, although important to our modern civilization, were of little use to the Mimbreños. More important to them was the wide variety of rocks created by the complex geological history and stratigraphy of this region due to a long history of extensive tectonic activity and volcanism. The oldest rocks, Precambrian schists, greenstone, and granites, are over 570 million years old. Paleozoic marine sediments that originated some 225 to 570 million years ago formed limestone, dolomite, shale, and sandstone. Late Cretaceous age rocks, formed during the Mesozoic era in the age of the dinosaurs 60 to 90 million years ago, include sandstone and shale. Extensive tectonic activity and volcanism occurred during the Tertiary period, 65 million years ago, and laid down many of the rock formations visible today across the landscape. The volcanic caldera that forms the Black Range was created during this time, along with the volcanic plug identified as Cooke's Peak and extensive formations of rhyolite, basalt, and associated pyroclastic rocks. Quaternary-age rocks that date from 2 to 3 million years ago to the present include conglomerates and sandstones. Through the natural processes of weathering and chemical action, the breakdown of these rocks provided the material constituents for soils throughout the region. Variations in soil chemistry, depth, and moisture created a mosaic landscape for the native plants. These rocks also provided the Mimbreños with material for construction, tools, and ornaments. Rhyolites, chalcedony, chert, and obsidian were used for stone tools, whereas certain minerals, such as turquoise, pyrite, mica, malachite, azurite, quartz crystals, talc or soapstone, schist, kaolin, iron oxide, and clays, were used for specific purposes to make paint, slip, ceramics, and jewelry.

The central Mimbres Valley lies on the border between the Upper and Lower Sonoran life zones. South of the NAN Ranch Ruin, the vegetation is dominated by grasslands with mesquite, creosote bush, acacia, and several species of desert succulents, including certain cacti and yuccas. In contrast to the desert, in the green belt along the Mimbres River Valley are found cottonwood, willow, ash, and walnut. In ancient times, common reeds also grew along the river's banks and in marshy areas.

The vegetation changes with elevation, and the grasslands of the Deming Plain and Lower Sonoran give way 5,000 ft above mean sea level (msl) to a mountain foothill parkland of oak and juniper. Succulents such as sotol, agave, cholla, yucca, and prickly pear cactus are found intermittently in this zone. Piñon pine occurs at a slightly higher elevation than the lowest juniper. The Transition zone that occurs from about 7,000 ft to 9,500 ft msl consists of ponderosa pine forest interspersed with grassy meadows. The Canadian Life zone is restricted to the slopes above 8,500 to 11,000 ft in the Mogollon, Mimbres, and Black Mountain ranges. Spruce and aspen are found on these high mountain slopes.[5]

Animals present in the Lower Sonoran life zone include jackrabbits, cottontails, rats and mice, prairie dogs, skunks, coatimundi, and squirrels. Various birds are also found, including the roadrunner, quail, doves, and hawks, and various reptiles, such as the diamondback rattlesnake. Pronghorn ranged in the grasslands, and whitetail deer could be found in the zone, ranging from the mountain slopes and upper valleys. The Upper Sonoran and Transition zones would have had all of these animals but in differing proportions. In addition, mule deer, elk, black bear and grizzly bear, wolf, mountain lion, mountain sheep, porcupine, and beaver inhabited or ranged into this zone.[6] Many of the birds and reptiles of the lower zone also lived here, with the addition of the golden eagle and the blacktail rattlesnake. All of these life zones are accessible to occupants in the middle Mimbres river valley and provided a wide range of plant and animal resources.

The Mimbreños

The ancient Mimbreños, like many cultures and civilizations in the past, were quite literally lost in time until discovered by archaeologists. No modern southwestern culture had any memory of or made any mythical reference to them as a people. They gained their archaeological identity through their pottery. It is appropriate, therefore, to identify the Mimbreños as the people who made exquisite black-on-white pottery. They were not the only people who used it, however. Mimbres pottery was obtained by neighboring groups, and the distribution of the pottery provides archaeologists with a means of identifying those groups within the Mimbres interaction sphere and the extent of the Mimbres regional system.

The Mimbres cultural system was part of and born out of a broader regional archaeological culture known as the Mogollon tradition, one of three broad regional cultural traditions in the Southwest prior to about A.D. 1200. The Anasazi and Hohokam were the other broad regional systems. The Mogollon area extended from the Mogollon Rim of east-central Arizona to the northern Chihuahuan Desert of far west Texas and northern Chihuahua, incorporating the Mogollon and Mimbres mountains and a series of block-faulted ranges in the Basin and Range province. Prior to A.D. 900 the Mogollon cultural tradition was characterized by pithouse villages and a brownware ceramic tradition. Separate regional expressions within this tradition were defined on the basis of house styles, locally developed painted pottery traditions, mortuary behavior, and overall differences in material culture. These regional developments include the Mimbres, Jornada, Cibola, San Simon, and Forestdale, among others.

To the north of the Mogollon area lies the Colorado Plateau. This arid landscape of deep canyons and high mesas contains the most impressive ancient ruins in the southwestern United States, preserved in such national monuments as Chaco Canyon, Mesa Verde, and Canyon de Chelly. The great Anasazi, or Ancestral Pueblo Chaco system, with its network of great houses and pueblos stretched from northwestern New Mexico to southwestern Colorado, southeastern Utah, and northeastern Arizona. Some of these great house communities were connected by roads, with major avenues leading to Chaco Canyon. The Chaco and Mimbres systems were coeval, but relatively little evidence exists of interaction between them, as shown by the lack of exchange in ceramics. Only rarely did Chaco system ceramics make their way into the Mimbres area.

The Hohokam cultural tradition lies to the west in Arizona, along the middle stretches of the Gila and Salt River valleys. These valleys contained networks of villages composed of shallow pit structures arranged around courtyards and sustained by extensive irrigation agriculture. Although the residential architecture of the pre–Classic period Hohokam, was not impressive (compared to the great Chaco ruins), the villages did contain ball courts and platform mounds, features not found elsewhere among the three regional systems.

The immediate ancestors of the Mimbreños lived in pithouse villages scattered throughout the region, perhaps as far back as 500 B.C. Before then, however, ancestral identities are much more obscure. Despite the uncertainty as to who the pithouse people were derived from and where they originated, archaeology does provide some clues. Prior to A.D. 200, the Mimbres Valley was not occupied on a permanent or semipermanent basis. During our survey of the NAN Ranch we found a mere trace of early and middle Archaic materials in the Mimbres Valley, but preceramic early agricultural villages do occur in the area. The main problem with identifying this crucial period in Mimbres chronology is that so little archaeological attention has been paid to either the early agricultural or the early pithouse settlements.

The earliest archaeological culture to appear in the American Southwest was that of the Ice Age hunters of the Clovis people, about 11,500 years ago. Artifacts of the Clovis culture, such as the Clovis spear point (Figure 1.4), are associated with mammoth bones and other now

1.4: Clovis point recovered from a Late Pithouse period midden at the NAN Ranch Ruin.

extinct large game animals. Drastic changes in the landscape and ecology followed the melting of the glaciers. Many of the large animal species living during the last ice age became extinct, including the mammoth, horse, camel, and large, straight-horn bison. Immigrant paleolithic hunters were likewise faced with extinction, and perhaps some did become extinct. Others, however, adapted to these changing conditions and became hunters and gatherers or, more precisely, gatherers with some hunting. These Clovis descendants at the end of the Ice Age sought out the optimal environments to sustain such a way of life through the beginning of the Archaic period. One such area was the Chihuahuan Desert.

Archaic people maintained a continuous and sustained presence in the Chihuahuan Desert from over 10,000 to 3,500 years ago, ranging from southern New Mexico and west Texas nearly to the Mexican Plateau. These seminomadic people lived off the land as bands of hunters and gatherers, moving from place to place. The desert supplied resources for all of their basic necessities—food, clothing, and shelter. Factors such as rainfall and seasonal changes largely dictated their movements.

Few noticeable changes occurred in their annual patterns until about 1500 B.C., when corn and squash were introduced from the interior of Mexico.[7] The first significant change seen in this early agricultural period from the preceding Archaic is the formation of pithouse villages across the southern Southwest. Two such villages have been archaeologically excavated in the Mimbres

TABLE 1.1. Chronological Scheme for the Mimbres Area Used in This Book

Date	Period	Phase	Painted Ceramics	Plain and Textured Ceramics
A.D. 1650–1880	Apache	Historic	None	Plainware
A.D. 1300–1450	Postclassic	Cliff	Salado Polychromes	Salado Red
A.D. 1200–1300	Postclassic	Black Mountain	El Paso Polychrome	Playas Red
A.D. 1110–1140	Classic	Terminal Classic	Late Style III B/W	Fully, partially corrugated
A.D. 1010–1110	Classic	Classic	Early, Middle Style III B/W	Fully, partially corrugated
A.D. 900–1010	Transitional	Late Three Circle	Style II B/W, Mimbres Red	Three Circle Neck Corrugated
A.D. 750–900	Late Pithouse	Three Circle	Style I B/W, Three Circle R/W	Three Circle Neck Corrugated
A.D. 650–750	Late Pithouse	San Francisco	Mogollon R/B, San Francisco Red	Alma Neck Banded
A.D. 550–650	Late Pithouse	Georgetown	Unnamed red slipped	Alma Plain
A.D. 200/400–550	Early Pithouse	Cumbre	Unnamed red slipped?	Alma Plain
1500 B.C.–A.D. 200/400	Early Agricultural	None designated	Preceramic	None
8000–1500 B.C.	Archaic	None designated	None	None
8000–8800 B.C.	Paleoindian	Folsom/Plano	None	None
8880–9500 B.C.	Paleoindian	Clovis	None	None

area: Wood Canyon and Forest Home.[8] The time span for these largely preceramic sites is from 895 B.C. to A.D. 350. Oval pit structures were found in the earlier components and round structures in the latter. Pit structures measured about 2.5 m in diameter and 15 to 20 cm deep with simple basin or rock-lined hearths. Bell-shaped storage pits were recorded at Wood Canyon. Both sites exhibited midden accumulations, indicating repeated seasonal occupation, as well as burials at Wood Canyon. Burial patterns, the earliest known for the Mimbres area, were flexed, with the dead placed in a supine position. The only accouterments were shell beads with certain burials. A red-tailed hawk burial was also found, indicating a rich body of symbolism that comes out in various material expressions later in time. Projectile points were all Cienega and San Pedro dart point types propelled by the spear thrower, or *atlatl*.

The introduction of domesticated corn and squash had an apparent impact on the way of life. Villages became more archaeologically visible with the construction of pithouses and midden accumulations, which resulted from more lengthy stays at one location. For reasons that are still unclear, ceramics were added to the material inventory in about A.D. 200 to 400. The addition of beans can be correlated with the first appearance of pottery since dried beans require soaking prior to consumption. This complement of storable vegetables allowed certain groups to stay in one place a little longer and make more intensive use of the resources immediately at hand. To be sure, as corn, beans, and squash increased in importance, a shift occurred in landscape use toward seeking out deeper, well-watered soils for cultivation. This shift in land use brought about changes in the settlement patterns of these early people. By about A.D. 200 to 400, seasonal pithouse villages had sprung up on the ridges and bluffs overlooking the Mimbres River. The first pottery was a well-made, thin, undecorated brownware. Vessel forms were modeled after the bottle gourd and included hemispherical bowls, neckless jars, and short-necked jars (Figure 1.5). These early pithouse villages initiated the long Mimbres sequence and ceramic tradition.

Population gradually increased through the pithouse period. Population increase and climate variables can be a stimulus for innovations within the inner workings of a culture in response to these potentially stressful factors. These innovations are more likely to involve food-getting technologies or population shifting in societies such as the ancient Mimbres. Substantive innovations such as changes in land use practices and organization of labor that would occur with a shift from dryland to irrigation farming could also require adjustments in the way the society was organized. When such major changes are adopted, they must be justified in regard to the people's worldview and traditional rituals. I believe these innovations toward the development of irrigation farming began to take by the Three Circle phase, if not somewhat earlier.

Development toward the Classic period took about 700 years. The Early Pithouse period culminated in the Georgetown phase, which represented a gradual shift in settlement location to the old terraces in the valley itself. This shift may have been associated with changes in agricultural strategies, but if so, they are difficult to recognize in the material culture. Change was gradual and slow at first but began to accelerate from about A.D. 650 to 700. During the San Francisco phase, the first substantive changes in architecture occurred with the shift from oval to subrectangular pithouses. Also, the first painted pottery began to be produced, and this phase marks the first placement of certain burials beneath the floor. These internments were infants unaccompanied with mortuary items. I believe these changes represent initial material responses to major adjustments in subsistence technologies and land use practices. Pithouses continued to change to more rectangular shapes during the early Three Circle phase, in about A.D. 800 to 850, when the first black-on-white pottery was produced. Certain adult females were now being buried beneath the floor along with certain infants and children.

Changes toward surface architecture began to take shape in the Late Three Circle phase, after A.D. 900. The accelerated pace of change during this time may have been brought about by a further increase in population (Figure 1.6), the introduction of a new variety of corn, and the expansion of irrigation agriculture. Some pit-

1.5: Pottery vessel forms modeled after bottle gourd shapes.

houses at the NAN Ranch Ruin were remodeled, and others were abandoned altogether and replaced by structures with freestanding walls. Pottery designs became more refined and complex, and certain houses became lineage shrines and contained family cemeteries beneath. Not all burials were placed under the house floors; a few individuals were buried outdoors, whereas others were cremated. At the NAN Ranch Ruin, cremated remains were buried in the east plaza either in pits marked by sherd concentrations or contained in vessels capped with bowls used as lids. Placing an inverted bowl with a "kill" hole at the head of a burial became a distinctively Mimbres pattern in the Late Three Circle phase and continued throughout the Classic period.

The scope of interaction with groups outside the Mimbres area may have increased, as suggested by the kinds of materials being exchanged. Villages in the Mimbres Valley and its tributaries were showing some signs of becoming organized into a regional system, with notable differences occurring between the Mimbres and Gila communities. Extraregional interaction also took on a different character than in previous times. More

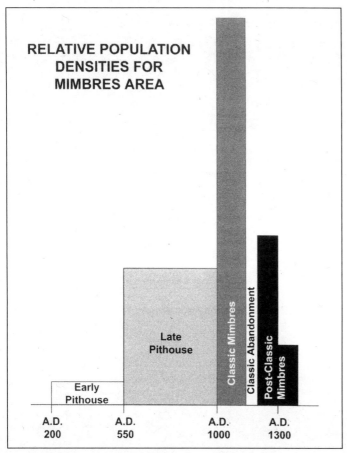

1.6: Model of Mimbres population estimates using 0.3 percent annual growth rate (from Blake et al. 1986).

exotic materials and concepts were beginning to appear. The origins for shell and other stylistic trends in certain material items such as palettes, stone bowls, and pottery designs presumably were the Hohokam area to the west,[9] where these items commonly occur. Shell artifacts were imported ready-made, but palettes and stones bowls were distinctively Mimbres in form and design. Mimbres Style II pottery is also found over a much wider geographic area, suggesting the Mimbres regional system was beginning to take shape.

This Hohokam flavor in certain Mimbres items may be due to the proximity of the Gila Mimbres populations to the Hohokam area downstream. Some archaeologists have speculated that the Gila Mimbres population density peaked in the A.D. 900s, with significant numbers drifting eastward into the already inhabited Mimbres Valley during the next century.[10] This intriguing notion is supported by three factors: large Mimbres towns in the upper Gila with surface architecture and Style II pottery, a significant decline in the population in the upper Gila during the Classic period, and a significant growth in the Mimbres Valley at this time (Figure 1.6). This proposed population shift could explain the rather rapid growth of such sites as Mattocks and NAN 15 after A.D. 1050, as well as the disappearance of Hohokam-inspired design motifs.

The Classic Mimbres phase marks the time when the move out of the pithouses was in essence complete: about A.D. 1000 or 1010. Aggregated residential units developed all over the Mimbres Valley, and some sites with multiple aggregated room blocks became large Mimbres towns. The larger towns developed in favorable locations near water and arable lands (Figure 1.7). Ceramics acquired the complicated geometrics and signatures in the naturalistic and geometric designs. Design styles changed every generation or so for the next 120 years. This artistic evolution of Mimbres painted pottery is presented in greater detail in a chapter 10. If the patterns at the NAN Ranch Ruin are characteristic, not all burials were placed beneath the floors. Approximately 10 percent were buried outside, and nine out of ten of these extramural burials were males. The practice of cremating a small percent of the dead also continued into the early Classic period but may have been abandoned in favor of extramural inhumations.

The apogee of the Classic Mimbres period at the NAN Ranch Ruin and throughout the Mimbres Valley was reached from about A.D. 1050 to 1110. After that time in the Terminal Classic period, signs of deterioration are evident in the architecture and ceramics. Clays used previously to bond the cobbles in wall construction were replaced by mud scraped up from fill in plazas and middens. Cobbles were often replaced by rhyolite slabs, perhaps to compensate the use of the poorer adobe mud. Habitation rooms became smaller, with walls and interior features less well constructed. Rules about framing the pottery designs, which were so standardized throughout the Mimbres region, began to be broken, and much greater variability is evident in the painted designs. Rooms or entire room suites were abandoned. By A.D. 1140, entire villages were depopulated or abandoned altogether. Whether the entire valley was abandoned by A.D. 1140 is a matter of debate, but certainly the bulk of the population had shifted and left the middle and upper valley vacant. The hallmark Classic Mimbres painted pottery ceased to be made.

The complex interplay within the infrastructure of the agricultural technology, including organization of labor and land rights, social structure and mechanisms of action, and ritual behavior, drastically changed in the early part of the twelfth century. With a breakdown in the subsistence technology for whatever reason and the supporting social and ideological mechanisms previously used to reinforce and justify technological organization, land rights ceased to be relevant. The diagnostic material culture associated with the technological, sociological, and ideological components of the infrastructure, such as the traditional cobble-adobe architecture, mortuary customs, and prestige ceramics, no longer existed. The disappearance of these diagnostic features in the archaeological landscape left archaeologists to wonder, What happened to the ancient Mimbreños?

I seriously doubt that the people we have labeled "Mimbreños" were, in truth, composed of a single homogenous population. The Mimbres may have been composed of a series of independent but related bands attracted to the oasislike environments along the Mimbres and upper Gila rivers. It may have become necessary for segments of these bands to work together through the construction and maintenance of irrigation networks and the sharing of a limited water supply. By adopting the infrastructure that constituted the Mimbres culture along with the diagnostic elements of ceremonies and beliefs, these people may have constituted a single ethnic entity composed of diverse groups from different areas. At least this is suggested by the way they dispersed into different regions, some to the south, others to the east of the Black Range, and perhaps still others to the Cibola area to the north. Certainly they shared a common religion and its associated material expression that left the indelible signature of "Mimbres."

The Mimbres Valley did not lie fallow for long.[11] By the early thirteenth century, desert farmers of the Black Mountain phase from the south and east moved into the lower and middle valley to reestablish claim to the arable lands and build adobe pueblos. There is some hint that at least some of these people were descendants of the former inhabitants: a vestigial inclusion of "killed" pottery vessels over the heads of some intramural interments. Also, burials were mostly placed in certain rooms, but we do not know enough about these sites to determine if these rooms were kivas. Painted pottery is dominated by the intrusive transitional, or Style II variant, of El Paso Polychrome.[12] Only culinary ceramics, Playas

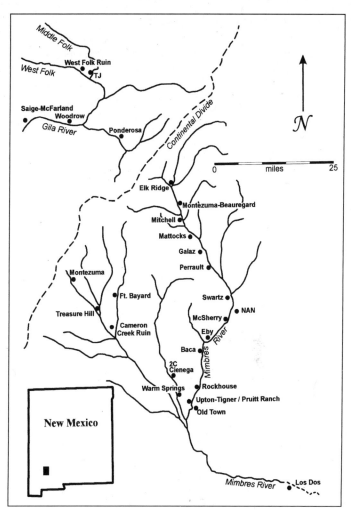

1.7: Locations of large Mimbres towns.

Red, were locally made; other imported pottery, such as St. Johns Polychrome and Reserve Filet Rim were imported from the Cibola region to the north, and Villa Ahumada and Ramos Polychromes were obtained from the Casas Grandes region to the south. Changes in mortuary customs were also evident: cremations dominated the pattern, although inhumations beneath floors also occurred, and some of these people continued the practice of placing a "killed" bowl about the head of the burial. Some of these Black Mountain phase pueblos were large, with an estimated hundred or more rooms. Most of these sites were not occupied for more than about two generations before they too were abandoned. Their short-term occupancy is suggested by the absence of thick midden deposits and large numbers of burials, which sharply contrast to Classic Mimbres pueblos. The process of moving in, building moderate- to large-size pueblos, and moving out in the Postclassic period continued for the next 200 years.

In late Postclassic times, about A.D. 1300, additional changes occurred. The interactions between the lower Mimbres Valley people and the Salado culture of Arizona became evident. Salado Red, Tucson Polychrome, Gila Polychrome, the late variant (or Style III) El Paso Polychrome, and Chihuahua polychromes were imported into the region. Playas Red continued to be locally produced. The mortuary custom of cremating the dead and placing the remains in plaza cemeteries was the dominant practice.[13] In Postclassic times, whole valleys in southern New Mexico were occupied for a short time, only to be abandoned and the people resettled in another valley. This process, termed short-term sedentism,[14] may represent an attempt to maintain an agricultural base in a region marked by highly fluctuating and unpredictable rainfall patterns. The agriculturalists abandoned the region by A.D. 1450, giving way to the Apaches, who migrated in and held the area until displaced in 1880 by U.S. expansion.

Spanish colonial exploration in New Mexico began with the arrival of Coronado in 1541. Permanent settlement was established in 1598 in the Rio Grande Valley, and missionary work among the Pueblo people was initiated shortly thereafter. The initial Spanish settlements skirted the Mimbres area, however, largely due to the Apache presence. But eventually Spanish, Mexican, and American miners discovered the rich mineral deposits in the region, including the famous Santa Rita copper deposits and silver deposits around Silver City, Pinos Altos, and Alma. The Apache wars, which began in 1837 with the massacre of Apaches at Santa Rita, continued off and on through the Mexican and early American occupation. The Apache presence, however, stymied Anglo development of the region, although Anglo mountain men, miners, and ranchers eventually pressured the U.S. government to do something about the situation. Famous Apache leaders such as Mangas Colorado, Cochise, Nana, and Geronimo made their presence known to those who ventured into the mountains. Following the Mexican war of 1846, a number of military forts were established to protect American interests, including Fort West in the Gila Valley, Fort Webster in the Mimbres Valley, Fort Bayard near Silver City, and Fort Cummings at Cooke's Springs near Cooke's Peak. The Butterfield stage line crossed the region from 1857 to 1861. Cochise surrendered in 1872, clearing the way for settlers. A brief return of the Apache, led by Geronimo after his escape from the reservation a few years later, was short-lived; Victorio was killed in Chihuahua in 1880 and Geronimo surrendered in 1886.

Archaeological explorations began in the area immediately after removal of the Apaches. Indeed, Adolph Bandelier, the first archaeologist to record Mimbres sites, came on the scene only a year after the battle of Gavilan Canyon and shortly after the Apaches had been driven from the area.[15] The history of archaeological work in the Mimbres region is the subject of the next chapter.

CHAPTER TWO
Mimbres Archaeology

Introduction

The archaeological discoveries that led to identifying the culture of the ancient Mimbreños were part of a cumulative process that involved the contributions of many people, both inside and outside the Mimbres area. As a result of these efforts archaeologists can work with a refined systematic classification, a detailed chronology, patterns in the material culture that serve to archaeologically identify the Mimbres, and knowledge of the geographic extent of ancient Mimbres material culture.

The history of Mimbres archaeology is characterized by sporadic periods of activity, with the most active periods in the 1920s and 1930s and again in the 1970s through the 1990s. The history of Mimbres research follows the general trend for southwestern archaeology as a whole, beginning with the early discoveries and pioneers such as Adolph Bandelier, Clement Webster, Jesse Fewkes, and Nels Nelson, who brought early awareness of the region's archaeology. As more archaeological activity across the Southwest generated new finds and filled in geographic gaps in the 1920s and 1930s, archaeologists progressed to a period of classifying and comparing artifacts and sites and defining regional cultural traditions and culture areas. One broad area label was the Puebloan Tradition of the American Southwest. Eventual awareness of differences across the Southwest by the 1930s resulted in the definition of three broad cultural regions: Anasazi, Hohokam, and Mogollon. The intensive archaeological activity in southwestern New Mexico in the 1920s and 1930s also served to define the Mimbres culture and its relative temporal or geographic extent.

Although Jesse Fewkes is credited with bringing the Mimbres to the attention of the archaeological profession, he was not the first archaeologist to explore the Mimbres area and record its ruins. Pioneer explorer-archaeologists Adolph Bandelier and Clement Webster were among the first to systematically record Mimbres ruins.[1] Bandelier spent several weeks in the Mimbres Valley in 1882–83, recording sites, making maps of ruins, and drawing pottery. One of the sites visited and mapped by Bandelier was on John Brockmann's property, which today is incorporated in the Y-Bar NAN Ranch.

A decade later, sometime between 1889 and 1892, Clement Webster, a geologist and amateur archaeologist, made several trips to the Mimbres region and investigated numerous sites in the valley.[2] Among the sites visited by Webster were the ruins on the Brockmann place as well as the site later known as the Swarts Ruin. Webster mapped part of the Swarts Ruin and excavated parts of three rooms, noting features and burials beneath the floors. Webster published some of his findings and deserves credit for presenting a rather mythical account of Mimbres burial practices.

The professional archaeological activity of Fewkes stimulated the already active plundering of sites by local and visiting collectors. Following the lead of Osborne, collectors soon learned they could profit from their digging, and with the growing popularity of Mimbres art, the market flourished. Even the Santa Fe railroad commissioned an artist to design a set of dinnerware based on Mimbres designs for serving their first-class passengers in the 1930s.

A flurry of archaeological activity focused on the Mimbres region during the 1920s.[3] Universities and museums in the Midwest and Southwest, such as the School of American Research at Santa Fe, Beloit College, the University of Minnesota, the University of Colorado, the Southwest Museum of Los Angeles, and the Peabody Museum of Archaeology and Ethnology, sponsored major excavations to explore the Mimbres pueblo ruins. These institutions carried out excavations of various scales at several large Mimbres sites to gain collections of Mimbres material culture, especially pottery. To

2.1: View of the Cosgroves' excavations at the Swarts Ruin (photo used with permission of the Peabody Museum, Harvard University).

underscore the primary purpose of these excavations, only two yielded substantive published contributions: those of the Peabody Museum and the School of American Research.[4] Unfortunately, digging into the ruins for recreational purposes and relic collecting became popular activities in the region, with some local relic hunters capitalizing on the expanding market for Mimbres pottery.

Not all local enthusiasts were bent on cashing in on their archaeological heritage. An avocational archaeology couple, Harriet and C. B. Cosgrove of Silver City, New Mexico, took measures to document and protect the rapidly disappearing Mimbres archaeology. Harriet and C. B. Cosgrove, a hardware merchant in Silver City, purchased a large ruin in the 1920s on the Rio de Arenas, a tributary of the Mimbres River between Silver City and Central (now Santa Clara), to protect it from looters. They named the site Treasure Hill and carried out limited excavations.[5] C. B. Cosgrove eventually quit his hardware business in Silver City and, accompanied by his wife and son, Burt Jr., sought professional training from leading archaeologists in the American Southwest, among them A. V. Kidder, the anointed father of Southwest archaeology[6] and excavator of Pecos Pueblo, and F. W. Hodge, who was excavating Hawikkuh at the time. Hawikkuh was one of the Zuni pueblos occupied at the time of Spanish contact.

Encouraged by Kidder, the Cosgroves leased the Swarts Ruin in the middle Mimbres Valley with the intention of conducting extensive excavations (Figure 2.1). These excavations were carried out with Kidder's support and were sponsored by the Peabody Museum at Harvard University. The Cosgroves spent four seasons from 1924 to 1927 clearing two large room blocks at the site, termed the "south house" and "north house." Explorations in the ruins also brought to light an underlying pithouse phase predating two superimposed layers of surface pueblo architecture. The pottery associated with the pithouses was similar black-on-white pottery, albeit with designs painted with bolder lines. These distinctions led the Cosgroves to establish the first systematic description of Mimbres pottery and to define Mimbres Boldface (which predominately occurred in the pithouse period) and Mimbres Classic Black-on-white. Analysis of the architecture, mortuary patterns, and subsistence at the Swarts Ruin provided a large body of information that allowed the Cosgroves to construct a model of Mimbres culture. Also in 1927, the Cosgroves carried out limited excavations at the NAN Ranch Ruin, about 3 km southeast of the Swarts Ruin.

The extensive archaeological work carried out in the 1920s firmly established the Mimbres as a major regional culture in the Southwest. None of this research, however, provided clear evidence as to the culture's origin: it was not until the following decade that the Mimbres' place in time and space was determined by Emil Haury.[7] In 1936, Haury excavated two large pithouse sites, Harris and Mogollon Villages, and used the information to define the Mogollon culture. Haury saw the Mogollon as a broad regional pattern separate from the Anasazi culture to the north and the Hohokam culture to the west (Figure 2.2). Harris Village was situated on a promontory near the town of Mimbres in the Mimbres River valley, and Mogollon Village was set on a mesa overlooking the San Francisco River north of Alma. Haury used material changes noted in the excavations and analyses at these two sites to define the Mogollon culture, as well as three temporal phases (Georgetown, San Francisco, and Three Circle) within its developmental continuum. Haury recognized that the Classic Mimbres phase represented a continuum from the Three Circle phase but hesitated to include it as Mogollon due to the similarity of the pueblo-style architecture to that of the Anasazi culture to the north.

A lull occurred in professional activity in the Mimbres area for the next 30 years. It was not until the 1970s that professional field work resumed with the survey in the Gila Wilderness by Donald Graybill[8] and limited excavations by James Fitting of Case Western Reserve University. Fitting carried out several seasons of field work in the Mimbres area, which included test excavations at several sites, such as Saige-McFarland, a large pithouse-pueblo ruin on the upper Gila River.[9] This research was especially significant since it suggested a dense local population in this part of the Mimbres area living in surface pueblos prior to the Classic period.[10] By the 1970s local collectors had begun to use mechanical equipment in their search for Mimbres pottery. This strip-mining procedure completely destroyed sites and left nothing for scientific investigations. It was partly this commercial destruction of Mimbres archaeology that stimulated Stephen LeBlanc to establish the Mimbres Foundation at the University of New Mexico and to carry out five years of field research that resulted in a redefinition of the Mimbres cultural sequence (Table 1.1). Of particular interest were under-

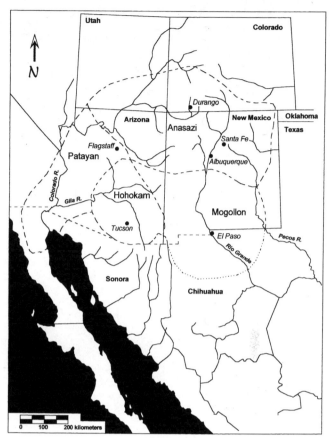

2.2: Regional archaeological cultures in the American Southwest.

standing the factors of population pressures on the landscape and finding explanations for why the Mimbres culture collapsed shortly after its apogee. To accomplish these goals, extensive surveys of the Mimbres River valley and limited excavations were carried out at sites in different environments that spanned the entire Mimbres sequence.[11] Among the important contributions made by the Mimbres Foundation were the refinement of the Mimbres chronology and development of models or interpretations of settlement and population changes through time that served as a basis for more intensive studies. Ecological studies by the Mimbres Foundation staff also provided a workable model suggesting that landscape degradation may have led to the collapse of the Classic Mimbres system.

From 1977 to 1979 the Amerind Foundation, under the direction of Charles Di Peso, conducted extensive excavations at Wind Mountain, a large Pithouse period site

2.3: Three Circle phase pithouse structure at the Old Town Ruin (LA1113) (photo courtesy of Darrell Creel).

overlain by a small Classic Mimbres ruin.[12] Di Peso excavated the entire site, exposing some 99 whole and fragmentary structures. His objective was to show that Wind Mountain was an economically important satellite community of Casas Grandes in Chihuahua, possibly established to exploit the rich mineral area near the site. Although the excavations failed to establish such a functional role for the site, an enormous amount of new data was provided on Three Circle phase architecture and associated features and artifacts. Di Peso's untimely death denied the archaeological community his full perspective on Wind Mountain, but the descriptive report produced by the Amerind Foundation presents the most complete information and view of a Three Circle phase village yet reported.

The next major project in the Mimbres area was Texas A&M University's investigations on the NAN Ranch, from 1978 through 1989, under the direction of the author, particularly the excavations at the NAN Ranch Ruin.[13] Surveys were conducted in the middle Mimbres Valley and Gavilan Canyon, and four additional sites, NAN 6, NAN 15 (Pueblo Vinegarroon), Y-Bar site, and Acequia Seca, were tested during the course of this research. Ancillary to the excavations was a detailed study of the rock art along the middle section of the Mimbres Valley.[14] The timing of the Mimbres Foundation research proved very important to our NAN Ranch project. We used the Mimbres Foundation findings and interpretations as the basis for interpreting our own discoveries, which are discussed in the next chapter.

The Old Town Ruin project, directed by Darrell Creel from the University of Texas at Austin,[15] was a direct spin-off of the NAN Ranch research. Originally this project was part of the work of Texas A&M University's Field School in 1989; one objective at Old Town was to provide an assessment plan for the Bureau of Land Management, Las Cruces office. Old Town is the site of some of Osborne's relic hunting that first attracted Fewkes's attention and was extensively ravaged by indiscriminate relic hunting and recreational activities. Creel's investigations have revealed that the site encompasses much more than just a Classic period ruin. A substantial Late Pithouse period village extends beyond the pueblo ruins, and a sequence of three great kivas at the edge of the pueblo largely escaped the ravages of the pot hunters (Figure 2.3). A large nearby Postclassic pueblo escaped much of the relic hunting as well. One of the surprises of Creel's work was the discovery of a prehistoric road leading into the large Classic community, reminiscent of the roads associated with the network of Chaco Canyon great houses and centers to the north. This road led to a great kiva constructed on the east side of the Classic period pueblo.

Another important contribution to Mimbres archaeology was Steve Lekson's report on the Saige McFarland site excavations conducted by James Fitting.[16] Lekson's descriptive report provides invaluable comparative information on the material patterns and is the most comprehensive study available on the upper Gila Mimbres. Lekson presents tantalizing notions about the early appearance of surface architecture in this valley, which he attributes to the Mangus phase, perhaps predating the developments in the Mimbres Valley.

On the eastern periphery of the Mimbres region is the research area of the Ladder Ranch project, directed by Margaret Nelson and Michelle Hegmon of Arizona State University. This long-term project has added research significant to our understanding of the geographic extent of the Mimbres culture east of the Black Range.[17] Situated along the Palomas, Seco, and Animas drainages, the researchers identified variations in the Mimbres settlement system that have not been seen in the more intensively occupied Mimbres Valley. Due to restrictions of water and arable lands, the population appears to have been more dispersed rather than concentrated in large towns. Important new information has also been gained on the Classic to Postclassic reorganization and transformation of Mimbreño society west of the Rio Grande. The Classic Mimbres settlements east of the Black Range include scattered residential and agricultural field houses and an occasional room block. This pattern is similar to that in the upper, mountainous reaches of the Mimbres and Gila rivers, as seen at the Lake Roberts Vista site, situated along an upper Gila tributary and excavated by Cynthia Bettison and Barbara Roth.[18]

The extensive amount of archaeological research carried out not only in the Mimbres area but in the adjoining Jornada area to the east within the past 30 years has helped to define the heartland of the ancient Mimbreños. The cultural center was the Mimbres Valley and its tributaries, where the greater population density arose during the Classic period. This population and settlement density in the Mimbres Valley in the Classic period, however, cannot be interpreted to mean that the populations were fixed on the landscape. Certainly one of the more significant findings of archaeological research has been indications of shifting populations from the Gila River valley to the Mimbres Valley, perhaps beginning as early as the Late Three Circle phase.[19] There are hints of groups moving about within the Mimbres Valley itself during the Classic period.[20] Interaction with the people in the Jornada area, especially during the Doña Ana phase, from about A.D. 1050 to 1120, is also well documented.[21] Doña Ana phase pithouse villages often contain substantial amounts of middle and late Mimbres Style III pottery. Despite the implied extent of interaction, the Jornada groups maintained their integrity and did not become a local manifestation of the Mimbres system.

NAN Ranch Ruin

Time has reduced to ruin this once thriving community, which lasted some 150 years and reached a population of perhaps 200 people, to an extensive rubble mound (Figure 2.4). The archaeologist's task of resurrecting an image of daily life in this community is accomplished by systematically excavating the site and analysis of a vast amount of information amassed over the years.

When we began our investigations at the NAN ruin in 1978, it appeared as a large, low mound of cobbles and adobe rubble partly obscured by scattered mesquite shrubs, sage, and succulent green tumbleweeds. The topography was dimpled with numerous holes from weekend pilfering of relic hunters in search of ancient skeletons with Mimbres bowls. The rubble mound was some 100 m long and 65 m wide, covering some 6,500 sq m. Traces of walls could be detected in a few places from the pattern of cobbles used in the construction.

The site is on the southwest part of a 5-hectare segment of the second (T-2) terrace on the east side of the Mimbres River. The site is about 5 m above the current river channel and 2.5 m above the first (T-1) terrace to the south. The ruins are partially buried by an alluvial fan emanating from an arroyo that drained part of the uplands to the east.

This setting must have been particularly attractive to the ancient Mimbres. In 1846 Lieutenant Emory of the U.S. Army described the Mimbres Valley as a truly

2.4: Condition of the NAN Ranch Ruin in June 1978.

beautiful valley of rich, fertile soil with a dense forest of cottonwood, walnut, and ash. He described the river as being 15 feet wide, three feet deep, and filled with trout.[22] Decades of mining in the upper part of the valley in the latter half of the nineteenth century, however, led to deforestation for fuel to supply the mines. The effects of the mining irreversibly changed the river's ecology from the time when the Mimbreños first settled its valley.

From the vantage of the NAN Ruin, the valley wall frames the terrace to the east; the east edge of an eroded segment of the Deming Plain extends east a few miles to Cooke's Range and Cooke's Peak. Cooke's Peak is a volcanic plug that forms a prominent feature on the landscape (Figure 1.3). The narrow valley is abruptly defined on the west by the foothills of the Cobre Mountains. In the distance to the north is the Black Range, an ancient Tertiary age volcanic caldera, or collapsed crater. Ash flows from this and other volcanoes were major events that created the formations that dominate the present landscape and formed the local rocks and minerals.

The river flows generally southeast and turns southward in the middle part of the valley, eventually emptying into a desert bolson or basin in the Deming Plain, south of Deming, New Mexico. The river channel today is clearly marked by the giant cottonwoods, ash, willows, and elms that shroud its banks (Figure 1.3). The topography of the Deming Plain, a broad, arid grassland, is broken by block-faulted mountains. These small ranges are part of the Basin and Range physiographic province, which stretches from west Texas to southern California.

Today the Mimbres River flows erratically. At times, it is a clear, cold mountain stream (Figure 2.5); modern irrigation may reduce it to a trickling stream in the spring or a totally underground flow during the late spring and early summer months. Only the summer monsoon rains fill its banks again with rushing brown water. These modern stream characteristics certainly do not mirror the more stable and predictable patterns of the river in prehistory.

History of Investigations

The NAN Ranch Ruin, or LA2465 (also reported as the NAN, Hinton Ruin, or LA15049), had been known for nearly a century when we began our investigations in 1978. The NAN Ruin was one of the sites visited and sketched by Adolph Bandelier. Bandelier spent several days in the winter of 1882–83 with the landowner, Mr. John Brockmann,[23] a year and a half after Chief Nana's

Apache band routed a contingent of U.S. Army and local miners in nearby Gavilan Canyon.[24] Bandelier did not excavate at the site, but he did provide a sketch map and several interesting observations, including a description of an enigmatic structure, which he called a reservoir, east of the main ruin.

Clement Webster also investigated the site, sometime between 1889 and 1892. Webster described a rubble mound and what he believed to be the ruins of a terraced, two-story structure. This rubble mound is likely the south room block defined by the Texas A&M University team. Another pioneer southwestern archaeologist, Jesse Fewkes, mentioned the site and noted the general condition of the ruins, but he did not carry out excavations.

Prior to 1978, the only recorded systematic excavations at the site were those of Harriet and C. B. Cosgrove of Silver City, who conducted limited excavations at the ruin in 1926 (Figure 2.6). A single page of notes and brief references in their report of the Swarts Ruin excavations describe the extent of their work at the NAN Ranch Ruin and their findings. According to their field notes, they excavated nine rooms and found 53 burials and 50 pottery vessels. Four of the rooms were described as "early rooms," and five were "late rooms"—one of the late rooms had some 40 burials beneath the floor. The pottery vessels and jewelry recovered from the burials were deposited at the Peabody Museum at Harvard University, along with the Swarts Ruin collections. No map is included with the notes, nor was one filed with their field records or pottery vessels at the Peabody Museum. An area in the northeastern part of the east room block, labeled disturbed rooms in Figure P.2, has been identified by local informants and from photographs taken by the Cosgroves as the location of the Cosgroves' work. The east room block was systematically excavated by Texas A&M University, and the area of disturbance fits the general description of the Cosgroves' excavations.

From 1930 to the 1970s, the site was subjected to intermittent, unscientific digging by various people in search of pottery vessels. One local relic collector claimed to have dug "58 rooms" at the site; much of his work seems to have been limited to the west room block, where partial looting of rooms appeared to be more systematic. At least two rooms (48 and 58) were excavated in the east room block by the late Virginia Wunder, an avocational archaeologist from Alamogordo, New Mexico. Other individuals conducted weekend excavations at the site between the 1920s and the 1960s. According to the late

2.5: Mimbres River in early summer 1980.

2.6: C. B. and Burt Cosgrove, Jr., and crew at the NAN Ranch Ruin in 1926 (photo courtesy of Carolyn O'Bagy Davis).

Colonel Burt Cosgrove, Jr., recreational pot hunting had occurred at the site prior to their work in 1926.[25] No record of the excavators or the findings from these earlier digs was made; only the remaining indiscriminate holes bear testimony to the destruction of the features and burials in the search for pottery.

Despite the extent of the damage done to the ruin over the years, surprisingly, much of the site remained intact. Entire room clusters in the east room block were largely undisturbed, and the south room block completely escaped the relic hunters' shovels. The relic hunters also

TABLE 2.1. NAN Ranch Ruin Tree-Ring Dates

Prov.	TRL No.	Field No.	Species	Date	Prov.	TRL No.	Field No.	Species	Date
Room 46	NAN-12	3-105	PP	1080vv	Room 29	NAN-126	8-967	PNN	1085+v
Room 41	NAN-29	2-580	DF	1107r	Room 29	NAN-121	8-963	PNN	1086+r
Room 9	NAN-36	3-353	PP	1071r	Room 29	NAN-123	8-966	PNN	1086+r
Room 9	NAN-37	3-356	PP	1071r	Room 29	NAN-124	8-1369	PNN	1086+r
Room 18	NAN-47	23-Apr	PP	1068vv	Room 29	NAN-135	8-1403	PNN	1086+r
Room 45/52	NAN-48	Apr-34	PP	1066vv	Room 29	NAN-134	8-1379	PNN	1088+r
Room 49	NAN-54	Apr-40	PP	1103v	Room 28	NAN-142	8-545	PNN	1109r
Room 49	NAN-52	Apr-36	DF	1108v	Room 79	NAN-148	9-772	DF	1060vv
Room 63	NAN-88	5-506	PNN	1064r	Room 79	NAN-147	9-772	PNN	1079+v
Room 11	MAM-89	5-114	PP	1041r	Room 94	NAN-149	9-705	DF	1098+vv
Room 11	NAN-90	5-510	PP	1087vv	Room 94	NAN-150	9-713	PNN	1098+r
Room 35	NAN-92	5-1429	PNN	1099+vv	Room 94	NAN-151	9-731	PP	1109v
Room 25	NAN-93	5-959	PNN	1098+r	Room 94	NAN-157	10-231	DF	1091vv
Room 25	NAN-94	5-942	PNN	1096vv	Room 109	NAN-165	10-726	PNN	1096vv
Room 25	NAN-95	5-944	PNN	1096vv	Room 109	NAN-168	10-826	PNN	1111vv
Room 25	NAN-96	5-967	PNN	1099+r	Room 109	NAN-162	10-830	PNN	1112vv
Room 25	NAN-97	5-946	PNN	1098+r	Room 109	NAN-159	10-699	PNN	1113v
Room 84	NAN-107	6-567	PNN	1128v	Room 109	NAN-163	10-820	PNN	1113v
Room 85	NAN-108	6-455	PNN	1073r	Room 109	NAN-163	10-927	PNN	1114r
Room 63	NAN-88	5-506	PNN	1064r	Room 25A	NAN-179	5-947(25)	PNN	1098v
Room 63	NAN-109	5-508	PNN	1062vv	Room 52	NAN-182	4-510/52	PNN	0859vv
Room 58	NAN-110	4-894	PNN	1105vv	Room 94	NAN-183	9-883(94)	PNN	1105vv
Room 76	NAN-139	8-606	PNN	1008r	Room 8	NAN-185	AF8SF1-2	PNN	1050vv
Room 76	NAN-140	8-607	PNN	1008+r	Room 8	NAN-186	AF8SF1-2	PNN	1065vv
Room 29	NAN-118	8-1108	PNN	1066r	Room 40	NAN-187	D1F1-1	PNN	1101+vv
Room 29	NAN-119	8-1106	PNN	1066r					

TRL = Tree Ring Laboratory number; field number represents NAN project reference; species: PP = ponderosa pine; DF = Douglas fir; PNN = piñon pine; date affixes: r: outside or ring date; +r, v, +v, vv, +vv indicate dates in order of decreasing confidence.

did not damage the pithouse settlement or the outdoor areas. Their focus was on the most visible parts of the surface ruin.

Prior to excavation in 1978, both horizontal and vertical data points were established for the site. A metric grid system oriented to the magnetic north was superimposed over the site. A vertical datum point arbitrarily set at 100.00 m and a secondary vertical data point of 99.77 m were established. All vertical elevations were taken from these vertical data points during the subsequent years of excavations. Although all excavations were keyed to these reference points, excavation

TABLE 2.2. NAN Ranch Ruin Archaeomagnetism Dates

Lab #	Sample #	Provenience	95% CL	63% CL	Best Fit Interval
ASMNR8	81#1	Room 12 hearth	A.D. 710–1050, 1100–1324		A.D. 990–1050
ASMNR9	81#2	Rm52 wall plaster	A.D. 660–720, 740–860	A.D. 810–860	A.D. 810–860
ASMNR8	82#1	Rm 64, U3, SF3-2	A.D. 700–1070 1190–1450		A.D. 920–1020
ASMNR9	82#2	Rm25 hearth SF2	A.D. 100–1050 1100–1150		A.D. 1000–1070
ASMNR10	82#3	Rm52 wall plaster	A.D. 700–990		A.D. 700–800
LA15049-1	F87#5	B175 cremation pit	A.D. 710–775 840–900		A.D. 840–900
LA15049-2	F87#5	B175 cremation pit	A.D. 700–920		A.D. 700–920
LA15049-3	87#3	Rm 102 wall plaster	A.D. 675–750 840–940		A.D. 840–940
LA15049-7	89#7	Rm 113 wall plaster	A.D. 675–710 900–925		A.D. 900–925

ASM: Arizona State Museum, Museum Laboratory. LA15049: Colorado State University Laboratory.

strategies varied depending on the goals or scale of the sample. Excavations were conducted in metric units of 2 m by 2 m, 1 m by 1 m, and 1 m by 2 m, depending on the specific intentions of the sampling, or within defined rooms. When walls were encountered in the excavations, the room or rooms involved were defined. Once rooms were outlined, they were often divided into four quadrants for excavation; smaller rooms were divided in half. Room excavations followed natural levels (e.g., room fill, wall fall, roof fall, below roof fall to floor, between floors, and below floor). Features and artifacts within rooms were recorded on plan maps keyed to the grid system. Metric units outside of architectural units, for example, in midden deposits, were excavated in arbitrary 10-cm or 20-cm levels, depending on the goal of the sampling strategy, unless adobe surfaces, adobe floors, or other distinguishable stratigraphic breaks were encountered.

All fill excavated from undisturbed deposits was screened through one-fourth-inch mesh. Fine screen sampling was selectively used when the situation dictated, such as in the excavation of the cremation cemetery in the east plaza, as was flotation for charred botanical remains and small faunal elements, to obtain quantitative samples.

Since the NAN Ranch Ruin is on private property, ownership of the excavated collection remains in the hands of the landowner. The entire collection is on an extended loan to Texas A&M University, where the collection and all field notes and records are currently housed. The owner continues to make the collection available to researchers for scientific study.

The NAN Ruin investigations have identified patterning in the architecture, mortuary behavior, ceramics styles, and subsistence technologies not previously recognized in Mimbres archaeology. None of these patterns would have had much meaning without the benefit of various dating methods. Stratigraphy, superposition, and stylistic seriation all provided relative means of dating structures, features, and artifact styles. Tree-ring, archaeomagnetism, obsidian hydration, and radiocarbon studies provided chronometric measures of time, which allowed us to give calendar dates to cultural phases and structural events. Tables 2.1 through 2.3 provide listings of all tree-ring (Table 2.1), archaeomagnetism (Table 2.2), and obsidian hydration (Table 2.3)

TABLE 2.3. NAN Ranch Ruin Obsidian Hydration Dates

AHC #88-	Provenience	Source	Rim width (um)	S.D.	Date	S.D.
812	Rm 39, FS574	Mule	2.58	0.04	A.D. 1063	30
813	Fl 39-103, FS977	Gwynn	2.73	0.06	A.D. 831	52
814	Fl 39-103, FS977	Gwynn	4.14	0.04	A.D. 673 B.C.	52
815	Fl 104-102, FS1397	Gwynn	2.56	0.06	A.D. 970	40
816	Rm 103, Fl.1-2	Gwynn	4.82	0.08	1619 B.C.	121
817	Rm 103, Fl.1-2	Mule	3.19	0.05	A.D. 620	92
818	Rm 39, FS420	Gwynn	2.73	0.06	A.D. 831	52
819	Fl 39-104, FS979	Gwynn	2.34	0.06	A.D. 1138	44
820	Fl 39-104, FS979	Gwynn	2.59	0.05	A.D. 947	41
821	Fl 39-104, FS979	Gwynn	4.79	0.08	1574 B.C.	120

AHC# = Archaeological & Historical Consultants, Inc., laboratory number; Source: Mule = Mule Creek; Gwynn = Gwynn Canyon. Gwynn Canyon and Mule Creek obsidian sources are approximately 60 km north and northwest, respectively, from the" NAN Ranch Ruin.

dates obtained for the site. Radiocarbon dates proved useless for the precision required at the NAN Ranch Ruin, with the exception of the NAN irrigation ditch. Radiocarbon dates used to assess the age of this feature are discussed in chapter 7. Dating allowed us to define patterns in the material record at specific points in time and through time. Awareness of these patterns has allowed researchers to reevaluate information from previous investigations and to raise our understanding of the ancient Mimbreños to a new level.

The following chapter begins the Mimbres story of the NAN Ranch Ruin with a look at the initial occupation and way of life during the early part of the Late Pithouse period, from about A.D. 600 to 650.

CHAPTER THREE
NAN Ruin Pithouse Communities

Introduction

The first people to settle on the site of the NAN Ruin lived in pithouses (Figure 3.1). Beginning with only a few separate houses, this settlement grew into a large community that eventually became the pueblo settlement of the Classic period. Clearly the pithouse dwellers were the ancestors of the people who lived in the pueblos; however, from the time of initial settlement to the time the pueblos were built, significant changes occurred in both the community and lifeway of its inhabitants. The differences were more of degree than of kind since there is a clear continuity of occupation and material traditions from the time the first village was established to when the surface ruin was abandoned.

This pattern of ancestral pithouse villages beneath Classic Mimbres towns is duplicated at all major Mimbres sites that have been excavated by archaeologists: Old Town, NAN, Swarts, Galaz, Mattocks, Cameron Creek, and Saige-McFarland. Such long-term fixed residence would require some kind of tethering factor, such as well-watered arable farmland. This tie began in the Georgetown phase.

The continuity of occupation at the NAN Ranch Ruin is shown by the repair and rebuilding within the settlement through time and the gradual evolution in the material and symbolic expressions of these people's beliefs. This kind of continuity indicates that a lineal sequence of generations, probably originating from the initial settlement, lived at the site for nearly 550 years. Cultural changes were slow in the Georgetown and San Francisco phases but became more frequent in the Three Circle phase.

The first community established at the NAN Ruin was during the period of round pithouses. This early settlement began in about A.D. 600 and became the foundation for a sequence of expanding and changing communities. To discover the earlier houses, we had to start from the surface and literally work back in time. Since the same space was used for later construction by

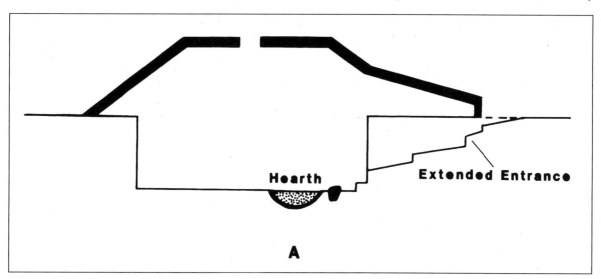

3.1: Schematic profile of a pithouse.

generations of inhabitants, earlier houses became buried or partially destroyed beneath later structures.

An estimated 75 to 100 pithouses (also called pit rooms) lie beneath the pueblo rubble and plazas at the NAN Ranch Ruin. These rooms cover an occupation span of about 400 years. Excavations in the pithouse community document the changes through time described briefly in chapter 1. What similarities and differences were there between the pithouse dwellers and their pueblo descendants? I will attempt to answer this question by summarizing the characteristics for each phase and how they changed through time.

Findings from the excavations in some of these pithouses provide a subtle contrast to the patterns of living seen in the later pueblo community. Both the pithouse and pueblo communities reveal a basic agricultural subsistence emphasizing the three major native North American domesticates: corn, beans, and squash. Permanent structures are found in both communities. Changes in the architecture and symbolism are reflected in the material culture, and it is here that both continuities and differences can be seen.

Pithouse architecture is characterized by small structures used by nuclear families for storage and refuge during cold nights and inclimate weather. A pueblo is a single, aboveground structure composed of multiple rooms, some with different functions; pueblos provide more flexible space to accommodate the habitation, storage, and ritual needs of extended families and family lineages.

What brought about this change in residence pattern? I present the case here that this change was correlated with a reorganization in Mimbres social groups brought about by implementation of irrigation agriculture. Increases in population required adjustments and re-alignments in household and community structures, social networks, and group and individual identities.[1] These changes eventually distinguished Mimbres populations from the greater Mogollon pool. Agricultural intensification and the role agriculture played in overall subsistence shifted the values and importance of land and land tenure, a subject discussed in more detail in the next chapter. Combined with the possible need for large cooperate labor forces, one means for establishing both land tenure and increasing the labor force is to redefine or reorganize the kinship group and the rules of inheritance. If we can assume that land tenure rights were similar to those of the Western Pueblos, then the first families to settle lands along the river probably claimed the choice lands for farming. For those that did, the most productive land was kept in the family, and these families tended to stayed put. Also following the Western Pueblo model, inherited rights to land included rights to the most important ceremonies associated with rain bringing and crop fertility. The powerful role of such ceremonial responsibilities in structuring Mimbres society will be addressed in chapter 12.

The first pithouses to be built at the NAN Ranch Ruin were not the earliest in the vicinity or the valley. When the first pithouse villages appeared in the Mimbres archaeological record, in about A.D. 200, as noted in chapter 1, they may have been little more than winter settlements, much like the small Late Archaic pit structures in the southern part of the American Southwest.[2] These early villages are typically situated along prominent, defensible ridges or mesas overlooking the stream valleys some distance from the fields but with commanding views of the countryside. The Mimbres Foundation tested two such sites, McAnally and Thompson.[3] The McAnally Site was on top of a high knoll in the middle part of the Mimbres Valley and consisted of about 15 pithouse depressions. The Mimbres Foundation excavated two pithouses at the site, both round with extended entrances to the southeast or south. One of the structures had burned, leaving a well-preserved floor assemblage consisting of several pottery vessels, manos, and a metate.[4] The Thompson site proved to be much more challenging and less informative. The two pithouses tested at that site were shallow and built on bedrock, and none contained floor assemblages.

Although some of the early pithouse sites were repeatedly used, others show evidence of only short-term use. Archaeologists speculate that such short-term pithouse sites may have been only seasonally occupied and suggest that a vestige pattern of Archaic mobility was practiced, albeit with seasonal changes to accommodate planting and harvesting and to incorporate stores of cultivated plants. In time, however, villages were occupied longer and field preparation and maintenance took time away from gathering and hunting.

A major trend can be seen in the location of pithouse settlements through time: movement from the ridge tops to low terraces and benches above the Mimbres floodplain. More villages were established up tributary drainages, especially near springs, where arable lands could be found. This shift to lower terraces and expansion in

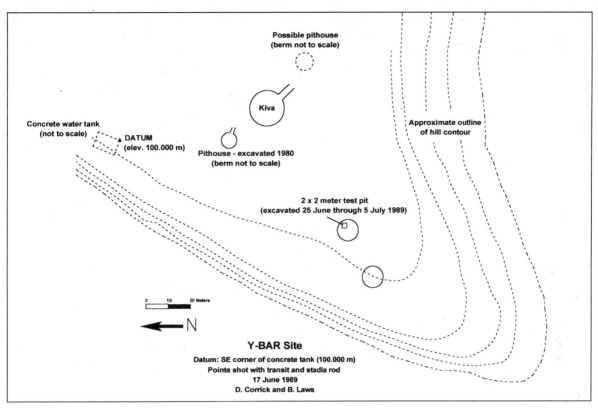

3.2: Y-Bar site map, showing visible pit structure depressions and the great kiva.

settlements up some drainages in search of farmlands was gradual and may have correlated with population growth.[5]

The first indication that one has found an early pithouse village is the presence of cultural material. Pieces of chipped stone residue, a few obvious stone artifacts such as hand choppers made by chipping flakes from one face of a small cobble or small fist-size stones used to batter and shape other stones, a rare projectile point, and small pieces of plain brown pottery mark the location of these sites. Sometimes the pottery is slipped on one surface with an iron-rich clay that fires to a earthy red. The projectile points are larger and heaver than the later arrow points and were used to tip small fleche spears propelled by a throwing stick, or atlatl (Figure 11.1).

Subtle circular depressions formed by abandoned, filled-in pithouses can sometimes be detected. The relative size of the pithouse village can usually be determined by the number of pit depressions and the area of artifact scatter. At some sites, the pit features only hint at what usually lies beneath the surface. Many more pithouses are usually present than surface pit depressions, especially at those sites that were occupied for one to three centuries.

Only one of these Early Pithouse period villages was tested during the NAN Ranch project. This was the Y-Bar site, situated about half a kilometer south of the NAN Ruin. This site consists of several round or D-shaped pithouses with extended entrances and a great kiva.

THE Y-BAR SITE

Situated on a high ancient terrace overlooking the Mimbres Valley, the Y-Bar site consists of at least five pithouses that are evident on the surface (Figure 3.2). Undoubtedly more lie buried beneath the fill and trash of these later structures. Among the unexcavated structures is an unusually large pit structure, often referred to as a "great kiva." This structure is either circular or rectangular (one cannot be sure, judging from the depression), about 8 m across. On the southeast side is the entryway,

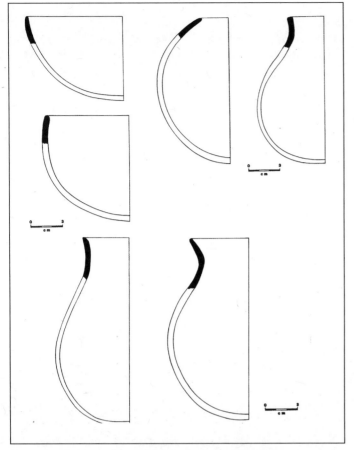

3.3: Reconstructed vessel forms from the Y-Bar site.

evident as a linear depression oriented to the southeast. Two pithouse structures have been partially excavated by members of the NAN Ranch project. The pithouse dwellers at the Y-Bar site laboriously dug the pits nearly a meter deep beneath the present surface in a consolidated gravel terrace; the walls and floors were plastered with clay. Entry to these structures was through a low ramp that began at the surface and gently sloped downward to near the floor level. One entrance of a tested pithouse at the Y-Bar site was excavated and found to face east.

Neither structure had burned, and no in situ floor assemblages were encountered. Chipped stone artifacts and potsherds were found in the fill of the pithouse, however. Items of chipped stone consist mainly of residual flakes from stone tool manufacture and small, fist-size chopping or battering tools. Fragments of grinding stones, or manos, were found, along with a dart or spear point. Ceramics consisted of plain wares, diagnostic sherds show that vessel forms included hemispherical bowls, *tecomates*–round, neckless jars—and small jars with necks (Figure 3.3).

It appears that the pithouses were abandoned after a short period of use. The structures eventually collapsed, and the pits became filled by natural processes. Judging from the sparse amount of refuse left on the surface around the pithouses, I doubt that the site was occupied for long. In fact, early pithouses may have been seasonal dwellings, used mainly for storage and shelter during cold winter days and nights. Pithouses, which were like small artificial caves dug into the ground, were well insulated and could be kept comfortably warm by a small fire in the floor. This is not where people spent most of their time, however. Most work was conducted outdoors and during the warm season. The pithouse villages may have been temporarily abandoned while the people pursued a seasonal hunting and gathering pattern or perhaps tended to small garden plots.

Archaeological evidence has revealed that the entryways faced east or southeast, toward the rising sun. The direction may have been determined by the location of other pithouses, whose entrances may have opened to a plaza area. Alternatively, the orientation may have been related to symbolic meaning rather than function; we simply do not know.

The amount of labor spent constructing these early pit structures indicates at least a semisedentary lifestyle.[6] Labor expended building the walls and roof of a structure was usually commensurate with the length of time the structure was to be used. Mobile hunters and gatherers in the southern North American desert spent little time building their houses. The labor needed to excavate the pits, then cut and procure the logs for the superstory contrasts sharply with the lean-to huts of sotol stalks built by the hunters and gatherers in the Chihuahuan Desert.[7]

No direct evidence was found for domesticated plants at the Y-Bar site, although their uses can be inferred from the ceramics and grinding implements. Evidence in the form of charred kernels and cobs recovered from other early pithouse sites in the Mimbres Valley indicates that corn was an important dietary item for these people.[8] Only traces of plant remains are found at these sites, and it is difficult to quantify how much of the diet consisted of cultivated crops such as corn, beans, and squash.

Meat from hunted animals was also important, of course, but again, because of lack of preservation and archaeological emphasis in Early Pithouse village archaeology, we know regrettably little about these people's hunting practices. Presumably hunting followed a pattern similar to that of the Chihuahuan Desert Archaic and early agricultural peoples, who hunted primarily small game such as rabbits and rodents, with a rare deer, mountain sheep, or antelope added.

Hunting methods included the use of the spear and spear thrower; spears were tipped with large stone points called dart points (as opposed to the smaller arrow points of later times) or simply with sharpened hardwood shafts. Traps, snares, and nets were undoubtedly used, as these were standard methods of procuring game during the earlier Archaic period throughout the Chihuahuan Desert and Southwest.

The earlier Archaic peoples did make small adobe-floored shallow pit structures in some areas of the Southwest.[9] No such evidence of sustained Archaic occupation has been found in the Mimbres Valley, and indeed none is really expected prior to the adoption of corn agriculture. The reason is that natural plant and animal resources in the Mimbres Valley are not plentiful and probably were not sufficient to sustain a resident Archaic population, as discussed previously.

Following the Archaic period, early preceramic agricultural settlements are known in the Mimbres region and very likely occur in the middle Mimbres Valley. These sites, as discussed in chapter 2, exhibit virtually the same patterns of material culture as the Early Pithouse period sites except that ceramics are usually absent. Such characteristics as small oval or round pithouses, cultivated foods such as corn and squash, thin midden deposits, virtually identical lithic assemblages, and emphasis on small game hunting suggest a clear continuity into the early ceramic phases in the Mimbres Valley.

Early Pithouse period villages were usually small, numbering anywhere from three or four up to 80 structures, but most have about five to 20. In most sites only three or four structures were probably occupied at any one time. These villages likely consisted of family groups, when several families occupied a single village. One pithouse often stood out as larger than the rest. Presumably these were the council houses for communal gatherings, housing for visitors, and space for council meetings and rituals during the colder months. The size and depth of the large unexcavated circular pit structure at the Y-Bar site, whose entrance points to the southeast, seems inconsistent with the small size of the Y-Bar pithouse village. The great kiva may belong to a later pithouse site known to have existed on a lower terrace immediately west of where the Y-Bar NAN Ranch headquarters are now.

Archaeological evidence for symbolism that could be interpreted as community or societal integrating themes is absent in the Early Pithouse sites. Such symbolism could appear on jewelry, ceramics, or rock art. No jewelry has been recovered from the Y-Bar site, and the ceramics are either plain or red slipped. Likewise, no burials were found in the Y-Bar site test excavations, and none have been found at other Early Pithouse period sites in the Mimbres Valley.[10] Burials reported from Early Agricultural sites in the Mimbres area, however, are isolated, flexed interments with few if any associated artifacts.[11] Although the mortuary practices of these first Mimbres farmers are at present unknown, I expect that time will show them to be a continuation of those of the Early Agricultural period, with the preponderance of burials single flexed interments placed outdoors.[12]

NAN VILLAGES OF THE ANCESTORS

Life in the succession of pithouse villages at the NAN Ranch Ruin was one of gradual change. Change was necessary to accommodate a growing population in the Mimbres Valley[13] as well as in the NAN community. With gradual population growth came the need to produce more food and provide more space for its storage. As any social group becomes larger, the structure of the social community becomes more complex. A village composed of a single family or an extended family of two or three houses usually functions well simply on the basis of division of labor and communal reciprocity. When a community is made up of two or more families, a higher order of organization is needed to bond the families against the outside world and to broaden the ties with neighboring communities. Leadership among many Native American cultures consists of a council of elders (usually males) chosen from residential kin groups who decide critical civic and war issues and enforce social rules and taboos.

In a separate dimension and apart from the councils who decide on civic issues are the family or lineage elders, some of whom were shamans and part-time priests. Shamans acted as healers and guarded their people against malevolent forces, while priests aided in connecting society members to spiritual worlds. These functionaries were responsible for holding and carrying

26 / CHAPTER THREE

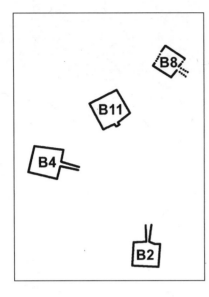

3.4: Pithouse courtyard cluster at the Old Town Ruin (LA1113) (after Lucas 1996: Figure 3.5).

on the sacred knowledge to organize and orchestrate ceremonies and provide individual curing (shamans) and community curing (priests) in times of subsistence or social stress.

The developing need for indoor and outdoor space for community rituals can be seen in the evolution of large civic-ceremonial rooms and the arrangement of structures around open plazas. Larger civic-ceremonial rooms have been a part of pithouse communities from the beginning, and the arrangement of contemporary structures facing or surrounding open areas may have been as well. However, definition of courtyards and plazas is difficult due to the abandonment of pithouses and the construction of later ones in old plaza space and to gaps in the archaeological record. To factor out such patterns requires extensive archaeological investigations.

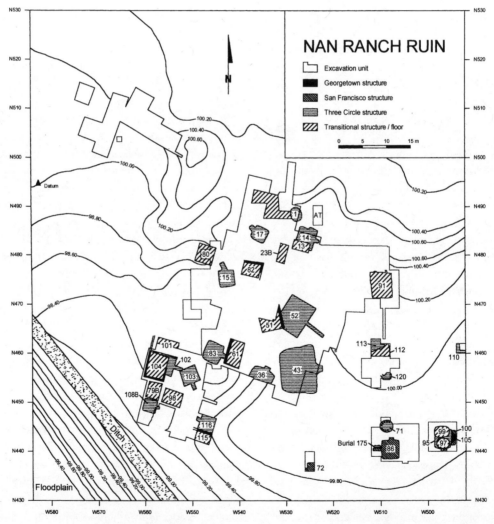

3.5: Pithouse villages at the NAN Ranch Ruin.

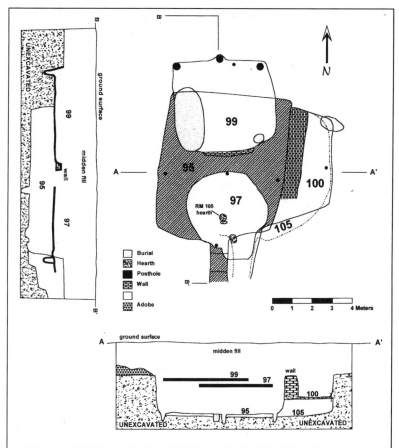

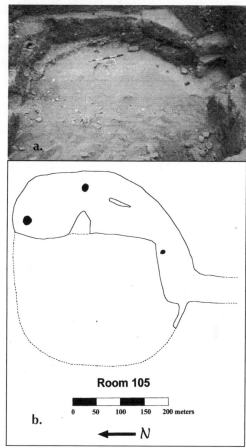

3.6: Plan of superimposed pithouse rooms 95, 97, 99, 100, and 105 at the NAN Ranch Ruin.

3.7: Georgetown phase room 105 at the NAN Ranch Ruin: a. photo of partially intact structure; b. plan drawing.

At first glance, a map of a Mimbres pithouse village shows pithouses randomly scattered across a site. These villages may have been organized, however, into clusters of pithouses, each representing some form of social grouping, such as an extended family. To determine such a pattern requires nearly complete excavation of several villages for each period of time. Hints of such clustering have been observed in the distribution and orientation of pithouses at the Old Town and NAN ruins. Darrell Creel's excavations at the Old Town Ruin have shed some light on this problem[14] (Figure 3.4). Unlike other Late Pithouse villages, where earlier architecture is obscured or obliterated by later construction, Creel discovered an isolated group of structures in area B whose organizational pattern was intact. The cluster of Three Circle phase pithouses at Old Town faced a central courtyard or plaza. The area B cluster at Old Town is a useful model for factoring out pithouse patterning at sites where the orientation for pithouses appears random. This model will be applied to interpretations of the NAN pithouse villages, which span the sequence from Georgetown phase through the Three Circle phase.

Beneath the NAN Ranch Ruin lies a sequence of pithouses starting from the time it was first settled and extending to the appearance of the first pueblo structures (Figure 3.5). This sequence of pithouses formed a continuum through the Late Pithouse period (Figure 3.6). The first pithouses built at the NAN Ruin were round or elliptical structures of the Georgetown phase (A.D. 550–650). Only one has been excavated (room 105). This elliptical structure was virtually identical to those built on the higher landforms and had an extended entrance toward the south (Figure 3.7). We were not able to excavate the entire structure because it was truncated by a later pithouse excavation. Its projected size is 8.5 m across by 6.5 m long.

The floor was composed of plastered adobe. About a meter in front of the entrance was a circular fire hearth with a cobble deflector. Deflector stones are a common feature of pithouses with extended entrances and were used to prevent a sharp breeze from blowing directly on the smoldering fire. The entry was "lobed"; that is, small projections into the room occurred on each side of the entry. Similar lobed features were found to be indicative of larger civic-ceremonial early pit structures,[15] but the size and floor assembly suggest that room 105 was a domestic structure.

Pottery recovered from the floor included both plain brownwares and the red-slipped wares. The vessel forms changed little from earlier times: hemispherical bowls, narrow mouth jars, and necked jars are the predominate shapes for this period.

We know that textiles such as sandals, basketry, matting, netting, and rabbit fur blankets were used since these items were found in protected caves in the region.[16] None, however, survived in this room, and few other diagnostic items were found associated with it.

No other features have been identified for this earliest settlement at the NAN Ranch Ruin. Since the pottery is virtually identical to that of the Y-Bar site and is duplicated in the subsequent phase, it is virtually impossible to identify outdoor features in the Georgetown phase unless they can be securely dated.

Pithouses of the San Francisco phase (A.D. 650–750) were subrectangular shaped as opposed to the elliptical or circular shape of the earlier structures. Pit walls, floors, and ramps are plastered; ramp entrances often have one or more steps. The roof was usually supported by three main support posts across the middle and posts at each corner and on each side of the entranceway. The number and position of the posts often varied, however, according to the degree of repair and longevity of use.

Domicile pithouses remain small, averaging from 10 to 12 sq m of floor space in the NAN Ruin community. That certainly seems small for four to six people by contemporary standards, but these structures were not actually "lived in" as we think of the way houses are used. Most work and activity was conducted outdoors. As mentioned above, these houses were used mainly for storage, sleeping during cold nights, and seeking respite from inclimate weather.

The San Francisco phase village was small, although the exact size is unknown. It probably consisted of no more than a few families, each occupying two to three pithouses. Four San Francisco phase structures were excavated at the NAN Ruin: rooms 72, 86, 95, and 100. Diagnostic ceramics recorded on or above the floor date the rooms to the San Francisco phase. The earliest painted pottery, Mogollon Red-on-brown, is one of the artifact types used to identify the San Francisco phase. No whole vessels of this ware were found, but ceramic cross dating of diagnostic sherds on the floor and in the fill above the floor can tell us about when the rooms were abandoned.

Room 100 was a subrectangular structure built over the ruins of room 105 (Figure 3.6). Both the east and north wall limits were the same as for room 105, but the original pit was enlarged to accommodate the straight walls and angled corners of the later room. Traces of a ramp entrance to room 100 were found to the south, partially cut into the entrance of room 105. The full extent of the room is unknown since the western part was destroyed by aboriginal excavation of the room 95 pit. Our estimate for the size of room 100 is about 13 sq m of floor space.

Room 100 burned, and remnants of the charred superstructure became visible as the floor surface was uncovered. The beam and thatch pattern suggests the room was framed by large timbers paralleling the walls; a single posthole in the east-central area near the east wall indicates that another beam was placed east-west. Smaller beams covered with layers of grass and reed thatch were placed over this log frame. Burned thatch consistently blanketed the floor, and a layer of adobe topped this nearly flat roof. We are not sure how the walls were constructed, but they were probably of adobe and freestanding above the walls of the pit.

The artifacts left on the floor were also revealing. Burned grass bedding was noted in the north end of the structure. Two pottery vessels, a San Francisco Red bowl and part of a neck-corrugated jar, were on the floor; part of a charred sandal was also among the charred plant materials littering the floor.

Room 95 was a late San Francisco phase room built over part of room 100. It had also burned, and charred contents littered the floor. Room 95 was a subrectangular pit structure cut into the ruins of rooms 100 and 105. Slightly over one-half of room 100 and traces of the west side of room 105 were destroyed in the process. Room 95 measured approximately 3.1 m along the north and east walls and 3.2 m along the west wall. The estimated floor space is about 10 sq m. The room opened to the south through a stepped ramp entrance 45 cm wide and about 2 m long.

No hearth was found in the floor of room 95, but this is not unusual for pithouses. Often fires were built directly on the floor, in which case the only indication would be residual ash deposits. Such deposits may have been on the floor of the room, but since it burned, ash was found throughout the structure.

When pits are excavated into unstable soils, the walls are often supported by cobble-adobe masonry. At first, this method of wall construction may have been merely an improvisation to stabilize a wall. As the cultural deposits at the NAN Ruin began to accumulate and newer pits for pithouses intruded into older ones, pithouse walls developed a general tendency to be unstable. The use of cobble-adobe construction provided an artificial means of ensuring a stable wall. A good example of this technique is the east wall to room 95, which was a thick cobble-adobe wall built across the loose, unstable fill of room 100. Masonry was used more frequently through time as less emphasis was placed on the pit wall as part of the interior structure. Clearly cobble-adobe masonry was not an invention of the Pueblo period; what was first a solution to overcome unstable deposits in the Late Pithouse period become a standard for aboveground construction in the Late Three Circle and Classic Mimbres phases.

Several pottery vessels were left on the floor in the southeast and central part of the room. Two large jars, one of which is Alma Neck Banded, were in the southeast quadrant of the room near the east wall. Another large plain jar was on the floor near the center of the room, and portions of two Three Circle Red-on-white vessels and sherds of Mogollon Red-on-brown were recovered from the ceiling debris. Since these sherds were burned, they either were on the roof, stored above the floor, or, less likely, used in roof construction. A large grass basket lay on the floor in the southwest section of the room near the entrance. Traces of grass or yucca mats, which may have been bedding material, were on the floor in the north end of the room. The storage basket was a narrow-necked form constructed of coiled bundles with interlocking stitch.

Whatever the range of functions for room 95, certainly one was for storage. Several large storage jars, including one Alma Plain and another Alma Neck Banded, were on the floor when the structure burned. We also found a large grass-coiled "bird's nest" basket, a type of storage container

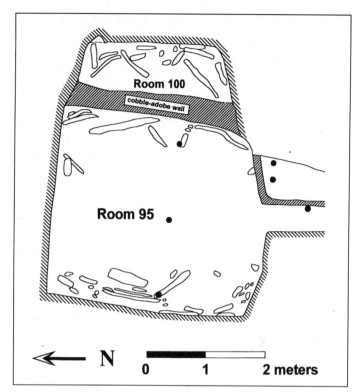

3.8: Floor plan of San Francisco phase room 95 at the NAN Ranch Ruin.

widely used by native inhabitants across the southern Southwest and northern Mexico for food storage.[17]

Subfloor features consisted of postholes, a pit, and a burial. The posthole pattern is shown in Figure 3.8. The pit was along the west wall toward the front half of the room. It had been filled in and capped with adobe. An infant (burial 209) was placed beneath the floor immediately west of the center post. Although the bones were mostly disarticulated, the few articulated elements indicate the body was flexed or semiflexed. No artifacts were associated with the burial.

The superposition of room 95 over room 100 allows relative dating of the two structures. Since the San Francisco phase lasted only about a century or less, room 95 falls in the late San Francisco phase. Its destruction may date to the beginning of the Three Circle phase since sherds of a Three Circle Red-on-white tecomate jar were found mixed among the burned roof material.

Another excavated San Francisco phase pit structure is room 86 (Figure 3.9). This subrectangular structure had an extended entry to the west. We were not able to precisely date room 86 because of the lack of association of diagnostic artifacts, but its relative placement was based on diagnostic sherds removed from the fill on and slightly above the floor, which contained an admixture of San Francisco phase and Three Circle phase sherds.

The bowl and jar sherds of plain brownware from the San Francisco phase deposits differ little from those of earlier periods and are not useful in ceramic dating. Two decorated types were found in the San Francisco phase. One is San Francisco Red, a red-slipped ware of earlier times that continued to be made; a partial vessel of this ware was found on the floor of room 100 along with part of an Alma Neck Banded jar. Neck banding is a technique of decoration with the coils of clay used to form the vessel during manufacture. The coils at the vessel's neck were left only partially smoothed rather than entirely smoothed, as was the case for other jars. Leaving coils only partially smoothed creates a roughened exterior at the neck that may have been an advantage in lifting a hot vessel of cooked food from a fire, especially if wooden tongs were used. Neck banding first appeared in the San Francisco phase and continued into the early Three Circle phase.

Burials at other sites assigned to the Georgetown and San Francisco phases are exclusively outdoors but not in formal cemeteries. Outdoor burials at the NAN Ruin rarely have ceramic associations. Therefore some of the flexed adult burials found in outdoor contexts undoubtedly date as early as the Georgetown and San Francisco phases, but here again, we cannot be certain. Burial 9, an adult burial found beneath two layers of surface pueblo architecture, is a good example. The grave, dug into the orange clay hardpan, was discernable only because the fill contained flecks of charcoal. (Hardpan is the clay capping of a Pleistocene gravel, sand, and clay terrace deposit of the Mimbres River.) The tightly flexed skeleton was placed on its left side with the head oriented to the east. No artifacts were found associated with the burial, and no covering rocks or slabs were placed over

3.9: Plan map of San Francisco phase room 86 and location of burial 127.

3.10: Artifacts associated with burial 127 in room 86. Top: cloudblower pipe; bottom left to right: small biface, turtle plastron, Olivella shell beads, and quartz crystal.

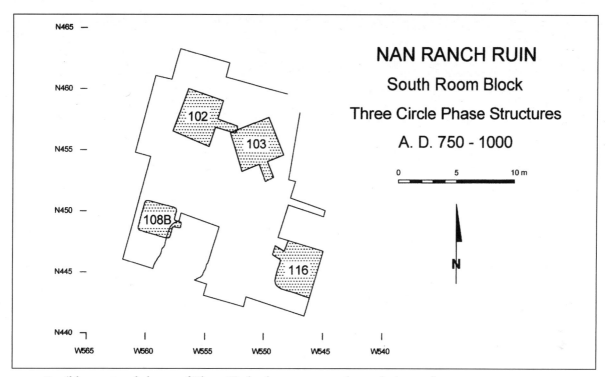

3.11: Possible courtyard cluster of Three Circle phase structures beneath the south room block at the NAN Ranch Ruin.

the body. The lack of associated artifacts and covering rocks is a clear indication that this burial dates to one of the pithouse phases.

Subfloor or intramural burials are rare during these early phases. Two early indoor burials were positively identified, however, based on room association: burial 209, the infant in the floor of room 95 mentioned above, and burial 127, an adult male placed in a sitting position in a specially constructed alcove off room 86 (see chapter 8). Burial 127 was unaccompanied by pottery, which is unfortunate since ceramics would have fixed a more precise date. Artifacts associated with this burial did include a cloudblower-type stone pipe, a small biface, a turtle plastron, three *Olivella* shell beads, and a quartz crystal (Figure 3.10). The unusual burial facility and the associated artifacts indicate that the individual held a special status; perhaps he was a shaman.

By the time of the Three Circle phase, approximately A.D. 750, the village had grown considerably, and evidence exists that some kind of structuring within the village had begun. Fifteen excavated or partially excavated pit structures, as well as a considerable accumulation of trash, were dispersed over the site that dates to this phase. We estimate there were at least 40 structures in the Three Circle phase village, but not all of them were used at the same time. Identified Three Circle phase habitation structures include rooms 14, 15, 17, 83B, 102, 103, 108B, 113, and 116. Rooms 14, 83, and 109 are discussed here as examples.

There is some evidence that pithouses were clustered, perhaps forming extended family compounds. Although it is difficult to factor out such clusters, given the problems of sampling components of the pithouse villages, which lie sometimes a meter or more beneath Classic Mimbres ruins, one possible cluster was found. Pithouse rooms 102, 103, 116, and 108B beneath the south room block form a cluster of structures that appear to face a small courtyard (Figure 3.11). Structures 115 and 108B face each other, and 102 faces east, whereas the earlier 103 faced southeast. The possible significance of this cluster of pithouses lies in the occupational continuity in this area of the site until the site was abandoned at the end of the Classic Mimbres period.

An example of a Three Circle phase domestic structure

is room 14, a subrectangular pithouse excavated 1.3 m into the underlying surface. Enclosed floor space within the room was approximately 9.5 sq m. The walls and floor were plastered with clay; the floor had received two separate coats of plaster. The entry (which was not excavated) lay to the east, and an adobe-line fire pit was situated in front of the entry. Two artifacts were recovered from the floor: a mano next to the hearth and part of a Three Circle Neck Corrugated jar in the northwest corner (appendix I: Figure A.28C). Beneath the floor in the northwest corner was burial 86, the tightly flexed body of an adult female (see chapter 7). The body was oriented with the head to the east. Accompanying this burial were from three to five small unfired, white-slipped, Mimbres Style I jars (Figure 8.4). Also included were the remnants of a coiled basket, a twilled basket, and a twilled mat wrapping the body. Associated with the remains of the coiled basket were seven worked potsherds, two pot-polishing stones, and a small Style I bowl (appendix I: Figure A.1F) with red pigment. In the fill above the burial were the sherds of a smashed Mimbres Style I bowl (appendix I: Figure A.1E) and a small, complete Style I seed jar (appendix I: Figure A.1G). Based on the unusual contents, I interpret this grave to have been that of a female potter.[18]

Another pit was found in the north-central part of the room. Although this pit had all of the appearances of a burial, no human remains were found. In the fill of the pit were sherds of two smashed vessels, a Mimbres early Style II bowl (appendix I: Figure A.1I) and a plain brownware bowl (appendix I: Figure A.27E). Also included in the grave fill were two worked potsherds and a pot-polishing stone.

The burial of a child (burial 93) was placed to the right of the entrance. Included with this burial were two small turquoise pendants near the right wrist, a string of shell beads on the left wrist, sherds of three vessels, a small mug embellished with random punctations (appendix I: Figure A.28G), a polished redware seed jar (appendix I: Figure A.1A), and a plain brownware elongated boat-shaped bowl (appendix I: Figure A.26E) with curved tabs at each end. Also included were a small turquoise and lead crystal inlayed object, a slate palette, two shell ornaments, and a shell pendant.

Mimbres Style I and early Style II Black-on-white ceramics provide a means for dating the occupation of this room to approximately A.D. 850 to 900. The burials in this room contained the most artifacts of the Three Circle phase burials at the NAN Ranch Ruin. Burial 86 is the first and only Mimbres burial identified as possibly that of a potter. We had suspected that women made pottery, based on the roles of women documented in pueblo society,[19] but this had never been confirmed archaeologically until we discovered burial 86.

Rooms 83B and 102 are more typical of the Three Circle phase pithouses we encountered. Room 83 was a square pit structure measuring 3.5 m by 3.5 m, with a floor area of 12.25 sq m (Figure 3.12). An extended ramp entryway opened to the east. It had two floors, the first of which was associated with the Three Circle phase, and the second, discussed in chapter 4, with the Late Three Circle phase transition. A rectangular, adobe-lined hearth was in the east-central part of the room in front of the extended entrance. This entryway was 50 cm wide and slanted upward 1.8 m to a slight 20-cm step to the top. A rectangular wall vent 20 cm wide and 15 cm high was placed in the south wall 30 cm above the floor. The vent shaft extended out 40 cm before it angled abruptly toward the surface. Assemblage of floor artifacts yielded only plain and Style I decorated sherds. A single adult female burial was found beneath the floor in a tightly flexed position oriented with the head to the east. Capping the burial was a deposit of sherds out of which two plainware jars were restored and a large early Mimbres Style II Black-on-white sherd (appendix I: Figure A.4B). One jar was polished black (appendix I: Figure A.27A); the second was a light brownware (appendix I: Figure A.27B).

Room 102, another Three Circle phase structure, was excavated about 60 cm into the underlying sand and gravel (Figure 3.13); the walls and floor were neatly plastered. Although the eastern one-third of the room had been disturbed in antiquity, enough was preserved to establish the room's dimensions: 3.25 m east-west and 3.85 m north-south, giving a floor space of approximately 12.5 sq m. The extended entrance ramp, which measured about 50 cm wide and 2 m long, was oriented to the east and partly cut into an underlying pithouse (room 103). The entryway began with a 20-cm-high step above the floor; the ramp sloped upward from the first step to another step at the end of the ramp. A circular clay-lined fire basin, 40 cm in diameter with a cobble deflector stone, was constructed in the floor 40 cm in front of the entry. Postholes were at each side of the entrance. The room had burned, and the only artifacts on the floor were several burned beams in the southeast corner. Unfortunately, these were of complacent species and were not suitable for tree-ring dating. No ceramic artifacts were associated with the room, so it was not possible to use ceramics for cross dating. We did, however, managed to get chronometric dates, using archaeomagnetism and obsidian hydration. The burned plaster yielded an archaeomagnetic date of A.D. 840 to 940.[20] A piece of worked obsidian from the fill yielded a date of A.D. 930 to 1010.[21] The obsidian could have been introduced into room 102 from numerous graves dug into the fill from room 104 above since the obsidian hydration date range overlaps with the age of the room 104 burials. Apparently room 102 was abandoned about A.D. 890 to 910.

Two Three Circle phase pit structures, rooms 43 and 52, are much larger than the average pithouse.[22] The relative sizes of these structures place them in the category of large civic-ceremonial rooms or great kivas. Room 43, shown in Figure P.2, was only partially excavated and had not burned; therefore I will not describe it further.[23] Room 52, however, was fully excavated and provided convincing evidence that it was a great kiva (Figures 3.14 and 3.15). It measured 7.2 m by 6.0 m, with a floor surface of 43 sq m. The ramp entry was oriented to the southeast and measured 4.3 m long and 0.6 m wide. The walls were smoothly plastered and well preserved to a height of about 1 m above the floor. Traces of white curving lines, possibly the remains of a painted serpentlike motif, were preserved along the west wall (Figure 3.16, p. 35). A large adobe-lined, basin-shaped fire pit 55 cm in diameter associated with a deflector stone was placed midway between the center post and the entrance. The room had burned, and except for the charred roof timbers, the floor artifact assemblage was meager but possibly revealing. Two pottery vessels, a small Mimbres Style I bowl (appendix I: Figure A.1H) and an untyped whiteware bowl (appendix I: Figure A.32E), were recovered along the west wall in proximity to three small postholes placed in a triangular pattern. Damon Burden, who conducted a study of the ceremonial structures at the NAN Ruin, interpreted this feature as the possible remains of an altar.[24] Burden also noted several suspicious holes in the floor, any one of which could have served as a *sipapu*, a sacred portal into the Underworld, a common feature in Pueblo kivas. The only other diagnostic pottery on the floor was a Three Circle Neck Corrugated jar. Surprisingly, no subfloor features were identified in this large room.

Rooms 43 and 52 are considered to have been places for communal activity. Typically the term *kiva* is used in reference to such large pit rooms in the Southwest, which implies a ceremonial function. The presence of one or

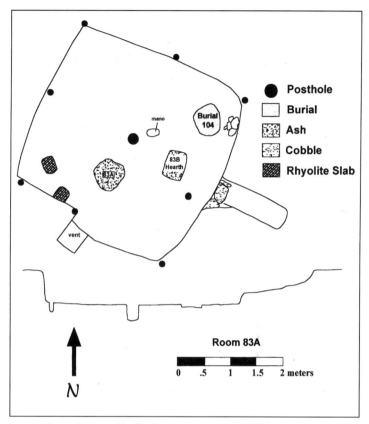

3.12: Plan of Three Circle phase room 83 at the NAN Ranch Ruin.

3.13: Photo of Three Circle phase room 102 at the NAN Ranch Ruin.

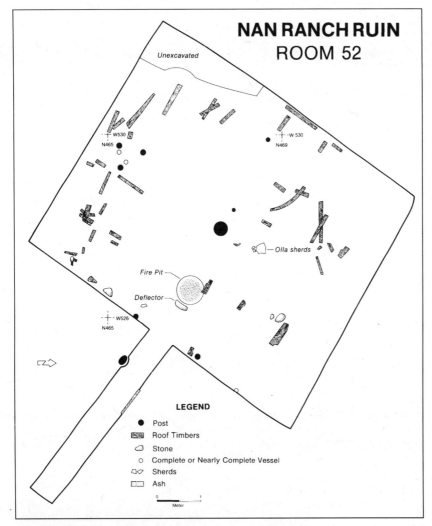

3.14: Plan of Three Circle phase great kiva room 52 at the NAN Ranch Ruin.

3.15: View of great kiva room 52 after excavation.

more holes in the floor that could have functioned as a sipapu, possibly painted walls, a possible altar, and deliberate burning or termination of room 52 provide strong support for a ceremonial function for this structure. Much less can be said of room 48 because it did not burn and was not nearly as well preserved as room 52. The absence of special artifacts or features precludes its identification as such here, but as we will see later in this chapter, outside features, particularly the cremation cemetery, may support the notion that these rooms did in fact have ritual significance.

Although the function of room 52 is quite certain, the times of construction and abandonment are not. The rectangular form clearly fits into the Three Circle phase and generally conforms to that of other Three Circle phase great kivas. The problem lies in conflicting dates for its construction and an ambiguous date for its abandonment. The single tree-ring date, NAN 182, obtained on the charred roof timbers is A.D. 737 to 859. The true cutting date for this beam is after A.D. 859, but we do not know how much after. A construction date of about A.D. 860 to 870 would fit well with the Style I ceramics associated with the room and associated material in the overlying fill, which dates mostly to the Late Three Circle phase. The accelerator mass spectrometer (AMS) dates, however, throw us a real curve (Table 3.1).[25] These dates are at least a century to a century and a half earlier than expected. Discounting LA2465-2, which is arguably too early, the remaining two dates (LA2464-1 and LA2464-3) indicate a construction date of about A.D. 700. The archaeomagnetism termination dates taken from burned plaster range from A.D. 660 to 720, 740 to 860 (ASMNR9), to A.D. 700 to 990 (Colorado State University LA15049-2) (Table 2.2) and are not inconsistent with the AMS dates. The construction of this great kiva may have taken place earlier than I previously assumed, and its abandonment may have occurred near the latter part of the ninth century. One other possibility is that the beam that yielded the single tree-ring date was not from a mapped construction timber, but rather from a large chunk of charcoal recovered from the floor. This timber could have been

TABLE 3.1. Accelerator Mass Spectrometer (AMS) Dates from Great Kiva Room 52 at the NAN Ranch Ruin

AA#	Lab #	Sample ID	d13C	14C	Age
AA46434	B3162A	LA2465-1	-23.4	1,368 ± 31	A.D. 613–759
AA46435	B3163A	LA2465-2	-22.6	1,475 ± 32	A.D. 540–643
AA46436	B3164A	LA2465-3	-24.2	1,333 ± 43	A.D. 638–778

Source: National Science Foundation–University of Arizona Accelerator Mass Spectrometry Laboratory, University of Arizona, Tucson.

used as fuel in the ritual termination of the structure and may date the termination rather than a construction or renovation phase. None of the dates are precise enough to know which of these scenarios is correct.

Room 43, which did not burn, also poses dating challenges. Its depth and form, including rounded corners, seem to conform to those of pithouses of the San Francisco phase. The floor assemblage of broken and possibly trampled sherds (based on small sizes) consists mostly of Style II, with an admixture of Style I and Mimbres Redware. The assemblage is consistent with a Late Three Circle phase structure, and that is the time when I assume this structure was abandoned.

Great kivas are a common type of structure in virtually all large Late Pithouse period villages in the Mimbres area, beginning with the Georgetown phase.[26] Three Circle phase great kivas are known from other large Mimbres sites in the valley, including Harris, Old Town, Swarts, Galaz, Cameron Creek, Hot Springs, Lake Roberts Vista, and Ponderosa Ranch. These types of structures reach their peak of development in the Three Circle phase. Great kivas were either deliberately destroyed by burning or were abandoned by the early Classic Mimbres phase, if not earlier. No functionally equivalent architecture exists in the Classic Mimbres phase, but there are arguably certain rooms with ceremonial roles and others with possibly civic roles. This change in ceremonial architecture hints of some kind of social restructuring. Perhaps it was a shift away from an emphasis on community integration as implied by the great kivas to one of corporate lineage integration, as suggested by the presence of a new type of ceremonial room described in chapter 5.

In addition to the domiciliary and civic-ceremonial structures in the Three Circle phase, we found another structure type at the NAN Ranch Ruin never before

3.16: Traces of painted lines, possibly a serpent motif, on a plastered wall of great kiva room 52.

reported in a Mimbres site. This is room 71, a round structure built in a shallow pit with a circle of interior postholes (Figure 3.17). Room 71 measures only 2.8 m in diameter, with the floor sunk slightly into hardpan. The floor surface consisted of packed adobe clay. No formal hearth was found on the floor; a shallow, extensively used ash pit was located in the south-central part of the room that served as the hearth. There were 15 confirmed and one suspected posthole (presumably lost to an intrusive pit disturbance); the postholes ranged from 16 to 20 cm across and 12 to 20 cm deep. Two older postholes were found in the hardpan beneath the floor surface, and one of these had been deliberately filled in and

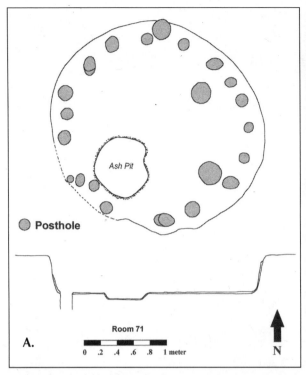 

3.17: Views of Three Circle phase round pit room 71 at the NAN Ranch Ruin: A, plan; B, photo.

capped at the time room 71 was constructed. No artifacts or features other than the ash pit and postholes were found in association with the room. A similar structure has been described for the Convento phase of the Casas Grandes culture in Chihuahua, Mexico.[27] The context of room 71, however, suggests that it was purely Mimbres and represents some of the architectural variability that occurs in the Three Circle phase. It is dated to the Three Circle phase on the basis of a few sherds found lying on and just above the floor and its stratigraphic relationship with the surrounding deposits. The function of this little structure is unknown, and its architecture is highly unusual for the Mimbres in that it is a structure built inside of a pit rather than the pit forming part of the walls. The room may have been used as a menstrual hut, a place to give birth, or a place for sweat baths for curing and purification rituals.

I gave examples of structures for each Late Pithouse period phase to provide the reader with a sense of the change that was taking place in the architecture at this time. I did not include all the investigated features that date to these phases, nor do the preceding discussions provide a true sense of the overall patterns used to define each phase or distinguish one from another. The remainder of the chapter presents information on certain diagnostic features, such as hearths, floor assemblages, ceramic design changes, and changes in symbolism that are used to infer significant patterns that occur in the Late Pithouse period, and sets the stage for recognizing changes that are either initiated in the Three Circle phase or are about to take place in the Late Three Circle phase.

Hearths in San Francisco and Three Circle phase structures were of three types: the most formal hearths were circular, adobe, or cobble lined, with deflector stones set slightly above the floor toward the entrance. These hearths were typically small (no more than 30 to 40 cm in diameter) in domestic structures. Examples were recorded in rooms 12, 17, 102, 103, 108B, 113, and 116. The second type of hearth was rectangular adobe lined, also placed in front of the extended entryway. Examples are in rooms 43 and 83b; the completely excavated hearth in 83b measured 30 by 48 cm. The third type is really not a formal hearth at all but an area of the floor on which fires were built. Rooms 115, 117, 86, and 95 contained these types of thermal features. Hearths were placed between the entrance and the room's center and may have served only for warming and light.

Subfloor pits are reportedly common features in Three Circle phase pithouses.[28] Most were shallow, irregular pits dug into the underlying gravel or sand beneath the floor and filled with rather clean loose gravel. The only evidence for the existence of a pit is traces of charcoal and an occasional sherd or lithic artifact. Presumably these features were contemporaneous with the excavation of the original pit and were filled to level the floors. No deep pits, which arguably were used for storage, were found in any of the NAN Ruin pithouses.

Extramural burial remains the primary means of disposal for the dead in the Late Pithouse period, although evidence for a changing pattern can be seen at the NAN ruin. A separate category of subfloor pits is associated with burials. Although rare, they reflect fundamental changes in mortuary behavior in the Three Circle phase. This is the first time that adults were also placed beneath the floor of pithouses at the NAN Ruin. In the previous phase, only certain infants were given this treatment. Two adult female burials were encountered beneath Three Circle phase room floors; both are described above. One was in room 14 and another in the floor of room 86; both were associated with smashed pottery vessels. Certain infants and children were also among those interred beneath room floors. An infant was beneath the floor of room 99, and a child was interred in the floor of room 14.

Cremation is yet another method of disposal that occurs during this period. Burial 175, a primary cremation, took place in the east plaza, near what was to become a major cremation cemetery in the next phase (see chapter 8). This is the only primary cremation found at the NAN Ranch Ruin and the only one ever reported from a Mimbres site. Since cremations were not uncommon in the succeeding phase, undoubtedly other primary cremations occurred at other Mimbres sites. Their lack of discovery is attributed to previous archaeological attention directed to architecture and not to exploring outdoor space.

Artifacts left on the floors of abandoned structures provide important information on how the space of a particular structure was used and specific information on storage behavior. Floor assemblages are usually meager except in those structures that burned with the floor contents. Rooms 43, 83b, 86, 116, and 117 were largely cleaned of floor contents at abandonment. Rooms 12, 52, and 113 had vessels left on the floors. Room 113, although only partially excavated, also had a slab metate and several manos on the floor near the entrance and a plain pottery jar in the entrance ramp.

Although most structures were thoroughly cleaned of floor artifacts when they were abandoned, enough information was left to suggest how the inhabitants used the pithouses. Sleeping areas were situated near the back of the rooms, whereas the front was used for storage and indoor domestic activity, as suggested by the location of storage vessels and metates. We suspect that most domestic activity was outdoors, although these activity areas and features associated with them were obscured or destroyed by the intensive activity of subsequent generations. Indoor hearths were used almost exclusively for warming, as suggested by white ash smoldering fires, which are less suitable for cooking than the higher-intensity outdoor fires with their constant flow of oxygen to fuel the flames.

The absence of storage pits in pit structures leaves open the question of how foods were stored. The finding of a possible quarry pit in the east plaza, partially filled by the burned contents of a large twilled storage container, may provide a partial answer. The contents of the container included several kilos of burned shell corn, suggesting that shelled corn was economically stored in various kinds of containers rather than in subfloor pits. Storing corn shelled rather than on the cob is consistent with the absence of formal granaries during the Three Circle phase. Storing corn shelled is a characteristic of mobile groups, whereas storing corn on the cob is more commonly found among sedentary groups.[29] Although I do not want to make too much of this single feature, the evidence that corn was stored shelled may indicate a greater degree of mobility during the Three Circle phase than in the subsequent phases.

Trough metates with one open end, cooking jars, serving vessels, ample traces of charred corn, and the storage of shell corn all point to an increased reliance on cultivated plants. A new and more productive variety of corn, *maíz de ocho,* was introduced into the region.[30] Perhaps more significant is the evidence of a growing permanence in occupation that is observed in the accumulations of midden deposits, burials, and labor commitments in the construction of pithouses. How much of the subsistence was gained through gathering is unknown since it is very difficult to measure these kinds of trends. Hunting, trapping, and snaring yielded a small quantity of meat from deer, antelope, mountain sheep, jackrabbits, cottontail rabbits, and rodents, as shown by the faunal remains recovered from the midden and pithouse fill, with jackrabbits and cottontail rabbits clearly dominating. The major hunting weapon until about A.D. 750 to 800 was still the atlatl thrown spear, but small corner-notched arrow points began to appear in the deposits and mark the introduction of the bow and arrow (Figure 11.1) and a major shift in hunting practices.

Changes in symbolism are evident during the Three Circle phase. For example, a gradual shift to indoor burial begins to take place, with selected infants and adult females placed beneath floors. Most burials, however, were still placed outdoors. Also, the ritual smashing of vessels and scattering sherds in the fill over the corpse occurred more frequently in the early part of the phase. Burials with ceramic or jewelry associations are still very much in the minority, but clearly a change in mortuary patterns was taking place.

The clearest change in symbolism can be seen in ceramics decoration and jewelry. The white-slipped wares so characteristic of Mimbres painted pottery were first produced in the Three Circle phase (see chapter 10). At first, the white-slipped pottery was painted with broad-line geometric patterns with a paint that fired to an oxidized red. This short-lived Three Circle Red-on-white, made from about A.D. 750 to 825, often displays four-quadrant designs similar to those seen on the Mogollon Red-on-brown, but greater variability in design layout occurs. The designs include frequent uses of scrolls along with opposed solid elements outlined with facing tooth-edged motifs. An evolution of the Mogollon Red-on-brown design layout can clearly be seen in the Three Circle Red-on-white and in the first black-on-white Mimbres Style I, formally called Boldface.

In the shift from red-on-brown to red-on-white to black-on-white the design became increasingly visible against the vessel background. Changing firing practices—perhaps simply by placing the vessel facedown in the outdoor bonfirelike kiln—allowed the paint to fire black in a reduced atmosphere. This early style of black-on-white evolved rapidly in terms of design style and execution.

From the early Three Circle phase (ca. A.D. 750–800) to its end (A.D. 800–900), Style I designs became more complicated and a distinct trend from thick, bold lines and motifs to a finer line execution can be traced (see Figure 10.6 in chapter 10). This topic will be discussed further in chapter 10. The Style I designs are not framed, and the decorations extend up to the rim. There is a liberal use of wavy lines—both to form circular designs and as cross-hatching—scrolls, and solid elements with toothed edges. Wavy lines give way to straight lines as hachure by the early A.D. 900s. Design layouts may be divided in quadrants, mirror opposites, circular, or in unbroken fields.[31] Style I designs vary from positive images at first to negative images, and, according to J. J. Brody and others,[32] anthropomorphic and zoomorphic motifs make their first appearance in late Style I. I do not see anthropomorphs and zoomorphs appearing in Mimbres pottery until Style II, however.

Archaeologists and art historians have noted similarities in early anthropomorphic and zoomorphic motifs to those of the Hohokam potters,[33] which may indicate the expression of a commonly shared symbolism among people in these arid lands.

An alternative explanation is that a gradual shift in population from west to east was taking place. This population shift has been documented for the Classic period by Margaret Nelson,[34] and the Hohokam characteristics of the Three Circle phase may have been introduced by people who previously were living on the periphery of the Hohokam and were influenced by them. Perhaps a more important question is why some of the pottery was elaborated in the first place. Certainly the labor required to slip and paint the bowls did not improve their function as cooking and serving vessels. So why elaborate the vessel?

Painted pottery represents only a very small percent of the pottery produced in the Three Circle phase, probably less than 10 percent of all vessels in the inventory at any one time. The frequency of painted pottery increased slightly toward the end of the Three Circle phase, from about A.D. 850 to 900, owing to increased ritual activity. Since so few of the vessels were painted during this phase, they may have first been used in ritual contexts, in altars, or as containers in ceremonial activities. This may account for their infrequent occurrence in the Three Circle phase and for their growing popularity in later phases with enhanced ceremonialism and public feasting.

This shift in method of embellishment on Mimbres pottery correlates with a general trend involving material culture that follows the transition from a mobile lifeway to a sedentary one.[35] This trend involves the shift from a utilitarian role of ceramics through the Georgetown phase to include utilitarian and symbolic roles of certain (painted) ceramics beginning with the San Francisco phase. As Mimbres society became more sedentary, the pottery designs became more elaborate due to the changing spheres in which pottery was used.

By end of the Three Circle phase, the community had begun to form some discernable structure. There is a hint that structures 102, 103, 108b, and 116 formed a cluster with a common courtyard when viewed together (Figure 3.11). This courtyard grouping is quite similar to that reported from area B at the Old Town Ruin and noted at other Mimbres pithouse villages[36] and may represent a Three Circle phase lineage grouping and the establishment of a residential space claim for this particular lineage in this part of the village. Such lineage courtyard clusters of structures is a common pattern in contemporary Hohokam communities to the west.[37] More will be said of this in discussions in chapters 4 and 6 of the south room block evolution. Probably other such clusters exist at the site, as suggested by the orientation of excavated pithouses, but the sampling did not reveal them.

Ceremonial space, like individual family and lineage residential space, was also defined. The location and orientation of the two great kivas, rooms 43 and 52, marked this area of the village as probably the ceremonial center. Although these structures were abandoned by the end of the Late Three Circle phase, if not before, the use of the space for ritual activity continued well into the Classic period, as shown by the placement of the cremation cemetery (see chapter 8).

Summary

The initial pithouse settlement of a few structures was established in about A.D. 600 in the Georgetown phase and grew to a substantial community of an estimated 50 or more pithouses by the end of the Three Circle phase, about A.D. 900. Substantive changes were beginning to take place in subsistence technology and organization of Mimbres society. The structure of the community began to take shape in regard to residential and ritual space. Social and ritual activities were becoming more inclusive, probably involving people living in nearby communities and perhaps beyond. Toward the end of the Three Circle phase, major changes were taking place that affected all aspects of Mimbres culture and society. These changes, seen in the architecture, subsistence, storage practices, mortuary customs, ceramic styles, and symbolism of the Mimbres, became manifest in the material culture of these people during the tenth century in the late Three Circle phase, the transition from the Late Pithouse period to the Classic Mimbres period.

CHAPTER FOUR
Pithouse to Pueblo Transition: Late Three Circle Phase

Introduction

A major transformation in Mimbres culture occurred in the Three Circle phase, but it was not until the Late Three Circle phase, in the tenth century, that many of these changes were expressed in the material record. Perhaps at no other time in Mimbres cultural history was the variation in material expression greater. It is hard to define the Mimbres area on the basis of architecture and artifact assemblage before the beginning of the tenth century. The pan-regional patterns used to define much of the Mogollon area from A.D. 200 to 750—round to rectangular pithouses, brownware pottery, early white-slipped pottery—encompassed a wide area of southwestern New Mexico and eastern Arizona, including the Mimbres Valley. These elements, however, gave way in the tenth century to more localized developments of architecture, elaboration in white-slipped brownware ceramics, and expressions of beliefs and symbolism that distinguished the Mimbres from the rest of the Mogollon.

The shift toward agricultural dependence and the establishment of land claims in the Three Circle phase probably preceded the ideological changes that materialized in the transitional Late Three Circle phase; that is, choices were made that required explanation in mythology and folklore. The subsistence shift was only a matter of degree since corn, beans, and squash were already in the subsistence inventory. The focus of landscape use, however, shifted from broad scale to localized sections of the valley or from hunting, gathering, and gardening to one with an unequal weight on agriculture. Probably three to four generations passed before this shift in subsistence and landscape use became fully ingrained in the ideology and symbolism, as it might have been expressed in rituals, ceremonies, and associated material culture. Certain ceremonies, especially those related to rain bringing and ancestor veneration, assumed paramount importance, as indicated by certain cultural behaviors that were expressed in the tenth century.

The archaeological evidence for this cultural transformation was one of the most significant findings of the NAN Ranch Ruin research. Previously archaeologists had assumed the processes occurred rapidly; we now know, however, that this was not the case. The process occurred in the A.D. 900s but was not uniformly accomplished, nor should we expect it to have been. In any community, including those of certain Pueblo groups, some individuals are conservative and hold to traditional ways, and some are progressive and willing to risk change.[1] Change during the transition comes in several forms: in architecture and associated features such as hearths and entryways; in special-function rooms such as granaries; in increased production of painted ceramics and the incorporation of new ceramic motifs; in mortuary practices, which now included bounded, subfloor cemeteries and cremation cemeteries; and in petroglyphs, which promote the same themes appearing on the painted pottery. All of the ingredients that characterize the Classic Mimbres phase were coming together, beginning in the later stages of the ninth century and throughout the tenth century, and constitute a major shift from the vestiges of semisedentariness of the Georgetown and San Francisco phases to a fully sedentary society by the Classic Mimbres phase.

Innovations in architecture provide some of the most compelling evidence for change during the pithouse-pueblo transition. Changes in the manner in which housing was arranged in a community and in traditional house types signal a reorganization in the composition of residential groups and in the ways the people believed houses should be built. Among these architectural changes are the use of cobble-adobe masonry for the construction of aboveground houses, change in hearth type and location, different method of entry, and greater variation in room function.

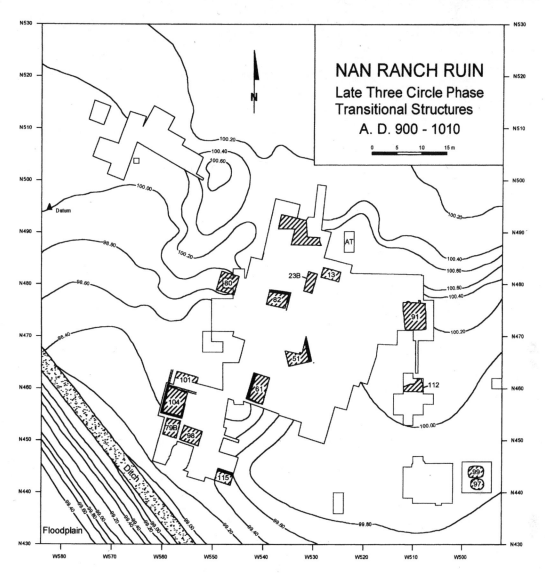

4.1: Map of Late Three Circle phase village at the NAN Ranch Ruin.

Architectural Evidence

We were able to document a clear evolution in the architecture from pithouses to pueblos in our excavations at the NAN Ranch Ruin. Information on 24 rooms provided critical evidence of the pithouse to pueblo transition (Figure 4.1). Some pit structures continued to be used, albeit modified to accommodate a change in architectural style (Figure 4.2A), whereas others were replaced by surface rooms (Figure 4.2B). These include one pithouse (room 91), three modified pithouses (43, 83, and 116), 16 early pueblo rooms that had either sunken floors or floors constructed on the hardpan surface (13, 23B, 51, 58, 57, 61, 79B, 80, 82, 89B, 98, 101, 104, 112, and 115), two constructed in the fill of an earlier pithouse (97 and 99), and three that were incorporated into early Classic period room blocks (12, 76A, and 89A). Sixteen structures are identified as habitation rooms, two are civic ceremonial (rooms 43 and 91), and two are granaries (rooms 51 and 76A).

Among the first changes in the traditional Three Circle phase was modification of existing pithouses by blocking the extended entrance and creating a hatchway in the ceiling. It is apparent that pithouses continued to

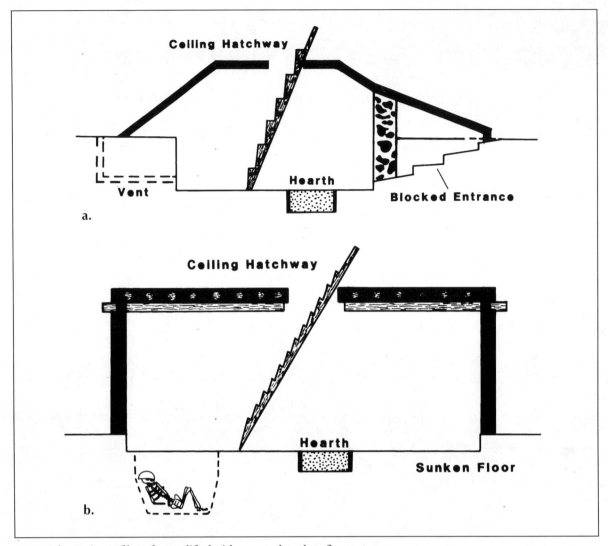

4.2: Schematic profiles of a modified pithouse and sunken floor room: a. modified pithouse; b. sunken floor room.

be used at the onset of the Late Three Circle phase at some sites, such as the Galaz and Cameron Creek ruins. Reconfiguring existing pit structures by blocking lateral entrances and constructing new ones is documented in the Three Circle phase but only to reorient a pithouse, as exemplified by room B4 at the Old Town Ruin[2] and unit 29 at Galaz.[3] In each instance in the NAN Ruin (rooms 43, 83, and 116), no evidence for new lateral entrances was found. Hearths in rooms 43 and 83B were rectangular and adobe lined, whereas the hearth in room 116 was partly cobble lined. Evidence for continued use of the pit structures and a relocation of the hearth area in room 83A (Figure 3.12) suggests the lateral entrances were converted to ceiling hatchways. Also, floor and deep fill assemblages for each of the structures yielded Style II Black-on-white pottery sherds, indicating that abandonment took place sometime in the tenth century.

Room 83 presents a good example of a modified pithouse. Two episodes of construction were detected in the excavations. The first episode, 83B, was a typical Three Circle phase structure, described in chapter 3. The next building episode, 84A, began with walling up the entrance, constructing an air vent in the south wall, and adding another coat of plaster on the floor, thereby capping the earlier fire hearth. No formal hearth was constructed in this episode, but an ash deposit in front of the wall vent showed that warming fires were built directly on the floor. The only subfloor feature that may be associated with 84A other than the postholes is the burial of a golden eagle near the north wall. The floor had been disturbed in this part of the room, and we were unable to confirm if the bird burial was placed in the floor before or after abandonment. Sherds on the floor of 84A included both Style II Black-on-white and Three Circle Neck Corrugated. One Style II jar was partially reconstructed from this sherd assemblage (appendix I: Figure A.5E) and helps to date the last use of the room to sometime in the tenth century.

Early pueblo-style structures had freestanding cobble-adobe or puddled adobe walls and floors formed out of or into the hardpan surface. The floors of 16 structures were constructed by either leveling or excavating 10 to 30 cm into the underlying hardpan surface. These rooms are superimposed over deeper and earlier pithouses and lie beneath later Classic Mimbres rooms. A similar architectural pattern was recognized at the Swarts Ruin[4] and was included in the category "Transitional period" architecture.

Walls consisted of cobble-adobe construction with an interior post arrangement similar to that for pithouses. Traces of cobble-adobe foundations were recorded for 14 rooms (51, 57, 58, 61, 76B, 76A, 79B, 82, 89B, 98, 99, 101, 104, and 115). Rooms 13, 97, and 112 appear to have had puddled adobe walls. Civic-ceremonial or kiva room 91, described separately in this chapter, was most unusual in that it had a wooden superstructure built in a pithouse but with a ceiling hatchway.

Previously, sunken floor rooms were described as shallow pithouses and generally attributed to the Three Circle phase.[5] It is clear, however, that at the NAN Ranch Ruin some of these rooms were single structures and represent a period of construction overlying Three Circle phase pit structures. There is some evidence to argue that one or more contiguous rooms may have been attached, based on the proximity of floor remnants and the orientation of wall bases. Possible cases include rooms 104, 79B, and 98. Room 104 was almost completely excavated, whereas 79B and 98 were identified only by wall base remnants and floors.

Preservation of these early pueblo rooms was generally poor because of their relatively shallow depth and disturbances from later construction and space use during the Classic period. Many were partially obliterated by later construction and can be identified only by sections of preserved floors and wall bases. Since few examples of burned rooms were found (e.g., rooms 51 and 91), evidence of superstructure construction details is scanty. Room 91 is an exception, but its construction is exceptional as well. Charred reeds and wattle-impressed daub in the debris of room 51 suggest roof construction was much like that of the Classic period. Clearly most sunken floor rooms had load-bearing cobble-adobe walls much like the later Classic rooms. The pattern of postholes for room 91 was similar to that in early Three Circle phase structures, but unlike the earlier dwellings, the walls were adobe and the entry was through the ceiling.

Hearths held both functional and symbolic importance and served as the defining feature for habitation rooms. When a change occurred in hearth design and location within the structure in the Late Three Circle phase, we can presume that such change involved functional and symbolic roles. As noted in chapter 3, hearths in Three Circle phase pithouses with extended entranceways consisted either of circular adobe-lined basins approximately 30 to 40 cm in diameter or ashy deposits on the floor. The patterned location of hearths was about midway between the room's center and the extended entranceway. A deflector stone was part of basin-shaped hearth construction; it was placed in the floor on the side of the hearth facing the entrance and protruded 3 to 5 cm above the floor. Sometime in the Late Three Circle phase, a change in hearth design occurred. The new hearth form was rectangular, either completely or partly framed with stone slabs set in adobe or simply adobe lined. The rectangular hearths lack deflector stones; such stones were no longer necessary with ceiling entrances and vented walls. Hearths were identified in rooms 58, 79B, 80, 82, 89B, 91, 97, 98, and 112 and are of three kinds: basin-shaped adobe lined (rooms 79B, 91, and 97), rectangular adobe lined (rooms 98, 104, and 112), and rectangular slab lined (rooms 58, 80, 82, and 89B) (Figure 4.3).

This shift in hearth design and location within the structures occurred at other Mimbres sites as well. Evidence from the Galaz Ruin shows that the shift to slab-lined hearths may have begun late in the Three Circle phase.[6] Seven pithouses with extended entrances from the Galaz Ruin[7] are reported to have had slab-lined hearths. A shift from basin hearths to slab-lined hearths was also noted at the Cameron Creek Ruin[8] in Late Pithouse period rooms both with and without extended entrances.

Rectangular hearths in pit structures with extended entrances are placed between the center post and the

4.3: Example of a Late Three Circle phase slab-lined hearth in room 80 at the NAN Ranch Ruin.

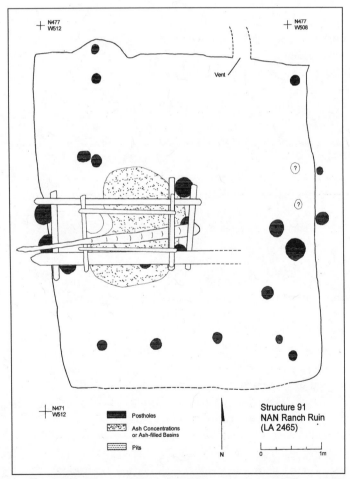

4.4: Suggested detail of ceiling hatchway for Late Three Circle phase room 91 at the NAN Ranch Ruin (after Burden 2001: Figure 3.21).

entrance. Similar hearths in sunken floor and surface rooms are placed off center; if the room had two vertical support posts, the hearth was between the posts about midway from the room's centerline to one wall. If the room had only a single center post, the hearth again was off center, about midway between the post and a corner. Air vents were usually in the wall nearest the hearth if that was an outside wall, but this was not a hard-and-fast rule. The shift in hearth location and type in sunken floor rooms presumably was to correlate with the location of the ceiling entrance, which may have been directly above the hearth.

Two types of entrances are either documented or inferred during the pithouse-pueblo transition: ramps and ceiling hatchways. The archaeological evidence for the presence of ceiling hatchways in transitional rooms is largely circumstantial but can be inferred on the basis of hearth location and type, absence of extended entrances, absence of deflector stones, and presence of ventilators. Hatchway frames were presumably of wood since no collapsed stone slab frames have been recorded in any Late Three Circle phase rooms (Figure 4.4). If stones were used, reuse of the space once occupied by the room and recycling the stones for later construction are probable reasons why the ruins of hatchway frames were not found. In Classic Mimbres period rooms hatchway slab concentrations often partly overlie hearths, indicating the entrance was above the hearths.

Along with the shift to pueblo-style architecture came changes in room function. Three functional classes of rooms were identified in the Late Three Circle phase: domestic, civic-ceremonial, and granaries. Domestic uses of rooms continued into the transition period, and certain rooms were constructed for civic-ceremonial use. Archaeologists assumed that pithouses were used primarily for habitation and civic-ceremonial functions and secondarily for storage. The intensification of agriculture and the accumulation of food surpluses, however, brought about the need for a change in storage facilities. Evidence for storage facilities in the San Francisco and Three Circle phases at the NAN Ranch Ruin came mostly from large jars and grass baskets in pithouses, as shown by the floor assemblage in room 95. Subfloor pits were commonly used for storage in the Three Circle and earlier phases,[9] but such features were not consistently found in the pithouses at the NAN Ruin. Postholes in the hardpan surface beneath Classic period rooms and in outdoor spaces suggest the

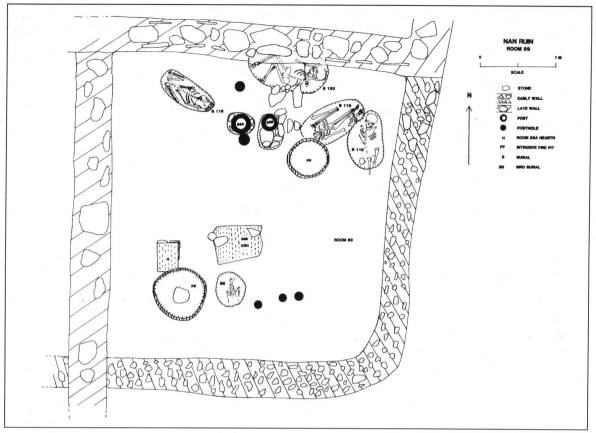

4.5: Plan of Late Three Circle/early Classic period room 89 at the NAN Ranch Ruin.

construction of arbors or elevated platforms that may have been for storage.[10]

Most transitional or sunken floor rooms with cobble-adobe walls were for domestic use. The presence of a formal hearth was one of the factors in determining domestic function. Although ceremonial rooms also had formal hearths, they had other features that set them apart. Twelve rooms fit the criteria for domestic rooms: rooms 12, 57, 58, 61, 76B, 79B, 80, 82, 89B, 97, 98, and 104. Rooms 12 and 58 were incorporated into early Classic period room blocks and are described in the next chapter. Examples of sunken floor domestic rooms are rooms 89 and 104, the most intact transitional rooms excavated.

Room 89 was a large room whose use spanned part of the Late Three Circle and early Classic phases. The room was nearly square and had 12 sq m of floor area (Figure 4.5). The south wall and west wall were constructed at one time, but not in typical Mimbres fashion. The walls, which varied from 30 to 50 cm thick, consisted of layers of small fist-size cobbles embedded in a matrix of compact adobe mortar. These walls were among the hardest we encountered in our excavations. The west wall continued beneath a Classic period wall that framed the eastern limits of a complex of previously excavated rooms, presumably by the Cosgroves in 1926. The east wall abutted room 76.

Room 89 had two distinct floors; 89A, the uppermost, was surfaced at least twice. This floor was badly disturbed by later activity, especially the construction of adobe-mixing pits (labeled fire pit—FP—in Figure 4.5) and postholes. A slab-lined hearth was in the southwest quadrant of the room. The floor of 89B was even in worse shape, but traces of another slab-lined hearth were found in the southeast quadrant of the room. The roof to both rooms was supported by a single post set in the approximate center. Several subfloor features were associated with the room, but it was impossible to determine from which floor the pits originated. Four human burials, 116, 118, 119, and

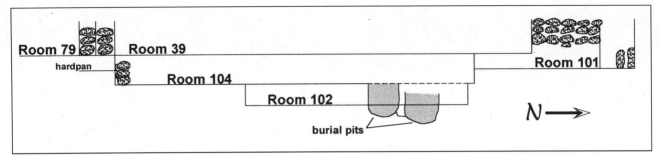

4.6: Schematic profile of rooms 79, 39, 101, 104, and 102 at the NAN Ranch Ruin.

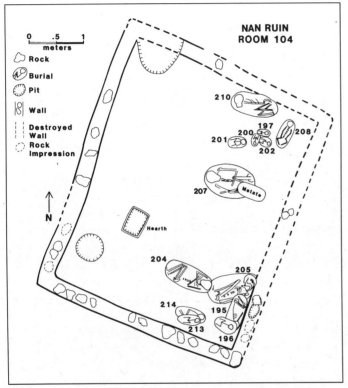

4.7: Plan of Late Three Circle phase room 104 at the NAN Ranch Ruin, showing floor and subfloor features.

statement. Also, the ceramics associated with two of the burials in room 89, a Style II bowl with burial 120 (appendix I: Figure A.5C) and an early Style III sherd with burial 118, provide an approximate date for the rooms' use. This time block also correlates well with that documented from transitional–early Classic period room 12, described in the next chapter.

Room 104 was overlain by room 39 (Figure 4.6). Its construction cut into room 102, a Three Circle phase pithouse. Room 104 (Figure 4.7) measured 5 m north-south and 3.5 m east and west, giving an overall floor space of 17.5 sq m. The west and south wall bases were intact, as was the southeast section of the east wall. The north wall of the room was apparently destroyed by Classic Mimbres construction activity; the wall's limits were determined by a small section of intact wall that extended eastward from beneath the west wall of room 39.

Walls were about 20 cm thick and constructed of cobble-adobe masonry. Wall bases were set in shallow wall trenches filled with adobe before the first coarse cobbles was laid. The floor was a thick layer of puddled adobe, however, that evidenced much leaching, obscuring pit or post outlines. The leaching also prevented recognition of separate flooring episodes, but the thickness of the adobe suggested that the floor was patched many times. The fire hearth was found approximately 1 m from the south wall and 1.5 m from the west wall. It was rectangular and adobe lined, measuring 35 cm north-south and 30 cm east-west. The hearth may have had a slab frame, but the adobe was not disturbed in the excavations.

Two subfloor pits were discovered beneath floor caps; one was in the southwest corner and measured approximately 30 cm in diameter and 20 cm deep. The second was an adobe-lined extramural cooking pit that measured over a meter across. No other features were found associated with the west end of the room, but 13 burials were found

120, and a turkey (*Meleagris gallopavo*), feature 89B-4, were associated with this room.

Room 89 may have been part of a small suite of rooms that the Cosgroves mentioned in their brief notes on their NAN Ranch Ruin excavations. In their notes, the Cosgroves describe excavating five late rooms and four early rooms. We have identified the area west of room 89 as the location of the Cosgroves' excavations, and the continuation of room 89's west wall beneath a later Classic period wall is consistent with the Cosgroves' beneath the floor in the eastern half. These burials provided a very important sample that stratigraphically predated the large sample from the Classic Mimbres room block that overlay room 104. The burials included three adult females (burials 204, 207, and 210), an adult male (burial 205), five children (burials 196, 200, 201, 208, and 214), and four infants (burials 195, 197, 202, and 213). Ceramics associated with room 104 burials showed a remarkably consistent stylistic continuum from the late Three Circle phase to the early Classic Mimbres phase (appendix I: Figures A.2D, A.3A, A.3C, A.3F, A.3G, A.4I, A.5D, A.5I, and A.8A). Furthermore, the mortuary population from room 104 demonstrates a fundamental change in mortuary behavior: the establishment of bounded subfloor cemeteries that included all sex and age categories.

Room 104 may have been used for as many as three generations, judging from the number of burials and intensity of use. We assume that the burials were placed in the floor over a period of time—and in some instances where intrusion is evident, a time lapse between burial intervals is clear. The projected temporal span of 60 to 75 years is also supported by the variability in ceramic styles spanning early to late Style II associated with the cemetery.

The most dramatic change in storage facilities at the NAN Ruin was the appearance of surface granaries during the Late Three Circle phase. Granary rooms are identified by such features as unusually thick adobe floors (room 51), an adobe floor reinforced by slabs or cobbles (room 76A), and the presence of burned corn (both rooms 51 and 76A).

Room 51 was only partially preserved, lying beneath rooms 40, 46, and 48 and above the ruins of the great kiva room 52 (Figure 4.8). Most of the room had been destroyed by the construction of the later rooms. The room was oriented 8 degrees west of north and measured approximately 4 m east-west by 5 m north-south with a projected floor space of over 20 sq m. Room 51 contained a large quantity (at least 40 liters) of dried corn on the cob when the room burned. The floor and wall base remnants beneath the floor of room 46 were preserved and show that the room had an adobe floor 6 cm thick and cobble-adobe walls with adobe footing. Although construction of rooms 47 and 48 had wiped out most traces of the room, we were able to project the approximate size based on patches of floor, wall base remnants, and burned corn. Efforts to date the room by dendrochronology and archaeomagnetism were unsuccessful. The room is securely dated to the Late Three

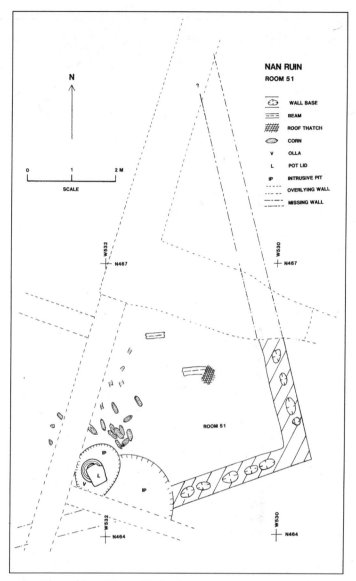

4.8: Plan of Late Three Circle phase granary room 51 at the NAN Ranch Ruin.

Circle phase based on its stratigraphic position above Three Circle phase room 52 and beneath room 40, an early Classic period room (Figure 4.8).

Room 76A was constructed over early transitional habitation room 76B at the end of the Late Three Circle phase and apparently continued to be used throughout the Classic Mimbres period. Two tree-ring dates, A.D. 1003r and A.D. 1003+r,[11] were obtained from burned construction timbers recovered from the floor. The original limits of the rooms are somewhat questionable since a pothole removed the western limits. A projection of

4.9: Late Three Circle/early Classic granary room 76, showing slabs beneath adobe floor.

4.10: Room 91 at the NAN Ranch Ruin, showing superposition of room 89.

room size made with fair confidence (measured from the inside) is 2 m by 3.5 m, with the long axes oriented east and west. The interior floor space was about 7.5 sq m. The floor comprised a layer of cobbles and slabs covered with a thick layer of adobe (Figure 4.9). When the adobe was removed, exposing the cobbles, a noticeable break was observed in the pavement pattern in the northwest quadrant of the room. Eventually burials 127 and 130 were found in this apparently patched area.

The wall bases of room 76 consisted of large cobbles set flat, forming the wall; vertical slabs set on edge were placed along both the inside and the outside of the cobbles, presumably to help guard against rodent intrusion. Vertical slab reinforcement of the wall bases is a characteristic feature of Classic period granaries. Along much of the south wall, the cobbles were anchored on top of the old room 89 wall base, suggesting that the conversion of this room to a granary at the early part of the eleventh century was after room 89 had been raised. The roof was supported by a single center post. Burning left a pattern of charred beams on the floor, providing some details of the superstructure construction. The burning also preserved ears of corn on the cob in the southwest part of the room.

Two civic-ceremonial rooms were dated as either being constructed or abandoned during the Late Three Circle phase: rooms 43 and 91. Room 43, the large pithouse kiva described in the previous chapter, presumably was abandoned in the Late Three Circle phase, based on the inclusion of Style II Black-on-white sherds on the floor. The shape of this structure is consistent with domestic structures of the Three Circle phase, and indeed, the room may have been constructed earlier than room 52. It is dated largely on the basis of the sherd assemblage on the floor, however, and is tentatively assigned to the transition phase.

Room 91 was situated in the northeastern part of the site, beneath rooms 89A and 89B (Figure 4.10). This unusual room measured about 5 m north-south and 4 m east-west, giving an overall floor area of about 20 sq m. The unusual architectural characteristics of room 91 coupled with the assemblage of interior features sets this room apart from other transitional period structures. First, the pattern of postholes across each end and another across the midline indicates that the posts supported a framework of three cross beams (Figure 4.11). This construction pattern is similar to that recorded for Three Circle phase pithouses. An air vent constructed in the north wall and the lack of evidence for a lateral entrance suggest entry was through a ceiling hatchway (Figure 4.4). The floor of room 91, however, was sunk from about 20 cm (south end) to nearly 80 cm (north end) into the uneven hardpan surface. The floor had been resurfaced at least three times. An extensively used basin-shaped, adobe-lined fire pit 35 cm in diameter was situated in the midline of the room, about 60 cm from the west wall. A number of less formal basin-shaped thermal features were found within a 3-m area in the western and southwestern part of this room (Figure 4.12). These features were oval or circular features filled with 10 to 15 cm of ash. One floor feature was a large kidney-shaped concentration of ash measuring about 1 m east-west and 2 m north-south in the west-central area of the room. These shallow pits also contained up to 10- to 15-cm-thick deposits of compact ash and provide clues as to how this structure was used. It is very clear that fire was an important element in the activities carried out in this structure. Furthermore, Damon Burden's detailed analysis of the structure identified three sets of small postholes possibly marking the location of altars and suspicious features in the southern part of the room along the midline that may have been sipapus.[12]

One hundred and eighty-five painted sherds were recovered from the various floor surfaces, 58 percent (n = 107) of which are Mimbres Style II, with a small admixture of Style I and Style III above the uppermost floor. Other artifacts include disk-shaped worked sherds, possibly used as gaming pieces, and two items of jewelry. No burials were found associated with this room. One extraordinary subfloor feature was found, however: a ritually cached Mimbres red-filmed seed jar covered with a plainware sherd lid, placed 15 cm beneath the uppermost floor surface in the approximate center of the room (Figure 4.13; appendix I: Figure A.1B). The jar contained 412 amethyst quartz crystals and may provide an important clue to the function of this room. Crystals were widely viewed among Native American peoples as having symbolic power and were often used in curing and healing rituals.[13]

The special subfloor cache of quartz crystals, multiple thermal features and associated ash deposits, lack of burials, and the overall character of the architecture and architectural features suggest this room served some kind of special function. Damon Burden presents a convincing argument that the room was a kiva, based on his detailed analysis of this structure.[14] Burden also suggests that during the course of the room's use, its primary alignment shifted from west to south, perhaps in response to the designation of the ritual space in the east plaza as the cremation cemetery.

Room 91 represents a departure from the large rectangular great kivas characteristic of the tenth century. The ashy deposits and quartz crystals cached beneath the floor suggest a function related to curing and healing, perhaps through the use of sweat baths. This possible shift in size and style of ceremonial structures may correlate with the designation of certain rooms, such as

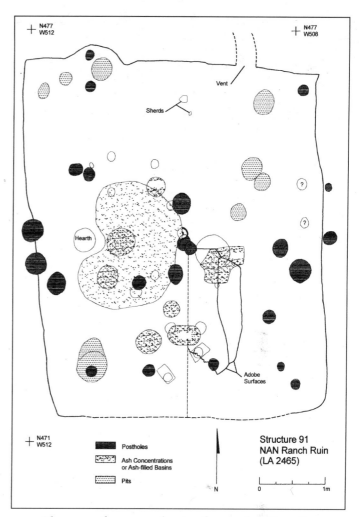

4.11: Plan map of room 91, showing floor and subfloor features (after Burden 2001: Figure 3.18).

4.12: Ashy deposits in the southwest part of room 91, suggesting possible thermal features for steam.

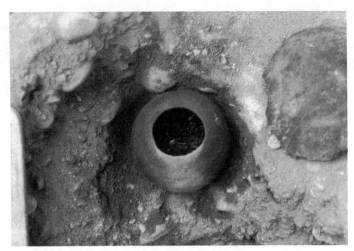

4.13: Subfloor cache of a Mimbres redware jar in room 91 at the NAN Ranch Ruin, containing 412 amethyst quartz crystals.

room 104, as the location of lineage cemeteries. In other words, the focus of ceremonial activity may have shifted from that of communitywide gatherings in great kivas to more lineage-restricted secret rituals in smaller structures. The use of lineage or corporate kivas was characteristic of the Classic Mimbres phase.

Changing mortuary patterns indicate transformations in the way people relate to their dead and the way these relationships are publicly symbolized. Earlier I correlated changes in mortuary practices with the process of agricultural intensification and changes in landscape use. Indeed, this shift in a custom that is so basic and fundamental to all human cultures–treatment of the dead and public acknowledgment of death and transformation–is complex and multidimensional. For example, both a culture's institutionalized beliefs and worldviews and the way the society is organized are ingrained in the religion and customs relating to the disposal of the dead. If a change occurs in the latter, then most certainly changes in either beliefs, social organization, or both can be inferred. The changes in mortuary customs during the Late Three Circle phase were sufficiently dramatic as to suggest a major restructuring of Mimbres society and belief systems at this time. If the shift in land use practices and ownership was established in the Three Circle phase, as argued in the previous chapter, then those changes had clearly become institutionalized in the Late Three Circle phase with respect to mortuary patterns.

The Three Circle phase burial pattern of isolated graves without surviving mortuary furniture placed outdoors near pithouses continued into the Late Three Circle phase, but only as a minor pattern. Of the 39 burials that can be assigned with confidence to the Late Three Circle phase, based on either stratigraphy, room association, or ceramic style, 24 (61 percent) were subfloor inhumations, seven (18 percent) were outdoor inhumations, and seven (18 percent) were cremations.

The dominant mortuary pattern during this transition was the use of bounded cemeteries beneath the floors of certain houses. These indoor cemeteries now included adults of both sexes, children, and infants, which contrasts with the few indoor burials of select females and infants during the Three Circle phase. Another major change was the inclusion of a bowl or a large sherd with a "kill" hole placed over or about the head of both children and adults. Small jars or pitchers, sometimes smashed, were also placed about the feet of children. The earlier practice of smashing several vessels and including sherds from each in a scatter above the burial also carried over in some graves, but this was not a widespread pattern.

Six rooms, 12, 57, 79B, 89, 98, and 104, provided information on indoor cemeteries during the transition. The largest was beneath room 104, where 13 burials were recorded. Rooms 12 and 89 bridge the time between the Late Three Circle and early Classic phases, and at least four burials in room 12 and one in room 89 were assigned to the period of transition, based on ceramic styles. The same can be said for four burials beneath room 57. A possible extramural cemetery was found in the fill of great kiva room 52, where burials (burials 51, 52, 54, 60, and 65) were placed. Only two (burials 51 and 65) of these were associated with ceramics. Burial 51 had a single Mimbres Redware bowl associated with it (appendix I: Figure A.1D), and burial 65 had a Style II bowl (appendix I: Figure A.2E). Additional isolated inhumations were found in the east plaza (burials 124, 218, 223, 225, 226, and 228) and beneath room 25/75 (burial 95). Burial 95 was associated with two Style II bowls (appendix I: Figures A.4A, A.4F) Other outdoor burials likely belong to this period, but unless ceramics were associated, it is not possible to place any of them in phases prior to the Classic Mimbres with any degree of confidence.

A cremation cemetery was established in the mid-tenth century in the plaza east of room 52 (Figure P.2). This cemetery, discussed in chapter 8, continued in use well into the Classic Mimbres phase and contained an estimated 50 or more secondary cremation deposits. The exact number, however, will never be known due to the limited area sampled, the extent of aboriginal disturbances, and reuse of the area. Eighteen secondary cremation features (11 cremations, four cremation deposits, and four possible cremation deposits), as well as bone from general fill contexts, were identified. All contained older subadults/adults (15-plus years). Approximately half (seven) of the cremation deposits date to the Late Three Circle phase, the remainder to the early and middle Classic Mimbres phase. We are not able to predict what percent of Late Three Circle phase burials were cremated because only part of the cremation cemetery was excavated, although the number is significant and may be as high as one out of three.

Artifacts associated with cremation features include whole or smashed pottery vessels, most of which appear to have been included in the cremation fire; burned shell artifacts (*Pecten* shells, *Glycymeris* shell bracelets, beads, tinklers, and pendants); stone beads and pendants; raw turquoise and beads; coral beads stone palettes, obsidian and chert arrow points painted stones; and, in one case (burial 236), fragments of a wooden object, possibly a *paho,* or prayer stick. The number and quantity of artifacts included in certain cremations are rarely equaled in inhumations. Only burial 93 in room 14 and burial 117 in room 62 are comparable. Vessels and vessel fragments associated with Late Three Circle phase cremations are shown in the appendix (Figures A.2B, A.F-I, A.3D, A.3I, A.4D, A.4G, A.4H, A.5G, A.5H, A.28A, A.28B, and A.28F).

The data on the east plaza cremation cemetery at the NAN Ranch Ruin have substantially expanded our knowledge of Mimbres mortuary practices. Previous investigations at Mimbres sites rarely encountered cremations, and when these data were synthesized, cremations accounted for less than 2 percent of all Late Pithouse period and Classic Mimbres burials.[15] Is the NAN Ruin an exception? I doubt it.

For much of the archaeological history of the Mimbres area, the focus of excavation was on masonry architecture, where inhumations, along with their mortuary vessels, were likely to be found.[16] If outdoor excavations were carried out at all, they were often conducted with less precision than for excavated rooms. In reconstructing the excavation history of Galaz, Anyon and LeBlanc[17] note that the initial excavations by the Southwest Museum in 1927 were "carried out at quite a fast pace" and that by the time the University of Minnesota began work there a year later, "there was some confusion as to exactly where the earlier work had been done." It should also be noted that the data from the early excavations in the Mimbres area often lacked the detail necessary to accurately identify even the general location of a burial, much less whether it was beneath a room or outdoors. In addition, the fast pace and lack of screening at these early excavations probably resulted in subtle features, such as sherd concentrations or small pockets of calcined bone, being overlooked entirely or their significance underestimated. For example, A. V. Kidder and C. B. Cosgrove, while searching for burials, noted only in passing a sherd concentration associated with calcined bone in the plaza at the Pendleton Ruin.[18]

At the NAN Ruin, arrow points (usually obsidian); shell, including *Glycymeris, Nassarius,* and *Pectan* (worked and unworked); stone beads; palettes; and burned corn were frequently associated with cremations. Jewelry and projectile points were commonly reported with Mimbres cremations, and the frequency of these inclusions varied over time.[19] Caches of turquoise and obsidian points, as well as sherd concentrations, were also present in the NAN cremation cemetery area. Although the relationship of the caches to the cremations cannot be determined, it should be noted that caches of obsidian points, beads (turquoise and *Olivella*), and sandstone pipes were found in the same area as the concentration of cremations identified by the Southwest Museum at Galaz.[20] Certain extramural pits at Wind Mountain contained quantities of ceramics. For example, pit 27 contained two Classic Mimbres bowls, a Mogollon Red-on-brown jar cover, and several other large sherds; pit 54 contained four Classic Mimbres bowls.[21] Both pits may have been cremation deposits similar to those found at the NAN Ruin. Other extramural pits at Wind Mountain contained apparent caches of stone artifacts and pigment.

Like most new discoveries, the cremation cemetery at the NAN Ruin raises questions rather than provides answers. Clearly an area of the east plaza was designated as a cemetery for cremated remains. Ceramic types indicate that the cemetery was used for about 100 years, from about A.D. 950 to 1050. Possible explanations that might account for the establishment of the cemetery separate from the lineage cemeteries beneath households include (1) cremation was the customary method of burial for one of the lineages at the site and the east plaza was the designated place for the cemetery; (2) cremation was used to dispose of the body of someone who died away from home, and a token deposit of the remains and associated material items was returned to the home site and interred; (3) burial of people who died from unusual circumstances; (4) individuals who may either have been considered victims of witchcraft or were themselves regarded as witches were given an atypical form of burial.[22]

Cremation as a method of disposal of the dead is widespread in American Indian cultures, both archaeologically and ethnohistorically. It was used both as a common pattern, whereby virtually all people from a group were cremated (as among the Hohokam contemporary with the Late Three Circle phase and Mimbres Salado), and one reserved for special circumstances (as among protohistoric Zuni). Historically it was reserved for someone who died under unusual circumstances, such as someone who died away from the village and could not be interred in the manner traditional to the people; for people who were killed in warfare; or for social outcasts such as witches.[23] Cremation was practiced historically, for example, by the Yuma-speaking groups of western Arizona and among the Cocopa of northern Mexico.

So why the differences at the NAN Ruin and how may we account for the variability in mortuary behavior and in the cremations themselves? For one thing, values and beliefs in regard to residency rules, access to lands, and ties to the ancestors were crystallized during the Late Three Circle phase transition. The creation of lineage cemeteries was directly tied to the establishment of a new architectural form, pueblo-style structure. Membership in the cemetery was defined on the basis of membership in the lineage and established a connection between the living and the ancestors from whom the living gained their knowledge and rights to prime lands. Assuming indoor cemeteries marked lineage households, we can define with some degree of confidence two areas within the site where long-term residence and space use was maintained. One is the northern part of the east room block, and the other is the area of the south room block, along with the east plaza. Continuity in both areas is demonstrated by a succession of structures overlapping each other from the Three Circle through the Late Three Circle and into the Classic phase, and the extent of remodeling of the same rooms and areas in the Classic phase. This continuity is demonstrated in the northeast part of the ruin by rooms 89A and 89B, 76A, 76B, 12, 58, and 57; in the bounded cemetery beneath rooms 12 and 89A; and in the Cosgroves' excavations, as shown by the succession of pottery styles identified in their 1932 report.[24]

The area of the south room block shows an architectural succession from Three Circle phase rooms 103, 102, 108B, and 116 to Late Three Circle phase rooms 104, 98, 76B, and 115, all of which were overlain by Classic period architecture. Bounded cemeteries beneath rooms 98, 104, and 79B are overlapped by Classic period room 29. I interpret these successions of architectural episodes and continued use of space for cemeteries as evidence for at least two firmly rooted lineages at the site, perhaps ranked in order of arrival and competing for power and prestige within the community, one in the northern part of the east room block and the other occupying the south room block space. Members of these lineages who died at home were interred in designated cemeteries, but some of those who died away from home or under unusual circumstances may have been cremated and their ashes symbolically interred in the common space of the east plaza.

Pottery associated with the transitional rooms and features in the Late Three Circle phase includes Mimbres Style II Black-on-white, Three Circle Neck Corrugated, Mimbres Redware (or red-slipped brownware), and plain brownware. Stylistic variation within late Mimbres Style II Black-on-white (formally included as Mimbres Boldface Black-on-white) is considerable (see chapter 10), however, more so than indicated by the original definition of Style II.[25]

Style II evolved subtly out of Style I, and where one draws the line is a matter of opinion. Initially the changes are only a matter of degree, with basic elements of the opposed or four-quadrant design layout remaining much the same at first, but with new twists and elements appearing later in Style II. This stylistic evolution is explained in detail in chapter 10.

The evolution and proliferation of stylistic variability in the Late Three Circle phase carried over and continued into the Classic phase. This proliferation of stylistic variation generally followed basic rules of technology and stylistic boundaries, which allows us to differentiate Mimbres Black-on-white from all other black-on-white wares in the Southwest. Within those broad stylistic boundaries, however, are clusters of vessels that seemingly follow rigid rules for motif combination, suggesting that a common producer may be responsible. In other words, the stylistic variability in Style II and later in Style III may be a factor of multiple loci of production (as discussed in chapter 10), with each production locus that of a prime lineage household.

Mimbres red-slipped brownware is probably derived from San Francisco Red. It first appears as a polished red-slipped brownware in earlier phases but becomes much less polished or more mattelike during the tenth century. Vessels are mainly bowls, seed jars, and narrow-neck jars. The red-slipped brownware vessels are more common during the Late Three Circle phase transition than at any other time but never number more than about 5 percent of all the vessels and ceased to be made after about A.D. 1000.[26]

Intrusive ceramics from features dating to the tenth century are rare, but sherds of Red Mesa Black-on-white and El Paso Brown occur among sherd assemblages, and partial vessels of these two types and a Mimbres redware bowl were found in feature 11-4, a possible cremation deposit in the east plaza. Sherds of Sacaton Red-on-buff were also recovered from the east plaza and elsewhere in the site.

Petroglyphs, pecking or incising designs and symbols on rock surfaces, occur throughout the American Southwest and northern Mexico. The faces of rock ledges, outcrops, and boulders in the Mimbres River valley often display one or more symbols pecked into the surface at some time in the distant past.[27] Since rock images were made throughout much of the ancient past, one cannot be certain when a specific image or motif was created. This problem certainly applies to the Mimbres Valley, but based on artistic style, individual examples were most likely made during the transitional and Classic period. Currently no accurate means of dating the rock art exists, but I have attempted to correlate some of the rock art motifs with certain motifs depicted on Mimbres Style II and III pottery. Although admittedly crude and somewhat subjective, I do think some valid correlations can be made.

One such example is a complex anthropomorphic figure on a rock ledge about half a kilometer south of the NAN Ruin (Figure 4.14, top). Certain stylistic features on this figure are notably similar to motifs on Mimbres Style II and early Style III pottery. The similarity is in the emphasis placed on the head and eyes, possibly depicting the "Tlaloc" eye motif (Figure 4.14, bottom) Furthermore, a scatter of sherds, including Mimbres Style II and Style III and Mimbres corrugated, in front of this pictograph suggests that it also served as a shrine and may have been

4.14: "Tlaloc" rock art figure overlooking the valley near the McSherry Ruin (above); early Style III bowl displaying prominent "Tlaloc"-like eyes (below).

ritually fed. Polly Schaafsma, a notable scholar in ancient rock art research, refers to such images as "Tloloc" motifs, suggesting a relationship between them and the rain deity of central Mexico.[28] In a sense I agree with her that these images probably served as icons or mnemonic devices, and that the emphasis may very well have been to evoke ancestor assistance in bringing rain. I do not agree that "Tlaloc" motifs are necessarily Mexican in origin. They may be symbols deeply rooted in ancestral belief systems of both areas.

Along with the intensification of agriculture through the implementation of irrigation came concern with summer weather and the need for rain at critical periods in the growing cycle. Although hunters and gatherers also were known to emphasize rain, it was for a different purpose. The Huichol, for instance, recognized that when the rains came, so did the deer.[28] The coming together of behaviors in the Late Three Circle phase that project similar themes, such as a shift to intramural burial, changes in architecture, and similar motifs appearing on ceramics and rock art, all point to a relationship between rain, clouds, and ancestors that became ritualized. These rituals became institutionalized in the Classic Mimbres phase.

Summary

The tenth century was one of the most dynamic periods in the Mimbres cultural sequence. Major changes occurred in domestic architecture, civic-ceremonial architecture, mortuary patterns, residential patterns, subsistence technology, and ideology. Changes in domestic architecture consisted of a gradual shift from pithouses to aboveground structures with sunken floors, freestanding cobble-adobe walls, flat roofs, and ceiling hatchways. With the new architectural style came a shift in the shape and location of interior hearths from the circular, basin-shaped hearths of the pithouse period to the rectangular adobe or slab-lined hearths beneath the ceiling hatches. Some circumstantial evidence shows that civic-ceremonial architecture also shifted away from the great kivas used for communitywide functions to smaller structures within household complexes used for secret lineage-based rituals. The creation of lineage cemeteries within designated structures marks a significant change in community organization and social structure. I attribute this change to a system of allocation of land rights, handed down from one generation to another. These land rights, which I believe correlate with the incorporation of irrigation agriculture and claims to prime lands, were defined on the basis of lineage membership. Lineage membership, in turn, determined residential membership and access to ancestor knowledge and ceremonial participation. The elaboration of Mimbres Style II pottery was an outgrowth of this process. Although the resolution of stylistic, contextual, and trace element studies is not finite enough to trace specific vessels back to the actual residence of the manufacturers, stylistic variability may very well be the result of a proliferation of prime lineages in the tenth and eleventh centuries. The interment of ancestors within the lineage residences established permanent places for them within the cosmos, which was symbolized in the architecture in the form of a conceptual metaphor. More will be said of these ideological changes and their possible meaning in chapter 12. The combination of all of these changes occurred by the early eleventh century and marks the onset of the Classic Mimbres period.

CHAPTER FIVE

Classic Period Architecture and Space Use

*At about the same time that the typical Pueblo III groups were shaping themselves
in the north, there sprang up in the Mimbres Valley a host of small villages....
But the northern influence played at least some part in whatever happened,
for after what seems to have been a short period of existence in clusters of
semi-subterranean hovels, the Mimbreños began to build rectangular,
above ground houses and to group them, albeit blunderingly, one against
another in a vague imitation of the northern arrangements.*

—A. V. Kidder 1932:xx

Introduction

In this chapter I describe Classic Mimbres phase architecture, associated features, and space use at the NAN Ranch Ruin. The structure and organization of most aggregated pueblo-style Mimbres communities of the Classic period required significant transformation from the communities of the earlier pithouse times, due to population growth and complexity in the organization of labor for irrigation agriculture. This transformation, which took place in the tenth century, was described in the previous chapter. By the beginning of the eleventh century, population residential space for the founding lineages at the NAN Ranch Ruin was firmly established, as evidenced by the extent of rebuilding and remodeling. Aboveground pueblo-style buildings with cobble-adobe wall construction had become the architectural preference (Figure 5.1). This remarkable shift in vernacular architecture is a strong indication that major reorganization of Mimbres society and its worldview had taken place. By the end of the eleventh century, the Mimbres population had reached its peak.

Something happens to societies when population reaches about 2,500 people. A vertical cleavage process that establishes a social and political hierarchy is predictable.[1] Previous efforts to assess population sizes by the Mimbres Foundation were admittedly crude and subject to criticism,[2] primarily because the estimates were based on surface assessments, such as counting the numbers of pithouse depressions and room counts at surface sites. Nevertheless, the relative growth recognized by this study has been supported by subsequent archaeological findings, which have documented behavioral changes that correlate with population changes. The overall estimates of population in the Mimbres Valley in the Classic Mimbres phase vary from 3,500 to over 5,000.[3] These estimates may appear to be on the high side, but our investigations have shown a significant influx in the population in the Mimbres Valley between A.D. 1050 and 1100, based on new construction and the establishment of sites such as NAN 15.

A. V. Kidder's Anasazi-centric description of Mimbres pueblos quoted above presents a false impression of how these communities once appeared. His description also

5.1: Excavations in the Classic period ruins of the south room block at the NAN Ranch Ruin.

misses the point that the Mimbres dwellings were constructed to accommodate the residential patterns of the Mimbreños and not in a subservient effort to copy someone else's architecture. The very social fabric of Mimbres society was different from that of their Anasazi neighbors to the north, and these differences clearly show in the individual expression of the corporate groups that formed in the early Classic period.

Large Classic Mimbres communities appeared as clusters of single-story tan pueblos with exposed beams jutting from the edges of the walls and slanted, single-pole ladders projecting upward from the ceiling hatches. Based on historic photos of similar structures in Southwest pueblo communities, one can predict that the cobble-adobe walls were coated with thick layers of adobe mud in various stages of erosion, some exposing the stone masonry beneath. Courtyards and plazas surround the buildings, the surfaces of which were dimpled with an occasional adobe-mixing pit or cooking pit. Arbors or storage racks stood adjacent to some of the buildings. A few outlier structures, possibly built to accommodate an overflow of visitors or for special events, had fallen into ruin and disrepair.

The excavation of the NAN Ranch Ruin is the only extensive scientific investigation of a large Mimbres pueblo that has been carried out since the Cosgroves excavated the Swarts Ruin in the 1920s. Therefore a descriptive overview of the architecture is warranted to support the interpretations that follow. A detailed description of each of the 55-plus rooms for which we have architectural data is beyond the scope of this book, but examples of each class of rooms are described, along with associated features and facilities, to convey the rationale behind room and feature classifications and interpretations.

Kidder may be blamed for the popular misconception that the Mimbreños had poor architecture, a reputation that unfortunately exists to this day. One archaeologist recently described Mimbres pueblos as poorly constructed of stones shaped like bowling balls.[4] In truth, wall construction varies greatly, and the Mimbres used whatever stones were available. The masonry was plastered over with liberal coats of adobe, giving the appearance of neat, single-story pueblos, contrary to the image presented by Kidder and others.

This reputation for poor architecture can partly be attributed to the fact that no standing ruins or great houses were visible to greet earlier visitors to the region.

In the Anasazi and mountain Mogollon pueblos of Chaco Canyon and Grasshopper, laminated stone was plentiful and dry-laid masonry possible; consequently, walls stood for centuries.[5] Mimbres pueblos, by contrast, did not weather well through time because of the liberal use of adobe and a general lack of tabular stone; structures were eventually reduced to rubble mounds.

We began our excavations of rubble mounds by clearing away surface debris to expose the tops of walls. When excavated, surviving walls rarely exceed 1 m in height. Thick deposits of wall fall partly filled most rooms, protecting a layer of burned roof material, charred stumps of roof support posts, floors, and floor artifact assemblages. Construction techniques are reconstructed from the patterned fall of charred beams and burned but intact segments of the ceilings. Sometimes, however, all that remains of a room are remnants of an adobe floor, traces of wall bases, and a hearth.

Construction materials were obtained both locally and from the surrounding region. Adobe for walls, floors, and plaster was mined on the site from the ancient river terrace clays beneath the ruin. Adobe quarry pits occur throughout the extramural areas that were sampled at the NAN Ruin, and adobe-mixing pits were frequently found in courtyards and plazas adjacent to buildings[6] (Figure 5.2). Stones used in wall construction were

5.2: Adobe mixing pit.

obtained from Mimbres River gravels or colluvial slopes of the valley or brought in from distant latite quarries. Building stones locally available consisted of rounded river cobbles or angular stones from outcrops of andesite and rhyolite along the valley walls. Imported stones were slabs of latite. Laminated outcrops of latite, locally termed Sugarlump rhyolite, occur in the southern end of the Mimbres River valley, just before it opens to the Deming Plain. Occupants of the Old Town, Prewitt Ranch, and Baca ruins used this material as a primary source in wall construction, and we have recorded masonry walls constructed of this material at both the McSherry and NAN Ranch ruins. Rhyolite and andesite cobbles for wall construction were obtained from Mimbres River gravels and from the colluvial slopes of the valley that border the site on the east. Broken metates, manos, and rhyolite slabs were also incorporated into wall construction.

Vent covers, door slabs, hatchway covers, hatchway frames, fire hearth slabs, and lentils and frames for vents and doors were made mostly of a laminated latite or tabular rhyolite (Figure 5.3). The latite (Sugarlump rhyolite) was probably mined about 8 km to the south, or imported tabular rhyolites from the Gila Wilderness to the west were used. These construction materials may have been obtained directly or from kinsmen in villages close to the outcrops.

Woods were obtained from the riparian belt along the river (cottonwood, willow, box elder, ash, and walnut), along valley and mountain slopes (piñon pine, juniper, and oak), and from distant forests (ponderosa pine, Douglas fir).[7] Vegetation along the river used in house construction included cottonwood, willow (*Salix*), common reed (*Phragmites communis*), and bunchgrass (sacaton); vertical roof support posts were mostly of juniper (65 percent) cut from the valley slopes. Piñon pine (13 percent), ponderosa pine (9.7 percent), and willow/cottonwood (6.5 percent) were also used for posts.[8] *Latias,* or cross timbers, placed on top perpendicular to the vigas were of any wood available, including cottonwood, willow, oak, juniper, piñon, and other pines. Common reed, willow, pine, and bunchgrass were combined and placed in perpendicular layers as closing material above the latias, and all of this was capped with a thick layer of adobe clay. Sometimes a layer of slabs and large sherds paved the exposed surface to reduce erosion. Construction woods such as cottonwood and willow were used throughout the Classic period and indicate

5.3: Room 55 south wall, showing use of Sugarlump rhyolite in construction.

that the riparian forest belt that traces the river today was not denuded, as has been previously reported.[9] The Mimbres, like the contemporary Maya in Guatemala and Belize, probably carefully managed important economic resources such as riparian trees and reeds so they would be available as needed for such important uses.

A study of wood timbers from 48 rooms showed some interesting trends in the selection of wood for room construction.[10] No preference overall was observed for any particular wood, but as noted above, juniper was preferred as vertical support posts, and this pattern extended throughout the Classic Mimbres period. The use of piñon remained unchanged throughout the period and amounted to about 20 percent of the woods used. We were particularly interested in determining if the selection of riparian species diminished through time since a previous ethnobotanical study in the Mimbres Valley showed a decline in the uses of these trees. The results did not support the previous study, and in fact, certain late rooms at the NAN Ranch Ruin (e.g., rooms 50 and 63) had very high counts of woods identified as cottonwood/willow. The continued use of riparian species may have been facilitated by timber management, although we cannot prove this. Cottonwood, willow, and alder, for example, tolerate a wood management technique known as coppicing, encouraging regrowth from the roots when trees have been cut. Coppicing ensures a supply of narrow, straight poles. Although we do not know if the Mimbres solved part of their construction needs by such methods,

5.4: Wall fall from room 25 at the NAN Ranch Ruin.

5.5: NAN Ranch room 40 after excavation, showing interior support posts.

timber management is known among other ancient agricultural peoples.[11]

Overall, the selection of woods appears to have been expedient, although we do not know what personal, social, or ritual factors may have been involved in selecting construction woods. How the distant timbers were acquired also is not known; each kinship group—lineage or clan—may have had ancestral claims to respective segments of forested lands where men traveled on timber-gathering expeditions. These resources could have been the rights of other villages, and some form of reciprocal exchange may have been necessary to acquire the needed timbers. Although we can trace the approximate source for certain resources, we cannot reconstruct the social mechanism by which those resources were acquired.

Walls were usually constructed of a single course of cobbles set in adobe mortar 20 to 30 cm wide. Wall height, calculated by measuring fallen walls at the NAN Ruin (Figure 5.4), was about 2.5 m. Walls two, three, and, in one case (room 39), possibly five courses wide occurred. Such reinforcement, however, was usually reserved for the outside walls of an aggregated unit or for extraordinarily large rooms.

The Classic period Mimbres used three methods to construct wall bases. One method, described in the previous chapter, involved excavating a narrow trench and filling it with puddled adobe before laying the first course of cobbles. The second was to excavate a narrow trench and set small boulders vertically to anchor the walls. Cornerstones often were small elongated boulders placed vertically. Mortar of adobe mined from the underlying hardpan clays was used to fill in around the stones before the first horizontal course of cobbles was laid. This latter method was noted for rooms constructed in the early Classic Mimbres period but apparently ceased to be used toward the end of the occupation. Walls were built up by adding courses of stones separated by thick applications of adobe and capped with flat stones or rhyolite slabs. The third method consisted of simply laying a horizontal course of stones or rhyolite slabs and adding courses of stones. Some walls added late in the sequence were constructed mostly of rhyolite slabs and mortar made of mud instead of the better-quality hardpan clay previously used.

Vertical support posts were found in most rooms (Figure 5.5), the exceptions being narrow storage rooms such as rooms 42 and 78. These main support posts included single posts set in the approximate center of the room or two posts placed along a midline approximately an equal distance apart and an equal distance to the nearest wall. Large, square rooms required additional posts; room 45 had three large posts placed along a midline, whereas room 39 had a square pattern of four posts. Additional posts were often used to shore up a sagging ceiling; the secondary support posts were in no particular pattern since they were incorporated only in specific instances for repair. The preferred wood for support posts was juniper, but pine and cottonwood were also used, although less frequently.

The presence and type of the formal hearth is the single defining feature in determining room function. Classic period hearths were of five kinds (listed as types 1–5 in Table 5.1, pp. 60–61): type 1, ash deposits on floor; type 2, adobe lined; type 3, rectangular slab lined or, 3A, rectangular adobe lined; type 4, rectangular slab lined with an adjacent floor vault; and type 5, circular, cobble lined. Type 1 hearths were merely ash deposits on floors. This hearth type occurred more frequently in the earlier pithouse periods but was also present in rooms 42 and 78/90. Type 2 hearths were also more common in the pithouse periods, but this type of hearth was encountered in rooms 60 (a storeroom) and 47 (a habitation room perhaps converted from a storeroom). Room 60, a Classic period storage room attached to room 55, had a small ash-filled basin 25 cm in diameter. Room 47 had an ash-filled basin hearth 30 cm in diameter.

A total of 25 (or 78 percent) of the 32 recorded interior hearths were type 3, rectangular slab lined. These consist of a box framed with upright slabs and sealed with adobe (Figure 5.6). Pit bottoms were often framed by rhyolite slabs. Slab-lined hearths were recorded in rooms dating throughout the Classic Mimbres period. Hearth size varied from 20 by 20 cm in room 25A to 50 by 60 cm in room 41. Most measured between these two extremes. Type 3A rectangular adobe-lined hearths were recorded in rooms 74 and 109, both large corporate storage rooms added very late in the architectural sequence.[12]

Type 4 hearths associated with a rectangular slab-lined vault (described below) situated next to the hearth occurred in five cases (rooms 12, 29, 41, 55, and 62). This hearth type is described in more detail below. Type 5 hearths appeared late in the architectural sequence, occurring in rooms 37, 39, and 84. Hearth diameters ranged from 33 by 40 cm in habitation room 84 to 60 to 65 cm in communal room 39.

Small rectangular bins 15.20 cm wide and 20 to 35 cm long were associated with hearth type 4 and were found adjacent to hearths in rooms 12, 29, 41, 55, and 62 (Figure 5.7). The construction was similar to that for hearths. They all were smaller than the hearths and, unlike the hearths, did not show evidence of burning. The contents of these features at the NAN Ruin are variable but generally include either ash or loose ashy fill, indicating that some of the vaults were empty at the time of abandonment. These features have variously been described as "double fireplaces,"[13] "double fireboxes,"[14] or double

5.6: Details of hearth construction in room 12 at the NAN Ranch Ruin.

5.7: Hearth and floor vault in room 29 at the NAN Ranch Ruin.

TABLE 5.1. Room Data for All Excavated Rooms and Structures at the NAN Ranch Ruin

Room no.	Hearth Type	Length (m)	Width (m)	sq m	Type	Burials	Probable Function
1	1	nd	nd	nd	pithouse	none	domestic
2	nd	nd	nd	nd	surface	1	habitation
3	3	nd	nd	nd	surface	1	habitation
4	3	3	2.8	8.4	surface	2	habitation
6	nd	nd	nd	nd	surface	1	habitation
7	none	2.5	3	7.5	surface	2	granary
8	3?	4	5.5	22	surface	3	habitation
9	3?	7.2	4.7	33.85	surface	1 plus	ceremonial?
11	none	3.4	2.25	7.65	surface	unknown	storage?
12	4	5.25	3.2	16.8	surface	15	corporate kiva
13	nd	nd	3	nd	transitional	none	unknown
14	2	3.2	3	9.6	pithouse	2	habitation
15	1	3	3	9	pithouse	2	none
16A	none	3.75	2.5	9.38	surface	none	storage
16B	3	3.75	2.5	9.38	surface	none	habitation?
17	2	3	3	9	pithouse	none	domestic
18	1/3?	7.5	3.75	28.13	surface	2	habitation
20	nd	3.2	3	9.6	surface	nd	unknown
21	nd	nd	3.2	nd	surface	nd	unknown
22	3	3.4	2.25	7.65	surface	6	habitation
23A	3	5	2.2	11	surface	1	habitation
23B	nd	nd	nd	nd	transitional	none	habitation?
25A	3	2.8	2	5.6	surface	none	habitation
25B	3	2.8	2	5.6	surface	none	utility
28A	3	4.1	3.45	14.1	surface	21	habitation?
28B	3	4.3	3.45	16.21	surface	–	habitation?
29A	4	3.8	3.6	13.5	surface	31+	ceremonial
29B	3	3.8	3.6	13.5	surface	6	habitation
30	3	3.6	3.1	11.16	surface	2	habitation
31	3	2.8	2.5	7	surface	1+	habitation
32	3	3.9	3.1	12.09	surface	yes	habitation
33	nd	4.0+	2.8	11.2+	surface	nd	habitation?
36	nd	nd	5	nd	pithouse	nd	habitation
37	5	4.5	4	18	surface	yes	habitation
38	nd	1.9	nd	nd	surface	nd	storage?
39	5	6	6	36	surface	4	ceremonial
40	3	6	3.7	22.2	surface	2+	habitation?
41	4	6.5	5	32.5	surface	10	habitation
42	1?	6	2	12	surface	2	storage
43	2	8	7.2	57.6	pithouse	none	great kiva?
45	none?	10	9.5	95	surface	none	communal
46	2	4.2	2.6	10.9	surface	none	storage
47	2	4	4	16	surface	2	habitation
48	3	6.5	3.5	16.75	surface	2	habitation
49	3	4.1	3.9	16	surface	2	habitation
50	3	4.6	4.2	19.32	surface	3	habitation
51	nd	4	5	20	transitional	none	granary
52	2	7.2	6	43 sq m	pithouse	4 in fill	great kiva
53	nd	nd	nd	nd	surface		
54	none	3.5	2.25	7.9	surface	–	storage
55	4	3.9	3	11.7	surface	3	corporate kiva
56	none	2	2.2	4.4	surface	none	storage
57	none?			29 (est.)	surface	6	habitation

TABLE 5.1. *continued*

Room no.	Hearth Type	Length (m)	Width (m)	sq m	Type	Burials	Probable Function
58	3	5.4	3.2	17.3	surface	yes	communal
59	none	5.25	2.8	17.7	surface	none	storage
60	2	2.6	2.4	6.25	surface	1	
61	nd	3.2+	3.0+	9.6+	transitional	none	habitation
62	4	3.3	3.4	11	surface	2+	corporate kiva
63A	2	5	2.2	11	surface	none	storage
63B	3	5	2.2	11	surface	3+	habitation
65	nd	–	–	–	surface	3	habitation?
67	nd	2.5+	2.2	5.5+	surface	1+	habitation
71	1	round	2.8 dia		pithouse	none	specialized
72	nd	nd	nd	nd	pithouse	nd	domestic
74	3A	7	5	35	surface	none	storage
75A	none	2.8	2	5.6	surface	none	granary
75B	none	2.8	2	5.6	surface	none	granary
75C	none	2.8	2	5.6	surface	2	storage
76	none	2	3.5	7.5	surface	2	granary
78 (90)	1	6	2.65	15.5	surface	none	storage
79A	none	2.35	4	9.7	surface	none	storage
79B	2	2.35	4	9.7	trans/sur?	2	habitation?
80	3	nd	nd	nd	surface	1	habitation
81	none	2	2.2	est. 6	surface	none	granary
82	3	4	2.7	10.8	trans/sur?	2	habitation
83A	1	3.5	3.5	12.25	mod. pitho		habitation
83B	3A	3.5	3.5	12.25	pithouse	1	domestic
84	5	4.4	3.8	16.72	surface	1+	habitation
85	3	3.7	3.4	12.6	surface	1+	habitation
86	1	3.5	3.5	12.25	pithouse	1	domestic
87	1	2?	2.5?	835	surface	none	ramada
88	none	2.4	2.8	6.72	surface	none	storage
89A	3	3.5	3.45	12	surface	4	habitation
89B	3	3.5	3.45	12	surface		habitation
91	2	5	4	20	pithouse	none	kiva
92	nd	2	3	6	surface	1 intrusive	storage
93	3A	3	3	9	surface	none	habitation
94	3	4.4	4.2	18.5	surface	6	habitation
95	1	3.1	3.2	10	pithouse	1	habitation
97	2	2.4	2.2	5.28	pithouse	none	domestic
98	nd	3.4	4.5	15.3	transitional	3	habitation
99	nd	2.4	2.5	6	pithouse	1	domestic?
100	nd	nd	nd	12.75	pithouse	none	domestic
101	nd	nd	nd	nd	trans/sur?	none	habitation?
102	2	3	4	12	pithouse	none	domestic
103	2	3	3.4	10	pithouse	none	domestic
104	3A	3.5	5	17.5	transitional	13	habitation
105	none	round	dia. 4		pithouse	none	domestic
106	nd	3.2	4.65	20.25	surface	nd	habitation
108A	none	3	2.5	7.5	surface	none	granary
108B	2	3	2.5	7.5	pithouse	none	domestic
109	2	5.7	7	39.2	surface	none	storage
111	none	2.8	2.4	est 7.0?	surface	none	storage
112	3	nd	nd	nd	transitional	1	habitation?
113	2	4.75	square?	est 22.6	pithouse	none	habitation
115	2	2.65	2.25	5.96	transitional	none	habitation?
116	2	3	3.2	9.6	pithouse	none	habitation?

5.8: Air vent in the south wall of room 28 at the NAN Ranch Ruin: A. covered; B. cover removed.

firepits."[15] The presence of floor vaults is one of the defining characteristics of corporate kivas. Their association with special rooms calls into question the previously assumed secular function of the vault. Its possible role and function are discussed further in the definition of corporate kivas given later in this chapter.

Air vents were constructed in outside walls to draw air into the room when the hearths were in use. These vents averaged 20 to 25 cm wide and 25 cm high (Figure 5.8). They were framed with rhyolite slabs and often were closed with subrectangular rhyolite slabs.

Doorways, or perhaps more aptly termed crawlways, provided access to and from secure storage rooms attached to habitation rooms. Doorways existed or had existed at one time between rooms 8 and 9, 16 and 25A, 28 and 29, 28 and 94, 29 and 79A (Figure 5.9A), 30 and 32, 41 and 42, 47 and 49 (Figure 5.9B, C), 50 and 54, 55 and 60, 58 and 48 (Figure 5.9B), 39 and 79/90, and 79A and 108. Doors ranged from 40 to 60 cm wide but averaged about 50 cm wide. Lentils and sills framing the doors were rhyolite slabs anchored in adobe mortar. Liberal coats of plaster usually covered the framing slabs and provided a smooth facing. Doorways were covered by large subrectangular Sugarlump rhyolite slabs (Figure 5.19A, B). The door between rooms 47 and 49 had a vertical slab set in the floor about 15 cm from the doorway in room 49 to anchor the door slab and to facilitate moving the slab from side to side to open and close the passageway (Figure 5.9C). The only surviving intact door encountered in the NAN Ruin excavations was between rooms 58 and 48 and measured 60 cm high and 50 cm wide (Figure 5.9D). No exterior doors were recorded in the NAN Ruin.

Ladder rests were not formal features as such but were constructed expediently in various forms. Possible ladder rests consisting of single slabs set upright in the floor near the hearths were in rooms 47, 50, and 63B (Figure 5.10). Two slabs set vertically in the floor at right angles marked ladder rests in rooms 12 and 94 (Figure 5.22). The ladder rest in room 28 was a bowl-shaped, cobble-lined, adobe-capped pit. The ladder rest in room 63 consisted of three cobbles set vertically in the floor, and in room 22 the rest was simply a bowl-shaped pit in the floor. Most ladders were probably anchored in floor depressions and were not generally visible archaeologically. In every case where rests were recognized, however, the use of single notched log ladders is indicated.[16]

Most ceiling hatches were probably partly framed with wood and rhyolite slabs. Collapsed frames that consisted of concentrations of rhyolite slabs were generally found in roof fall above the hearth area of habitation rooms (Figure 5.11). The number of slabs in the concentrations varied and suggested that some were entirely framed with slabs, whereas others may have had only one stone slab at the entry point. At least one slab was used in virtually all cases where hatch remnants were found. Collapsed hatch frames were documented in rooms 29, 40, 47, 49, 80A, and 84. The hatch side opposite the ladder must have had a slab that served both as

5.9: Doors at the NAN Ranch Ruin: A door between rooms 29 and 79; B. door between rooms 47 and 49; C. door slab anchor in room 49; D. intact door between rooms 48 and 58.

a frame and a seat, judging from the extensive smoothing and wear observed on specific examples.

Subfloor features associated with room use consisted mostly of pits; subfloor pits were of two kinds, burial and storage. Burials of all ages and both sexes were placed beneath the floors of all Classic period habitation rooms used for any duration of time. The size and depth of the burial pit was usually commensurate with the size of the individual. Adults were placed flexed or semi-flexed in oval pits that measured 90 to 100 cm long and 50 to 60 cm wide (see chapter 8). If subsurface conditions merited, adult burial pits were about 60 to 80 cm deep. Shallower adult burials occurred when dense consolidated gravel was encountered. Children and infants

5.10: Possible ladder rest in room 50 at the NAN Ranch Ruin.

5.11: Ceiling hatchway fall in room 47 at the NAN Ranch Ruin.

5.12: Corrugated storage jar beneath the floor of room 46 at the NAN Ranch Ruin.

were placed in smaller, shallower graves sufficient to accommodate the body. Cairns were composed of cobbles, small boulders, discarded metates, manos, other stone artifacts, and occasionally large sherds capped the pits of adults and children but usually not of infants. Mortuary vessels were placed over the face or head of 60 to 70 percent of the subfloor burials. Classic period mortuary practices as a whole are presented in chapter 8.

Only three instances of subfloor caches have been found. One was a *Glycymeris* shell bracelet broken into four pieces and cached west of the hearth in room 28. The second was a small corrugated mug (appendix I: Figure A.29G) beneath the floor of room 85, and the third was a sherd-lined pit in room 78/90, possibly associated with a carved *Glycymeris* shell bracelet fragment, two turquoise pendants, and a caved zoomorphic pendant.[17]

Deep subfloor storage pits with either straight-sided or bell-shaped forms were found in habitation rooms, corporate kivas, and private storage rooms (see chapter 7). Such pits were noted in rooms 40, 41, 42, 46, 47, 50, and 79B. In two instances (rooms 41 and 46), these pits contained large corrugated jars (Figure 5.12). In room 40, one grass-lined pit contained a large Mimbres Style III jar capped with a Style III lid bowl; inside the jar were the remains of desiccated squash (*Cucurbita pepo*; see chapter 7). Most storage pits, however, were empty at the time of discovery.

We were able to define several types of Classic period rooms based either on construction details or associated features. These room types are habitation, restricted storage, cooperate storage, cooperate granaries, communal, and cooperate kivas. Table 5.1 (pp. 60–61) lists all of the surface rooms for which some data are available. Habitation rooms and cooperate granaries were used throughout the sequence and were a carryover from the Late Three Circle phase. Cooperate kivas were firmly established in the early Classic Mimbres period and may have evolved from certain Late Three Circle phase pit structures. Storage rooms with restricted access were also in use at least by middle Classic times, if not earlier. Large communal rooms and large cooperate storage rooms, however, were late room types that became part of larger households in the latter half of the Classic Mimbres period.

A single room may have been used in different ways at different times. Functional change for rooms was a common feature in the Classic Mimbres period. Certain rooms, such 11/22, 28, 29, 25/75, 58, and 63/23A, among others, were floored multiple times, with the function of the room often shifting through time (Figure 5.13). Two rooms, 63/23A and 25/75, illustrate this process and demonstrate just how complicated the architectural stratigraphy can be, even within the confines of a single room. The sequence of superimposed rooms identified as 63/23A includes three separate renovation episodes within the same four walls. Room 23A was a small habitation room measuring 2.2 by 5 m with a slab-lined hearth in the east-central part of the room. One burial, 89, was associated with the use of this room. The room did not burn but apparently went into a period of disrepair.

5.13: Room 63/23, illustrating functional differences in room use through time: A. 63A, showing absence of hearth; B. slab-lined hearth and ladder rest; C. 23A, floor with slab-lined hearth.

About 10 cm of fill covered the floor. Later modification (63A) involved the construction of an adobe floor and a new slab-lined hearth and a vertical slab ladder rest in the west-central part of the room. The use of 63A as a habitation room was sufficiently long, perhaps a generation or so, for three burials (81, 84, and 88) to be interred beneath the floor. Another floor, room 63A, was constructed about 10 cm above 63B. This floor did not contain a hearth or evidence of a collapsed hatchway. It may once have been a storage room connected to another room, perhaps room 24 to the west, although the preservation of the walls was not such that evidence for a door was found.

The functional history of room 25/75 is even more complex (Figure 5.14, p. 66). This small room, measuring 2.8 by 2.0 m, had been remodeled three times and refloored five times. The room began as a storage room, possibly a granary (75C), with a thick adobe floor. The next episode, 75B, involved the construction of a granary by placing a dense layer of cobbles on the 75C floor and capping this with a 7-cm-thick layer of adobe. After a period of use, yet another dense layer of cobbles was placed on 75B, and again this was capped with a 7-cm-thick layer of adobe, forming the floor of 75C. This floor was capped with a layer of fill 15 cm thick and the application of an adobe surface (25B). Its function is uncertain; for a while the space may have been a small courtyard since an adobe-mixing pit 15 cm deep and 60 cm in diameter was constructed in the floor, perhaps to be used during renovation. It was also during the span of 25B that a walled bin enclosing a space 27 by 34 cm was constructed in the southwest corner. The wall to the bin was 20 cm thick and was cobble-adobe construction, much like that used for wall construction (Figure 5.15, p. 66). The wall rested on the floor of room 25B, but the interior extended beneath the floor. The function of this walled feature is uncertain, but it may have been used as a turkey pen. Turkey pens have been reported from Elk Ridge, a large Mimbres site in the upper Mimbres River valley.[18] The structure was again roofed, an event dated to about A.D. 1100 based on tree-ring dates (A.D. 1098+r, 1098+r, 1099+r, 1096v, and 1096vv), and the mixing pit was later filled in and smoothed over.

Room 25B burned, and the wall bases were used to rebuild the 25A room. A small slab-lined firebox was constructed in the floor of room 25A, and two concentrations of corrugated jar sherds were recovered on the floor. A door leading into room 16 (which itself was razed later) was constructed in the west wall. Room 25A also burned, but the space was never reclaimed after that event.

Twenty-nine rooms that were used at one time for habitation were completely or partially excavated.[19] Classic Mimbres habitation rooms were identified by the presence of formal hearths, which were rectangular and framed with upright rhyolite slabs ($n = 25$, or 83 percent) or circular lined with cobbles ($n = 5$, or 17 percent),

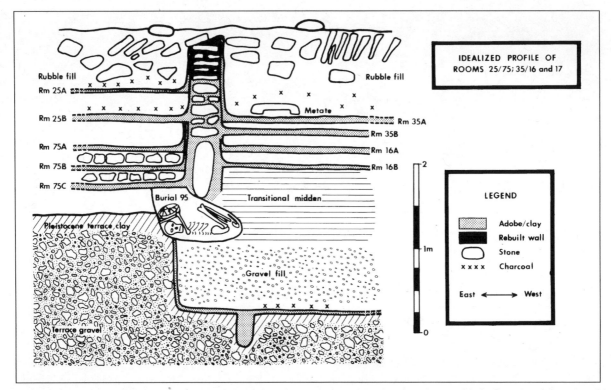

5.14: Schematic profile of rooms 75/25 and 35/16 at the NAN Ranch Ruin, showing multiple floors and functional changes through time.

5.15: Walled bin in room 25B at the NAN Ranch Ruin.

adobe floors, and wall vents. Entry into the room was by a ladder through a ceiling hatchway, as shown by the presence of collapsed hatch frames and ladder rests. Habitation rooms were generally better constructed than rooms without hearths. Walls were thicker and heavier, and floors, walls, and ceilings were plastered.

Room size could be determined for 23 habitation rooms (Table 5.1). The mean size is 16.41 sq m, with a variance of 7.66. The size of Mimbres habitation rooms is larger than reported for later Mogollon sites such as Turkey Creek: 12.22 sq m.[20] The size of the Mimbres rooms is, however, consistent with Hopi room size at Orayvi, which is 15.6 sq m.[21] Five habitation rooms either served as or were converted into corporate kivas (rooms 12, 29, 41, 55, and 62).

Habitation rooms were mostly cleaned of their contents, as abandoned rooms rarely had many artifacts left on the floors, but there are exceptions. The most common artifact found on habitation room floors was smoothed-flat kneading slabs of fine-grained rhyolite; less frequently manos, metates, pottery vessels, bone awls, and three-quarter grooved axes were left on the floor as well. Room 30 contained a large Mimbres Style III bowl (appendix I: Figure A.14G), a white-slipped seed jar (appendix I: Figure A.26B), and a Mimbres Style III seed jar (appendix I: Figure A.24F). Room 47 had a corrugated cooking pot, a bone awl, and a polished slab; room 50 had a metate and two manos; and room 94 had a metate, three manos, two bone awls, and a corrugated cooking pot (appendix I: Figure A.30E).

Two habitation rooms, rooms 22 and 28, are featured here as examples to illustrate specific room characteristics as well as the dynamic changes that occurred in rooms that were used over a long period of time. Room 22 was one of four long, narrow rooms that included rooms 10, 22, 63/23, and 26, constructed along a north-south axis in the center of the east room block (Figure P.2). Rooms 22 and 63/23 were built onto the existing west walls of rooms 12 and 58, whereas room 75/25 abutted room 22 to the west. Both rooms 22 and 63/23 were apparently constructed at the same time, as indicated by the bonded juncture of the dividing wall. There is no evidence, however, to indicate that the two rooms were ever connected by a crawlway.

Room 22 was a small rectangular interior room with a floor space of about 7 sq m (Figures 5.16 and 5.18). The room had undergone a series of modifications and functional changes, the last of which was ended by burning. The room was initially constructed about A.D. 1041. The plaster floor was resurfaced at least three times, as indicated by thick layers of superimposed adobe. Each time the floor was resurfaced, the plaster was extended up the walls. A vent once opened into the west wall, and a sill slab in the north wall may also have marked the location of a vent or small crawlway into room 10. A rectangular, slab-lined firebox was constructed in the northwest quadrant of the room. Two adobe depressions found south of the firebox and associated with the second flooring presumably represent anchor holes for ladders. The original posts used to support the roof of room 22 were the same used in later modifications. The third flooring capped the firebox, which may have changed the function of the room.

An oval pit capped by the third flooring cut through the second floor in the south-central part of the room (Figure 5.17). This basin-shaped pit measured 75 by 55 cm and contained a concentration of large sherds and lumps of yellowish organic material intermixed with the sherds. Two partially corrugated jars were reconstructed from the

5.16: NAN Ranch room 22, illustrating slab-line hearth, floor and wall patches.

5.17: Pit with sherds in the floor of room 22.

sherds (appendix I: Figures A.31H, I). The form and structure of the organic nodules suggests that they may be coprolites–desiccated feces–but this could not be confirmed in the laboratory. Although the pit's function is unknown, it may have been a termination or desecra-

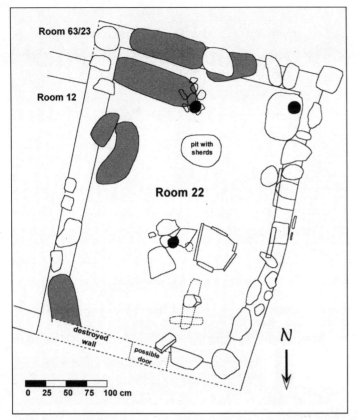

5.18: Plan of room 22, showing the location of floor and subfloor features and burials (dark areas).

tion ritual since the room ceased to be used for habitation after this time but was not burned.

Six burials were interred beneath the floor of room 22 (Figure 5.18): five adults (one male, two females, and two indeterminate) and an adolescent. An adobe patch in the floor above burial 82 represented an aboriginal disturbance to the grave. The disturbance involved the excavation of the grave pit for burial 83, an adult female placed east-west beneath the south wall. The burial 83 grave pit disturbed burial 82, disarticulating the skull and a few other bones near the skull. A Style III bowl associated with burial 82 (appendix I: Figure A.16C) and fragments of another vessel (appendix I: Figure A.16I), a warped Style III bowl segment possibly used as a scoop in the excavation of burial 83, were mixed in the fill of both graves. Burial 91 was also placed beneath the south wall. Vertical slabs were placed along the wall at the juncture with the floor to seal the grave and reinforce the wall. A similar feature was observed with the closure of

the grave for burial 85 in the east wall. An adult burial placed beneath the floor in the northeast part of the room was removed by relic hunters.

Loose organic fill containing desiccated corn husks accumulated above the floor of room 22, suggesting the abandoned habitation room may have been temporarily used as a granary or a place to dry corn. These fill deposits reached a depth of about 20 cm and were capped by a thin adobe floor designated as room 11. The original superstructure of room 22 remained in use, but some renovation took place with room 11 modification. Room 11 was terminated by burning.

The use of room 22 as a habitation room probably began in about A.D. 1041, based on a single tree-ring date, and likely continued for no more than two generations. At some time after A.D. 1087 renovation took place and the room was used as a storeroom. The ceramics associated with room 22 interments are middle Style III Black-on-white and fall within the 50 or so years this little room was used for habitation (see appendix I: Figures A.11D, A.12I, A.16C, A.16H, and A.16I). The function as a habitation room probably ceased when it became an interior room with the addition of either room 10 to the north or room 24 to the west. Interior rooms lacked a direct means of venting with air from the outside and were usually abandoned as habitation rooms when direct venting was no longer possible. Their functions often shifted to that of storage rooms or kivas, rooms with more limited use and restricted access.

Room 28, another habitation room, was constructed onto the east side of room 29 in the south room block (Figure 5.19). It too had undergone several episodes of remodeling. The floor area was about 14.1 sq m. The room had burned, and some defacto refuse was left on the floor at the north end, including two manos, a smoothed slab, a bone awl, and portions of three vessels: half of a Mimbres Style III bowl, sherds of a partially corrugated jar, and approximately one-third of a fully corrugated jar (not illustrated).

Excavations revealed that the history of room 28 was complex and involved at least two major construction episodes. Each construction event involved new wall and hearth construction. The first construction may have taken place in A.D. 1066 or about 1088, when major renovations were done to adjacent room 29. At some point early in its history, room 28 was connected to room 29 by a doorway. This doorway was later closed, perhaps with the A.D. 1109 renovation. Room 28B was the earlier floor. Floor features included a square, slab-lined firebox ritually(?) dismantled in the southwest-central part of the room and a large posthole in the center of the room. A wall vent that may have been in the south wall was later enlarged by the addition of a crawlway into room 94. We suspect that several burials were placed beneath the floor during this episode of use, but burials could rarely be seriated, and it was not possible to separate early pits from later ones.

Extensive modifications occurred in the renovations of room 28, not all of which can be chronologically ordered. Another wall course was added to the west wall, blocking the doorway into room 29. At some point room 94 was added to the south of room 28, and a common doorway was constructed between the two rooms. One or both rooms burned, and both were rebuilt in A.D. 1109, based on tree-ring dates. The ceiling was rebuilt as the single support post of room 28 was replaced by two posts set in a north-south centerline of room 28A. A new floor was laid and a new firebox constructed in the east-central part of the room between. A vent in the middle of the east wall was sealed and a new one constructed near the northeast corner when room 109 was added four years later, in A.D. 1114. Other features associated with this floor include a ladder rest consisting of a small stone-lined pit and a dedicatory cache consisting of a *Glycymeris* shell bracelet broken in four pieces that was placed on the west side of the room 28A firebox. In addition, several postholes, most of which presumably predate the structure, were found in the hardpan surface beneath the east and central part of the room.

A large cemetery beneath the floors of room 28 contained 21 individuals: 11 children, two adolescents, and eight adults (Table 8.1).[22] Burials were placed beneath the floor in each phase of room use, as indicated by pit origins. Not all burials could be assigned to floor since later burials often destroyed the evidence of earlier pits. Ceramics associated with the burials include middle, middle-late, and late Style III Mimbres Black-on-white, indicating the period of cemetery use may have spanned about 80 years, or from about A.D. 1060 to 1140, consistent with tree-ring dates from construction phases.

In summary, Mimbres habitation rooms are defined as rooms with the following features: well-plastered floors and walls, formal slab- or cobble-lined hearths, and subfloor cemeteries that contain adult burials. Mimbres habitation rooms probably represented a scaled-down version of Mimbres cosmology, and there-

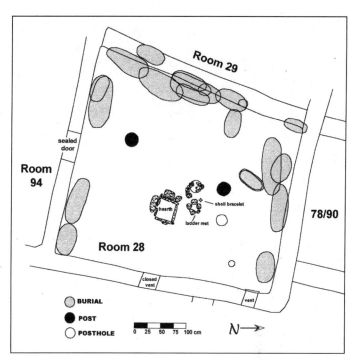

5.19: Floor plan of NAN Ranch room 28, showing floor and subfloor features.

fore virtually any sacred or profane activity carried out inside a ceremonial structure could have taken place within these rooms. This multipurpose role could account for their use as domestic habitation rooms, cemeteries, and places for ritual caches and conversion into corporate kivas.

Corporate kivas can be identified, in part, on the basis of roles that originated in habitation rooms, such as their use as cemeteries. The primary differences between habitation rooms as defined here and corporate kivas are the addition of the floor vaults, continued use as cemeteries, and other special features for corporate kivas. Each corporate kiva, however, also contained individual attributes that usually set the kivas apart from other rooms.

A subset of habitation rooms are classified as corporate kivas, or special rooms that served as the focal points of family rituals.[23] Five rooms fall into this class: 12, 29, 41, 55, and 62; other rooms may have fallen into this category, such as rooms 9, 49,[24] and 58, but in 9 and 49 relic hunters had destroyed the hearths. Room 58, described separately as a communal room, stands out from all other rooms in that it has benches around three walls

5.20: Hearth, vault, and ladder rest in room 12 at the NAN Ranch Ruin.

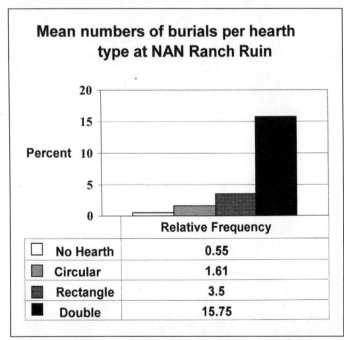

5.21: Graph showing mean number of burials per hearth type at the NAN Ranch Ruin.

but lacks a floor vault, or at least one was not present in the preserved parts of the room. Rooms classified as corporate kivas are virtually identical in appearance to habitation rooms, with two notable differences: in addition to a slab-lined hearth, each has a smaller, rectangular slab-lined floor vault or bin next to the hearth (Figure 5.20), and rooms with floor vaults characteristically have the highest density of burials compared to all other rooms (Figure 5.21). The NAN burial pattern for rooms with floor vaults also is consistent with that of other large Classic Mimbres sites. Rooms with floor vaults usually held the largest cemeteries at both the north and south house at the Swarts,[25] Cameron Creek, Mattocks, McSherry, and Saige-McFarland sites.[26]

Floor vaults do not show evidence of burning like the adjacent hearths. Contents of these features at the NAN Ranch Ruin are variable but generally include ash or loose, ashy fill, indicating some vaults were empty at the time of abandonment. The specific function of floor vaults is unknown, but they may have been floor drums or sipapus, symbolic openings to the Underworld and to the house of the ancestors buried below. Other features that may have had ritual significance include wall niches in room 29, wall shelves in room 12, and benches in room 58; the niches and shelves may have held ritual items or been components of shrines, further strengthening the interpretation that these were indeed special rooms.

Floor vaults are special features that required an additional construction investment beyond that for habitation rooms.[27] These rooms probably served not only as habitation rooms but also as focal points for coresidential rituals, similar to that of corporate kivas among the Anasazi. Mimbres corporate kivas were special rooms within the coresidential household, which probably contained a shrine and where religious activities were practiced and paraphernalia stored. Such rooms were not previously recognized because they are not that obvious. They lack a form that contrasts with habitation and storerooms and a set of diagnostic interior features such as those found in Pueblo II and Pueblo III round kivas. The ratio of rooms with floor vaults to total rooms at both the NAN and Swarts ruins is about 1:8. This is about the same ratio of circular kivas to Pueblo II and Pueblo III rooms at small sites in the Chaco cultural system (i.e., 1:6.5) and Cliff Palace at Mesa Verde (1:10). One major difference between Anasazi kivas and Mimbres corporate kivas (besides the distinguishing architectural details of the former) is the presence of subfloor cemeteries in the latter.

CLASSIC PERIOD ARCHITECTURE AND SPACE USE / 71

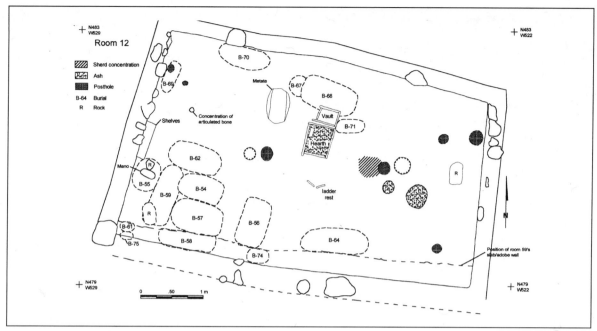

5.22: Room 12 floor plan (after Burden 2001: Figure 5.20).

The abandonment of the Mimbres great kivas during the Late Three Circle phase transition and early Classic Mimbres period correlates with the mortuary pattern shift to bounded, intramural cemeteries in rooms with formal hearths and eventually in rooms with floor vaults. Rooms with floor vaults may have replaced great kivas in large Mimbres towns as the society reorganized and became structured around prime landholding families. The kivas may have served to integrate members of corporate lineages through ancestral ties. Two corporate kivas, rooms 12 and 29, are described to provide details on the characteristics of this class of rooms.

Room 12 is one of the earlier structures at the NAN Ruin with a floor vault (Figure 5.22). The room was one

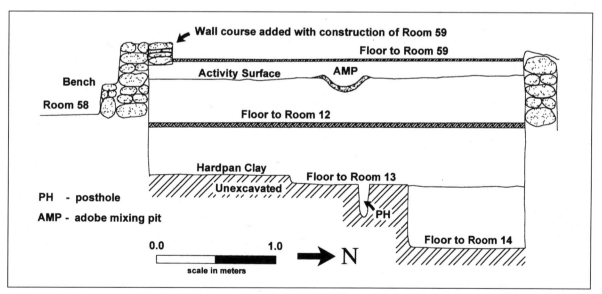

5.23: Schematic profile, floors above and below room 12.

5.24: Wall shelves (subfeature 18) in the west wall of room 12.

of several rooms constructed along an east-west axis in the northern part of the east room block. Originally it may have been part of the Cosgrove suite to the east, a suite of rooms excavated by the Cosgrove family in 1926. Room 12 stratigraphically overlay Three Circle phase room 14 and transitional room 13 (Figure 5.23). Room 22 was constructed onto the west wall of room 12, and part of the south wall was shared with room 59. Room 12 had an overall floor space of about 16.5 sq m.

An elaborately constructed firebox with an adjacent vault was in the north-central part of the room (Figure 5.6). When we dismantled the hearth to record construction details, we discovered a layer of juniper twigs and bows beneath the flooring slab and at the bottom of the pit dug to construct the firebox. These items were scorched from the heat but otherwise well preserved and easily identifiable. Juniper was used widely among Pueblo people in healing and purification rituals.[28] Its presence in the hearth is attributed to a dedication ceremony in conjunction with the hearth construction and possibly to the room's special importance as a corporate kiva or an ancestor shrine.

Other features in the room include a ladder rest, consisting of two slabs oriented at right angles (Figure 5.20), set vertically in the floor about 0.5 m south of the fire hearth. In the west wall of the room were two carefully placed shelves of well-shaped Sugarlump rhyolite slabs, identical in size (52 cm long), placed horizontally 42 cm above the floor (Figure 5.24). These slabs were spaced 5 cm apart, one above the other, and extended out 15 cm from the wall. They are interpreted as the remnants of a shrine.[29] Wall shelves are rare in Mimbres rooms and have been reported at only two other sites, Swarts and Treasure Hill.[30]

Room 12 was floored twice and had been both resurfaced and patched multiple times. Fourteen burials were identified beneath the floor: four infants, two children, one adolescent, and seven adults. Charred beams on the floor of room 12 failed to yield tree-ring dates. Ceramic styles associated with the burials, however, include three late Style II vessels (appendix I: Figures A.3B, A.4C, A.4E), three early Style III (appendix I: Figures A.6C, A.6G, and 9A), and four middle Style III (appendix I: Figures A.10C, A.10E, A.10G, and A.15G), indicating cemetery use spanned three to four generations, beginning late in the tenth century through about A.D. 1060.

The room was burned, and the space was converted to a small enclosed courtyard. Half a meter of windblown and midden fill accumulated in the courtyard. At least one activity surface associated with an adobe-puddling pit was detected in this accumulation. The space was eventually incorporated into room 59, which was built directly over room 12. Room 59 was constructed very late in the east room block sequence; its function is unknown.

Room 29, an interior room, was situated immediately west of room 28 and separated from it by a thick, double-course wall. The overall floor space was about 13.5 sq m. The room was originally constructed with single-course walls; through renovations and additions of other rooms, the east and north walls became double course (Figure 6.2). We detected two major construction episodes and at least three flooring episodes in the stratigraphy. The original construction is referred to as room 29B, whereas the later episode is room 29A. Room 79A, a small storeroom, was later attached to room 29 and connected by an interior doorway.

Room 29B was built over the ruins of transitional room 98 (Figure P.2), and at least two separate flooring episodes were associated with its use. A rectangular, slab-lined firebox was situated in the south-central part of the room. The roof was supported by at least two posts set against the west and east walls at approximately midline; traces of a center post were removed with the remodeling that followed. A possible doorway was in the east wall, which led into room 28; this possible doorway was

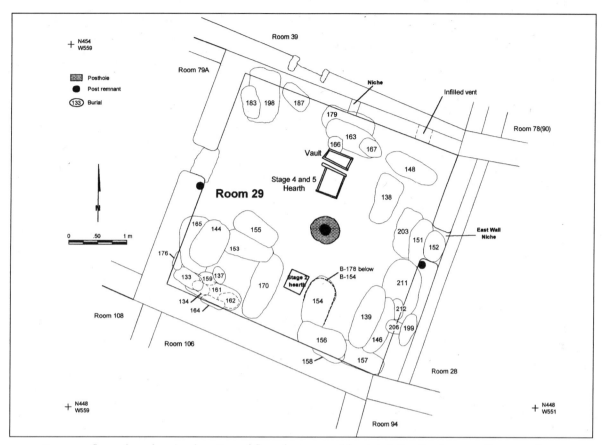

5.25: Room 29 floor plan, showing location of floor features and burials (after Burden 2001:Figure 5.15).

later blocked by the added wall course from room 28, creating a niche or recess.

Room 29A represents the remodeled room; the firebox was moved and a new roof was constructed (Figure 5.25). The roof was supported by a single upright center post of juniper, and the burned stumps from the lateral support posts for room 29B were incorporated into the wall and plastered over. A doorway in the west wall led into room 79, which was added on to the south room block. The door slab on the room 29 floor was a well-shaped Sugarlump rhyolite slab. A slab-lined firebox and an adjacent rectangular floor vault were situated between the center post and the north wall (Figure 5.7). An air vent 17 cm wide and 24 cm high was constructed in the north wall in line with the hearth, 1.65 m from the northeast corner (Figure 5.7). This vent was blocked with the addition of a second course to the north wall when room 39 was constructed, converting the vent to a wall niche. The niche was open and the contents

5.26: East wall niche in room 29.

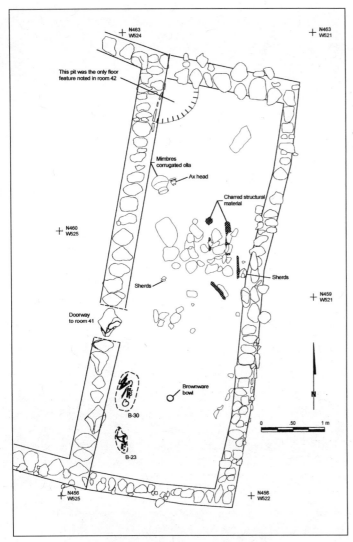

5.27: Room 42 floor plan at the NAN Ranch Ruin (after Burden 2001:Figure 5.29).

removed; the cover slab was on the floor next to the opening. This was the second air vent constructed in the north wall. An earlier vent, possibly associated with room 29B, was constructed nearer to the northeast corner and had been completely closed and filled when the original north wall of room 29 was refurbished. The second and larger of the two niches was created by closing a doorway in the south wall leading into room 28 (Figure 5.26). This niche measured 54 cm wide and 34 cm deep; the interior was well plastered and the bottom was flush with the room floor. This feature may have housed a shrine, not unlike the wall shelves in room 12.

With the addition of room 39 to the north, room 29 became an interior room without an outside wall. Venting the room for habitation became a problem, which may have been one reason the room was converted to a corporate kiva.

The floor assemblage was sparse at abandonment. A single Mimbres Style III jar (appendix I: Figure A.25A), three kneading slabs, and a *tschamahia* (a stone blade to a digging stick) were on the floor; a metate and two restorable Style III bowls (appendix I: Figures A.17F, A.21E, A.21F) were in the roof fall debris.

The largest cemetery reported from a single Classic Mimbres room was beneath the floor of room 29: forty separate burials were documented. This does not include all burials placed beneath the floor since graves of several infants and small children were completely destroyed by later interments. The disarticulated bones of infants and children and sherds of associated mortuary pottery were common in the fill of adult graves along the walls or in the corners in the southern half of the room. At this time there is no way to accurately estimate the minimum number of individuals buried beneath room 29, but a reasonable guess would be at least 45. Four (burials 168, 169, 188, and 193) are assigned to transitional room 98 beneath room 29B (Table 8.1). Although burials can be seriated in specific cases, it is not possible to determine from which floor or building episode all burials originated due to the extensive number of grave pits. The pits of the earlier burials are identified by the relative degree of leaching present, relative depth, stratigraphic position relative to other burials, and location within the room. Burials tentatively identified as early Classic period interments are 157, 165, 170, 179, and 198. The remainder are simply assigned to room 29. As a group, room 29 burials also were the most wealthy in terms of associated artifacts, such as the number of burials with vessels, the number of vessels with burials, and the number of burials with jewelry and other items.[31] Burials and associated artifacts are listed in Table 8.1. Vessels associated with burials in room 29, identified in appendix II, Table 1 and illustrated in the appendix, provided crucial information for microstylistic seriation of Mimbres Style III pottery.[32]

Room 79A was connected to room 29 by a crawlway and lacked evidence of a ceiling entry. Restricted access or private storerooms lacked ceiling hatches and could be entered only through a small door or crawlway from the adjoining room. Most such rooms were associated with corporate kivas. These rooms were often added to an existing room, such as rooms 29, 39, 41, and 55. Floors of some rooms were simply dirt and lacked any traces of adobe (42 and 78), whereas floors of others had thin veneers of adobe (60, 63A, and 79A). Rooms 42, 60, 63A, 78, and 79A are excavated examples of private storerooms. If present at all, hearths were variously basin shaped (60) or merely ash deposits (42, 78, 79A). Floor assemblages were present in rooms 42 and 60. Room 42 contained a partially corrugated jar, a smudged brownware bowl, and a grooved ax (Figure 5.27). The assemblage in room 60 included a partially corrugated jar, a Mimbres Style III Black-on-white jar, half of a Style III flare-rim bowl, and a small plainware bottle with suspension lugs. A grinding slab and a mano were on the floor of this room. A subfloor storage pit was found in room 42, and burials of infants or children were recorded in rooms 41, 60, and 63A.

I had originally associated these storerooms with domestic space use,[33] but I am more inclined now to attribute most of their uses to activities associated with corporate kivas (especially rooms 42, 60, and 79A) and to the storage of ritual paraphernalia. Rooms 60 and 79 are described below to illustrate examples of private storerooms.

Attached to the west end of room 55, room 60 consisted of a small private storeroom accessible only by a crawlway from room 55. It measured only 2.6 by 2.4 m, giving an overall floor space of 6.25 sq m. The floor was covered with a thin coat of plaster. A single room support post was set in the approximate center of the room, and a shallow, oval ash basin was northeast of the center post. A rhyolite grinding slab and a mano lay on the floor in the northeast corner. Four pottery vessels were left on the floor in the northwest part of the room. One was a large Mimbres partially corrugated jar (appendix I: Figure A.31G), one was a large Mimbres Style III jar (appendix I: Figure A.25B), and the third was a small plain narrow-necked jar with suspension lugs (appendix I: Figure A.26F). Half of a Mimbres Style III flare-rim bowl was on the floor just inside the crawlway (appendix I: Figure A.23E). Beneath the floor along the east wall near the southeast corner was a child burial associated with a much used Mimbres Style III bowl (appendix I: Figure A.22B).

The Mimbreños apparently made a distinction in regard to storage space depending on what was to be stored. Rooms 42 and 60, like other rooms in their class, served as restricted access storerooms that could be

5.28: Granary rooms 7 and 75A; A. room 7 beneath room 8 showing slab-reinforced floor; B. room 75A showing cobble reinforced floor.

entered only through an adjoining room. The restricted access to these rooms suggests they served not only as private storage rooms for the occupants, but also possibly for storage of ritual paraphernalia, since most corporate kivas have attached storerooms. Rooms used for communal storage, while accessible via ceiling hatches, were also built into corporate households. Such storage rooms were of two kinds: granaries and large communal storage rooms.

Classic period granaries are usually identified based on special construction details, such as vertical slabs set along the interior and exterior wall and floors paved with slabs or cobbles and plastered over with thick layers of adobe (Figure 5.28). Entry was through the ceiling. All of these construction features presumably were to help secure the room from burrowing pests. Hearths were absent. Rooms with diagnostic construction attributes included 7, 75A, 75B, 76, and 81. Rooms 108A and 54, although they do not fit the norm, may also have been used as granaries. The subfloor of room 108A was consolidated gravel, and the floor assemblage included a metate and a sherd baffle. The room had both a ceiling hatchway, identified by the fallen slab frame, and a doorway leading into room 79A. If this room was used as a granary, it was the only one with a lateral entry. No interior entry was evident for room 54, but this tiny room also lacked wall or floor reinforcement. One room, 76, had deposits of burned corn on the cob. Only rooms 7 and 76 had burials beneath the floor. Two infant burials were beneath the flagstone floor of room 7, and an adult female and the disarticulated remains of a child were recorded beneath the floor of room 76. Both burials in room 76 are attributed to 76B, however, and may predate the room's use as a granary.

Two large communal storage rooms, rooms 74 and 109, were attached to separate corporate households late in the architectural sequence. Tree-ring evidence suggests that room 109 was constructed in about A.D. 1114, and room 74 was added on to room 84, which was constructed in about A.D. 1128. These large rooms had only thin adobe floors and lightly used rectangular adobe-lined hearths. Both were entered through ceiling hatchways, and none had burials beneath. The floor area of room 74 was 35 sq m, whereas room 109 was about 40 sq m. What is remarkable about these rooms is the floor assemblage. Room 109 had several large sherd concentrations (but no restorable vessels), manos, worked slabs, and bone awls.

The contents of room 74 deserve special attention not only because of the amount, but also because of the character of the assemblage (Figure 5.29). Twenty-five manos, one flat abrading slab, one grooved greenstone ax, and at least 15 pottery vessels were left on the floor. Some of the vessels were placed on checker weave *petates*, or mats, the charred remnants of which were scattered on the floor, beneath the broken vessels.

The vessel assemblage included one large El Paso Bichrome jar (appendix I: Figure A.32D), one large Chihuahua indented corrugated jar (appendix I: Figure A.32C), five large Mimbres partially corrugated jars (appendix I: Figures A.31D, A.31E, A.31F), three large Mimbres fully corrugated jars (appendix I: Figure A.30B), three Mimbres Style III Black-on-white jars (appendix I: Figures A.24H, A.25C, A.25D), one unusual Mimbres partially corrugated jar (appendix I: Figure A.32B), and half of a late Mimbres Style III bowl (appendix I: Figure A.19H). The jars in this assemblage are the largest reported in a Classic Mimbres site.[34] The two intrusive vessels and partially corrugated jars have capacities ranging from 42 to 113 liters, far beyond the 8- to 13-liter range generally associated with household use.[35] Were these vessels used for storage of dry foods, or were they reserved for feasts? Given the fact that no traces of burned corn or other foods were found in the room or among the sherds, it seems probable that these large jars were used for cooking and serving during large social gatherings rather than for storing dry foods.

Two rooms, 9 and 58, are classed here as communal rooms, based on their large size and internal features, although both could have served as habitation rooms as well. Room 9 was mostly destroyed by relic hunters, but enough of the walls was exposed to provide basic information about the room. The room had approximately 34 sq m of floor space, and the roof was probably supported by two posts set along a north-south midline, although we found evidence for only one post in our excavations. The room was constructed over earlier Classic period ruins during the middle Classic period, as indicated by two tree-ring dates, both 1071r. Disturbed ashy deposits in the west-central part of the room probably identify the location of the hearth. Aside from the room's relatively large size, two interesting floor features consisting of two posts set apart were recorded in the southwest corner along the south wall. These posts, while possibly reinforcing a weakened corner, may also have been part of an altar, raising suspicion that religious activities were carried out in this room. A sherd concentration consisting of parts of a partially corrugated jar was recovered in the southwest quadrant. Unfortunately, lack of data on hearth type and the absence of other features in the room preclude any further assessment of the room's function.

Room 58 is classed as a communal room despite its rather average size because of benches along three walls (Figure 5.30). It measured 5.4 m north-south and 3.2 to 3.4 m east-west, giving an overall floor area of 17.82 sq m. The room had been previously excavated by avocational archaeologist Virginia Wunder,[36] but she left floor remnants and certain interior features that provided important information about the room. Benches were

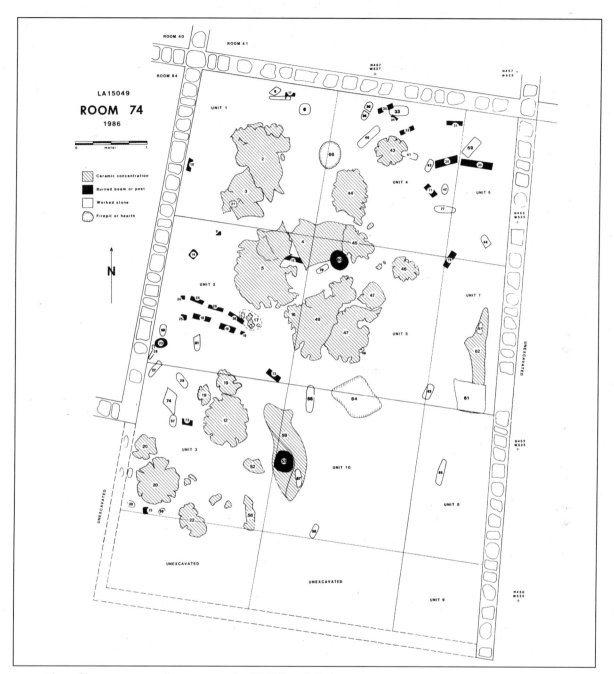

5.29: Plan of large communal room 74 at the NAN Ranch Ruin.

present along the north, west, and south walls, and a vent was placed in the north wall. The construction of the benches was much like that for regular walls, with cobbles set on edge at the base and adobe and smaller cobbles laid in courses above this base. Benches averaged about 20 cm wide and extended 40 to 50 cm above the

floor. Other room features included a door near the west end of the south wall, leading into room 48; a wall vent; postholes; and a slab-lined hearth. If a floor vault was present, it was destroyed by previous excavators. The door was the only complete door found at the site with the top still intact. It was rectangular and plastered,

5.30: Photo of room 58 at the NAN Ranch Ruin, illustrating benches along the west, south, and north walls.

5.31: Photos of room 39 at the NAN Ranch Ruin: A. viewed from the west; B. viewed from the north.

measuring 60 cm high and 50 cm wide. A vent was constructed near the west end of the north wall, leading into room 12; this vent became closed when the reinforcing wall for room 59 was added.

The room revealed a history of renovations, including two major construction episodes.[37] The first construction episode consisted of the addition of a single center post with support posts set along the north and south walls and what was probably a slab-lined hearth in the northeast quadrant of the room. The floor was resurfaced twice during this interim. Renovations occurred at a later time, and the single center post was replaced by two juniper posts set along the room's north-south midline. A new slab-lined fire hearth was constructed in the east-central area immediately east of the abandoned center posthole with the paving over of the older hearth. At least two additional floor surfaces were applied following this renovation.

Information on subfloor features was largely unavailable due to previous excavations. A number of burials were interred beneath the floor of the room, but since all were destroyed by previous digging, the exact number is unknown. At least five separate concentrations of human bone fragments were found while we were cleaning out the subfloor disturbances; infants and adults were represented among the remains.

Damon Burden's detailed analysis of this structure convincingly shows the room was used throughout the Classic period. A single tree-ring date of 1105vv dates one of the later renovations. The fact that room 58 was a core room in the east room block and the room's long and complicated history suggest multiple functions. The benches certainly distinguish this room from habitation rooms. Its interior position suggests that the room was converted to either a storage room or to one used to hold special functions. The hearth, benches, and history of renovation support its use as a communal room, perhaps one reserved for secret religious gatherings such as a corporate kiva.

Two large communal rooms, 39 and 45, form a subset that deserves special attention because of the rooms' physical attributes and associated artifacts. Room 39, with 36 sq m of floor area, was the second-largest room in the south room block, surpassed only by communal storage room 109, measuring 39 sq m. The north wall of room 39 was a massive five courses thick, contrasting sharply to the typical one-course walls that characterized the east block rooms. Originally the north wall was two courses thick,

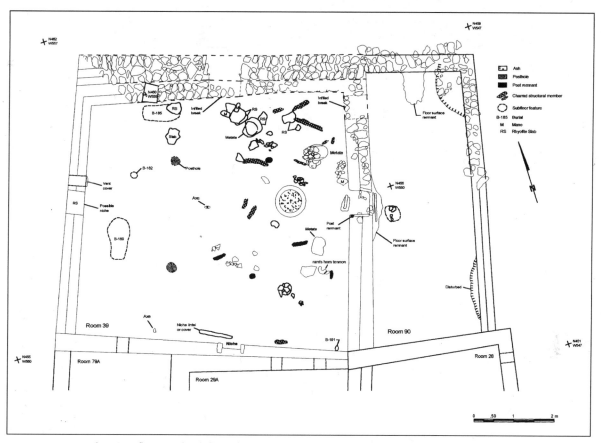

5.32: Room 39, showing floor and subfloor features (after Burden 2001: Figure 4.28).

but a thicker three-course reinforcement was added as a buttress. The three-course east and west walls were also massive compared to the walls of other rooms at the site (Figures 5.31A, 5.31B; Figure 5.32).

The roof to this large room was supported by a square pattern of four support posts and constructed of riparian species (cottonwood or willow). An unusably large circular hearth, 60 to 65 cm in diameter and outlined with cobbles, was in the east part of the room, 1.3 m from the door leading into room 78. The floor and walls were coated with plaster, but multiple floorings were not evident.

Architectural features were noted in each of the four walls. In the center of the north wall was a filled-in space 50 cm wide built into the original two-course wall. This may have been a niche or, more likely, a filled-in doorway used during the room's construction.[38] A niche was preserved in the south wall. This feature also measured 50 cm wide and was constructed into the course added to the north wall of room 29. Another similar wall feature was once in the east wall in line with the hearth; this feature may have been a doorway into the storeroom 78/90 west and may have been converted to a niche when the storeroom fell into ruin. Another possible niche was in the west wall, which was intact except for the footing stone. An air vent was found in the west wall as well.

Unlike in habitation rooms, a large domestic assemblage of artifacts was left on the roof or floor at the time the room burned. Among the artifacts were two trough metates; one was found north of the hearth and associated with a Mimbres Style III flare-rim bowl (appendix I: Figure A.22E) and a large sherd baffle from a Style III seed jar (appendix I: Figure A.24D); the second metate was faced down, south of the hearth. Along the south wall was a partially corrugated cooking jar (appendix I: Figure A.32A) and a fully corrugated jar (appendix I: Figure A.30I) on the floor near the hearth. At least three late Mimbres Style III bowls (appendix I: Figure A.20I, A.21G), a Style III plate (appendix I: Figure A.15B), and a small

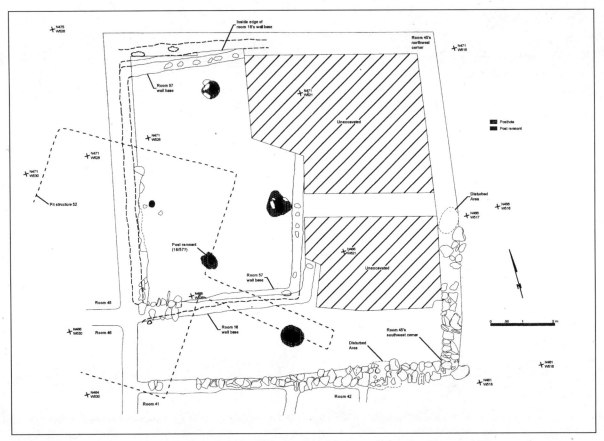

5.34: Plan of room 45 at the NAN Ranch Ruin, showing floor features (after Burden 2001: Figure 4.9).

function difficult. More likely, size alone allowed for both civic and ceremonial activities to take place; the rooms may have served as a place to house visitors as well. I am inclined not to consider them as kivas, but this certainly does not preclude them from having served just such a function, especially room 39. One peculiarity about these rooms is that neither room was used for the burial of individuals who merited mortuary vessels; indeed, no burials were found associated with room 45. If room 39 served in the same capacity, it would be the exception in the NAN Ruin sample.

Porches, ramadas, and drying racks were either attached to an outside wall or constructed as separate structures. Postholes and burned roofing material adjacent to pueblo structures were interpreted as porches or arbor-type shades covering outdoor activity areas. Such structures may also have been used as drying racks for vegetables. Porch structures were found on the north side of room 55 (designated as room 65) and on the south side of rooms 92 and 93 (designated as room 87). Both had thin adobe surfaces. Postholes encountered in plazas and courtyards may have been associated with detached arbor structures common in Pueblo architecture, but none were positively identified.

Traces of possible special function structures constructed near the pueblo were encountered during the extramural excavations. Two small detached Classic period structures had special features that set them apart from pueblo buildings: one may have been a granary and the other a special function building. The remains of the possible granary (feature 85.62) consisted of the remnants of a subrectangular floor paved with cobbles constructed over the ruins of room 92 at the southern end of the east plaza (Figure 6.1). Although the southeastern half of the floor was missing due to later disturbances, the projected floor area of the structure was 4 sq m. Cobbles were capped with a thin layer of adobe, and the floor was outlined with a cobble wall base. The feature was not burned.

5.33: Ram's horn tenon on the floor of room 39.

plain jar were also represented in the roof/floor assemblage (appendix I: Figure A.26I). Other floor artifacts include two three-quarter grooved greenstone axes, three bone awls, and an unusual ram's horn tenon that was probably once set into the east wall (Figure 5.33).

The large domestic assemblage in room 39 suggests yet another possible function for this room: for the ritual activities of women, a corollary to the presumably male-oriented corporate kiva room 29. The presence of the two metates and what appears to be a domestic assemblage of bowls, jars, awls, and axes might indeed suggest such a function for this room. Comparable spatial segregation of gender-related activities (albeit more formal) has been suggested for the northern Anasazi.[39]

Four burials were placed beneath the floor. Two were infants, one of which may predate the room. Two were adult males, one placed along the north wall and the other in the southwest quadrant near the west wall. None were associated with mortuary vessels, suggesting that these individuals may not have been members of the coresidential groups occupying the south room block and therefore were not give the status of lineal ancestors. This interpretation is based on the functional role for the inverted, "killed" mortuary vessels discussed in chapter 11.

The extraordinarily large room 45 (Figure 5.34), built mostly with double-wall construction, was added to rooms 41 and 48 late in the Classic period, possibly after A.D. 1107. The proposed dating is based on a single tree-ring date of 1107r from room 41 and on the fact that the walls are abutted to room 41. Also, earlier dates of 1066vv and 1068vv were obtained on burned room material from room 18, which underlay room 45. Approximately half of room 45 was excavated, but most or all of the four walls were outlined. The giant room measures 10 m north-south and 9.5 m east-west, giving an overall floor area of 95 sq m.

The floor consisted of a thin adobe surface that was better preserved in the western half of the room. In the eastern part that was sampled, the floor was almost completely lost to weathering. The room was supported by three large juniper posts set in a north-south line through the approximate center of the room. No formal fire pit was found in the excavated portion, but a thick ash deposit in the north-central part may have marked the hearth area.

Ceiling construction in the northwest part of the room included the incorporation of thin rhyolite slabs and large sherds. These flat items were probably laid on top of the adobe, capping the ceiling to retard erosion. Another interesting architectural feature was a fallen wall or column constructed of flat rhyolite slabs. The function of this wall or column may have been to shore up a sagging roof or to salvage the west half of the room.

Artifacts found within the room were few, owing in part to the possible reuse of the room space. Two cloud-blower pipes,[40] one of sandstone very similar to one reported from the Swarts Ruin,[41] and another of a light green stone were found on or above the floor of the room. Sherds of a restorable Mimbres Style III plate were recovered from the floor fill along the southern wall. No subfloor features were assigned to the room.

The use of this room was short-lived, probably because of the difficulty in maintaining such an extraordinarily large room. Erosion of the floor on the east side of the room and the compacted nature of the fill above the floor in this area point to an early collapse of the roof on the east side. The western half of the room may have been salvaged for a time, as suggested by the much better preserved floor and possible shoring up of the roof. No identifiable architectural features other than size suggest how this room was used. The association of the two pipes and plate, however, suggest both communal and ritual activities may have taken place here.

Parallels to rooms 39 and 45 can be found at other Classic Mimbres sites. With the exception of room 39, the lack of formal features other than relative size to distinguish these rooms makes interpretation of their

5.35: Circular structure in the east room block courtyard at the NAN Ranch Ruin

This feature may have been a temporary detached granary, since Classic period granaries characteristically had similarly paved floors.

The second structure is more unique. Its remains consisted of rhyolite slabs placed in a circular alignment 1.5 m in diameter and capped with a thin adobe floor (Figure 5.35). This enigmatic structure was in the courtyard overlying a thick Classic period midden deposit in the east room block. A concentration of cobbles surrounded part of the alignment, indicating its walls were of cobble-adobe construction. Presumably the slabs were a foundation for some kind of structure, but its function is unknown. It may have been a temporary birthing or menstrual hut.

Exterior Space

Outdoor space associated with household activities included roofs and a courtyard immediately surrounding the structures. Roof space was used for a multitude of purposes: for dry storage of wood, as a drying area for garden produce, for food preparation, as a lighted area for hand-working chores, and for leisure activity. Communal space extends beyond the household roof into courtyards shared by other households. Plazas are defined as public space between architectural units, usually open on one or more sides. The distinction between plazas and courtyards is based on size and the ranges of activities that may have been carried out in each. Courtyards are partly or mostly enclosed, are smaller in size, and served mostly for domestic use. Both were surfaced one or more times with thin layers of wet adobe, and adobe-lined pits and outdoor hearths are associated with both.

Data on courtyards at the NAN Ruin are limited to the east room block. One, designated as room 35 and 35 West (Figure P.2) and referred to here as the room 35 courtyard, was an unroofed enclosed space bordered by rooms 24, 37, and 82. It was originally bordered on the north by room 16, but this room was razed and the courtyard extended into room 16 space. A total of 23 sq m of space was contained within the room 35 courtyard. The courtyard surface was paved with adobe and two features, a metate and an adobe-lined fire pit containing burned rocks, were in association with the courtyard. No human or animal burials were found in the sampled area.

The second courtyard was a midden and activity area in the east room block, open to the west. It was bordered by rooms 37 and 82 on the north, rooms 26 and 48 on the east, and rooms 50 and 47 on the south. The space became smaller with the addition of rooms 55, 60, and 65. These rooms were constructed on midden fill after most of the deposits had accumulated. Although we are describing this as a courtyard because it appears to have been an enclosed space containing evidence of numerous outdoor activities, it was also used as a midden during the Classic Mimbres period. Midden accumulation reached 1.0 m in depth. Several features were found within this courtyard midden, including four adult burials (three males and a female), a circular structure, and two adobe-lined pits. Relic hunters had disturbed other burials, indicated by human bones scattered in the back dirt of their pits.

Although none of the defined courtyards were enclosed by low walls as described for Classic Mimbres sites elsewhere,[42] two small enclosed courtyards were documented in the east room block. Both represented open spaces created when rooms burned and fell into disuse. The open space created by the destruction of room 12 was converted to a small courtyard. An activity surface 30 cm above the floor of room 12 yielded traces of two adobe-mixing pits. This space was later claimed with the construction of room 59.

Another possible courtyard was the temporarily open space in room 25B described above, which had an adobe-mixing pit and a walled bin as associated features. Adobe-mixing pits were found in both enclosed courtyards (room 25A and above room 12). The room 12 courtyard measured 12 sq m in space, whereas that of room 25B was only 6 sq m. In both instances, several centimeters of fill had either accumulated or was brought in and capped the floors. Also in both instances, later rooms were constructed over the courtyards (rooms 59 and 25A respectively).

The space between the east and west room blocks was a paved plaza open at the south end (see Figure P.2). This plaza capped previous activity space that included one pithouse (room 83), a transitional room (room 80), and adobe quarry pits and exhibits at least two paving episodes separated by midden fill. A total of 70 sq m of the west plaza was sampled. Among the features associated with the two plaza surfaces were six adobe-lined pits, two male burials (one adult, one subadult), three bird burials, two ash deposits with burned *Artiodactyla* bones (mule deer, mountain sheep, or pronghorn), and a concentration of corrugated jar sherds. Based on the dominant Mimbres Black-on-white ceramic styles, dominated by middle Style III found between the two paved surfaces, we conclude that the use of this area as plaza space dates back at least to the middle of the Classic Mimbres period (A.D. 1060–1110).

The main plaza at the site is designated as the east plaza (Figure P.2). The space was extensively used and repeatedly modified. It was open at the north and south ends and had a raised border on each side created by architectural units. The orientation and wear suggest it served as the main corridor and perhaps even as a road into and through the site. Approximately 157 sq m of space were excavated in the plaza. A sequence of 11 adobe surfaces was documented in the northern part of this area, overlying pithouse room 91 (Figure 5.36), but although multiple surfaces are indicated elsewhere, it was not possible to determine how many separate pavements existed. Stratigraphic dating on the basis of architectural associations and ceramic styles from associated features and cremations suggest a time range for public use of the east plaza from the Late Three Circle phase through the Classic Mimbres phase, or from about A.D. 950 to 1125. The density of adobe-lined pits in this plaza is remarkably high (Figure 5.37).[43] In one 6-by-6-m excavation block, 27 pits were encountered, with some overlapping one another. Across the east plaza as a whole, an average of one pit per 1.25 sq m was excavated. The high density

5.36: Profile showing multiple surfaces in the east plaza at the NAN Ranch Ruin.

5.37: Concentration of adobe-mixing pits in the east plaza at the NAN Ranch Ruin.

of pits decreases as one moves away from surface architecture toward the east, indicating their close association with domestic space. The presence of pits indicates a dual role for plazas: the space could have been used for both domestic and public functions.

The numerous resurfacing episodes and associated features in the east plaza suggest this was the main plaza at the site, perhaps analogous to the "dance plaza" at the Swarts Ruin.[44] This interpretation is supported by the variety and density of domestic and ritual activities documented. Domestic use of plaza space is indicated by the location and frequency of adobe-lined pits and thermal features or outdoor cooking pits; public use is indicated by the presence of other features, such as artifact caches composed of isolated vessels, turquoise concentrations, a set of two large bone pins, and burials in the form of inhumations and cremations (see chapter 9).

Adobe pavements were discovered in various outdoor contexts throughout the site and were clearly associated with the activities carried out around each household. These adobe surfaces were found bordering all Classic Mimbres structures. Arguably, in some instances these work surfaces may have been courtyard or plaza surfaces that extended to the pueblo building, but where surfaces were not bordered by courtyards or plazas, this was clearly not the case. Examples of adobe pavement were also found capping abandoned architectural space (rooms 12 and 25, as noted above, and room 88). The basic purpose of these prepared surfaces may have been to keep the grounds around the structures relatively clean.

Excavations around and beneath Classic period rooms yielded traces of older paved surfaces with associated adobe-lined pits. Space south of room 94, north of room 12, and south of room 74 all had one or more paved surfaces. Traces of extramural work surfaces were found beneath Classic period rooms 39 and 109 in the south room block and beneath rooms 8, 41, and 82 in the east room block.

One of the more surprising findings in our extramural excavations was the high frequency of adobe-lined extramural pits, which had not been previously described at large Mimbres sites.[45] These features were very common in courtyards and communal plazas, as were paved work surfaces adjacent to standing structures. More than 100 adobe-lined pits have been documented at the NAN Ruin. Their common occurrence and location in paved work areas, communal plazas, and courtyards adjacent to pueblo buildings indicate that each household maintained such features as part of its daily facilities. Most of the pits were used to mix adobe, whereas some were used as outdoor hearths, presumably for cooking.

The Mimbreños' abundant use of adobe for wall mortar, flooring, and plaster and the need for refurbishing and repair are ample justification for one to expect some kind of adobe-mixing facility. Presumably if such features were left in the open for the residue adobe to become sun dried or baked, then archaeological detection might be possible. Expected attributes of adobe-mixing pits would include evidence for puddling around the rims, nodules of adobe left in the basins, and being filled with adobe or plaza trash upon abandonment. As a source of comparison, adobe-mixing pits have been amply described in Classic Hohokam sites in Arizona[46] and at modern Pima sites.

The pits were constructed into virtually every surface that accumulated adjacent to standing architecture. The extramural pits were generally circular basin shaped, although shape varied to oval and even to subrectangular; all were lined with puddled adobe. Cross sections of the rims often clearly showed a laminated pattern created by the application of multiple layers of wet adobe during construction. Adobe-lined pits range in size from 18 to 120 cm at maximum dimension and an average of 62.7 cm across. Depths vary from 2 to 39 cm and average 15.1 cm. As discussed above, the pits were almost always associated with adobe pavements; some were clearly in plazas and courtyards, but others were in paved surfaces abutting outside walls. Most pits were abandoned, filled with loose midden soil or cobbles and sealed over. Approximately 18 percent of the adobe-lined pits were thermal features that contained gray ash and burned rocks. Several of the features in the east plaza were described as filled with adobe when they were paved over in the application of new work surface.

Eighteen percent of the adobe-lined pits were thermal features or hearths. They were distinguished as such by rims discolored gray or orange and burned rock and dark ash contents. When the fire pits are cleaned of the contents, the adobe lining is identical to that of pits that do not contain ash and burned rock, suggesting either that their construction was identical to that of adobe-mixing pits or certain adobe mixing pits were also used as outdoor hearths. Flotation samples taken from outdoor hearths did not yielded definitive patterns of plants cooked in these fires.[47] Charred seeds and fuel woods were the most common items recovered from both outdoor and indoor features.

In addition to the outdoor hearths, three large roasting pits or earth ovens were discovered during the course of the excavations. Two were associated with different age activity surfaces beneath room 109 in the area of the south room block, and the other was beneath room 8. The latter feature (designated as 2-AFSF32) (Figure 5.38) provided botanical evidence that yielded clues to the items roasted. The pit beneath room 8 measured 1.15 by 1.25 m across and 88 cm deep and had nearly straight sides. The bottom was relatively flat. The pit was dug from a layer of cultural fill on which the floor of room 8 was laid. The upper part of the pit was filled with clean river sand and gravel. Loose middenlike fill containing sherds was beneath the sand and gravel. A layer of burned rocks was encountered about 20 cm above the floor, and beneath the rocks was a layer of charred grass and twigs. A thin layer of ash lined the bottom of the pit. The clay subsoil was burned orange from a fire at the pit's bottom. The pit is dated to the Classic Mimbres phase, based on its stratigraphic origin and the Mimbres Style III sherds mixed in with the fill.

5.38: Circular roasting pit beneath room 8 at the NAN Ranch Ruin.

Macro- and microbotanical analysis was conducted on matrix samples collected from the floor of the pit and from pit fill. These samples yielded evidence that the pit's probable function was to roast green corn. The frequency of *Zea mays* (corn) pollen was significantly higher in both samples than in other contexts at the NAN Ruin, including granaries.[48] Other economic plants represented in the pollen counts included both high spine and low spine composite (sunflower family), Cheno-Am (weeds in the *Chenopodium* and *Amaranthus* genera), *Opuntia* (cactus), *Echinocereus* (cactus), *Poacea* (grasses), and *Cyperaceae* (sedge). Grass and weed pollen may be accidental inclusions since these plants were used for insulation and are represented in the layers of charred grass and other plant material in the pit's bottom.

Nearly identical pits have been described in the ethnographic literature for the American Southwest that served as earth ovens for roasting green (or sweet) corn.

The Hopi consumed sweet corn shortly after harvest. Once roasted, the corn was consumed immediately. The facility to roast the corn was large roasting pit, virtually identical to earth oven baking pits used by Native Americans throughout western North America. The pits were located near the fields, and were used repeatedly. To roast the corn, pits were first cleaned out and filled with wood. The ignited wood was allowed to burn down to a bed of coals. Rocks were placed over the coals and heated. The green corn was then added. The pits were refilled and the corn was allowed to roast overnight. The roasting event involved both sexes and was associated with both ritual and gayety.[49]

Burials were placed outside of structures during all periods of occupation at the site. Although the pattern of subfloor burial became dominant in the Classic period, approximately 10 percent of the burials excavated were found in courtyards, plazas, or middens. Classic period inhumations were identified on the basis of rock cairns placed over them. Infant burials, however, lacked cairns and so were indistinguishable from those of earlier periods; these burials could be placed chronologically only on the basis of stratigraphy. The bodies of subadults and adults were treated much like the bodies in subfloor burials: they were placed flexed or semiflexed in elongated pits. Burial 109, placed in a sitting position without an associated cairn, was an exception. Classic period extramural burials also lacked mortuary vessels. This very significant finding provides a subtle distinction between extramural and indoor burials and perhaps aids in determining the affiliation of the extramural burials, a topic discussed in the next chapter. As noted above, a significant number (perhaps as many as 10 percent) of Classic period burials were secondary cremations placed in the east plaza. Most, if not all, were associated with mortuary vessels and shell artifacts that had been included in the funerary pyre. At least one cremation was covered with a "killed" covering bowl.

Animals have often been given special status treatment in death, not unlike that reserved for humans in the Southwest and northern Mexico; the Mimbres region is no exception. Burials of animals, mostly birds, are reported from several professionally excavated Mimbres sites.[50] Dogs, bears, rabbits, and several species of birds, including turkeys, hawks, and macaws, are among the animals represented. Twenty-three animal burials, described in chapter 8, were recovered from courtyards, plazas, and subfloor contexts at the NAN Ruin.

Historic accounts describe a canal and a reservoir on the terrace on which the NAN Ruin lies. An 1867 General Land Office map records an "old acequia" in the position of the NAN canal, and Adolph Bandelier mentioned the reservoir when he visited and mapped the site in 1883.[51] Field explorations and testing by Lain Ellis confirmed the existence of both features and also provided relative and absolute dating that placed them in the Classic Mimbres period.[52] Exploring these features and finding a method to date them were complicated by the fact that both the ditch and the reservoir were modified and used historically. Factoring out the origins and history was indeed a complex exercise, but Ellis seems to have resolved the issue satisfactorily. Further discussion of this reservoir and ditch system is presented in chapter 7.

Summary

The NAN Ranch Ruin excavations yielded an enormous amount of new information about how the Mimbreños lived and how they may have structured their community. Prior to the NAN Ranch project, little was known of these aggregated communities except that they were composed of contiguous cobble-adobe rooms, some larger than others. Little was known of room function or indoor and outdoor space use. It was assumed that larger rooms were for habitation and smaller ones were for storage, but no study had been conducted to explore room variability and to determine if rooms of different function could be identified on the basis of features within the rooms themselves. Nothing was known about how such aggregated pueblos grew or if they were constructed all at one time. And it was not known how the mortuary patterns fit in with all of this: the popular notion was that many burials were placed beneath floors but with no explanation why. The model of a Classic Mimbres town was based on the Cosgroves' field map of the Swarts Ruin, which was presented as the "typical Mimbres site."[53] The implication was that all rooms were occupied simultaneously. The NAN Ruin evidence has helped to fill some of these interpretive gaps by identifying room variability and function and demonstrated just how dynamic these communities were: changes in room use occurred frequently. Furthermore, we found more variability in mortuary behavior than previously recorded and that room variability and space use correlated with mortuary variability.

Habitation rooms were the focal point of domestic activities. Individual family space was private, accessible only through entry into the room through a ceiling hatchway. Domestic space may also have included private storage rooms entered only through interior crawlways, but the evidence whether such private storage rooms were associated with domestic dwellings is ambiguous. These restricted access storage rooms also occur with corporate kivas. Rooftops of dwellings may have been for private use and for external storage of dry goods.

Corporate space was shared by households affiliated through kinship or residence. One room within each coresidential unit was designated as a sacred room or kiva reserved for corporate rituals and cemetery. Features used to identify Mimbres corporate kivas included small rectangular floor vaults built next to the hearths. Although these features may have been floor drums, they could have served as sipapu, or symbolic entries into the Underworld containing the remains of the ancestors below. Corporate kivas held the largest cemeteries of any room in each coresidential unit. These rooms are regarded as corporate kivas, analogous in function to structures built by the Anasazi cultures to the north, although little architectural similarity exists between the two.

Other sheltered corporate space needs were met by constructing granaries and large storage rooms. Communal space needs, possibly for civic gatherings or to house visitors, were met by constructing large rooms attached to each coresidential unit. Features and floor assemblages suggest these rooms probably had multiple functions.

Courtyards and plazas immediately next to the corporate households provided space for coresidential outdoor activities. Public facilities included plazas, middens, a reservoir, and a canal feeding the reservoir. The canal and reservoir were the first such features identified at a large Mimbres site; the reservoir may have been used in opportune circumstances to catch and hold flash flood runoff when the river discharge was low. Or it may have been simply for the convenience of keeping pooled water handy to mix adobe, as some modern pueblos have done.

The east plaza may also have been the main thoroughfare through the site. The idea of the Mimbres having a formal road system not unlike that documented for the Chaco culture to the north came about with Darrell Creel's discovery of a prehistoric road leading into the Old Town site.[54] The striking similarity in shared behavior recognized among large Mimbres sites and the knowledge of intervillage ceramic exchange between sites indicate that a great deal of traffic traveled between sites. Well-beaten trails or roads undoubtedly connected all large towns to provide a network of communication and interaction. Traces of such roads probably have been lost through time, with the exception of the unusual preservation situation at Old Town, but archaeologists have not looked for them.

Room variability and function is but one way to understand the structure of a large Mimbres town. To understand how the site shown in Figure P.2 came to be, it is necessary to consider the dimensions of both time and space. Imagine a time-lapse series of photos, the first showing a community of individual pueblo-style buildings, some clustering near one another. The second frame shows some of these joined, while rooms were added to others. The third shows more rooms added to the existing structures, with public plaza space more clearly defined. And finally, the frame shows some rooms being abandoned while new rooms are added. This scenario is precisely what has been interpreted from the archaeological evidence.

The NAN village began as a community of single structures whose primary function was to house an extended family. These households clearly evolved from the previous pithouse settlement at the beginning of the eleventh century and looked much like the pithouse community except that the structures were built aboveground. As the population of the communities continued to grow, social cleavages between families, lineages, and community evolved, creating a cluster of independent corporate entities in each large Mimbres town. Community growth in population and complexity is reflected in the social organization, architecture, and dimensions of space use. Space dimensions included private, corporate, and public. The next chapter examines the various scales in the residential groups as defined by the architecture. The model presented applies to the organization and structure of large Mimbres towns throughout the valley.

CHAPTER SIX
Classic Period Community and Social Organization

Introduction

How was the NAN Ruin community organized? I will attempt to answer that question in this chapter, where I examine architecture and other material patterns in regard to household composition and community organization. Four tiers or scales of community structure can be recognized on the basis of architecture. I assume these various levels of architectural integration had meaning related to the social organization within the community. Therefore I assigned social components to each of these tiers. In this model, the first tier is single families, graduating to larger and more integrated social components within the architectural units.

In the first tier, single-family households are defined as habitation rooms with no demonstrable connection or attachment to other households. The second tier in Mimbres society consists of two or more habitation rooms incorporated to create a corporate extended family household. Corporate groups were coresidential and shared common economic interests.[1] Corporate residential units shared communal rooms that included large storage rooms, civic-ceremonial rooms, and granaries. The third tier is larger aggregated units or room blocks composed of two or more extended family clusters, and the fourth tier is the village as a whole. Although these tiers are defined on the basis of patterning among habitation rooms, they can also be considered as analytical units for intrasite and intersite comparisons. A fifth tier of Mimbres society integration is the intercommunity network of towns and outliers throughout the Mimbres Valley.

Classic Mimbres households were more complex than those of previous phases. I attribute this complexity to three related factors: the importance of maintaining social unity of the extended family, the importance of maintaining lineage rights and holding on to inherited productive lands, and labor requirements needed to sustain and manage irrigation agriculture. For the sake of projecting time depth into the foregoing hypothetical model, I define lineage residences as extended family households that were occupied for multiple generations. In other words, the extended family household is the horizontal dimension and refers to the number of rooms occupied by a family at any one time, while the lineage household is the vertical dimension, which implies a longevity of multiple generations. Granted, we will never know just how Mimbres society was organized in regard to architectural space at the family and extended family level since ethnographic studies have shown such structures can be highly flexible and dynamic.[2] The model suggested here, which is supported in part by cemetery patterns, is my interpretation of how such an organization may have occurred.

As noted in chapter 5, rooms with formal hearths, adobe floors, and cemeteries beneath the floors were occupied by social groups that probably consisted of nuclear and extended families. Large extended family households may have consisted of a cluster of habitation rooms in the same contiguous architectural unit, sharing communal rooms such as granaries and large storage and civic-ceremonial rooms. The size of the architectural space accommodating an extended family probably depended on the size of the family and how long they occupied the same space.

I believe the key to understanding social unity is the composition of the extended family and its duration as a lineage household. Lineage households were the products of the successful growth cycle of a family and successful corporate economic strategies. Primary lineage households formed the core structure of large Mimbres towns in the valley and probably defined community structure as a whole, based on how lineages or corporate groups were ranked in regard to hierarchy within the community.

Mimbres extended family and lineage households were probably equivalent to pre-Classic Hohokam courtyard groups[3] and comparable to the Anasazi Pueblo II unit pueblos[4] and corporate group structure.[5]

The excavated part of the south room block represents a cluster of related extended family households that formed a single lineage household and corporate group. A lineage household is equated with Dozier's[6] lineage residence. The composition of a lineage household was defined by traditional rules of residence, which kept certain members together through time. Size and success of a lineage household was determined, in part, by such factors as survival and accumulated or inherited wealth and political prestige. Survival simply means holding a family together, whether by keeping key members alive or economically secure. A relative measure of survival is evidence for repeated reflooring and accumulated burials in cemeteries. Accumulated or inherited wealth and political prestige were assets most likely defined in the Mimbres sense by first-arrival rights or ownership of productive lands, that is, lineages that first laid claim to prime agricultural lands. As argued previously, corporate groups formed by lineage households had rights and access to the most productive lands and were sustained in place so long as they survived. Primary lineage households probably grew out of Three Circle and Late Three Circle phase courtyard groups, while others may have been families that resettled in the Mimbres Valley or from extended families split from existing lineage households.

Classic period coresidential lineage households shared special function ancillary rooms. These common rooms included granaries, both small and large storage rooms, and large civic-communal rooms. Linage households or residences emerged when additional households and ancillary rooms were added or incorporated into the nuclear family household through time.

Single Households: The First Tier

As with previous phases, the fundamental and first-tier social and economic unit in Classic period society was the nuclear family unit. Nuclear family units occupied a household composed of a habitation room with a formal hearth and any room or rooms connected via a lateral crawlway. The social composition of this occupying group of a habitation room could have been either a nuclear or an extended family, but the former is the minimal unit occupying such structures. These households can be somewhat equated with nuclear family residence as described by Dozier.[7] Dozier's nuclear family residence consisted of no more than two or three rooms connected by interior doorways and outside entrances affording access only to the nuclear family unit. For the Mimbreños, in certain instances this definition would apply to habitation rooms and their interconnected storerooms.

Single-family households existed throughout the Classic Mimbres period, both within large settlements and in outlier sites. In large sites single-family households appear as attached rooms (e.g., room 84) and as unattached architectural units (e.g., the 92/93 suite of rooms) (Figure 6.1). Use of these rooms tend to be short-lived, suggesting that they may have been occupied by low-ranking families within the community. Most single households had burials interred beneath the floors if the rooms were occupied sufficiently long for someone in the family to die.

Cemeteries were integral components of residential space, whether it was occupied by a single family or a corporate group.[8] The placement of ancestors in formal cemeteries may have been used as justification for inheritance of land rights and access to resources. The evolution of cemeteries beneath lineage households may have signified the inheritance of that space and the fields that were tied to a particular lineage. Presumably people who lived in the household and died at or near home were buried in the lineage cemetery. Family and lineage cemeteries were maintained beneath occupied rooms in Classic Mimbres times in the Mimbres Valley regardless of age. Variability in this pattern occurred with isolated extramural burials in plazas and courtyards and primary and secondary cremations in the main plaza. Presumably the extramural exceptions either were not members of residing families or died under unusual circumstances.

The south room block at the NAN Ruin yielded the most comprehensive data set available for Classic Mimbres lineage households and how they evolved. Using the south room block as a model, I believe it is possible to identify other lineage households at the NAN Ruin and at other sites as well. A closer look at the south room block is essential in interpreting the composition of the east room block and Classic Mimbres communities in general.

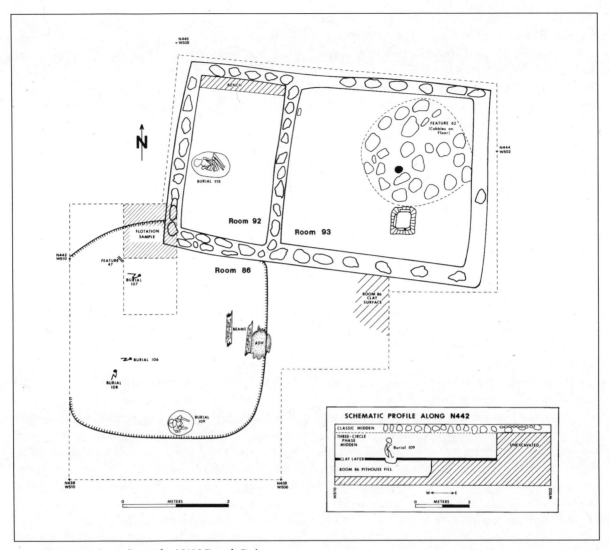

6.1: Rooms 92/93 suite at the NAN Ranch Ruin.

A LINEAGE HOUSEHOLD: THE SECOND TIER

The south room block is an example of a lineage household and the residential unit of a corporate group (Figure 6.2), and the unexcavated northeast room block may have been such a household as well. The south room block evolved over many generations, and evidence suggests that this locus may have been in the same lineage since the Three Circle phase. The surface pueblo component was composed of 11 rooms, three or four of which were once habitation rooms occupied by nuclear or extended families; the remaining rooms were either for restricted or communal space use.

The architecture of the south room block appeared to have been extraordinary from the beginning when compared to that of the east room block. Walls were generally two courses thick instead of the one-course walls typical of the east room block, and the massive north wall of room 39 was five courses thick. The double roof fall layer of room 29, coupled with the massive walls, was seen as possible evidence for a two-story architectural unit. The interiors of rooms 28 and 29 seemed to be unusually well finished, and the burials encountered beneath the floors of these rooms were among the most concentrated and wealthiest reported in the Mimbres area. The architectural and mortuary variability alone is sufficient justification to focus primary attention on the south room block.

The chronology of the area beneath the south room block, underlying the surface pueblo room block, is documented in a sequence of structures beginning sometime in the Three Circle phase. The architectural chronology is complex, but the reconstruction is aided by excellent stratigraphy and the use of such dating methods as ceramic microstyles, dendrochronology, archaeomagnetism, and obsidian hydration. The architectural sequence at this location began with the construction of four Three Circle phase pit structures (Figure 3.11).

As shown in chapter 3, the earliest pit structure beneath the south room block was room 103, a rectangular pithouse with an extended entrance to the southeast. A single obsidian hydration date of 620 + 92 was the only chronometric date for this room. The date is clearly too early for the architectural style and predominately Style I among the painted sherd assemblage. The early obsidian hydration date may reflect the mixing in of earlier fill. The extended entryway to room 102 (see chapter 3) cut into room 103, documenting the superposition of the latter structure. The destruction of room 102 occurred in approximately A.D. 890 + 50, based on a single archaeomagnetism date.

Another shallow pit structure dating to the Three Circle phase lay immediately beneath room 108; in fact, the dimensions of surface room 108 follow those of the pit structure almost identically. The shallowness of the pit structure beneath room 108B was due to a cemented gravel deposit immediately beneath the floor. Although the complete outline of 108B was not preserved due to the construction of surface room 106 and a nineteenth-century barn, the entryway was oriented to the east, as indicated by the location of the hearth and deflector slab. The fourth structure of this grouping was pithouse room 116, another subrectangular pithouse whose entryway faced west. A late Mimbres Style I Black-on-white sherd was recovered from the entryway of this room, which provided a ceramic style date of approximately A.D. 850 to 900.

The clustering of rooms 103, 102, 108B, and 116 may represent a courtyard grouping when viewed together. This clustering is quite similar to the courtyard grouping of Three Circle phase pithouses reported from area B at the Old Town Ruin and noted at other Mimbres pithouse villages[9] and may represent a Three Circle

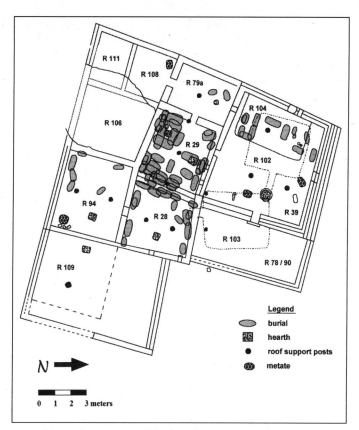

6.2: Plan of south room block at the NAN Ranch Ruin.

phase courtyard group comparable to Hohokam lineage clusters.[10]

Overlying the pit structures was a cluster of at least five Late Three Circle phase transitional rooms: 79B, 98, 101, 104, and 115 (Figure 6.3). These are all of cobble-adobe wall construction, with floors either sunk into the hardpan or constructed directly on top of it. A transition may have begun in this area with the blocking of the entry to room 116, possibly converting it to a room with a ceiling entryway.[11] Overlying room 102 was sunken floor Late Three Circle phase room 104, described in chapter 4. This room, built sometime in the early or mid– A.D. 900s, was used for approximately three generations and perhaps best establishes the argument for continuity of space use and tenure. Two obsidian hydration dates were obtained from samples associated with this room. The earliest, A.D. 947 + 41, was from fill above the floor, and the second, A.D. 970 + 40, was from the fill of a burial pit dug beneath the floor. The cemetery beneath the floor contained at least 13 interments: three adult

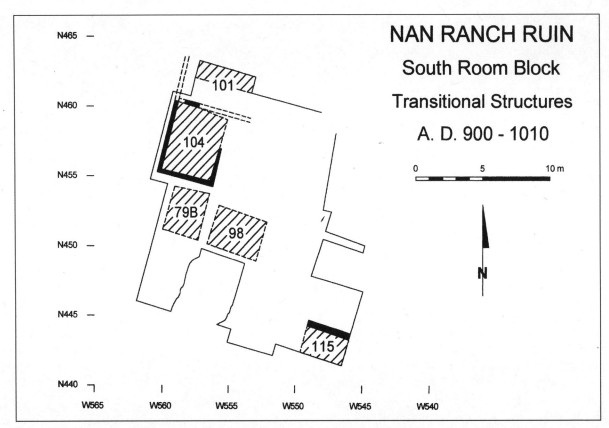

6.3: Cluster of Late Three Circle phase rooms beneath the south room block at the NAN Ranch Ruin.

females, an adult male, five children, and four infants. Associated ceramic microstyles show significant stylistic changes from middle to late Style II during the time the cemetery was in use.

Room 79B was constructed at some interval during this time, but little remains of the original room. It was a small extended household that had a thick adobe floor and a small circular clay-lined hearth. Two large subfloor pits, both capped with thin rhyolite slabs, were associated with the room. Two burials were placed beneath the floor of 79B, a child (burial 194) and an adult (burial 215) whose grave was later cleaned out in antiquity, save for a partially articulated foot. Burial 194 was associated with a late Mimbres Style II vessel (appendix I: Figure A.3H). The style of this vessel suggests contemporaneity of this burial event with the occupation in rooms 104 and 98. We were not able to connect room 79B, 98, or 104 with certainty. Apparently room 79B had burned and was almost completely razed, along with rooms 98 and 104, prior to the construction of room 29.

Additional Late Three Circle phase structures beneath the south room block include rooms 98, 101, and 115. Room 98, discussed in chapter 4, was in use in the late A.D. 900s and early 1000s, based on stratigraphy and ceramic microstyles associated with the burials. Floor remnants of room 98 were detected beneath the floors of room 29. The floor surface was very difficult to trace due to the large number of burial pits that cut through the room from the overlying floors of room 29.

Room 101 was identified by the remnant of a wall base consisting of vertically placed stones on the northwest side of room 39 and a floor remnant that extended beneath room 39. Room 115, a sunken floor room, was only partially excavated, and no chronometric or stylistic dates were available. Stratigraphically, however, the room overlay the southern part of room 116 and traces of yet another room identified only by the remnant of a slab-lined hearth; room 115 was beneath room 109. The sunken floor pit style suggests architectural contemporaneity with room 104.

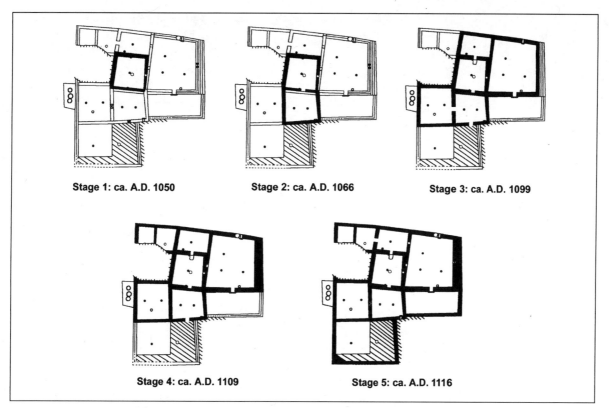

6.4: Proposed five-stage construction sequence for the south room block at the NAN Ranch Ruin.

Although no pattern of arrangement could be ascertained for the Late Three Circle phase structures, once again their clustering suggests that some occupational continuity existed, perhaps the initial stages of development of corporate groups. The establishment of lineage cemeteries in at least three of the extended households also supports this interpretation. Furthermore, granaries have been identified elsewhere at the site, dating to the Late Three Circle phase, which indicates increased variability in the functional role of architecture.

The examination of wall bonding patterns and intra-room stratigraphy has yielded a sufficient body of data to infer a general model of growth for the surface pueblo component of the south room block. A model of room block growth is illustrated in Figure 6.4 and is described here in stages 1 through 5. Renovation and modification probably occurred annually, and all renovations cannot be associated with each stage. Nevertheless, the relative and absolute sequence that follows is based on a number of criteria: tree-ring dates, wall bonding patterns, ceramic microstyles, and burial stratigraphy.

Stage 1: Rooms 101, 104, 79B, and 98 were all razed, perhaps at different times. The south room block pueblo was begun in about A.D.1020 with the construction of habitation room 29, which incorporated much of the space taken up by room 98. Room 104 may still have been in use, but if so, it was razed shortly thereafter. The ceiling to the original room 29 was supported by a three-post pattern oriented east-west, with a center post and posts set in the east and west walls. A hearth was constructed in the southern side of the room.

Stage II: Room 28 was added about two generations or so after the initial construction of room 29, or in about A.D. 1066, and was connected to the latter via a crawlway. Room 28 initially may have been a storeroom, but eventually a formal rectangular slab-lined hearth was constructed in the southern part of the room. This construction episode followed the burning and remodeling of room 29. The three-post pattern of room 29 was replaced by a single center post, and the hearth was relocated to the north side of the room. Room 106 may have been constructed at this time, but it was destroyed by the construction of a horse barn by Mr. John Brockmann in the late nineteenth century. Therefore we cannot be sure when this room was constructed or how it was used. We can only say its west wall abutted onto the south wall of room 29. The courtyard north of room 29 was used as an outdoor activity area. Two features, an adobe-puddling pit and an infant burial, were discovered in this area, but we had no way of assessing age except that they predated the construction of room 39.

Stage III: The crawlway between rooms 28 and 29 was closed with the addition of a second wall course dividing the two rooms; this modification probably took place in about A.D. 1098 or 1099, when extended household room 94 was constructed. Room 94 was connected to room 28 via a crawlway. Room 28 was refloored, and a new hearth was constructed in the eastern part of the room. This renovation also replaced the old south wall of room 28 with a long wall shared with room 94. A long wall was also added onto the north side of room 29 and extended westward to become the new north wall of room 79A. Apparently the original wall had been razed with the modifications to that room.

Several other major construction episodes took place at about this time. Room 39, the large civic-ceremonial room, was added to the north side of the unit, and with its construction, room 29 became an interior room, perhaps changing its function from a habitation room to a corporate kiva. Also room 79A, now a storeroom, was connected to room 29 via a crawlway, and the room was refloored with a thin sandy clay surface. Approximately 11 cm of loose fill containing large pieces of wattle-impressed daub had accumulated on the floor of burned and abandoned room 79B.

Stage 4: In about A.D. 1109, the doorway between rooms 28 and 94 was blocked off and room 28 was extensively remodeled with the application of a second flooring and construction of a new fire hearth. Room 78/90 was added to the east wall of room 39 and connected via a narrow crawlway; rooms 108A and 111 were added to the southwest corner of the unit onto the west side of room 106, where other extensive modifications had taken place.

Room 108A was a small utility room, perhaps once a granary, connected to 79A by a crawlway; room 108A also had a ceiling hatchway. The previous function as a granary is assumed but not demonstrated by the presence of corn. The assumption is based on observation that the adobe floor covered an old pithouse floor constructed on extremely hard cemented gravel. A metate with a large sherd baffle, a door slab, several rectangular slabs from the fallen hatch, a ceiling hatch cover slab, and several smoothed slabs were found on the floor.

Room 111 was a small storage room probably connected to room 106, although the wall between the two rooms was destroyed. Only an ephemeral adobe floor remained; no floor or subfloor features were associated with this little room.

Stage 5: A new long wall was constructed along the entire southern end of the room block when communal storeroom 109 was added in A.D. 1117. A new air vent was constructed in the east wall of room 28 when the old vent was blocked by the addition of room 109. No tree-ring dates are later than A.D. 1117, so we must assume no new construction occurred after this time. Room 94 was abandoned and began falling into ruin despite continued occupation of room 28. Two burials were interred into the debris accumulated on the floor of room 94 prior to its termination by burning. These burials were very shallow and were slightly scorched from the fire.

While room 29 was being excavated, we observed two separate layers of burned roof timbers in the southwest quadrant of the room. We initially interpreted this as the remains of a possible second floor. Subsequent analysis of the notes and photographs, however, suggests otherwise. The collapse of the room after ritual burning apparently took place over a period of time rather than all at once. We were not able to confirm the presence of a second-story unit, nor has confirmation of second-tier rooms in large Mimbres sites been reported elsewhere, although it has been suggested for the Treasure Hill Ruin by the Cosgroves,[12] the Old Town Ruin,[13] and my own observation at the TJ Ruin in the West Fork of the Gila River. As noted in chapter 2, the NAN Ranch Ruin was visited by Professor Clement L. Webster sometime between 1889 and 1892 while conducting an archaeological and geological study of southwestern New Mexico. Webster's[14] description of the ruin raises an interesting point on this issue. He says:

> It is in external appearance quite similar to others already described; although judging from the amount of debris from the ruins, the buildings were somewhat more massive than was usually the case in these villages; in fact *some of the rooms may have been terraced* (emphasis added).

By terraced, Webster presumably meant multistoried. Evidently he did not provide a map of the ruin to indicate where the "terraced" area was. According to the ranch manager, the south room block rubble mound was the highest on the site until he partially leveled it to construct a ranch road. This high rubble mound where the south room block is was probably due to the massive construction of the north wall of room 39 and the use of double wall construction elsewhere. Also, Webster may have been misled by the fact that the NAN Ranch Ruin itself was noticeably mounded as a result of repeated rebuilding over the same space.

Large lineage or corporate group cemeteries were beneath rooms 28 and 29, and a smaller cemetery was beneath room 94 (Figure 6.2), all of which served as habitation rooms at one time or another. Four burials assigned to the Classic period were beneath room 39, but these were either infants (two) or adult males (two) and lacked associated mortuary bowls.

The south room block is the best example of a corporate residential unit at the NAN Ruin. In terms of social makeup, it is perhaps analogous to the cookie-cutter Pueblo II and Pueblo III unit pueblos of the Anasazi to the north but with some very important differences in terms of architecture and cosmology. Both have rooms suggesting multifamily occupancy, specialized ceremonial rooms (key-shaped kivas vs. corporate kivas), and perhaps even rooms set aside for women's ritual space (mealing bins[15] vs. room 39). Very important differences exist, however in orientation, mortuary patterns, and disposal patterns. Much has been written recently about the north-south meridian relating to Chaco Canyon,[16] and the decidedly north-south orientation of the Pueblo II/III unit pueblos indicates the orientation had important significance in Anasazi cosmology. Apparently this was not the case among the Mimbres, where corporate lineage residences, if anything, trend east-west, although this is hardly definitive. An east-west orientation is suggested since most corporate kivas and storerooms are oriented that way (29/79, 41/42, 55/60), which may be descended from the easting orientation of the Late Three Circle phase great kivas. Distribution of trash among the northern Anasazi was more formalized and consistently deposited south of the kivas; no such attention was paid to trash among the Mimbres. Burials among the northern Anasazi were in the trash mounds, whereas the Mimbres placed their lineal dead beneath the floors of the corporate kivas or habitation rooms. If there was a pattern to the corporate lineage residences of the Mimbres, it was not recognized until now; the unit pueblos of the Anasazi, however, have been recognized for over a century. In sum, the Mimbres corporate households emerged largely out of necessity from previously independent family groups of the earlier pithouse periods and display numerous structural and cosmological differences with the Anasazi unit pueblos.

An important component of the Mimbres corporate households is lineage cemeteries. Burials in these cemeteries varied from two to over 40, the number depending on the size of the corporate group and how long the lineage residence was occupied. I attempted to determine approximately how long, or how many generations, the south room block was occupied by roughly calculating how long it took to inter the number of individuals in the respective cemetery.

A total of 87 individual burials were recorded in the south room block area. Specific information on provenience, age, sex, position, and association is given in Table 8.1. Twenty of the burials are assigned to the transitional phase on the basis of room provenience, artifact association, and stratigraphy; 13 were associated with room 104, four with room 98, two with 79B, and one was extramural. The remaining interments are dated to the Classic Mimbres phase. Room 29 contained the greatest concentration of burials (Figure 5.25). Forty individual burials were recorded beneath the floors of room 29, but 36 individual burials and an unknown number of disturbed graves of infants and children are associated with Classic period use of the space. As described above, room 29 was remodeled at least three times, and at least three separate flooring episodes were documented. Space use in the room shifted, as indicated by relocation of the firebox. Burials occurred during all episodes of room use. Twenty-one burials were recorded from room 28 (Figure 5.19), which had the second-largest cemetery, and room 94 had six burials recorded.

Critical to defining lineage residences and multigeneration occupancy is assessing how long a specific residential complex was occupied. The occupation of the south room block spanned several generations, as shown by the stratigraphic superposition and horizontal stratigraphy of the architecture, the range of ceramic microstyles, tree-ring dates, and the relative numbers of burials in the cemeteries. How many generations occupied specific household rooms, however, can only be guessed, based on the above criteria. One method of measuring the span of occupation is based on calculating the estimated number of deaths per household per

TABLE 6.1. Estimated Number of Deaths per Household in the South Room Block at the NAN Ranch Ruin

No. of Houses		House life in Years		People per House		Crude Death Rate		Total
3	X	20	X	5	X	0.0503	=	16.599
3	X	20	X	5	X	0.036	=	11.88

generation multiplied by the number of estimated generations. This estimate is then compared to the actual number of burials recorded for each habitation room. Two things are assumed with this method: first, that burials placed in the floor of a household room were of people associated with the household through kinship, and second, that the cemeteries are a true mortality population not skewed by selection of age, sex, or social status. These estimates, for obvious reasons, exclude those interred in nonaligned rooms (such as room 39) or in midden deposits and those who were cremated.

The projected death rate per generation was calculated from rooms 28, 29, and 94. The formula for calculating the death rate is taken from studies based on the estimated average house use life, multiplied by the number of people per household times crude death rate.[17] Both high and low estimates are calculated, depending on which house use life (22 or 15 years) and crude death rate (.0503 high or .036 low[18]) was used.

Estimating use life of ancient vernacular structures is problematic for a number of reasons. How long a structure is used depends on social, technological, and physical factors.[19] In the Classic Mimbres case, such technological factors as maintenance, repair, remodeling, reuse, and razing are all among the processes that come into play. Erosion and human wear and tear are the foremost physical factors affecting structure use life. Natural growth and evolution of a family and changing space needs can result in realignment of rooms and shifting room function. Mimbres predominately single-story cobble-adobe architecture would subject exposed surfaces to moderate to severe erosion from the often torrential summer monsoonal rains, making frequent maintenance and repair necessary. Burning, whether accidental or intentional, occurred periodically in most rooms occupied for lengthy periods and in the majority of abandoned rooms regardless of how long they were used.

The south room block calculations are generally based on the assumption that the average use life was 20 years. This was based on the estimates of 15 and 22 years used in a Hohokam study. Since the architecture of a Mimbres pueblo is much different from that of a Hohokam pithouse, where these figures were derived, in that pueblo walls and interior space were usually unchanged through renovation and reuse, Classic Mimbres use life could have been highly variable and have lasted longer than 22 years for interior rooms. Therefore use life is equated here with the estimated average length of a generation of about 20 years. This estimate approximately correlates with the clusters of tree-ring dates from the south room block (e.g., A.D. 1066, 1088, and 1109). Estimating the average number of people per household is equally problematic, but I used an average of 5.5 based on Catherine Cameron's recent study of Hopi architecture.[20] Both the high and low crude death rate figures were used to provide an expected mortuary population for the excavated area of the south room block. The results of these calculations are shown in Table 6.1.

The formula for estimating the death rate requires that the number of households be known. The estimates below are projected with the assumption that a minimum of one and a maximum of three households were occupied at any one time. Each household consists of at least one room with a slab-lined hearth but also includes other rooms connected by interior doorways. Thus rooms 28, 94, and 29 are the three household units defined for the south room block.

Table 6.2 provides both high and low death rate estimates based on a generation length of 20 years and crude death rate figures of .0503 and .036, respectively. The

TABLE 6.2. Projected Death Rate per Generation/House Life in the South Block at the NAN Ranch Ruin

Room No.	No. of 20 yr Generations		Crude Death Rate	Estimated	Actual
28	3	@ .0503	5.533	16.599	21
28	4		5.533	22.132	21
94	1		5.333	5.333	6
94	2		5.333	10.666	6
29	5		5.333	26.665	36
29	7		5.333	37.31	36
28	3	@ .036	3.77	11.88	21
28	4		3.77	15.08	21
94	1		3.77	3.77	6
94	3		3.77	7.92	6
29	5		3.77	18.85	36
29	7		3.77	26.39	36

TABLE 6.3. Inferred Number of Generations for Each Household in the South Room Block at the NAN Ranch Ruin

28	4	@ .0503	5.33	22.13	21
94	1		5.33	5.33	6
29	7		5.33	37.31	36

figures provided in the total number of deaths column indicate the number of deaths that would be expected for each generation in three households. The duration of occupation from the south room block is about 140 years, or about seven generations of 20 years each. But since all households were not occupied all of the time, figures were calculated using one to seven generations. Table 6.3 shows the best match for the number of generations a room was occupied compared to both the high and low crude death rate figures (0.503 and .036) and the actual number of burials recorded for each room. Based on these crude estimates, room 29 was used for about seven generations, 28 for four, and 94 for a little over one. Overall, the expected number of burials for the three rooms with these generation estimates is 64.77, whereas the actual number is 63. The expected number for room 29 is 37.31, compared to 36 actual; for room 28, the expected number is 22.13 and the actual 21; and for room 94 the expected number is 5.33 and the actual six.

The chronological sequence of occupation for each of the three households is discussed in the architectural growth models presented above. Room 29 was the oldest and was first constructed in the early part of the eleventh century, based on early Style III ceramics associated with deeper burials. It was used for about three generations, or some 60 years, before room 28 became a household. Room 28 was used for about 80 years; this estimate is based on tree-ring dates for additions to room 29 (A.D. 1066), construction dates for room 28 renovations (A.D. 1109), estimated terminal dates for the south room block occupation (ca. A.D. 1140), and the presence of only middle and late Style III ceramics. Room 94, added in approximately A.D. 1109, had only late Style III pottery associated. I am aware that the assumptions on which these estimates are based are open to challenge and that the interpretations involved a bit of circular reasoning. The purpose of this exercise, however, regardless of its flaws, was to show occupational longevity of specific households and to support the interpretation discussed in chapter 10 that these were not only the functioning households for the living, but also the residences of the lineage ancestors.

The outdoor area around the south room block was not extensively sampled, but limited excavations revealed evidence for a number of activities whose traces were sealed beneath various layers and lenses of adobe and other fill. Features encountered include four adobe-mixing pits, adobe quarry pits, two roasting pits, a Late Three Circle phase burial (burial 226), and a bird burial (feature 10–9). Not surprisingly, these features indicate that the space around the pueblo was repeatedly used for both domestic and ritual activities.

Aggregated Multihousehold Unit: The Third Tier

The third tier of architectural units at the NAN Ranch Ruin is represented by the east and west room blocks. Both are large, complex aggregated structures incorporating several corporate residential units comparable to the north and south houses at the Swarts Ruin. The south room block provides an architectural model for identifying other corporate lineage households at the NAN Ranch Ruin. The east room block, however, poses some challenges in identifying lineage households because it is a larger aggregated architectural unit. Extended households, corporate kivas, granaries, and civic-ceremonial rooms can be identified individually within the east room block, but it is not always possible to be certain which extended households connected to which corporate kivas or other special function rooms because of the aggregation. In most cases a corporate kiva is the identifying factor for the presence of a lineage household, and merely counting corporate kivas, or those rooms with floor vaults, is one way of recognizing the numbers of possible lineage households (Figure 6.5). Five rooms with floor vaults were excavated, and one is proposed to be a lineage household based on the Cosgroves' findings. It would be easy to leave it with that figure, but there are reasons for attempting to go a step farther. Unlike the south room block and the Cosgroves' suite, which appear to have been prime lineages in the sense of internal ranking,[21] certain lineage households appear to have been added at later times. This evidence of community growth may be tied to optimal years for agriculture, a topic discussed in chapter 7.

Four corporate kivas are identified among the rooms in the east room block, rooms 12, 41, 55, and 62 (Figure 6.5), but there may have been as many as three others. This class of rooms was described in chapter 5. Rooms 41 (rooms 41/42 suite; Figure 6.6A, p. 100), 62 (rooms 62/85/84 suite; Figure 6.6B, p. 101) and 55 (rooms 55/56/60 suite; Figure 6.7A, p. 102) are, however, illustrated to show the variability within this class of rooms. Room 47 (Figure 6.7B, p. 103) in the 47/49/50 suite may also be a kiva room, but a looter's pit destroyed the hearth to the extent that we could not determine if a vault was associated. Reference to the above corporate kivas will be used, however, to expand the discussion of corporate households in the east room block. We can assume a kiva was present in the Cosgroves' excavated suite east of room 58 since one of these rooms had a large lineage cemetery that contained many burials. The Cosgroves report excavating five late rooms and four early rooms, 53 burials, and 50 pottery vessels in this location. The presence of both early and late rooms is consistent with the architectural stratigraphy we observed in our excavations of rooms 12, 76, and 89. One excavated room contained 40 burials according to the Cosgroves and most assuredly was a corporate kiva. I suspect that this was the highest-ranking corporate household in the east room block, probably encompassing room 45, and may have been at least ranked on par with the south room block.

Other possible lineage households were the rooms 9 and 48 suites. The room 9 suite, consisting of rooms 8, 9, and 10 (Figure 6.8, p. 104), may have been a lineage household with room 9 as the nucleus, but relic hunters' excavations destroyed the hearth features in this large room. The rooms 48/58 suite was also badly disturbed by relic hunters but yielded some extraordinary information nevertheless. Several lineage households undoubtedly were present in the west room block, although our testing of this aggregated unit was limited and did not identify corporate kivas. Using the known figures from the east and south room blocks, I would guess that anywhere from 12 to 15 lineage households or corporate groups were present at the NAN Ranch Ruin during its peak around A.D. 1100.

Room 12 (Figure 5.22), as described in chapter 5, is defined as a corporate kiva on the basis of the floor vault, wall shelves, and about three generations of burials beneath the floor. The cemetery spans the time from the late 900s to about A.D. 1050, based on ceramic styles that include late Style II and early Style III vessels. We were

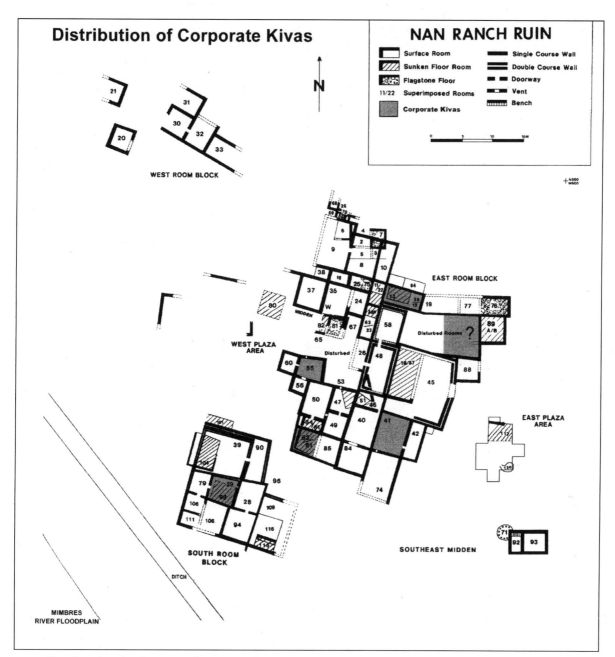

6.5: Site plan showing location of rooms at the NAN Ranch Ruin with floor vaults.

not able to connect room 12 to any other room due to extensive disturbances in this area of the site. Room 12 was presumably part of the Cosgroves' suite to the east and southeast, but even though these rooms were all but destroyed, no connecting doorway was found. Such a connection is possible in the south wall since only the wall base remained at the time of our excavation.

The corporate kiva identified as room 41 was built relatively late in the NAN Ruin sequence, in about A.D. 1060, and was remodeled at least once.[22] It was added to the linear suite of rooms that included rooms 58, 48, and 40. Room 42 was later attached to the east side of room 41 and connected by a crawlway. No other extended household could be convincingly tied to room 41. Room 40 was

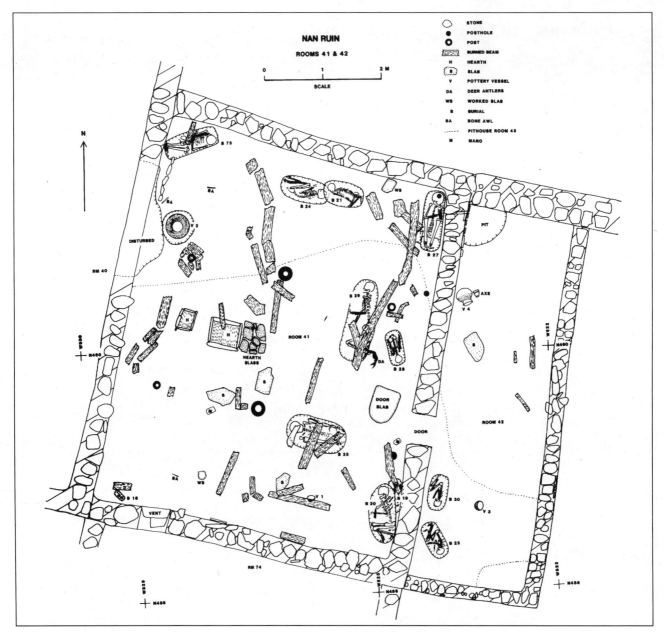

6.6A: NAN Ranch Ruin room suites: plan of rooms 41/42 suite, showing corporate kiva room 41 and subfloor features.

abandoned by the time room 41 was constructed and had gone into ruin, as indicated by accumulated midden deposits over the ruins. Renovated room 84A—mentioned earlier as a possible nuclear family household—may have been connected to this lineage household. The construction of communal storage room 74, which also converted room 41 to an interior room, supports this theory. The very large and short-lived civic-ceremonial room 45 was added to the rooms 41/42 suite and may have been associated with it, with the Cosgroves' suite north of room 45, or, more likely, with the room 48 suite.

Room 41 had been resurfaced numerous times, and the room had undergone some renovation, the last of which was in A.D. 1107.[23] Based on the 12 burials interred in this

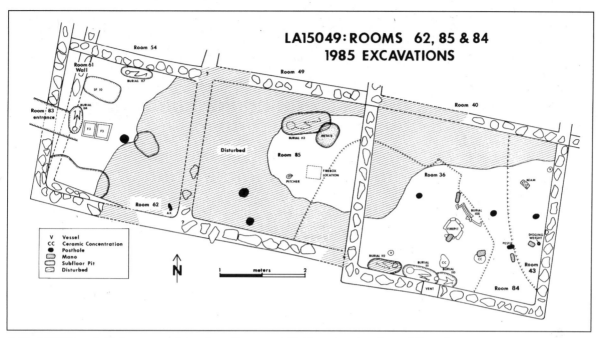

6.6B: NAN Ranch Ruin room suites: plan of rooms 62/85/84 suite, showing subfloor features.

suite, I estimate this lineage household was used for at least three generations. Initial construction probably began sometime shortly after A.D. 1060, based on ceramic microstyles present in the burials. Only middle and late Style III ceramics were recovered from mortuary contexts, and a single late Style III bowl was on the floor.

Room 62 was a small lineage household that was probably connected to rooms 85 and 84B. These rooms were badly disturbed by relic hunters, who removed numerous burials from each of the rooms. Despite the extensive damage, we were able to salvage some important information from this suite. Classifying room 62 as a corporate kiva was based on the presence of the compartmentalized hearth, one side of which may have been a floor vault, although both sides were filled with ashes. Numerous burials were beneath the floors. The room was constructed over transitional room 61. The wall connecting room 62 to room 85 was destroyed save for a small remnant, and relic hunters had clearly also removed burials from the west end of room 85. At least 10 burials were interred beneath the floors of rooms 62 and 85, a figure calculated based on the minimum number of individuals represented in the remains recovered from both undisturbed and disturbed fill.[24]

The room 62 suite also included rooms 85 and 84B.

Room 85 was an extended household with an unknown number of burials; at least four are estimated, based on extant burial pits and scattered bones. No minimum number of individuals was calculated for this room specifically. Room 84B was completely razed, but its presence was revealed by three burials (110, a child, and 111 and 112, both adults) placed against an old wall base beneath 84A. The south wall of room 85 may have joined to this wall, but we could not be certain due to the amount of disturbance. A later room, 84A, was constructed using the old wall base.

Another lineage household was created with the construction of rooms 47, 49, 50, and 54 (Figure 6.7B), and the addition of rooms 55, 56, and 60 may have enlarged the household. The construction began with a common wall extending west from the room 46-48 juncture. This wall served as the north wall to both rooms 47 and 50. Two tree-ring dates from room 49 (1103v and 1108v) provide an approximate construction date for this suite. Rooms 47 and 49 were joined by a crawlway, as were rooms 50 and 54. Both rooms 49 and 54 had been disturbed by relic hunters, but enough of room 49 was left to ascertain its function. It was the main room of the two-room suite, having a slab-lined hearth, and the door between the two rooms was closed from the room 49 side.

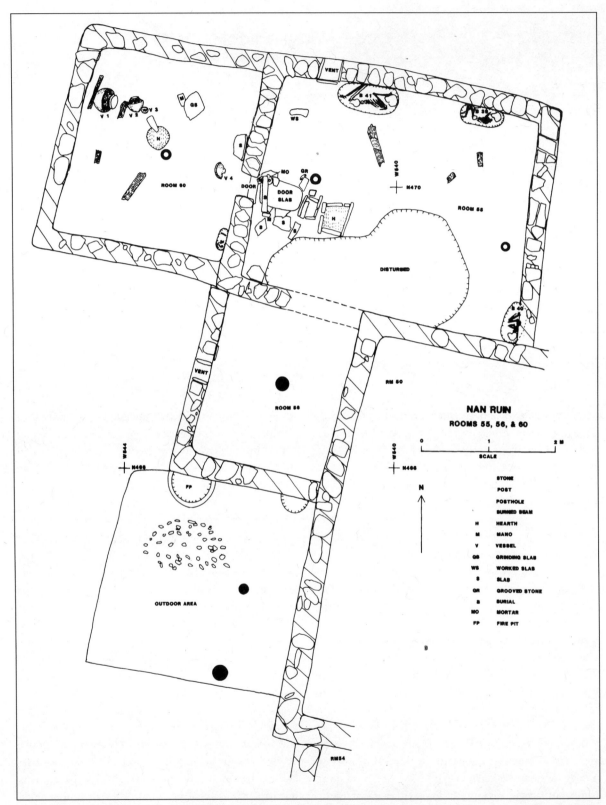

6.7A: NAN Ranch Ruin room suites: plan of 55/56/60 suite, showing corporate kiva and associated floor and subfloor features.

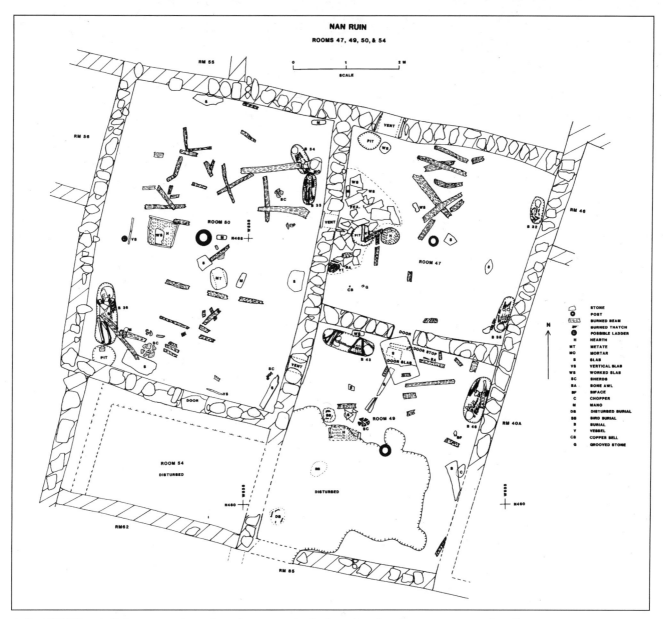

6.7B: NAN Ranch Ruin room suites: plan of rooms 47/49/50/54 suite, showing common north wall.

Room 47 had a circular cobble-lined fire hearth, and room 50 had a slab-lined hearth. Little can be said of room 54 due to its disturbed state, other than to note that it was constructed over the ruins of room 61. The suite may initially have incorporated three extended households: 47, 49, and 50.

Shortly after the construction of this suite, another suite, consisting of rooms 55, 56, and 60, was added. Room 55 was a corporate kiva and may have served both suites of rooms. Room 60 was attached to room 55 by a crawlway, but no horizontal entry was detectable for little storage room 56. Since no corporate kiva was identified in the 47/49/50/51 suite, we can assume that room 55/60 served that function. Room 49 may have been a kiva room, but only the north edge of the hearth was present; the remainder, and possibly a floor vault, was destroyed by relic hunters.

Two very interesting patterns occurred in architecture

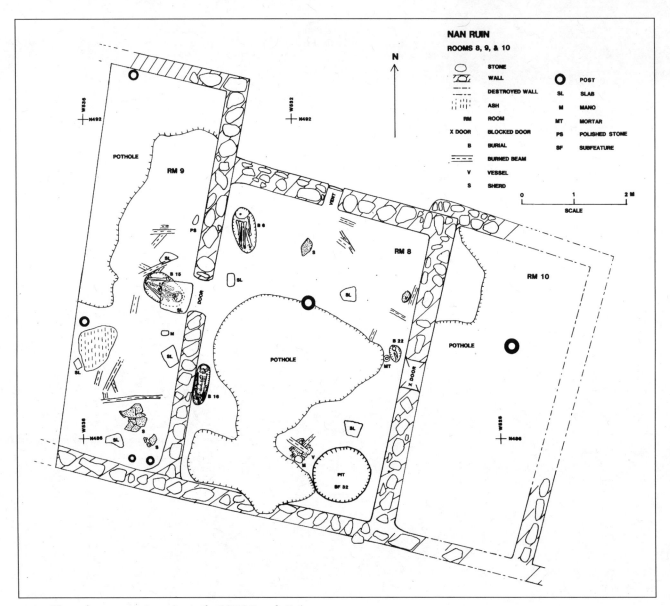

6.8: Plan of rooms 8/9/10 suite at the NAN Ranch Ruin.

and burials from the 47/49/50/51 suite of rooms that add further support to the assumption that these suites do represent a corporate lineage household. Both rooms 47 and 50 had a vertical slab ladder rest placed west of the hearth. Also, three burials—burial 46, an old female adult in room 49; burial 34, a young child in room 47; and burial 35, an infant in room 50—were buried flexed but facedown. These are the only such facedown burials found in the entire site except for burial 157 in room 29, which was placed headfirst into a deep pit. This deviance in mortuary patterning also hints that decisions on how and where a body was placed were family based rather than dictated by overriding cultural mores.

One other possible lineage household is represented by rooms 8, 9, and 10, all overlying a razed suite of earlier Classic period rooms (Figure 6.8). Two construction dates of A.D. 1071 were obtained from burned timbers in room 9, the larger of the rooms in this suite. Rooms 8 and 9 were joined by a doorway. Looters' disturbances were extensive in this area of the site and had destroyed most of room 9, including the hearth. Therefore it was not possible to determine if a floor vault was present. Based on the quantity of disturbed human remains scattered throughout the potholes, a number of burials were associated with room 9 and the underlying rooms. The argument that this suite is indeed a lineage residence is bolstered somewhat by the complexity in the architectural stratigraphy at this location. Rooms 8, 9, and 10 overlie a series of structures including rooms 3, 4, 5, and 7 and beginning with pithouse room 1 (Figure 6.9, p. 106). The degree of rebuilding at this location is also illustrated in Figure 6.9.

The suite composed of rooms 48, 58, 46, and 26 is another likely candidate for a lineage household, although none of these rooms had floor vaults preserved. Room 48 was probably the primary residence for this suite since all other rooms were connected to it by crawlways. We reexcavated rooms 48 and 58 and, despite the damage, were able to retrieve valuable information on these rooms. Room 48 was a habitation room with a complicated history of renovation, including the addition of reinforced second courses to all exterior walls, the only two-course wall structure in the east room block. Not destroyed by previous excavations was a floor section with a slab-lined hearth; the floor where a vault would have been was destroyed. At least two adult burials had been disturbed by previous excavators. Room 58 (described in the previous chapter), connected to room 48 by a crawlway, was extraordinary in that benches were around three walls. Room 26 was almost totally destroyed, but room 46 was intact. Room 46 was a small storeroom converted from a salvaged end of room 40. A metate, a sherd tool, and a mano(?) were on the floor of the room, and a sealed cache pit in the floor contained a corrugated jar (Figure 5.12).

The NAN Community: The Fourth Tier

Earlier in this chapter I presented a model that large Mimbres towns were composed of multiple tiers of architectural units. The first tier consisted of habitation rooms forming the core of nuclear or extended family households. The second tier incorporated two or more habitation rooms and formed corporate lineage households such as the south room block. The third tier consisted of integrated, large aggregated units such as the east and south room blocks. The fourth tier represents the integration of all of these residential units and surrounding space, including the courtyards and plazas that defined the town as a whole. Clearly, however, the town was not composed of a clustering of egalitarian families.

Previous attempts to define social ranking in Mimbres archaeology were based on mortuary evidence.[25] References to lineage ranking is often made in Western Pueblo social organization, and inferences to such ranking have been made using architectural and mortuary data.[26] The conclusions were that Mimbres society was in essence egalitarian and lacked evidence for social hierarchy. When we completed the first season's excavations at the south room block, I was struck with the seemingly extraordinary efforts that went into the construction of that structure compared to the east and west room blocks. If there was indeed a ranked lineage at the NAN Ranch Ruin, I felt that the south room block was a good candidate. With this consideration in mind, when I analyzed the mortuary data, I found some interesting contrasts between the south room block and the east room block as a whole. Comparatively speaking, the south room block stood out in relative wealth of graves, based on frequency and numbers of mortuary vessels and adornment jewelry. These differences in architecture and mortuary data could translate as evidence for lineage ranking. This hypothesis was tested in independent studies conducted by Elizabeth Ham[27] and Diane Holliday. Ham used the superordinate/subordinate model proposed by Peebles and Kus[28] in a study to determine if the NAN Mimbres society was in essence egalitarian (as previous studies had suggested) or ranked. Holliday searched for differences in health between the east and south room block populations in an effort to determine if the south room block folks were somehow better off.

Ham examined the mortuary data from the east and south room blocks for evidence of social differentiation. Using the superordinate/subordinate model, she sought to identify both the vertical and horizontal elements that may be present in a society. The superordinate dimension is used to define an apical class, whereas the subordinate dimension applies either to the lower level of a two-level hierarchy or to a true egalitarian society. She compared the south room block mortuary population with that available from the east room block. Her findings revealed some interesting, although not conclusive patterns. The south room block did have "wealthier" graves, as defined by the amount and class of associated mortuary furniture, than did the east room block. Furthermore, more female burials were found to have ceramics, with more ceramics per burial than males. Females also tended to be buried

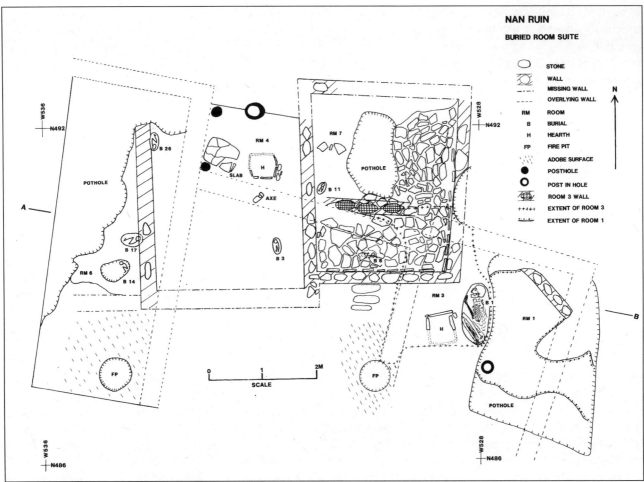

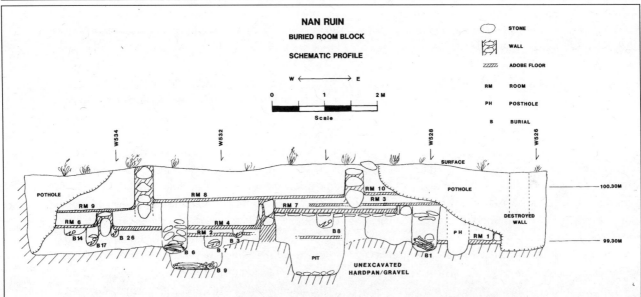

6.9: Suite of rooms buried beneath room 9 suite, room plan is shown at the top; cross section at the bottom illustrates the extent of renovation that took place in this part of the site.

with a pelvis/spine direction to the east. No Classic period burials showed any extraordinary energy expenditure in grave preparation, however, to suggest one individual standing above the others. None of these patterns were explained by the ranked or egalitarian definitions as presented in the superordinate/subordinate model. Clearly something was going on, but it could not be explained by the overly simplistic ranked or unranked assumptions used in the analysis. Ham did, however, suggest that the Mimbres social organization was matrilineal, based on the differences in mortuary treatment between the sexes, which seemed to place more emphasis on females.

Holliday compared the south and east room block skeletal samples for differences in health based on skeletal pathologies.[29] She found no significant differences in the two populations to suggest one group experienced better health and nutrition than the other group; however, if these social differences indeed existed, they could not be distinguished on the basis of dietary or hygienic behavior.

Both of these studies have an inherent weakness in that they compare the south room block population, which is arguably largely that of a single lineage, to a composite sample probably composed of two or more lineages, as suggested previously. We could not isolate a sufficiently large mortuary sample from a single lineage cemetery in the east room block and so were forced to combine all of the burials from that part of the site. The 40-plus burials excavated by the Cosgroves contained an unknown number of wealthy graves. One grave contained a large collection of worked shell items, which the Cosgroves illustrated and identified as coming from the NAN Ranch Ruin in their 1932 report.[30] Furthermore, the vessels recovered from this cemetery contained two Mimbres polychrome vessels, perhaps the most prestigious of the Mimbres ceramics. The only other polychrome vessel from which provenience information is known was from room 29, in the south room block. It is possible that polychrome vessels may be indicators of relative importance when recovered in association with a particular lineage assemblage.

Although the material evidence for social ranking among lineages is not very strong, I still believe it is possible to identify at least one primary lineage and infer others. Archaeologists usually relate wealth based on quality and quantity of material items. Wealth may also be reflected in the longevity of a lineage household. Such longevity would imply that these households were able to hold on to productive lands for generations, thereby gaining prestige and power through agricultural success. Certainly the south room block is the best candidate for a primary lineage household, but others, such as the Cosgrove suite and the room 48 suite, may have been occupied by a primary lineage as well.

Summary

In this chapter I have defined four tiers of social groupings based on architecture: single habitation rooms, which may have formed nuclear or extended family households; corporate households, composed of clusters of habitation rooms and auxiliary rooms, which may have been occupied simultaneously by members of larger extended families or lineage members; aggregated architectural units composed of two or more clusters of habitation rooms; and clusters of households and an aggregated unit forming the village as a whole. A fifth tier, consisting of the network of Mimbres towns and outliers, is discussed in chapter 12.

Households are defined by material patterns in the architecture, mortuary customs, and other material items. Lineage households were a phenomenon that evolved, some occupying the same space through time, as suggested by the south room block, the rooms 8/9/10 suite, and the Cosgrove suite. A more detailed description of the growth and development of the south room block was presented, along with estimates for the lengths of time in generations each extended household was occupied. This information demonstrated the process of growth for a lineage household and how special function communal rooms became integrated into the lineage household suite.

In contrast, other lineage households may represent new families that either joined the community or families that split from prime lineages, as suggested by the 47/49/50/51 suite. Extended family households that did not evolve or survive may include the 91/92, 84A, and 16/25 suites, among others. It was not possible to establish suite affiliation for several rooms (e.g., rooms 11/22, 24, 37, 67, 63/23, 18, 81, and 82) or any of the excavated rooms in the badly disturbed west room block.

The south and east room block findings also show that lineage households can stand alone or may become incorporated into a much larger aggregation. Other examples of this have been suggested by Mara Hill in her reconstruction of aggregation units at the Swarts Ruin.[31]

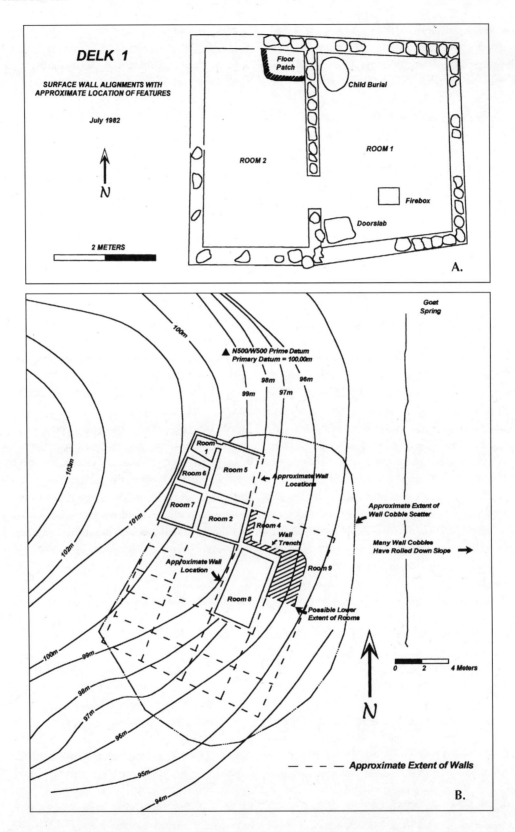

6.10: Plan of Delk and NAN 15 ruins: A. Delk ruin; B. NAN 15 ruin.

Larger aggregations are common in large Mimbres sites, as shown by the east and west room block at the NAN Ruin, the north and south houses at the Swarts Ruin, the Old Town Ruin, and the Galaz Ruin.

The NAN Ruin lineage household model can now be applied to Classic Mimbres settlement pattern schemes. When tied to their economic function, the distribution of households also provides some insight into the strategies for dispersing or concentrating populations during the Classic Mimbres phase and into the growth and decline of this phase. The most comprehensive settlement pattern study done in the Mimbres area was of the Rio Arenas Valley, by LaVerne Herrington.[32] This settlement pattern model will be used to describe the Classic period settlement pattern and how it relates to large pueblos. Herrington ranked Classic Mimbres sites into a five-tiered structure based on the number of rooms that could be discerned. This classification is very useful in defining functional components among the sites and examining the distribution of those components. First-order sites are pueblo ruins of more than 100 rooms; second-order sites have 20 to 30 dwelling rooms; third-order pueblos have approximately nine to 18 dwelling rooms; fourth order, two to eight; and fifth order, one to two rooms. Herrington notes that sites of the first four orders have a full range of artifact types: manos, metates, chipped stone tools and debitage, and plain, corrugated, and painted ceramics. Items of jewelry or sculptured stones are present even in fourth-order sites along with burials. No burials have been reported from fifth-order sites.

Lineage households formed the core to large Classic Mimbres towns in the Mimbres Valley, or Herrington's first- and second-order sites. The archaeological data from the NAN Ruin and other large ruins such as Swarts, Cameron Creek, Mattocks, and Saige McFarland suggest that large communities evolved from not a single extended family household but a cluster of several.[33] Some of these became primary lineage households around which the communities grew.

Extended family and lineage households also occur as small outlier sites throughout the Mimbres region. These fall into Herrington's second- to fourth-order site. Some extended family households such as the Delk Ruin (Figure 6.10A), a fourth-order site, show short-duration use, perhaps less than a generation.[34] Such sites may be indicative of short-lived attempts to cultivate secondary lands that were only watered during good years. Lineage households that contained accumulated midden deposits and numerous burials, Herrington's third-order sites, on the other hand, probably represented more successful households and predictably were situated in proximity to arable plots of land. The Wheaton Smith Ruin[35] and NAN 15 are examples of third-order sites (Figure 6.10B). Single-room field houses and one- to two-room jacal structures were special-function structures associated with specific lineage households.

The enlargement of the basic economic unit from the extended family households in the Three Circle phase to the more inclusive lineage households and multilineage communities in the Classic period was a response to the increasing complexity of the economic organization associated with food production and distribution. I present the argument here that successful food production in the early and middle Classic period served as a magnet attracting near and distant kinsmen into the valley and major settlements. As discussed in chapter 2, a population drift eastward out of the upper Gila into the Mimbres Valley occurred in the Classic period. A similar shift may have occurred out of the deserts to the south as well, swelling the Mimbres Valley population to its zenith from about A.D. 1050 to 1100.

CHAPTER SEVEN
Foods and Subsistence

INTRODUCTION

In this chapter, Classic Mimbres foods and subsistence technologies are described, based on material evidence from the NAN Ranch Ruin and supplemented by information from elsewhere in the Mimbres Valley. Production of surplus food within the constraints of the local ecology and climate was the ingredient that solidified the Mimbres into a cohesive regional system. Their inability to sustain the production of food surpluses presumably led to their downfall.

It is no surprise that the central element in the diet of the ancient Mimbreños was corn, combined with a mixture of other cultivated plants, gathered wild plants, and hunting. Hard evidence of agriculture and subsistence, in the form of charred corncobs, corn kernels, discarded animal bones, projectile points, and broken and discarded food-processing tools, is common in the cultural deposits at the NAN Ranch Ruin. More subtle indications of subsistence and the capability to produce food reserves come from such sources as granaries, irrigation systems, processing tools, ceramics, ceramic designs, and even implications drawn from mortuary practices.

The evolution that took place in Mimbres culture from the Late Pithouse period to the Classic Mimbres phase is related to agricultural intensification and its organizational requirements (labor organization, food preparation and storage, ceremonial and ritual components), whereas the demise of the Classic Mimbres phenomenon is attributed to a collapse of the agricultural system and its supporting sociocultural infrastructure.[1] I make the case that in the Late Three Circle phase, irrigation agriculture began to impact Mimbres society in many ways, subsistence being primary, but societal restructuring also became necessary to establish the infrastructure to maintain and expand the irrigation systems and establish a reciprocity network for food distribution. The irrigation systems necessitated corporate labor groups who were held together by obligatory rules of kinship and a common belief system. Evidence for such social restructuring and formation of corporate groups is the appearance of lineage cemeteries in the Late Three Circle phase.[2] Other consequences include a restructuring in storage and food-processing technologies, broader networks of social relations, and ceremonies and symbolism that tied villages together and defined the inner and outer boundaries of Mimbres culture and society.

In cultures with subsistence-oriented economies, food is power. A family who can produce a food surplus will attract relatives from near and far and may build a powerful network of reciprocal obligations that significantly enhances their prestige. A prime reason food is power is that it cannot be banked for long and must be distributed or lost. Providing relatives with food through exchanges and feasts establishes obligatory responses that can be recalled when needed. Reciprocity can be in kind, including providing labor or resources not produced by the family itself. Families that can produce food surpluses therefore are in the position to establish a powerful network of relatives to muster when the situation demands it. If we can assume the Mimbres were organized in a similar fashion to other nonindustrial societies that practiced agriculture, including Western Pueblo culture, rules governing rights to fields and food distribution networks were probably complex and followed kinship alliances, such as membership in lineages and the more inclusive lineage clans.[3] In other words, the structure of the irrigation system in regard to the allocation of water and fields probably mirrored the social organization of the village.

Numerous aspects of the behavioral system involving Mimbres agriculture are evident in the material record. The botanical record is unequivocal about the importance of agriculture, but empirical evidence for agricultural intensification is not so dramatic when botanical evidence alone is considered. Such correlates as changes in hunting and gathering practices, storage, food processing, labor management, water control, social restructuring, increased ritual activity, and changes in symbolism and cosmology are all regarded as evidence for restructuring social and technological organizations around an expanding commitment to irrigation agriculture.

Two lines of thinking can explain the appearance of agriculture in the American Southwest. One line postulates that it was brought in by immigrant populations from the south, the other that agriculture became incorporated into the subsistence regimes of indigenous Archaic hunters and gatherers. Recent archaeological evidence from southern Arizona, New Mexico, and northern Chihuahua shows the latter view to be more correct, but the process was much longer and more gradual than previously thought. The general assumption has been that agriculture gradually became more important through time in Mogollon culture at the expense of hunting and gathering, beginning with the initial early pithouse villages. The process actually began long before the Early Pithouse period. Corn was available to Archaic hunting and gathering people at least 1,000 years before the first fixed villages were constructed in the Mimbres Valley. Corn was not domesticated in central Mexico until about 3000 B.C.[4] and it took only 1,500 years for it to become an important cultivated plant in the American Southwest. The earliest corn in the Southwest is a type called *chapalote*, small-cob popcorn. Squash was introduced at about the same time and beans from about 500 to 300 B.C.

The site Cerro Juanaquena in northern Chihuahua, Mexico, has shown the co-occurrence of corn with the extensive construction of many man-made terraces around a high, natural hill, signifying a shift toward intensive land use and economic reorganization from about 1500 to 1200 B.C. This and other sites in Arizona show that some of the hunter-gatherer cultures were quite capable of mustering significant labor to construct elaborate earthworks for agriculture.[5] Early agricultural sites dating from about 1500 to 200 B.C. have been discovered in southern New Mexico and Arizona, including the sites of Wood Canyon and Forest Home in the Burro Mountains in southwest New Mexico.[6] These sites are preceramic but contain substantial midden accumulations and small pit structures. The Early Pithouse period in the Mimbres Valley represents not so much a change in subsistence emphasis, but rather a regional relocation of populations already living in shallow pit structures and utilizing corn. The relocation into an oasis valley was strategic in that the venue was set for feeding an expanding population. The continuity of material culture and lack of evidence for new technologies such as storage and food-processing facilities between late Archaic and early agriculture assemblages across the southern Southwest discounts the theory that distant immigrant populations from Mesoamerica supplanted indigenous Archaic people.

The specific method of growing corn during the Early Pithouse period is unknown and could have involved several choices. In ancient times marshy areas may have been present along the river and up major tributaries below springs. These subirrigated plots would have been ideal for dry farming, where natural conditions were relied upon to provide the necessary moisture. It is also possible that some form of *akchin* agriculture was practiced, whereby runoff waters are allowed to flow across alluvial fans where crops might be planted. One such fan on the NAN Ranch Ruin terrace may have been cultivated by the first pithouse dwellers at the site.

The evolution of Mimbres agriculture has been attributed to a response to food stress brought about by increasing population from the Early Pithouse to the Classic Mimbres period. This Mimbres Foundation model of Mimbres subsistence was based on estimates gained from population studies, climate, and available agricultural lands.[7] Unpredictable fluctuations in the climate were thought to have placed severe stress on the Mimbres capacity to produce enough foods to sustain their growing population. Climate conditions were favorable for dry farming during the first two-thirds of the Classic Mimbres period[8] but turned unfavorable during the last third, or after A.D. 1100. Less favorable rainfall patterns, decreasing frequency in the use of riparian woods at the expense of upland species, and changes in faunal assemblages were interpreted as evidence for degradation in the local environment due to overpopulation.

The Mimbres Foundation model has been widely accepted among southwestern archaeologists[9] despite its inherent weaknesses.[10] One weakness is that chronological resolution within the Classic Mimbres period was nonexistent at the time the model was formulated and the scale of comparison was only by broad blocks of time represented by periods. In other words, it was not possible to detect changes in material responses at the very critical time the Classic system failed, approximately A.D. 1100. The chronological resolution provided by the NAN Ranch Ruin data helps to fill this serious gap and allows some reevaluation of the model.

Mimbres agriculture remained small scale until the Three Circle phase, when the first stages of irrigation agriculture arguably began. Early varieties of chapalote corn hybridized, were supplemented, or were replaced by a new corn, *maíz de ocho,* by the San Francisco phase.[11] Improved growing conditions are also reflected in the crop yields. The ubiquity of maize kernels and cobs in midden deposits increase threefold from the Three Circle to the Classic phase.[12] Analyses of corn from Classic Mimbres phase deposits showed a decrease in the eight- and 10-row cobs common in the earlier phases and an increase in 12 and 14 row, reflecting the boom period for Mimbres irrigation farming from about A.D. 1000 to 1100.[13] The success of irrigation farming was unequivocal.

The evolution of Mimbres agriculture can also be seen in changes in processing facilities such as manos and metates. The morphology of metates, for example, changes from the oval basin shape of the Early Pithouse period to trough metates in the Late Pithouse period or certainly by the Three Circle phase.[14] The first trough metates were open at one end, but by the Late Three Circle phase, trough metates open at both ends were preferred. Manos evolved from the oval one-hand variety to the subrectangular two-hand variety from the Three Circle phase on. These changes denote growing efficiency in milling technology to compensate for greater food demands.

By the Late Three Circle phase social and technological correlates for agricultural intensification began to kick in, such as construction of granaries. The inauguration of riverine irrigation was arguably in place by the Late Three Circle phase, with continued expansion well into the Classic period. Knowledge of irrigation systems was probably part of Mimbres mental technology gained through interaction with their Hohokam neighbors to the west. Information exchange between the two cultures can be seen in several kinds of material culture. Mimbres potters incorporated elements of Hohokam designs in their ceramics,[15] and ceramic designs and physical exchange of Hohokam vessels and sherds occur in Mimbres sites.[16] Additional evidence of physical interaction includes the exchange of shell artifacts from the Gulf of California and Pacific coast where trade routes crossed Hohokam territory. It would indeed be naive to assume rigid information boundaries existed between the Mimbres and major cultural systems such as the Hohokam, Chaco Anasazi, and Jornada Mogollon. Buffer zones in which a mixture of characteristics occur generally separate the heartlands of each of these systems. The West Fork Ruin, once situated along the West Fork of the Gila River near the TJ Ruin, for example, shows a mixture of Mimbres and Cibola ceramics and ceramic characteristics. A different kind of situation existed in the San Simon Valley, where intrusive Classic Mimbres pottery accounts for 2 percent of some samples,[17] and Doña Ana phase sites in the Jornada area have anywhere from 2 to 6 percent admixtures of Mimbres Style III pottery.[18] Intrusive ceramics from each of these surrounding areas occur at the NAN Ranch Ruin, albeit in very small amounts. Jornada brownwares are the more frequent. Trace element analysis has demonstrated that the Mimbres ceramics made in the Mimbres area were intrusive in both the San Simon and Jornada sites.[19]

For over a century, the scientific community has known about the existence of ancient irrigation canals in the Mimbres Valley. Adolph Bandelier observed what he described as garden beds and canals or ditches near the ruins in the Mimbres Valley.[20] There is, of course, no way of knowing to which phase the features Bandelier mentions belonged since the middle and lower sections of the valley were also intensively occupied by Black Mountain and Cliff phase people. The very existence of extant canals that could easily be repaired may have contributed to a rather rapid reoccupation of the valley following the Classic period depopulation. This may partly explain why Black Mountain phase pueblos were situated in proximity to the Classic period ruins.

Archaeological evidence for prehistoric irrigation and water management has been documented across the Mimbres River drainage by LaVerne Herrington,[21] Darrell Creel,[22] Lain Ellis,[23] and others. These water control features include canals, ditches, diversion dams, check dams, and terraces. An exceptionally well-preserved canal system feeding into bordered fields similar to the features mentioned by Bandelier was documented on the Rio de Arenas, a tributary of the Mimbres River. Canal systems have also been observed on Cameron Creek, Lampbright Draw and Gavilan Canyon[24] and in the middle Mimbres Valley.[25] Evidence that all of these systems are Classic Mimbres in age is not unequivocal but is certainly strong in the Rio de Arenas case and supported by radiocarbon dates in the Gavilan Canyon and by radiocarbon dates and stratigraphic evidence in the Mimbres Valley example.

By the most liberal estimates, dryland farming simply could not reliably feed many people.[26] Irrigation farming accounts for the marked increase in Mimbres population from approximately A.D. 650 to 900 and especially after that time, in my opinion. Direct and indirect evidence convincingly points to water conservation and irrigation agriculture. Direct evidence for irrigation agriculture is the irrigation systems in the Rio de Arenas, Gavilan Canyon, and middle Mimbres Valley. Sources for indirect evidence of irrigation are the correlates of agricultural intensification, such as new varieties of corn in the Three Circle phase, Late Three Circle phase changes in storage facilities to accommodate food surplus,[27] and restructuring of Mimbres society to accommodate, among other things, the labor requirements.

A complex of water control structures in the Rio de Arenas drainage, documented by LaVerne Herrington, includes water conservation structures such as check dams and terraces and water diversion structures such as ditches, canals, and dams that are convincingly Classic Mimbres in age. All the water control methods she describes have ethnographic correlates among native groups in the American Southwest.[28]

Check dams are linear arrangements of stones, laid in drywall from one to several courses high and placed across short drainages perpendicular to the water flow (Figure 7.1). The height of the dam depended on the gradient of the drainage. Herrington estimated that some 700 such structures were built in the upper Arenas watershed alone, and some 400 were situated within 1 km of a large Classic Mimbres site. Similar structures have been noted in upper Lampbright Draw and in other upland drainages in the Mimbres and upper Gila watersheds. The effectiveness of such structures in retaining moisture and checking soil erosion was demonstrated by the depths of fill behind tested check dams, which averaged about 75 cm, with a maximum of 165 cm.

Small upland clearings of 100 to 500 sq m are also present in the northern part of the upper Arenas watershed. These are naturally nearly flat but have been cleared by removal of scattered stones downslope from the area.

Stone-faced terraces three to four courses high were recorded in and around the larger Classic Mimbres sites

7.1: Check dams in the upper Rio de Arenas watershed.

in the upper Arenas Valley. The walls, like the check dams, were constructed of drywall masonry. Herrington believes these terraces probably functioned more to retard erosion around the pueblos than as agricultural features.

A surprisingly well-preserved system of canals and diversion structures was discovered by Herrington in the midsection of the Rio de Arenas watershed. Even today, this system is visible by subtle topographic and vegetation differences (Figure 7.2A, B). Here the stream crossed several igneous dikes that created natural check dams for pooling water. Artificial diversion structures of stone were placed at these natural dikes to divert water into a network of canals and ditches feeding into bordered fields. Overall, some 185 square hectares of arable land were available to the farmers of a nearby large Mimbres pueblo.[29]

Dating the Arenas features is somewhat problematic

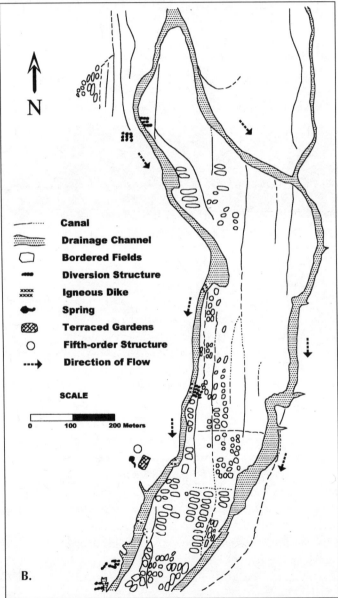

7.2: Mimbres irrigation system in the Rio de Arenas valley: A. infrared image of Rio de Arenas irrigation system (courtesy of LaVerne Herrington); B. map of bordered fields and water control structures of Rio de Arenas system (used with permission from Herrington 1979: Figure 35).

due to the lack of adequate chronometric measures, such as radiocarbon dating. Herrington, however, makes a convincing case that these water control features date to the Classic Mimbres phase, based on their proximity and/or association with known Classic Mimbres sites and the minimum age of the Style III Mimbres ceramics caught in the fill of the check dams and canals. Granted, the ceramics could easily have eroded into the fill long after abandonment, but the context of the ceramics in the bed of the canal, the proximity of the water control features to the largest Mimbres sites in the upper and middle Arenas watershed, and Herrington's observations that many of the features were part of planned construction events lend credence to her case.

Another well-preserved water control system was discovered in the lower section of Gavilan Canyon, only about a kilometer above its confluence with the Mimbres River.[30] This system, on the first terrace of Gavilan Canyon, is an irrigation ditch complex, at least two reservoirs, and a canal that tapped rainfall runoff into two floodplain fields. Gavilan Canyon has a permanent flow of water for short distances from three springs along the lower 6 to 7 km and surface flow from an occasional flash flood. The soil on the terrace is permeable, deep fine sandy clay overlying gravel. The soil on the steep slopes of the late Tertiary conglomerate is shallow. The first terrace is 50 to 100 m wide and has the same gradient as the stream, at 2 m vertical drop per 100 m horizontal distance.

A ditch could be traced for approximately 400 m at the base of the terrace edge (Figure 7.3). This main ditch and its one main lateral are about 1 m wide and 30 cm deep. The main ditch captured runoff from the narrow rocky slopes above the terrace and from one of the reservoirs. Eventually the ditches emptied water into two lower floodplain field areas, each about 1 hectare in size (Figure 7.4).

The two small reservoirs associated with the system

were constructed in a side arroyo. The impoundment basin of one dam was about 300 sq m and about 1 m deep. A V-shaped notch was excavated into a narrow ridge behind the dam to divert water into the main ditch (Figure 7.5). From the V cut, the water dropped nearly 2 m into a cobble-filled channel that fed into the main ditch 10 m below. A second impoundment dam at the mouth of the arroyo may be historic in age, constructed long after the first had filled with sediment and broke. A third diversion dam, constructed across a possible ditch channeling water from the uplands terrace to the arroyo, is historic and was constructed in the 1970s to pond water for livestock.

Another unrelated ditch system (NAN 37) was discovered across the canyon and downstream from NAN 20, and a Mimbres Style III sherd was found in the fill of that ditch. No other Mimbres sites that would otherwise explain the presence of the sherd were near the ditch. The association of the sherd and the ditch raised the possibility that the latter was at most Classic period in age. Therefore we assumed the features at NAN 20 were prehistoric and possibly Classic period in age.

The well-preserved nature of NAN 20 was at first suspect until the results of dating efforts were obtained. Soil organic matter was the only source for radiocarbon dating of the ditch and dam features since they did not involve activities in which woody charcoal would be present. Soil organic matter is composed of organic carbon from a variety of sources with different ages, and carbon from each source decomposes at a different rate. A radiocarbon date from soil organic matter does not date the time a particular stratigraphic layer behind the dam was deposited but provides a date for the average amount of carbon-14 decay as a whole and how long the organic matter has been in place. Radiocarbon dates were obtained from sediments behind the diversion dam. One date on carbon present in soil humates was from the upper 5 cm of a horizon composed of humic soils buried beneath the dam and beneath the laminated sediments that accumulated behind it. This date was A.D. 1140 to 1270 and should provide a maximum date for the dam construction. Two samples from the lowest sediments caught behind the dam yielded dates of A.D. 720 to 890 and A.D. 1300 to 1420. Although these dates seem ambiguous, soil humate dates are commonly used by geoarchaeologists to assess the geologic age of sediments, and they seldom have the precision that satisfies archaeologists. Nevertheless, these dates do confirm our suspicions that the system is

7.3: Main ditch of the Gavilan Canyon rainfall irrigation system.

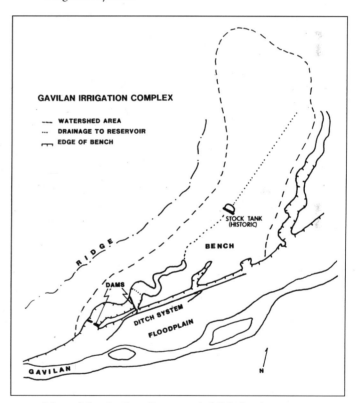

7.4: Map of the Gavilan Canyon rainfall irrigation system.

prehistoric and does not discount the possibility they are Classic Mimbres in age.[31]

The suspected fields were sampled for fossil pollen in hopes of detecting evidence of cultivars. Five soil samples

7.5: Photo of gap between the reservoir and main ditch to the Gavilan Canyon rainfall irrigation system.

were taken from the upper field, 10 to 20 cm below the surface. All tested samples had very high counts (85 to 90 percent) of Cheno-Am (Chenopodiaceae and the genus *Amaranthus*) pollen. Chenopodiaceae and/or *Amaranthus* are both weedy plants commonly used by indigenous groups in the Southwest. The analyst, Richard Holloway, interpreted the evidence as indicating an ancient field despite the absence of maize or other primary cultivars. Holloway felt that the high Cheno-Am pollen counts indicated disturbed soils expected in agricultural fields and that Cheno-Ams may have been one of the economic plants grown in them.

A relic reservoir and canal system was discovered on the NAN Ranch Ruin terrace east of the ruin during geoarchaeological investigations of the site by Lain Ellis. Both modern and relic canals occur on the NAN Ranch Ruin terrace. Investigations identified canal features that were not only prehistoric, but probably Classic Mimbres in age.[32] The surface of the NAN Ranch Ruin terrace had never been cultivated and was an excellent candidate for exploring for water control features. Hand and backhoe testing yielded evidence of several relic canals in addition to the modern canal dispensing water from a head gate created around a natural dike in the Mimbres River at the north end of the terrace.

The most ancient canal can be traced about 160 m on the east side of the terrace, emptying into a man-made reservoir on the east side of the NAN Ranch Ruin (Figure 7.6). The canal was about 3 m wide and half a meter deep, with a slope of 0.8 percent; walls were lined with adobe and small cobbles where it crossed permeable midden deposits. Excavators of the original canal and reservoir cut into terrace paleosurface or Late Pithouse period midden deposits. The original canal could deliver about 615 cubic meters, or 0.5 acre-feet, of water per hour. Sometime later, perhaps in historic times, the canal was reexcavated, cutting into sediments filling the original canal. The later canal was deeper with respect to width than the original, and Ellis suggests it was dug using different technologies and relates the later canal to the occupants of Camp Mimbres, which was occupied from about 1863 to 1867. Interestingly, however, Bandelier made no mention of a canal feeding into the reservoir, suggesting that the alluvial deposits that cover the ditch today also obscured it from view during Bandelier's visit. Webster made no mention of either a reservoir or a ditch system when he visited the site a decade later.

The reservoir was formed by shallow excavations into underlying deposits of terrace paleosurface, Late Pithouse period midden deposits, and alluvial fan fill. It was bounded by an excavated berm composed of underlying midden or terrace fill. The canal fed into the northeast side of the reservoir. Ellis speculates that the function of the reservoir may have been to capture discharge from upland drainage and divert it to fields on the terrace below; the holding pond may have conserved water for adobe construction secondarily, but since the drop-off from the second to the first terrace below the reservoir is rather steep, a holding pond may have been necessary to slow down the flow. Another possibility explored by Ellis is that gardening occurred on the second terrace around the site and was fed in part by the canal system.

The reservoir was enlarged historically at least twice: once prior to the present ownership of the ranch and later, in 1981, following a damaging flash flood that spewed out of one of the arroyos that spills onto the NAN Ranch Ruin terrace. The later modification was quite extensive and hampered our efforts to trace the full extent of the original reservoir, so capacity estimates are not possible. With the discharge rate provided by the canal, however, it would not take much rain to fill the basin. Radiocarbon dates from the NAN reservoir and ditch system (Table 7.1, p. 118) have been thoroughly analyzed by Ellis.[33] Taking the problems of soil organic matter dating into consideration in his age assessments

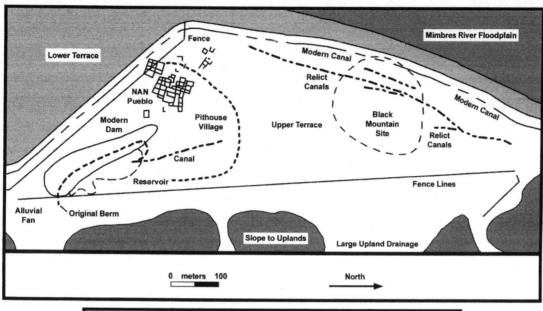

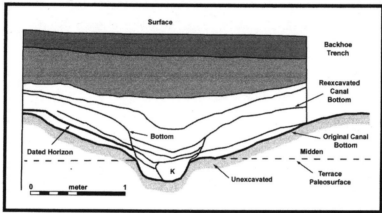

7.6: Map of ditch and reservoir on the NAN Ranch Ruin terrace (after Ellis 1995: Figure 11.2).

of the NAN features, he dates the reservoir and overflow sediments in the canal to the early to middle Classic period and canal sediments to the Classic period. None of the dates preclude, however, uses of these features in the Black Mountain phase.

Knowledge of how to conserve water using ditches and hand-dug reservoirs was not out of the ordinary in the Mogollon area, as shown by the Mimbres' neighbors to the east. The use of ancient reservoirs fed by drainage ditches has been documented among the Jornada people in the Tularosa Basin. These water conservation features may date as early as the Doña Ana phase and were used in the El Paso phase; the Jornada phases were coeval with the late Classic Mimbres and Black Mountain phases, respectively.[34]

Diet

Archaeological indicators of diet can be direct, such as charred remains of plants, butchered animal bones, and desiccated human fecal material, or indirect, such as the presence of fossil pollen from economically important plants, storage facilities, processing implements, and scenes on pottery. In this section, I review both direct and indirect indicators of Mimbres cuisine.

TABLE 7.1. Radiocarbon Dates Associated with the NAN Ranch Ruin Ditch and Resevoir (after Ellis 1995)

Sample	Laboratory Number	Radiocarbon. Years B.P	Delta C13*	Calibrated 95% C.I.	Calibrated Intercepts
Reservoir Sediments					
Humin sample (HM)	GX-15934	825±75	-19.2	A.D. 1030–1280	A.D. 1223
Canal Overflow Sediments					
Humin sample	GX-15932	815±155	-15.3	A.D. 900–1420	A.D. 1227
Humic Acid Sample (HA)	GX-15933	690±165	-15.4	A.D. 1010–1490	A.D. 1281
Canal Sediments					
HA-1	GX-17643	725±65	-19.7	A.D. 1190–1390	A.D. 1278
HA-2	GX-17644	870±65	-20.1	A.D. 1002–1280	A.D. 2263, 1174, 1188
HA-3	GX-17645	1055±115	-21.6	A.D. 687–1220	A.D. 987
HA-4	GX-17646	445±110	-22.8	A.D. 1280–1660	A.D. 1438
HA-5	GX-17888	460±110	-20.6	Uncalibrated	Uncalibrated

GX = Geochron Laboratory number.

Charred plant remains occur throughout the cultural deposits at the NAN Ranch Ruin and provide direct empirical evidence for the use of cultivars, especially corn. Although the easiest way of studying subsistence shifts might seem to be comparing the botanical remains from each period, there are problems with such an approach. Charred plants are preserved in the archaeological record accidentally, and the changes in frequency may or may not have anything to do with the frequency of their use. Most microfossils are recovered by systematically floating out charred plant remains from a measured volume of matrix. Desiccated plant remains, like those recovered from rock shelters and caves in the American Southwest, were not found at the NAN Ranch Ruin except in rare circumstances. Charring could be considered a random event, so any changes in the botanical assemblages detected through time would have some statistical validity. The ubiquity index is one method used to partially overcome this bias in measuring changes in the uses of each plant taxa in the macrofossil record. Ubiquity indices provide a means of comparing percentages of specific plant parts in one sample and comparing one sample (or time period) with another. Changes in percentage may signify shifting preferences in the uses of certain plants or perhaps better preserved archaeological deposits. Paul Minnis[35] used this method to test for frequency shifts in uses of cultivars through time and found virtually no distinguishable differences from A.D. 750 to 1150.[36] This is not the case with the NAN macrobotanical studies. Corn increases nearly threefold from the San Francisco through the Classic phases,[37] a finding that strongly supports the notion of agricultural intensity during this period.

Corn, beans, and squash were the main constituents of the Mimbres' diet throughout the site's occupation. Botanical remains of corn and other cultivated plants such as common bean, tepary bean, squash, sunflower, pigweed, goosefoot, and cotton have been recovered from Mimbres archaeological sites. These cultivars were supplemented by either gathering of wild plants or, in some instances, possibly even cultivating or creating favorable conditions for wild plant growth. Cultivated and wild plant remains recovered from Mimbres sites (including sites tested by the Mimbres Foundation,

TABLE 7.2. Wild and Domestic Plants Identified from the NAN Ranch Ruin and Other Mimbres Valley Sites

Taxon	Part Recovered	Taxon	Part Recovered
Cotton	Seed, seed hair	Chokecherry	Seed
Maize	Cob, kernal	Saltbush	Fruit
Common bean	Seed, seed hair	Mesquite	Seed, fruit
Tepary bean	Seed, seed hair	Acacia	Seed
Squash	Fruit rind	Canyon grape	Seed
Goosefoot	Seed	Stickleaf	Seed
Pigweed	Seed	Hedgehog cactus	Seed
Purslane	Seed	Prickly pear	Seed
Pepper grass	Seed	Banana yucca	Seed
Bugweed	Seed	Spanish bayonet	Stem
Sunflower	Seed	Grama grass	Seed
Tansy mustard	Seed	Brittle grass	Seed
Beeweed	Seed	Rice grass	Seed
Knotweed	Seed	Dropseed	Seed
Walnut	Nut	Love grass	Seed
Alligator-bark juniper	Seed	Paspalum sp.	Seed
One-seed juniper	Seed	Bulrush	Seed
Piñon	Nut		

Wind Mountain, and the NAN Ranch Ruin) are listed in Table 7.2[38] and include such items as fruits from mesquite, prickly pear cactus, cholla cactus, and banana yucca and seeds from grasses, purslane, juniper, piñon, and chokecherry. The hearts of agave (*Agave* sp.), yucca, and sotol were used throughout much of the Archaic period in the Chihuahuan Desert to the south and by the Mimbres' Jornada neighbors to the east and were likely used by the Mimbres as well. Marshy areas supported stands of cattails, which were also harvested opportunistically.

Opportunistic recovery of plant microfossils, especially in a primary context, is very important since it does provide direct indication of use. As noted earlier, identification of charred beams on room floors and wood identification of charcoal from hearths are direct indications of which woody plants were used and which types were preferred. The recovery of charred corn on the floors of burned structures such as rooms 51 and 76 helped to assess their function as granaries. Desiccated squash (*Cucurbita moschata*) from a subfloor storage cache provides a glimpse of storage behavior and value placed on certain plants.

Fossil pollen is sometimes well preserved in archaeological deposits in the American Southwest and is an indicator of economic plants used for dietary and ritual purposes. For that reason, archaeological deposits were systematically and opportunistically sampled throughout the site, providing some interesting information that confirmed our suspicions about the function of certain features and our interpretations of ritual behavior. Pollen is well preserved in its natural state in the archaeological deposits at the NAN Ranch Ruin, so the potential for gaining useful information from pollen analysis is good.

Pollen is distributed in three ways: by wind, by animals and insects, and by self-pollination. Such plants as pines, juniper, spruce, oaks, cottonwood, grasses, sedges, and Cheno-Ams are wind pollinated and produce large quantities of pollen each year. A single anther of pigweed (*Amaranthus*), for example, may produce 100,000 pollen grains, whereas insect-pollinated plants, such as beans and squash, may produce far fewer, 100 grains or so per anther. When relatively high amounts of pollen from insect-pollinated plants occur in a sample or feature, for example, it is very possible that the insect-pollinated plant was used in some economic way. Wind-pollinated plants, such as grasses and weeds, often produce the majority of pollens found in archaeological sites, which are considered to be background contaminants unless the circumstances suggest otherwise. The high Cheno-Am pollen counts in the Gavilan Canyon fields mentioned above are an example of this.

Factoring out the background pollen is necessary to get some indication of the uses of and changes in economic pollen types, that is, those pollen grains from plants thought to be used by the inhabitants. One method of determining background pollen is to collect samples of modern pollen from various elevations away from but in proximity to the site. These findings are then compared to fossil pollen to identify background types, and gross changes in the local vegetation might also be detected. Concentrations of economic pollen recovered from sealed contexts such as fill in roasting pits, burial pits and burials, subfloor caches, and storage pits can be very important in defining uses for specific plants. When pollen from a specific plant dominates a sealed sample, the likelihood that the plant was used in the activity is increased.

Pollen studies in archaeology are mostly related to reconstructions of past environments through the construction of pollen diagrams showing changes in pollen frequencies through time. Such reconstructions can show gross changes in plant communities due to climate change (as with changes from the late Pleistocene to Holocene environments) or help to gauge the impact of human occupation. The Mimbres Foundation's study of pollen from sites dating throughout the Mimbres sequence, for example, showed that plant communities were affected by the size of the human populations in the valley.[39] Weedy plants increased in proportion to population. Also, *Opuntia* (e.g., cholla, prickly pear cactus) and tree legumes such as mesquite were more plentiful in ancient times than today, especially in the Classic Mimbres period.[40] Cattail (*Typha*) also was found to be present throughout the sequence but increased in the Black Mountain phase, perhaps reflecting reestablishment in marshes along the river or in relic canals after the Classic period.

Pollen studies from the NAN Ranch Ruin have been used primarily to assess artifact or room function and to identify possible dietary and ritual plant uses from specific contexts. Archaeological samples were compared to modern transect samples as a baseline for determining differences in ecology and to identify potential economic plants. We found economic plant pollen in all the samples we examined and listed potential economic plants present in the pollen spectrum. Specific dietary information, however, requires very tight control on the origins of samples from specific features, and the pollen from these samples is compared with the pollen spectrum from the surrounding fill to identify relative concentrations. For this reason, pollen analysis was used mainly to confirm the function of suspected features (roasting pits and possible granaries) and to search for concentrations in burials that might provide hints of dietary or ritual behavior.

Pollen samples were systematically taken from burial fill and from the stomach/colon areas of the skeleton. The purpose was to compare the fill samples with those taken from the area of the body cavity in hopes of detecting both dietary and ritual uses of plants. Pollen samples from 14 burials were analyzed to see if any conspicuous patterns related to diet or rituals might be detected. The results of this test were not overwhelmingly positive: pollen spectra from burial cavities and burial fill in most cases showed no significant differences. With the exception of burial 109, the results were not particularly informative, but did provide some hints of both dietary and ritual behavior.

The only coprolite (fossil feces) specimen recovered from the NAN Ranch Ruin excavation came from the colon contents of burial 109.[41] Tissue was preserved in certain burials from the NAN Ranch Ruin, including 109, and the preservation of the colon contents provided a rare opportunity to examine the individual's last meals. The burial was that of a male approximately 35 to 40 years old at the time of death, who suffered from numerous pathological disorders, including a deformity of the sacrum.

Burial fill samples were dominated by pollen from Cheno-Ams, a common pattern in midden fill samples from the site. The next most common midden pollen was maize, which represents a cultural phenomenon. Wind-dispersed pollen from asters, pines, and willows represented environmental types from the normal pollen rain.

The burial fill pollen contrasted with the sample from the colon, in which pollen was found from mustard (Brassicaceae) at 53 percent, willow (*Salix*) at 26.1 percent, and maize at 10.3 percent. Although willow is normally considered an environmental type since it is partly wind pollinated, the large percentage (26.1 percent) seems to indicate natural ingestion. Hence willow pollen may have been ingested as part of a medicinal concoction. The ingestion of the willow pollen through drinking water is discounted; otherwise, one might expect other common environmental types to be present as well. Cattail and squash were other dietary pollen types in the colon, and the coprolite also contained fragmented seed coats from maize and an unidentified black seed, possibly an amaranth. The last item ingested by the individual in burial 109 appears to have been a maize gruel, possibly mixed with a medicinal tea brewed from willow and mustard plant parts (including flowers and/or anthers). Colon pollen also suggests the season of death was in the late spring, when willow and mustard plants pollinate.

Additional dietary and behavioral information was obtained from three of the burial pit fill samples examined: burials 12, 73, and 86. Burial 12 was that of an adult male buried in a tightly flexed sitting position in midden fill accumulated over the ruins of room 40. Elevated levels of grass and phacelia pollen were found in the sample from the stomach area. Grass seeds may have been part of a gruel. Phacelia is a purple flower that blooms during the spring and is used extensively by southwestern Indians for its medicinal qualities. It is very likely that this individual ingested parts of this plant for medicinal purposes shortly before his death. Burial 73 was a subadult female buried semiflexed in the northwest corner of room 41. Pollen samples were collected from the chest and stomach and the burial fill for control. The chest sample had a high frequency of juniper pollen (12.5 percent), much higher than any other burial sample. Various parts of juniper were used aboriginally, especially for medicine and ritual purification. Juniper pollen (or bows) may have been introduced into this burial through ceremony, and if so, the interment probably took place in the early winter. Elevated frequencies of grass and *Cucurbita* sp. pollen from the stomach area

probably relate to the consumption of a concoction that included grass seeds and squash. Burial 86 was an adult female buried flexed beneath the floor of Three Circle phase pithouse room 14. The burial was associated with an array of artifacts (pot-polishing stones, worked potsherds, unfired vessels, red ochre paint, kaolin clay), indicating she was a potter. Pollen samples were taken from north of the cranium, the stomach/colon area, and grave fill. The sample north of the skull yielded grass (32 percent), maize (20 percent), and cattail (34 percent) pollen. These three pollen types were also present in the stomach/colon sample but in lower percentages (28, 6, and 15 percent respectively). The results of the pollen studies suggest that a mixture of pollen or plant parts containing pollen may have been ritually sprinkled over the head of the individual at the time of burial.

The lack of consistent patterns in pollen concentrations from burial contexts may not necessarily be due to the absence of pollens per se, but rather to the problems of sampling. Concentrated pollen may have been present only in very small areas, and if these areas are missed, then the samples taken would be similar because they represent pollen spectra from the general fill. Therefore when pollen concentrations are detected, they may indicate dietary or ritual behaviors that were more widespread than sampling indicated. This is especially true in regard to the uses of medicinal plants, whose parts (anthers, leaves, flowers) would yield greater concentrations than processed corn or squash, for example.

Food storage facilities, such as pits and formal granaries, often provide direct information on food habits. Granaries, as special function structures, were first constructed in the Late Pithouse transition, in approximately the late 900s. Prior to the Late Three Circle phase, food was probably stored either in containers such as jars or baskets or placed on arbors or racks to dry. We found no evidence for subfloor pit storage prior to the Classic period. Large storage jars and a coiled grass storage basket were found in the charred interior remnants of pithouse room 95 and a late San Francisco/early Three Circle phase structure. Also, about 10 kilos of burned shelled corn was disposed of in a deep pit feature dating to the Three Circle phase in the east plaza. The corn was in a twilled basket when it burned, and the entire mass was tossed into the pit and covered over. Although this feature was clearly a secondary deposit, it suggests a change in storage strategies. Corn was stored shelled in earlier phases and stored on the cob in the Late Three Circle and Classic times.

7.7: Photo of squash seeds from subfloor cache in room 41 at the NAN Ranch Ruin.

Storing shelled corn is a strategy often associated with mobile groups, whereas storing corn on the cob is characteristic of more sedentary groups.[42]

Mimbres granaries were identified for the first time at the NAN Ranch Ruin on the basis of one or more of the following characteristics: thick adobe floors; reinforced subfloors, usually consisting of a layer of cobbles or slabs; vertical slabs placed around the wall, either on the inside, outside, or both; and quantities of burned corn on the cob. In two cases, charred corn on the cob was found on the floors (rooms 51 and 76). Room 51, dating to the Late Three Circle phase, was the earliest granary, stratigraphically situated beneath rooms 40 and 48, both early Classic period rooms, and above Three Circle great kiva room 52. Room 51 contained several kilos of burned corn on the cob. Room 76 (built in A.D. 1008) is another early granary. Other Classic period granaries included rooms 75b, 75c, 81, and possibly 108. We also found an outlier feature constructed late in the Classic period that may have been the remnants of granaries, but we were not able to confirm their specific function. One extramural feature, possibly a granary, consisted of the remnants of a rectangular slab/cobble paved area capped with adobe at the south end of the east plaza.

Pollen samples from selected rooms were also systematically examined to aid in assessing their function. One of these, room 7, was defined as a granary on the basis of the architecture (thick adobe floor with a slab-paved subfloor and vertically placed slabs lining the walls on the inside). Six samples were examined from the context of room 7, and in each Cheno-Am pollen dominated (varying from 75 to 92 percent). Pine, juniper, prickly pear cactus, maize, and grass pollen were all found above the 1 percent frequency, but none in percentages high enough to argue for storage of any of these items.[43] If the corn was stored husked, as suggested by charred ears from rooms 51 and 76, then we might expect pollen percentages to be low.

Opportunistic discoveries at the NAN Ranch Ruin have also provided some interesting insight into Mimbres storage behavior. Three Classic period subfloor storage pits were found to contain large jars, or pit containers. The use of such jars was obvious: their contents could be easily sealed from moisture and invading rodents. Large corrugated jars with volume estimates of 25,000 to 27,000 cc were found in subfloor pits in rooms 41 and 46. The jar in room 46 was sealed with a thin rhyolite slab (Figure 5.12). Unfortunately, both jars contained loose fill and yielded no discernable pollen or plant macrofossil concentrations. This was not the case, however, with a cache found beneath the floor of room 40. This cache consisted of a large Style III jar with a capacity of about 17,000 cc, capped with a Style III bowl placed in a grass-lined pit. This jar contained dried squash seeds and rind. Variability in the sizes and shapes of the seeds suggests two varieties were present: the cultivated *Cucurbita moschata* and an unidentified variety (Figure 7.7).[44]

In addition to the subfloor pits containing jars, deep subfloor pits were found in rooms 42 and 79A. The pit in room 79A was over 60 cm deep, with a maximum dimension of 50 cm, and covered with rhyolite slabs. It appeared to have once contained a vessel, but if so, it had long since been removed.

The most conspicuous items used in processing foods were manos, metates, and cooking pots. Efforts to trace the growing importance of maize agriculture in the Mogollon region were based on the size, shape, and wear on western Mogollon manos and metates.[45] The results showed that the dietary importance of maize remained low and stable from the Early Pithouse period through the Georgetown phase. The consumption of maize increased during the San Francisco phase and continued to increase through the Three Circle phase. This trend holds true for the NAN Ranch Ruin as well.

Although the number of whole and broken manos and metates recovered from the NAN Ranch Ruin is well over a hundred, few were recovered from sealed primary contexts. The one Three Circle phase metate recovered from a burned structure, for example, was a trough metate open at one end. By contrast, the one Late Three Circle phase metate found came from room 104 and was a trough metate open at both ends. Classic Mimbres phase metates were recovered from rooms 46, 85, 29, 39 (three metates), 94, and 106 and courtyard 35. Metates also were included in cairns over burials 1, 21, 88, and 151. Manos also varied in size from the small, single-hand variety more frequent in Three Circle phase deposits to two-handed varieties, which occur throughout the sequence. Three Circle phase manos were generally two handed but smaller and more ovoid in shape, whereas in the Late Three Circle phase and Classic period, manos were more rectangular in shape. The open-ended-trough metates with two-handed manos were simply more efficient milling implements. The need for this efficiency was probably brought about by demands to feed larger social groups and a greater reliance on corn during these phases.

Unlike the graded metates found in the Anasazi metate bins (coarse, medium, and fine grained), the Mimbres millers used a single-grade metate but varied the coarseness of the mano. The single metate in room 94 was accompanied by three manos of different texture: one of vesicular basalt, one of coarse rhyolite, and one of fine-grained rhyolite. Also in this assemblage were two bone awls; worked jackrabbit pelvises were recovered in proximity to this concentration of milling implements and may have been a tool used in processing corn.

The pattern of special mealing rooms, widely documented in Anasazi and later mountain Mogollon sites, does not hold for the Classic Mimbres. No mealing bins of multiple metates are known from Classic Mimbres sites in the Mimbres Valley. The distribution of single metates at the NAN Ranch Ruin suggests that foods were prepared at the extended family level indoors, on roofs, and in courtyards and that each family owned at least one functioning metate. The three metates in room 39, a large communal room, were found in separate locations and not side by side. This room had a large floor assemblage composed of manos, smooth slabs, bone awls, two grooved axes, and several vessels, including both jars and bowls. The three metates and vessels might suggest corporate participation in food preparation, perhaps during feasting events. Alternatively, as suggested in the previous chapter, the role of room 39 may have been gender related; the room may have served as the female corollary to male corporate kiva room 29.

In archaeological circles it is generally assumed that ceramics occur mostly in cultures engaged in agriculture. So many exceptions to this rule exist that it can no longer be considered valid. Many hunting and gathering cultures, for instance, made pottery for domestic uses. Conversely, hunters and gatherers existed for thousands of years in the Southwest and elsewhere who did not make pottery. Pottery first appears in this part of the Southwest in about A.D. 200, long after corn and squash were introduced into the area. By the time pottery appears in sequence, it is associated with economies engaged in food production.

Mimbres potters produced pots as needed for immediate consumption or for exchange. Size, form, and elaboration reflect function and a functional role for ceramics. Context further defines the last roles in which vessels were used but not necessarily the role for which their manufacturer intended them. As contexts changed, so did function. For example, large jars previously used for cooking, based on exterior soot concentrations, were sometimes used to line subfloor pits. Exquisitely painted bowls that may have originally been used in ritual feasts were secondarily used in a domestic context; certain vessels from this context were then selected for mortuary purposes.[46]

Vessel size and volume may vary according to relative degrees of residential mobility and size of the social groups using the ceramics.[47] This pattern holds true in the Mimbres sequence at the Galaz site,[48] and it has been demonstrated elsewhere in the Southwest as well.[49] Therefore one potential measure for detecting change in group size is vessel volume. Vessel volume may be used as a criterion to assess vessel function.[50] If one assumes that as larger social units evolved with the inception and expansion of irrigation technology, more food would be needed, larger-capacity vessels for food preparation and storage would be required.

Patterns of production of Mimbres pottery, discussed in more detail in chapter 10, show that one or more producers resided in each of the large Mimbres towns and probably in each lineage household. Given the lack of centralized hierarchy in this segmented society, each lineage household probably was capable of producing its own culinary ware, that is, pottery used for cooking, serving, and storage. The social contexts creating a need for the production of white-slipped ware probably occurred in corporate household settings. Here preparations for important ceremonies, rituals, and feasts may have involved the production of the prestigious black-on-white pottery. This scenario suggests some degree of specialized production of painted ceramics but probably not at the level of individual craft specialization. Ceramic craft specialization will be addressed in more detail in chapter 10.

Ceramics fall into two broad technological and functional categories: plain/textured and slipped/painted. Plain and textured vessels are mostly jars, with the exception of a rare plain or textured bowl. Texturing includes such embellishments as neck banding, corrugating, incising, brushing, and punctating. Plain and textured jars were used mostly for cooking and storage, whereas slipped and/or painted vessels were used mostly for serving and liquid storage, although there are exceptions in both categories in terms of secondary and tertiary uses, such as the textured pitchers and mugs of the Late Three Circle and early Classic Mimbres phases. Mainly we are concerned here with the primary roles for textured and slipped jars and bowls. Size and shape of vessels do provide important information on how vessels may have been used.[51]

The sample of whole or restorable jars from Three Circle phase and Late Three Circle phase contexts is small and does not provide an adequate means for comparing volumes with those of the Classic Mimbres phase. The extant samples do, however, show some trends supporting the notion that cooking and serving to increasingly larger social groups requires increasingly larger vessels. For example, jars from Three Circle phase contexts range in capacity from 3302 cc to 24,171 cc ($n = 4$). Style II and Three Circle Neck Corrugated jars range from only 179 to 3903 cc ($n = 3$). Classic Mimbres Style III jars, on the other hand, range in size from 9,992 cc to 17,536 cc ($n = 16$). The real contrast is seen with the Classic Mimbres partially and fully corrugated jars and in two intrusive vessels. Two corrugated jars fall in the 4,000 to 8,000 cc range; five are in the 8,000 to 13,000 cc range, four have a capacity of 13,000 to 21,000 cc, two are 21,000 to 42,000 cc, and four are over 42,000 cc. Two of the latter are large intrusive jars; one, the largest, at 147,316 cc, is a Convento Corrugated jar traced to northern Chihuahua, and the other (80,343 cc) is an El Paso Red-on-brown traced to the El Paso area. Both vessels were recovered from the assemblage left in room 74, the large communal storage room in the east room block. Style III jars ranged from 13,000 to 17,536 cc.

Exterior sooting on vessels shows that partially and fully corrugated jars in the range of 4,000 to 26,500 cc were used to cook stews and gruels. Secondarily, such jars were occasionally used in subfloor storage pits. Large Style III jars were probably made primarily for use in carrying and storing water.

There is a trend toward large size in the corrugated/neck banded category through time, but this is just a trend. Large jars do occur in San Francisco/early Three Circle times, but none equal the size of the jars in the late Classic Mimbres period. Relative jar size may be indicative of the size of the social groups being fed. Evidence of cooking is preserved on many of the jars, even some in the larger size range, suggesting the preparation of feast-size meals. The very large jars that appear late in the Classic period are reminiscent of the large jars or "fiesta pots"[52] used to brew corn beer (*tesquino*)—a feasting beverage—among the Tarahumara. Large jars are also common in the Viejo and Medio periods at Casas Grandes.[53]

Bowl size, however, does not change significantly from the Late Three Circle to the Classic Mimbres phase. Bowls can be used for both serving and food processing, and vessels classed as individual serving bowls have a capacity of 3,000 cc or less, whereas those used in food production are larger.[54] Bowls constitute the largest vessel class for which volume measurements could be obtained. Style I hemispherical bowls number only four specimens: two are under 1,000 cc capacity, one is 1,972 cc, and the fourth is 3,035 cc. Volumes were calculated for 32 Style II hemispherical bowls measured and 101 Style III bowls mostly from burial context. The volume comparisons for Styles II and III are shown in Figure 7.8. These trends show virtually no difference in the sizes of bowls for Styles II and III, at least for bowls selected for use in burials. The graphs may be skewed somewhat by the selection of burial bowls and may not accurately reflect the frequency of the larger vessels. The higher frequency of painted vessels in Style III compared to Styles I and II does suggest some significant behavior differences in regard to the production and distribution of pottery from the Three Circle to Classic Mimbres phases. This shift suggests greater expansion in the social spheres and the bringing of larger groups into the sphere through feasting and ceremonies. A case will be made in chapter 10 to suggest that the production of Style III pottery is related to a increase in attendance and participation in ceremonies.

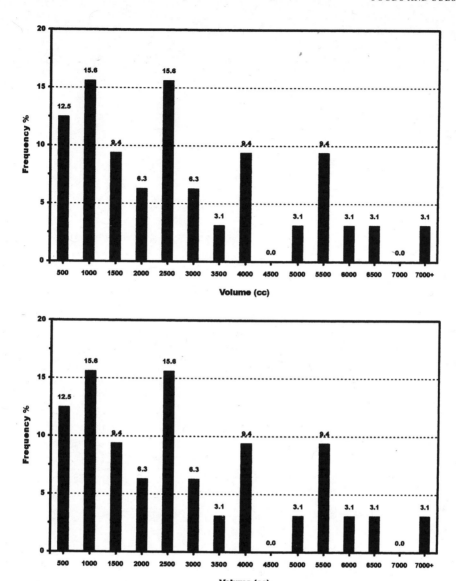

7.8: Frequency distributions of Style II and Style III hemispherical bowl volumes at the NAN Ranch Ruin (after Lyle 1996: Figure 5.2).

Gathering

Gathering and seasonal mobility define the late Archaic in this part of the Southwest. We have seen that corn was introduced into the Archaic subsistence in approximately 1500 B.C. but did not change the mobility patterns until about A.D. 200 to 400. The Mimbres Valley, however, for the most part lies on the northern periphery of the Chihuahuan Desert and the block-faulted mountains of the Basin and Range province. The valley does not have the same plant communities or density of certain economic species as does the Chihuahuan Desert to the south. In other words, most of the Mimbres Valley did not have the plant diversity that could sustained hunting and gathering groups year-round.[55] The addition of cultivars made sustained occupation in the Mimbres Valley possible. Given the long-term association of these populations with the Chihuahuan Desert, gathering would continue to play an important role in regard to the plants available.

Macrofossil evidence for gathering of wild plants, like that for cultivars, is basically a laundry list interpreted on the basis of ubiquity. Here again Paul Minnis has done the most extensive analysis to date, listing quite a range of wild plants in the flotation inventories from the Mimbres Foundation sites. Identified charred seeds of economically important wild plants include goosefoot, pigweed, purslane, sunflower, tansy mustard, knotweed, mesquite, prickly pear, banana yucca, and grasses. The plants identified through macrofossil and pollen studies are listed in Table 7.2, providing a glimpse of a wide range of economic plants used by the Mimbres for food, fuel, medicinal, and ritual purposes.

Hunting

Hunting successes yielded limited amounts of animal protein. These successes were determined by the kinds and densities of animals available and the technologies used to procure food and raw material. Principal species hunted throughout the NAN Ranch Ruin sequence were cottontails, jackrabbits, rats, mice, gophers, and an occasional artiodactyl (deer, pronghorn, mountain sheep). All animal species identified in the NAN sample are listed in Table 7.3.

The first major model of Mimbres faunal exploitation was based on an analysis of bones excavated from the Beaugard, Mitchell, Montezuma, Mattocks, and Galaz sites by the Mimbres Foundation.[56] According to this model, intensified agriculture and population increases during the Late Pithouse and Classic period altered habitats around Mimbres settlements. Natural vegetation was altered by clearing lands for cultivation and replaced by weedy and brushy vegetation, which formed a different type of habitat. Local animal populations were altered by these changes, resulting in a decrease in available habitat for and populations of cottontails and artiodactyls (deer and pronghorn) and an increase in jackrabbits and rodents. The Mimbres Foundation assumed that Mimbres predatory behavior would mirror changes in local animal communities.

Two very important studies have been completed on the faunal remains from the NAN Ranch Ruin by Brian Shaffer[57] and Julie Sanchez.[58] Together these studies identified 28 genera of fauna. Shaffer provided the most comprehensive analysis of faunal remains from any Mimbres site. He examined 11,648 specimens excavated from east room block and east plaza midden deposits and identified 24 genera from systematically sampled deposits throughout the occupational sequence. Sanchez examined 8,932 specimens recovered from the south room block excavations and identified 17 genera. Genera not in Shaffer's analysis but present in the south room block were *Bufo* sp. (toad), *Procyon lotor* (raccoon), *Felis rufus* (bobcat), and *Urocyon* sp. (fox). The most common genera identified in both studies in order of frequency were *Lepus* sp. (jackrabbit), *Sylvilagus* sp. (cottontail), *Thomomys* sp. (pocket gophers), and *Neotoma* sp.(wood rats). Shaffer calculated indices using jackrabbits, cottontail, rodents, and artiodactyls to examine changes in the exploitation of these animals through time (Figure 7.9, p. 126). The jackrabbit/leporid index, for example (Figure 7.9A), was calculated by dividing the number of jackrabbits by the total of leporids, the cottontail index (Figure 7.9B) by dividing the number of cottontails by the total number of leporids, and so forth. According to the Mimbres Foundation model, the number of jackrabbits should have increased toward the Late Pithouse and Classic periods, but they did not. Jackrabbits decreased slightly in the Late Pithouse period, only to increase in the Classic. Cottontail and artiodactyl indices showed fluctuating frequencies throughout the sequence (Figure 7.9B). The one significant change was in gophers and rodents, which increased during the Classic period (Figure 7.9C). Shaffer attributes the increased utilization of gophers to garden hunting with snares and traps set to catch gophers attracted to the soft soils and produce of the garden.

Another interesting finding Shaffer made was the unexpectedly high frequency of fish remains. Fish bones were virtually unreported from Mimbres sites prior to Shaffer's study. One reason is that most archaeologists use either one-quarter-inch or one-half-inch mesh screen in excavations, if screens are used at all, which are too small to detect fish bones. One-quarter inch-mesh was consistently used in our excavations at the NAN Ranch Ruin. We systematically collected flotation samples as part of our ethnobotanical study, and Shaffer used one of the flotation control units to examine for tiny bones that would otherwise be missed in conventional screening. Using the volume of a 1-by-1–m-sq control unit, Shaffer found fish bones in deposits dating from the Three Circle, Late Three Circle, and Classic phases. The bones were from small chubs, suckers, and minnow-size fishes. The frequency in Classic period deposits equaled that of cottontail rabbits, indicating

TABLE 7.3. Animal Species Recovered from the NAN Ranch Ruin (after Shaffer 1991: Table 5.1)

Taxon	Common Name	NISP	Taxon	Common Name	NISP
Vertebrata	Vertebrates	4828	Mammalia (small/medium)	Small/medium mammals	2
Osteichthyes (small)	Small bony fish	19	Mammalia	Medium mammals	2
Osteichthyes (medium)	Medium bony fish	1	Mammalia (medium/large)	Medium/large mammals	1459
Osteichthyes (medium)	Bony fish	2	Mammalia (large)	Large mammals	3
Cypriniformes	Suckers, minnows, etc.	4	Mammalia	Mammals	1169
Testudinata	Turtles	8	Vespertilionidae	Bats	1
Lacertilia	Lizards	1	Leporidae	Rabbits and hares	150
Phrynosoma sp.	Horned lizards	1	Lepus sp.	Jackrabbits	1708
Serpentes	Snakes	7	Sylvilagus sp.	Cottontail rabbits	594
Viperidae	Pit viper snakes	1	Rodentia	Rodents	88
Colubridae	Colubrid snakes	14	Sciuridae	Squirrels and chipmunks	4
Aves (small)	Small birds	39	Sciurus sp.	Squirrels	6
Aves (small/medium)	Small/medium birds	12	Spermophilus variegatus	Rock squirrel	18
Aves (medium)	Medium birds	22	Spermophilus sp.	Rock, ground squirrels	10
Aves (medium/large)	Medium/large birds	22	Cynomys sp.	Prairie dogs	19
Aves (large)	Large birds	6	Geomyidae	Pocket gophers	188
Anatidae	"Ducks, swans, geese"	2	Thomomys sp.	Pocket gophers	128
Falconiformes	"Vultures, hawks, falcons"	5	Perognathus sp	Pocket mice	4
Accipitridae	"Hawks, kites, eagles"	4	Dipodomys sp.	Kangaroo mice	6
Phasianidae	"Turkeys, grouse, quail"	39	Cricetidae	New World rats and mice	56
Meleagris gallopavo	Turkey	2	Onychomys sp.	Grasshopper mice	2
Strigiformes	Owls	1	Baiomys taylori	Northern pygmy mouse	1
Picidae	Woodpeckers	3	Peromyscus sp.	Mice	9
Colaptes sp.	Woodpeckers	1	Sigmodon sp.	Cotton rats	11
Passeriformes	Perching birds	12	Neotoma sp.	Wood rats	123
Corvidae	"Jays, crows, ravens"	7	Ondatra zibethicus	Muskrat	5
Mimus sp.	Mockingbirds	1	Carnivora	Carnivores	2
Emberizidae	Perchng birds	2	Canidae	Dogs and relatives	2
Molothrus sp.	Cowbirds	1	Canis sp.	Dogs	6
Mammalia (micro)	Micromammals	27	Artiodactyla	Even-toed ungulates	160
Mammalia (small)	Small mammals	547	Odocoileus sp.	Deer	25
			Antilocapra americana	Pronghorn	28
			Bovidae	"Cows, bison"	3
			Ovis canadensis	Bighorn sheep	3
			Total		**11,636**

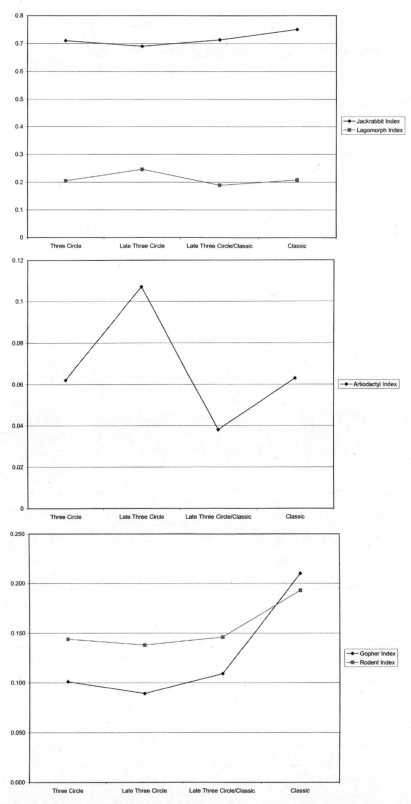

7.9: Indice graphs showing fluctuating exploitation of jackrabbit, cottontail, artiodactyl, and gophers through time at the NAN Ranch Ruin.

that taking fish was not a rare event. The implications of this finding in understanding how the Mimbres may have managed their resources are considerable. Did the Mimbres construct retention dams that held deeper pools of water secondarily for the purpose of harvesting fish? Or was the riverine ecology such that pools of water existed that allowed fish populations to be harvested by trapping and shooting? Fish are also prominent images depicted on Mimbres pottery (see appendix I: Figures A.14C, A.14D, and A.14E for examples). The stylized depictions often resemble saltwater species,[59] but the Mimbreños had access to a variety of fishes from the Gila, Mimbres, and Rio Grande rivers, including sunfish, trout, chub, minnows, suckers, gar, and catfish.

Shaffer's study was site focused, but Sanchez's study was more comprehensive. She examined faunal samples from both the NAN and Old Town ruins and extended her analysis to include extant data from sites throughout the Mimbres Valley. Using data from the NAN Ranch and Old Town ruins, she tested the Mimbres Foundations model on the increase in jackrabbit exploitation as an indicator of environmental stress. She examined 8,932 specimens from the south room block at the NAN Ranch Ruin and identified 44 percent to the level of genus; 17 genera were identified. The sample from Old Town was smaller (4,093 specimens), with 38 percent identified to genera and 10 genera identified. The Mimbres Foundation model of changes in species predation for the valley as a whole was not supported by the NAN and Old Town data. Sanchez discovered that the indices for jackrabbits, cottontails, and artiodactyls did not change significantly from the Late Pithouse to the Classic periods. She argues that although the Mimbres Foundation model was not disproved for certain upper valley sites, it did not hold for sites in the middle and lower valley.

Many factors can affect faunal samples and how they are to be interpreted. Butchering or consumption patterns could change through time, affecting the visibility of identifiable elements while procurement remained relatively stable. Incorporating new technologies or hunting methods or new social factors such as feasting, whereby large amounts of food were massed in anticipation of a major ceremony as described historically for Zuni Pueblo, for example, would change faunal samples.[60] Feasting as an explanation for such changes cannot be discounted outright since examples of communal rabbit hunting are depicted on Mimbres bowls.[61] Also, exchange or movement of pottery and other material items from village to village has been demonstrated by trace element and other raw material studies. We can presume that food was exchanged in similar ways. In other words, it is not difficult to imagine a feast at Mattocks Ruin, for example, attended by kinsmen from NAN or Old Town who were called upon to bring jackrabbits or antelope, thereby skewing the faunal record.

Hunting, snaring, and trapping methods may also have changed through time in response to a more sedentary lifeway. The most significant technological change in hunting was the introduction of the bow and arrow sometime in the Late Pithouse period, probably in the San Francisco or early Three Circle phase, around A.D. 700 to 800. The bow and arrow first appeared in the Great Basin in about A.D. 600.[62] Larger dart points were replaced by small, lightweight corner-notched arrow points in the NAN Ranch Ruin sequence. Corner-notched arrow points first appear in the Three Circle phase, A.D. 750 to 900. These were later replaced, at the onset of the Classic Mimbres period, by three styles of side-notched arrow points (Figure 11.1). More will be said about Mimbres stone technologies in chapter 11.

ICONOGRAPHIC EVIDENCE

I have discussed empirical evidence for agriculture, its importance, and changes in overall subsistence strategies, but the Mimbres left us a very unique graphic legacy showing their agricultural practices. Much like the graphic depictions of ancient Egyptian daily life left on the walls of the tombs of the nobles, the Mimbreños left us with scenes on pots showing many mundane activities, such as the cultivation of corn in waffle gardens, hunting rabbits using rabbit drives, trapping birds, tracking deer and other game, and killing deer, antelope, sheep, and bear (Figure 7.10). Bows and arrows were frequently depicted on Style III vessels, and arrow points are shown on Style II vessels.[63] These rare examples should be taken as emic depictions of the Mimbreños' lives even though they may have been, in fact, metaphors for myths and religious themes. Certainly the scenes shown are as interpretable, if not more so, than any of the patterns that we as archaeologists see emerging from masses of excavated information. In other words, the scene of a rabbit drive tells us not only that jackrabbits were sometimes procured through corporate hunting endeavors, but what kinds

7.10: Mimbres scenes depicting subsistence pursuits: A. gardening; B. rabbit drive; C. hunting; D. fishing (drawings by Karen Gardner).

of tools were used in this method of capture (Figure 7.10C). What we cannot know, however, is whether or not the specific scene was to illustrate a jackrabbit per se or whether the depicted rabbit drive was a metaphor for a specific ceremony or ritual.

Changes in ritual space and graphic symbolism on Mimbres Style II and Style III pottery are arguably signs of increasing importance placed on ritual and ceremony.

Scenes on Mimbres pottery often depict public rituals and ceremonies, some of which may have counterparts among historic Pueblos. Rain ceremonies and an emphasis on rain bringing are common elements in Puebloan religions. Given the unpredictability of rainfall in the Mimbres Valley and the degree to which Three Circle and Classic period folks were dependent on agriculture, rain bringing was predictably an important element that permeated their belief systems. This topic will be discussed further in chapter 11.

As mentioned above, the size of and participation in public ceremonies and feasting increased as part of the cultural elaboration during the Classic period. One of the purposes of such feasts and ceremonies was to attract people from outside the community and to enhance the power and prestige of the hosts of such events. I also suggest that the production of the Mimbres painted pottery was tied to these special occasions as a means of promoting prestige and displaying the accouterments of feasting ceremonies. Pueblo feasts and ceremonies are colorful events, in which the finest costumes and wares are displayed. I see no reason why we should expect the Mimbres to have been any different in that respect.

I also posit that the growing importance of agriculture in the late Three Circle phase and Classic Mimbres period is tied to the creation of bounded cemeteries for the dead. These subfloor cemeteries did not exist prior to the late Three Circle phase. The creation of such cemeteries is presented as evidence for the formation of corporate groups distinguished by inclusion in respective lineage cemeteries. As argued in chapter 6, the evolution of corporate cemeteries is tied to the restructuring of Mimbres society from a cluster of families solidified by communal great kivas in the Late Three Circle phase to corporate groups solidified by their own corporate kivas in the Classic Mimbres phase.

The placement of "killed" vessels over the face of the deceased may well have been tied directly to rain-bringing rituals and ultimately to *Katcina* worship. If the house was regarded as an extension of the field and vice versa, cemeteries provided a lineal connection between the living and the dead in regard to land rights and access to the best farmlands. But the placement of the vessel over the face may symbolize yet another important connection to the ancestors, a topic of the next chapter.

Summary

To reiterate, the Mimbres Foundation model to explain the Classic Mimbres phenomenon, as articulated by Paul Minnis and others, is that the Classic Mimbres evolved in response to efforts to combat severe food stresses brought about by population increase, coupled with annual fluctuation in rainfall. Furthermore, the inability to overcome environmental stress caused by repeated years of poor rainfall after A.D. 1100 led to the demise of the Classic Mimbres system. The NAN Ranch Ruin data provide a new body of information to reevaluate parts of this model and to suggest alternative interpretations. In essence, I argue that the implementation of irrigation agriculture by the Late Three Circle phase provided periodic food surpluses that attracted people to the valley, thereby inflating the population. The warm, moist period from about A.D. 1000 to 1100 was an optimal time for agriculture, and the Mimbres apparently took advantage of it. The population reached its peak between about A.D. 1050 and 1110, after which families began to move out for a generation or so until all of the large towns in the upper and middle sections of the valley were abandoned.

Perhaps one of the more compelling arguments for Mimbres irrigation, in addition to the physical features described above, is the settlement pattern along the river. The linear arrangement and spacing of some 14 large pueblos along the river itself allowed each village to use the water. The location and spacing of villages were presumably due to the location of arable lands but perhaps also to the placement of diversion dams along the river. Each village, however, would be dependent upon each other villages in regard to water rights and scheduling, and so some stringent means of cooperation among all of the villages in the valley would have been required.

An extensive irrigation network might necessitate some form of hierarchal administration. Efforts to define vertical stratification in Mimbres society have failed,[63] but evidence has been presented for vertical ranking among corporate groups. No evidence of a centralized administrative center has been recognized among the various Mimbres pueblos, but if some form of centralized leadership existed, it may have been in the form of a council whose members represented each of the villages or a central figure whose tenure shifted from village to village. Another possibility is that the valley irrigation system was administered via the religion, with priests serving a dual role. Certainly religion is closely integrated with water management in similar situations where villages depended on a common source of water.[64] In Bali, for example, a network of communities shared the same water source for irrigation; embedded within this structure was a network of water temples, each headed by a priest.[65] The priest's role was to oversee the administration of the water under his jurisdiction and to ensure that all of the villages received their share. Although the Bali case is more complex than the Mimbres one, I am suggesting that the Mimbres system could have been administered through a similar, albeit less complex organization. A set of related features discovered by Darrell Creel at Old Town may shed some light on the hierarchal issue.[66] A complex series of features at this site included an elaborate burial and evidence of ritual activity capped by an artificial mound that is unique in Mimbres archaeology. We do not know if, or how, these features might be related to the administration of irrigation networks, but certainly Old Town would have been in a pivotal place in the overall system.

The peak population period at the NAN Ranch Ruin came between A.D. 1050 and 1110, during an optimal period for agriculture in the American Southwest. The climate cycle during much of this time was warmer and wetter than usual (Figure 7.11),[67] allowing for agricultural expansion into marginal areas and higher altitudes. But something happened to cause the Mimbreños to abandon their fields, homes, and ancestors after about A.D. 1130. The culprit may indeed have been environmental change, but not in the form that Minnis and his colleagues envisioned. Recent evidence for environmental change comes from the middle Gila Valley in Arizona. Michael Waters and John Ravesloot[68] have documented evidence of episodes of severe channel entrenchment and widening along the middle Gila from about A.D. 1050 to A.D. 1150, between the pre-Classic and Classic Hohokam. They suggest that these changes could have resulted in the disruption of irrigation systems, crop failures, and the need to abandon older canal systems and construct new ones. They also suggest that this regional episode of channel erosion may have contributed to social, political, economic, and demographic changes in Hohokam culture at this time. The origin of these flooding episodes was in the Gila Wilderness, which is also where the Mimbres River originates. According to Waters and others,[69] this period of down cutting was widespread across the American Southwest, from west Texas to Arizona.

That the timing and severity of climate episodes is responsible for channel entrenchment makes good sense when applied to the Mimbres case, even though little empirical evidence at this time supports the theory. Preliminary geoarchaeological studies on the NAN Ranch in the middle section of the Mimbres River showed that Mimbres-age deposits in the river corridor were cut away and replaced by more recent floodplain deposits.[70] When the Mimbres-age deposits were cut away is not known, but radiocarbon dates from sediments exposed along the river indicate the floodplain was reestablished centuries later.

Another factor may have helped to change the course of the Mimbres culture. A significant cooling trend in the northern hemisphere began in about A.D. 1100 and may have shortened the growing season in the higher altitudes. Repeated crop failures in the upper part of the valley may have created such reciprocal hardships that site abandonment became necessary. Abandonment of sites in the upper part of the valley would have interrupted the Mimbreños' irrigation systems and led to disintegration of the systems in place. This scenario is supported in part by the fact that when reoccupation of the valley took place in the Black Mountain phase in the early A.D. 1200s, the upper reaches of the Mimbres and Gila valleys were largely unoccupied.

The down-cutting model does support the theory that Mimbres agricultural success rode the wave of irrigation, and when that was no longer possible, the systems it supported collapsed. If corporate groups formed around the development of irrigation dams and canals, then a disruption, whether by down cutting or climate change, would put these agricultural technologies and the ideologies behind them to a real test. Corporate groups achieved their prominence and power from their abilities to produce food, seek advice from ancestors, and host important ceremonies and feasts. If they lost the ability to produce food, they lost their prominence and power, and reinforcing mechanisms no longer were necessary.

The changes from the community organization of pithouse times to that of the pueblo period, as noted in chapters 3 and 4, were substantial. These changes reflect the reorganization of Mimbres society necessary to meet labor requirements for the irrigation systems needed to feed a growing population. The Mimbres shifted the emphasis of their subsistence economy to more labor-intensive irrigation, whereby the waters in the river or its major tributaries were diverted into fields and holding ponds.[71] Prior to the Late Three Circle phase, corn was stored shelled in baskets and jars. But in this phase, the Mimbres constructed formal granaries to protect corn stored on the cob and other products of their harvests. These changes also included the adoption of a new surface pueblo architectural style, establishment of corporate cemeteries with restricted access, and production of prestige pottery embellished with corporate iconography. Architectural changes included a shift from extended

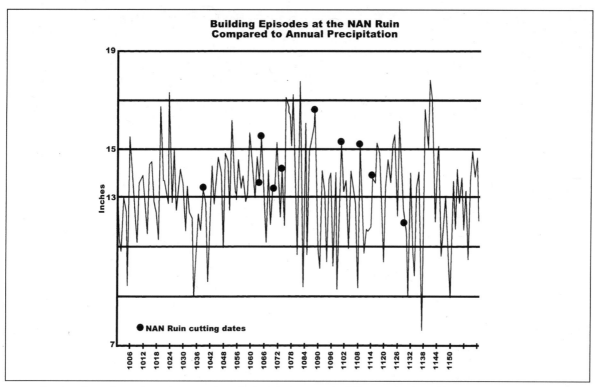

7.11: Cutting dates from the NAN Ranch Ruin in relation to rainfall patterns through time.

entrances to ceiling hatchways, from circular to rectangular hearths, and the location of hearths within the rooms. These changes occurred throughout the Mimbres heartland and signaled a common reorganization in attitudes, values, and material expression of their worldview. For reasons that might be related to below-normal rainfall patterns, the system began to break down after that time until the final stages of abandonment in approximately A.D. 1140.

In a nutshell, the NAN Ranch Ruin data show an almost threefold increase in population from the Three Circle phase to the peak of the Classic Mimbres period. Although actual population estimates are hard to come by, this estimate is based on the numbers of households identified for each period and estimations of the total number of extended family households at the site during the Three Circle phase (eight), Late Three Circle phase (12), and Classic period (24-plus). In regard to population increases, the trend Minnis used, based on Mimbres Foundation survey work,[72] is supported by the NAN data. Tree-ring data used by Minnis have been refined by more recent evaluation and additional dates[73] and reflect sharp short-term fluctuations. The years between A.D. 1006 to 1030, 1046 to 1090, and 1114 to 1130 were generally favorable times, whereas the periods from 1031 to 1045 and 1091 to 1113 were generally unfavorable. Within each of these brackets, however, were interspersed good and bad years. We noticed that good precipitation years, especially those that followed on the heels of bad years, were times when buildings were either refurbished or added at the NAN Ranch Ruin (Figure 7.11). These data can be interpreted in several ways, but I think they reflect a certain degree of mobility among the Mimbres populations, which served as a built-in mechanism to offset food stresses for some families, who could simply pick up and go where food was available. This does not imply that the whole population was equally mobile, since some corporate households were continuously occupied throughout the period, as shown in the previous chapter. The mobile segment of the population may have been composed of those families who had poorer choices of irrigated lands or no land at all. One problem in interpreting the tree-ring data for short-term fluctuations is that precipitation shortfall may be offset by prolonged river discharge from previously wet years, which could have been used for irrigation. Also, what may appear to have been a bad year may not have seriously affected Mimbres agriculture if the rains that did fall came at the right time.

Environmental degradation to the degree argued by Mimbres Foundation staff is not upheld by the NAN data. Certainly packing 2,500 to 4,000 people into the Mimbres Valley during the height of the Classic period did have a significant impact on the local ecology: draining marshes and diverting the river altered the wetland landscape and associated plant communities, and perhaps overhunting of some species occurred. But the extent of degradation posited by the Mimbres Foundation model does not seem to have taken place in the middle part of the valley. As noted previously, riparian woods were not wiped out but were extensively used in hearths and in construction right up to the end of the Classic period at the NAN Ranch Ruin. Furthermore, faunal studies by Shaffer, Sanchez, and Shaffer and Baker[74] failed to support the Mimbres Foundation model of ecological changes as reflected in the animal communities.

In sum, irrigation agriculture and the infrastructure to support and maintain it provided the ingredients for sustained growth in the Mimbres Valley until about A.D. 1100 or shortly thereafter. The implementation of irrigation agriculture obviously did change the ecology of the river valley by altering the stream course, probably draining ciénagas, or swampy areas, expanding habitats for small fishes, and creating new field microenvironments that attracted gophers, rabbits, and other game as well as expanded habitats for such plants as pigweed and goosefoot (i.e., the Cheno-Ams). The Mimbres' ability to sustain food surpluses allowed for rapid growth in the population, which peaked in the middle Classic period through increased extended family sizes and probably in-migration. Population increase may also have led to the formation of a hierarchy of social spheres not seen previously whose participation was, in part, defined by shared symbolism and cosmology. Expanding food surpluses placed additional demands on labor requirements, thereby expanding kin networks and lineal obligations. Increased emphasis on ceremonial activities, rituals, feasts, and ceremonies, reinforced by a shared iconography and symbolism, led to the production of classes of prestige material items such as the painted pottery. How successful the Mimbres were in providing healthy living conditions, however, is quite another matter. The next chapter will examine mortuary data from the NAN Ranch Ruin, including burial patterns, life expectancy, and overall health and nutrition.

CHAPTER EIGHT
Mortuary Customs

Introduction

Treatments of the dead and associated rituals are celebrations of termination and continuity. Mortuary customs are outward expressions of a group's beliefs about the transformation of the dead into the spirit world (if one is believed to exist), where the dead reside, and how their spirits are integrated into the world of the living.[1] Mimbres mortuary practices, distinct from all others in the American Southwest, stand as a testament to the Mimbrenos' belief in their own spiritual world, not that of some distant regional system.

Mortuary customs from the San Francisco phase through the Classic Mimbres phase are discussed in this chapter. Documentation, recovery, and analysis of human burials constitute one of the most important sources of information about ancient social customs and organization, beliefs and worldviews, and patterns of affiliation. I will show how mortuary customs at the NAN Ranch Ruin evolved over time from isolated interments in the early Three Circle phase to formal lineage cemeteries in the Late Three Circle and Classic Mimbres phases.

In the animistic world of the Mimbreños, animals were also interred into the spirit world through formal burial. Animal burials occurred at the NAN Ranch Ruin, and these too are discussed. Presumably these animals embodied some form of sacred power to justify their transformation into the spirit world.

Human Burials

Data gathered on 222 human burials at the NAN Ranch Ruin have provided a wealth of information about changes in Mimbres attitudes toward social organization, institutionalized beliefs, and worldviews (Table 8.1). Treatment of the dead, in regard to beliefs and worldviews, provided a symbolic structure for sociopolitical relations and helped to define rank among corporate groups. Mortuary patterns, which include intramural inhumations, extramural inhumations, and extramural cremations, are examined in both temporal and spatial contexts to model changes in Mimbres mortuary behavior and social organization through time. The sample is also examined for evidence of hierarchal ranking among members of the population in relation to the way the dead were treated. Placement of the dead, inclusions in graves, and formal rituals associated with burial and funerals provide some insights into Mimbres belief systems and how the dead were regarded by the living. I will show how mortuary patterns and rituals corresponded to changes in subsistence patterns and community organization and infer a generalized model of Mimbres beliefs and worldviews based on the mortuary evidence.

Myths abound in the archaeological literature about Mimbres mortuary practices. Central among the myths is that the Mimbres buried their dead beneath their houses and placed a "killed" bowl over the head of the deceased,[2] a pattern that applies to some burials, but certainly not all. Another myth is that the Mimbres buried their dead both inside and outside the houses and that bowls occur with burials regardless of where they were placed, which is only partially correct. Since men only recently began to adorn themselves with jewelry in American society, another myth assumes that Mimbres men did not.[3] The ritual of placing a "killed" vessel very rarely occurred with extramural burials, and the cases in which this happened at the NAN Ruin involved two Late Pithouse period burials and a Classic period cremation. Jewelry is almost exclusively male adornment. Part of these modern myths can be blamed on local folklore; part on Clement Webster and Jesse Fewkes,[4] who illustrated skeptical views of vessels placed over sitting skeletons

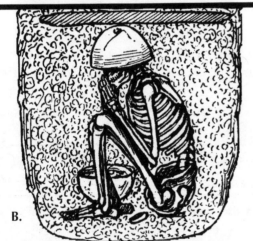

8.1: Early interpretations of Mimbres burial practices: A. by Clement Webster (1912); B. by J. W. Fewkes (1914).

burials and changes in mortuary practices through time. More specific information on both temporal and spatial patterning in the mortuary practices was not obtained until the NAN Ruin sample became available.

Approximately 2,500 Mimbres burials were excavated by various institutions during the first half of the past century. In the majority of cases (the Mattocks, Galaz, Eby, McSherry, NAN, Cameron Creek, and Old Town ruins) burial information was either scanty or nonexistent. The earlier reports of Bradfield and Nesbitt suffered from a lack of understanding of chronology. In these studies, a crude seriation of burials was based on house types, which were described only as pit rooms, middle period rooms, and late period rooms. Since the depth of the room may have not had much bearing on the time period of occupation, these investigators' conclusions were often ambiguous. The Cosgroves provided a much more accurate, albeit generalized, description of Mimbres mortuary practices, which has still been used as the comparative model by some even in recent times.[6] More importantly, data recovery by the Cosgroves was superb for their time, and their extensive and detailed notes on room, depth, and grave association provide a wealth of information on the mortuary practices at the Swarts Ruin. Unfortunately, a detailed descriptive account of their notes has never been published. Their report should no longer be used as the standard reference for Mimbres mortuary practices, however, for several reasons. First, the report condenses information on over 1,000 burials to merely six pages. Second, the distribution map shows each burial only as a dot and does not indicate temporal groupings of the burials, which we now know spanned the Three Circle, Late Three Circle, and Classic phases.[7] For any given dot, burials could be above the floor or below the floor or predate the room entirely. The Cosgroves did record the placement of burials within the confines of a surface room and measured the depths from either the surface or the floor level in their field notes, but specific placement is not indicated on their map. Uncritical viewers see the dots and relate their placement in reference to the surface rooms shown. The generalized image presented by the Cosgroves and cited as fact by later archaeologists[8] is that burials occur both intramurally and extramurally in about equal numbers and that mortuary vessels are found with both in about equal frequencies.[9] We now know this to be a distorted image of Mimbres mortuary customs, which were more varied than previously thought, and that Late Pithouse period burials occurred mostly outdoors,

(Figure 8.1); part on misinterpretation of the Cosgroves' burial location map from the Swarts Ruin; and part on a lack of information from previous excavations as to sexing and context. The characterizations of Mimbres burial practices by Webster and Fewkes were altered by the Cosgroves', Nesbitt's, and Bradfield's excavations at the Swarts, Mattocks, and Cameron Creek ruins, respectively, and the widely disseminated reports of their works published in 1931 and 1932.[5] These early contributors provided only general information on intramural and extramural

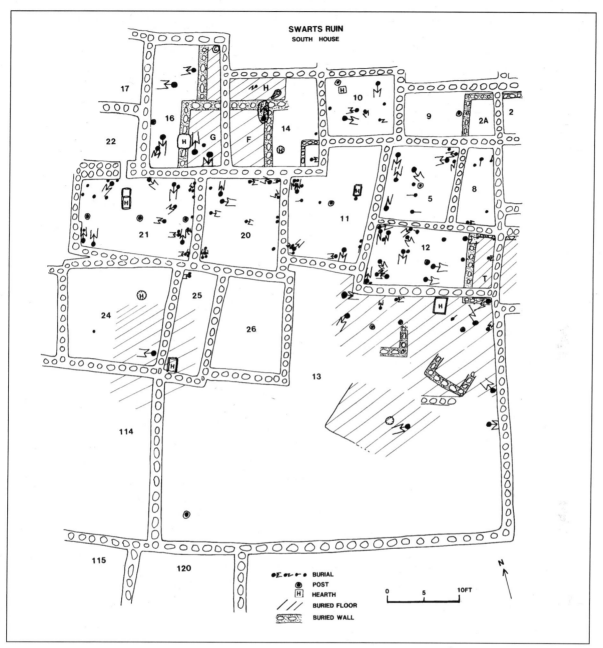

8.2: South house at the Swarts Ruin, showing location of burials; some burials reported as extramural were actually beneath buried adobe floors (reconstructed from field notes prepared by Hattie Cosgrove, courtesy of the Peabody Museum, Harvard University).

whereas Classic period burials occurred beneath floors. I examined the field notes from the south house at Swarts and found instances where certain burials shown to be "extramural" on the map were in fact beneath the floors of razed rooms (Figure 8.2).[10]

The ritual of placing a "killed" (perforated) bowl (or, in rare instances, a large sherd) inverted over the head of the deceased of all age groups did not begin until the Late Three Circle phase. The practice began in the San Francisco phase, with the smashing of one or more vessels and scattering of the sherds in the grave. Placing "killed" bowls over the heads of corpses did not become a significant trait until the Late Three Circle phase, when the majority of intramural burials in large Mimbres Valley sites had bowls associated.[11] This practice carried over into and throughout the Classic period. Cremations are scarcely mentioned in any report because they were found to be quite rare.

Another myth about Mimbres mortuary practices concerns the mortuary vessel. Some scholars assert that Mimbres pottery was made for mortuary purposes. Use-wear studies conducted on NAN Ruin ceramic samples clearly show that this assertion is incorrect. Over 75 percent of the pottery vessels used in burials show distinct signs of domestic use (sooting, chipping, scratching, or abrasive wear), suggesting they were drawn from a domestic assemblage.[12] Although Mimbres painted pottery might have been initially produced for ceremonial or feasting purposes, it eventually ended up in household assemblages.

The intramural pattern does not hold for the entire Mimbres area, however. When excavated Classic period sites in the upper Gila Valley were compared to those in the Mimbres Valley, the frequency of intramural burial dropped from five burials per room in the Mimbres Valley sites to about one burial per room in the upper Gila sites.[13] These differences suggest one of three things: the sites are not comparable in age, geographic differences existed in behavior between the two Mimbres populations, or both. Some evidence suggests that the Mimbres pueblo sites in the upper Gila are somewhat earlier than those in the Mimbres Valley,[14] and the more restricted area of potentially irrigated lands in the upper Gila Valley may have influenced lineage land ownership rights and land inheritance to the degree that ancestors were handled a bit differently.

More recent studies of Mimbres mortuary patterns at the Galaz Ruin and Wind Mountain site have helped to alter the generalized view. Roger Anyon and Steven LeBlanc[15] did a yeoman's job of synthesizing the extant data on earlier excavations at the Galaz Ruin conducted by the Southwest Museum and the University of Minnesota, but their interpretations were hampered by the overall poor quality of the records. Regardless, very significant information on mortuary patterns at Galaz was salvaged. One serious problem with the Galaz data is the absence of detailed information about room features and room function to correlate with the mortuary evidence. I see this as a critical weakness of many of the earlier works since room function clearly dictated the locations of corporate cemeteries in the Classic period. This is not a problem with the excellent information from the Swarts Ruin, however, where it is possible to correlate burial data with vessel and room type.[16]

The mortuary data from the Wind Mountain site provide some of the best comparative information available for the Late Pithouse period.[17] The Wind Mountain patterns reveal the extent to which extramural burial occurred in that period. Of the 124 excavated burials (122 inhumations and at least two cremations), only three were described as intramural (burials 1, 91, and 100). Overlying a large Late Pithouse period village was a small Classic period room block or extended family household suite. Classic period occupation at the site was apparently short-lived, judging from the fact that I can assign only seven burials (burials 1, 3, 18, 24, 27, 32, and 45) to this phase on the basis of either associated ceramics or burial treatment. Of these, two were probably intramural (1 and 24) and the remainder were in the fill of abandoned structures. Two additional intramural burials clearly date to the Late Pithouse period: the one in room TT was a small child, one to two years old, and the other, in room AF, was a neonate infant. Like many pre–Classic Mimbres sites, it is difficult to assign burials to phases at Wind Mountain without diagnostic mortuary pottery. The ceramic types Alma Plain and San Francisco Red may occur in burials from the Georgetown through Late Three Circle phases. Woolsey and McIntyre's classification of all red-slipped plainware as San Francisco Red is unfortunate; the thin, polished, dimpled San Francisco Red is a San Francisco phase type, but the thicker mattelike finish of Mimbres Redware, as defined in chapter 10, is a type that lasted until about A.D. 1000, or throughout the Three Circle and Late Three Circle phases. Therefore it is not possible to segregate the true San Francisco Red from the later Mimbres redwares in the Wind Mountain burials to better examine mortuary variability. I would venture to guess that all burials with "killed" "San Francisco Red" bowls in fact date to the Late Three Circle phase, as the construct is used here. The significant pattern at Wind Mountain is the near absence of intramural burials for any time period.

Cremations at Wind Mountain were few (only cremations 1 and 2 were recognized), but I would venture to suggest at least one more exists since pit 54 had all the earmarks of a cremation feature, including "killed" Style III bowls. The paucity of cairns over graves at Wind

Mountain, a Classic period trait, is in keeping with the pattern at the NAN Ranch Ruin.

In sum, Webster and Fewkes's myths were dispelled by excavations in the Mimbres area during the first half of the twentieth century at the Swarts, Galaz, Mattocks, and Cameron Creek ruins. In these excavations, burials were rarely found in a sitting position; more often they were placed on the back or side in a flexed or semiflexed position, and some had mortuary vessels inverted over or about the heads. The NAN Ranch Ruin patterns also help to dispel the intramural versus extramural treatment myths and give a much clearer insight into the importance of cremations in the Late Three Circle and Classic periods. Use-wear studies, which showed wear on the majority of NAN mortuary vessels, also dispelled the myth that Style III bowls were made for mortuary purposes.

Previous mortuary studies in the Mimbres region have mostly emphasized temporal changes and the search for evidence of social differentiation. The rich symbolism surrounding Mimbres mortuary patterns also provides a unique opportunity to explore the topics of beliefs and worldviews, especially in the context of change and social reorganization.

Previous Mimbres mortuary studies have been carried out primarily to look for evidence of social differentiation. The main goal of Roger Anyon and Steven LeBlanc's synthesis of the Galaz Ruin mortuary data, for example, aside from providing basic descriptive information, was to explore for evidence of social ranking based on grave facilities and relative wealth. The conclusions drawn from this study showed that the Mimbres society at Galaz was in essence egalitarian and tribal in nature. There was no indication that the society was structured in a vertical hierarchy. Elizabeth Ham drew similar conclusions from a spatial analysis of data from 200 burials at the NAN Ruin.[18]

Ham's analysis of the NAN Ruin mortuary sample sought to identify social differences through the use of the Superordinate/Subordinate Dimensional model, created by Christopher Peebles and Susan Kus.[19] Ham established comparative categories to test for evidence of status differentiation and sexual preference. Her categories included sex, age, time period (Three Circle, Transition or Late Three Circle, and Classic), spatial location (east room block, south room block, Classic midden, or southeast midden), body position (flexed, semiflexed, extended), body side (left, right, back, sitting), cardinal direction, presence or absence of jewelry items such as beads, pendants, bracelets, inlayed objects, and associated artifacts such as vessels and palettes. The spatial clusters she used for comparison were drawn from the south and east room blocks and middens. Differences did exist in the relative "wealth" of graves in those room blocks, based on the number and quality of associated artifacts, but these were not found to be statistically significant. South room block burials trended toward the more wealthy in regard to such association items as jewelry and multiple vessels. The strongest bias was toward individuals buried extramurally. These burials lacked mortuary vessels and were predominately males. Ham found no significant evidence to suggest social ranking during the Classic period among the individuals in NAN society, but she did find some hints indicating that adult females were favored in regard to grave content (more female burials were found to have ceramics) and orientation to the east. She concluded that although no convincing evidence of vertical ranking existed, some hints of horizontal ranking did when the populations of the east and south room blocks were compared.

Other Mimbres mortuary samples for which a similar comparison is possible come from Patricia Gilman's research at the Mattocks Ruin[20] and Mara Hill's and my analysis of the Swarts Ruin field notes.[21] Gilman examined the mortuary sample collected by both the Mimbres Foundation and Paul Nesbitt's[22] earlier excavations at that site for evidence of social differentiation. Her conclusions were virtually identical to those drawn by Ham and Anyon and LeBlanc in that she found no evidence for vertical social differentiation during the Classic period, nor was there evidence of differentiation among age groups. She, like Ham, found hints for differentiation in regard to mortuary inclusions among certain families or kin groups.

Several new developments in Mimbres archaeology aided cemetery studies. One was architectural stratigraphy at the NAN Ruin, which allowed us to place the burials in a better time framework. Having a qualified bioarchaeologist on the staff during all field seasons provided a more accurate assessment of sex and age based on infield analysis, which was later checked in the laboratory. Another new development was the recognition of a microstylistic series in both Style II and Style III pottery. This microseriation allowed us to recognize temporal dimensions within mortuary vessel assemblages and therefore to identify the relative time span over which a cemetery was used. Also, the excellent body of information gathered on the south room block provided detailed information on room block growth over time and on room function. Yet another development was the recognition of the significance of the floor vault, a feature in certain rooms. Rooms with floor vaults are identified in chapter 6 as corporate kivas. Rooms with floor vaults usually contained large intramural lineage cemeteries, and large cemeteries often showed a range of painted pottery styles, indicating use over several generations. Only one room with floor vaults occurred in each multiroom residential unit and more often than not contained the largest cemetery in that suite.

When all of these factors are taken into consideration, the temporal and spatial clustering of cemeteries throughout the east and south room blocks suggests the presence of lineage cemeteries. The sex and age information allowed us to take a closer look at Mimbres society as expressed in mortuary behavior. As mentioned in chapter 6, the south room block and the Cosgrove suite probably were occupied by two of the ranking lineages at the NAN Ranch Ruin.

Important confirmation of our NAN Ranch Ruin patterns came from Mara Hill's analysis of the burial data from the Swarts Ruin.[23] Armed with information on microstyles in Mimbres painted pottery and with Hattie Cosgrove's detailed field notes in hand, Hill was able to reconstruct vessel assemblages in some of the rooms of the North House, using microstyles. From this she could show that certain cemeteries were used over many generations. Keyed in on rooms with floor vaults, mortuary assemblages, and ceramic styles, her findings suggested that at Swarts, like at NAN, the surface pueblo was constructed around core rooms that often became corporate kivas and that the North House originally was composed of a number of separate corporate households, based on the location of kivas and lineage cemeteries. Partly on the basis of her findings, Hill inferred that the Classic Mimbres society at Swarts was organized around matrilineal corporate groups.

Explaining Mimbreño mortuary patterns in terms of beliefs and symbolism has been a subject generally avoided by archaeologists simply because such interpretations are not considered verifiable through independent means. The rich corpus of symbolism that stands out in Mimbres material culture such as the images on the painted pottery and the unique mortuary tradition, however, tempts scholars to make some meaning of it all.

A question I am frequently asked is: "Why did the Mimbres punch a hole in the bowl and place it over the head?" This question has at least two parts: placing the bowl and punching the hole. A common folk answer I have heard is that the "kill" hole was either to let the spirit pass or to render the bowl unusable for domestic purposes. As for placing the bowl, no one in folk culture seemed to know the answer. Another frequent question is: "Why did they bury the dead under the house floor?" A Hopi informant from a group that still practiced this tradition of burying some infants beneath house floors[24] told the late Florence Ellis that it was done in hopes the spirit would be conceived again. This belief may have played a role at some point in time in the intramural burial of certain infants (such as in the Three Circle phase) but not necessarily for adults. I will consider an alternative explanation within an overall context of American Indian beliefs and material expressions of those beliefs.

Despite the inherent problems of drawing meaning from symbols in the archaeological record to infer past beliefs and cosmologies, some Mimbres researchers, myself included, have ventured into this Post-processual realm. More will be said of this in chapter 12. Symbolism on painted pottery, placement of mortuary vessels, and body placement beneath the floors have been interpreted as indications of Mimbres belief in a layered universe.[25] Because of the rich body of artistic and historical sources from Mesoamerica, other scholars see a connection between the Mimbres and certain Mesoamerican civilizations.[26] My own perspective on this is that it is not fruitful to use such far-reaching examples for specific beliefs and explanations. Since non-Athabaskan-speaking Pueblo and non-Pueblo people in the western United States and Mexico share common roots, it is presumptive to believe the Mimbres were not part of the common pool who shared a broad cosmology. Surface expression of that cosmology in the form of material style and tradition was precisely what separated one archaeological culture from another. In other words, we can, and I do, draw broad comparisons with Mesoamerican and Puebloan cultures, but in doing so, I do not mean to imply that one directly influenced the other.

We were able to assess the time period and context of almost all of the 222 in situ human burials at the NAN Ruin (Table 8.1, pp. 141–145). Burials disturbed by relic hunters are not listed in Table 8.1 since critical information about them was not available. For the most part,

text continues page 146

TABLE 8.1 Nan Ranch Ruin Burial Data

Burial No.	Sex	Age	Temporal Location	Room No.	Spatial Location	Body Postion	Body Side	Direction	Bds*	Pen	Bra	Inl	Ves	Pal	CB	Pnt
1	Male	Adult	Classic	3	East RB	Semiflexed	Right	North		X			1		X	
2	Ind	Infant	Classic	30	West RB	Flexed	Right	West					0			
3	Ind	Infant	Classic	8	East RB	Flexed	Right	North					0			
4	Female	Adult	Pithouse	30	West RB	Flexed	Back	NE					0			
5	Ind	Adult	Classic	31	West RB	Flexed	Back	West					1		X	
6	Ind	Adult	Classic	5	East RB	Flexed	Back	North					1			
7	Ind	Infant	Classic	5	East RB	Flexed	Back	West					1			
8	Ind	Infant	Classic	7	East RB	Flexed	Left	NE					0			
9	Male	Adult	Pithouse	ex	East RB	Flexed	Left	East					0			
10	Ind	Infant	Classic	7	West RB	ND	ND	ND					1			
11	Ind	Infant	Classic	7	East RB	Flexed	Right	North					0			
12	Male	Adult	Classic	I 40	East RB	Flexed	Sitting	NW					0			
13	Male	Adult	Classic	40	East RB	Flexed	Right	North					1		X	
14	Ind	Infant	Classic	9	East RB	Flexed	Right	South					0		X	
15	Female	Adult	Classic	6	East RB	Flexed	Back	East					1		X	
16	Ind	Adol	Classic	8	East RB	Semiflexed	Back	East	X				1			
17	Ind	Infant	Classic	5	East RB	Flexed	ND	East					1			
18	Ind	Infant	Classic	41	East RB	ND	ND	ND					0			
19	Ind	Infant	Classic	41	East RB	ND	ND	South					0			
20	Male	Adult	Classic	41	East RB	Flexed	Right	North					1		X	
21	Ind	Adult	Classic	41	East RB	Flexed	Right	East					0			
22	Ind	Infant	Classic	8	East RB	Flexed	Sitting	South		X			0			
23	Ind	Child	Classic	42	East RB	Semiflexed	Back	South		X			0			
24	Ind	Child	Classic	41	East RB	Flexed	Right	West					1			
25	Male	Adult	Classic	41	East RB.	Flexed	Left	West	X	X			1		X	
26	Ind	Infant	Classic	8	East RB	Flexed	Back	South					0			
27	Male	Adult	Classic	41	East RB	Flexed	Back	North					1		X	
28	Ind	Adol	Classic	41	East RB	Flexed	Back	South	X				1		X	
29	Ind	Adult	Classic	41	East RB	Semiflexed	Left	North					1		X	
30	Ind	Adol	Classic	42	East RB	Semiflexed	Left	South					0			
32	Ind	Adult	Classic	47	East RB	Flexed	Back	North					1			
33	Ind	Child	Classic	50	East RB	Flexed	Back	South	X	X			0			
34	Ind	Child	Classic	50	East RB	Flexed	Stomach	NW	X	X			3			
35	Ind	Infant	Classic	47	East RB	Semiflexed	Stomach	South	X	X	X		1			
36	Male	Adult	Classic	50	East RB	Flexed	Back	North	X				0		X	
37	Ind	Infant	Classic	8	East RB	ND	ND	South					0			
39	Ind	Child	Classic	55	East RB	Semiflexed	Left	West					1			
40	Ind	Child	Classic	55	East RB	Semiflexed	Left	South					0			
41	Male	Subadult	Classic	12	East RB	Flexed	Right	East					0		X	
43	Female	Adult	Classic	49	East RB	Semiflexed	Back	East					1		X	
44	Ind	Infant	Classic	57	East RB	Semiflexed	Back	North					1			
45	Ind	Infant	Classic	60	East RB	ND	ND	ND	X				1			
46	Female	OA	Classic	49	East RB	Flexed	Stomach	South					1		X	
47	Ind	Infant	Classic	57	East RB	ND	Back	East					0			

*Bds = Beads, Pen = Pendants, Bra = Bracelet, Inl = Inlay, Ves = Vessel, Pal = Pallet, CB = Cobble Burial, Pnt = Point

TABLE 8.1 Nan Ranch Ruin Burial Data *continued*

Burial No.	Sex	Age	Temporal Location	Room No.	Spatial Location	Body Postion	Body Side	Direction	Bds*	Pen	Bra	Inl	Ves	Pal	CB	Pnt
48	Female	Adult	Classic	57	East RB	Flexed	Back	West					1		X	
49	Ind	Infant	Classic	57	East RB	Flexed	Left	SE					0			
50	Ind	Infant	Classic	57	East RB	Flexed	Back	South					0			
51	Female	OA	Trans	EM	East RB	Semiflexed	ND	SW					1			
52	Male	Adult	Trans	EM	East RB	Flexed	Back	North					0			
53	Ind	OA	Trans	EM	East RB	ND	ND	ND					0			
54	Ind	Child	Classic	EM	East RB	Flexed	Back	East		X			1		X	
55	Ind	Infant	Classic	12	East RB	Flexed	ND	North		X			1			
56	Female	Adult	Classic	12	East RB	ND	ND	ND					0			
57	Female	Adult	Classic	12	East RB	Flexed	Back	East					1		X	
58	Female	OA	Classic	12	East RB	Flexed	Back	East					1		X	
59	Ind	Adult	Classic	12	East RB	Flexed	Back	South					1		X	
60	Male	OA	Trans	EM	East RB	Flexed	Back	South					0			
61	Ind	Infant	Classic	12	East RB	Flexed	ND	ND					0			
62	Male	Adult	Classic	12	East RB	Flexed	Back	West					1		X	
63	Ind	Child	Classic	57	East RB	Semiflexed	Back	North		X			0			
64	Male	Adult	Classic	12	East RB	Semiflexed	Back	West					2			
65	Ind	Infant	Trans	57	East RB	ND	ND	ND					1			
66	Ind	Child	Classic	57	East RB	ND	ND	ND					0			
67	Ind	Infant	Classic	12	East RB	ND	ND	ND					1		X	
68	Male	Adult	Classic	12	East RB	Flexed	Back	East					0			
69	Ind	Child	Classic	12	East RB	Flexed	Back	South					0			
70	Female	Subadullt	Classic	12	East RB	Flexed	Back	West					1			
71	Ind	Infant	Classic	12	East RB	Flexed	Back	East					0			
72	Ind	Child	Classic	12	East RB	ND	ND	ND					0			
73	Female	Adult	Classic	41	East RB	Semiflexed	Back	East					1		X	
76	Female	Adult	Classic	18	East RB	Semiflexed	Back	South					1		X	
77	Male	OA	Classic	EM	East RB	ND	ND	SW					0		X	
78	Female	Subadullt	Classic	65	East RB	ND	ND	East		X			0			
80	Ind	OA	Classic	EM	East RB	ND	ND	South					0			
81	Ind	Infant	Classic	63B	East RB	Flexed	Back	South					0			
82	Male	Adult	Classic	22	East RB	Flexed	Back	West					1		X	
83	Female	Adult	Classic	22	East RB	Flexed	Back	West					1		X	
85	Ind	Child	Classic	23A	East RB	Flexed	ND	North					1			
86	Female	Adult	3-Circle	14	East RB	Flexed	Back	East					6			
87	Female	Adult	Classic	22	East RB	Flexed	Back	South					0		X	
88	Male	Adult	Classic	63B	East RB	Flexed	Back	South					1		X	
89	Ind	Child	Classic	23A	East RB	Flexed	Back	SW					0			
90	Ind	Ind	Trans	14	East RB	ND	ND	ND					1			
91	Ind	Adol	Classic	22	East RB	Semiflexed	Right	West					1		X	
92	Male	Adult	Classic	EM	East RB	Semiflexed	Back	NW				X	0			
93	Ind	Infant	3-Circle	14	East RB	Semiflexed	Back	East	X	X		X	3	X		
94	Ind	Infant	Trans	EM	East RB	ND	ND	ND					0			
95	Male	Adult	Trans	EM	East RB	Flexed	Back	East				X	2			
96	Ind	Child	Classic	CM	East RB	ND	ND	ND					0			

*Bds = Beads, Pen = Pendants, Bra = Braclet, Inl = Inlay, Ves = Vessel, Pal = Pallet, CB = Cobble Burial, Pnt = Point

TABLE 8.1 Nan Ranch Ruin Burial Data continued

Burial No.	Sex	Age	Temporal Location	Room No.	Spatial Location	Body Postion	Body Side	Direction	Bds*	Pen	Bra	Inl	Ves	Pal	CB	Pnt
98	Ind	Child	Classic	CM	East RB	Flexed	Left	SW					0			
99	Male	Subadullt	Classic	WP	CM	Flexed	Back	South	X	X			0		X	
100	Male	Adult	Classic	WP	CM	Flexed	Right	NW					0		X	
101	Ind	Adult	Classic	82	East RB	ND	ND	ND					0			
102	Ind	Infant	Classic	82	East RB	Extended	ND	South					1		X	
103	Male	Adult	Classic	67	East RB	Semiflexed	Back	West					1			
104	Female	Adult	3-Circle	83	East RB	Semiflexed	Back	East					2			
105	Female	Adult	Classic	84	East RB	Extended	Stomach	ND					0			
106	Ind	Infant	3-Circle		SEM	Flexed	Back	East					0			
107	Ind	Infant	3-Circle		SEM	ND	ND	West					0			
108	Ind	Infant	3-Circle		SEM	ND	ND	North					0			
109	Male	Adult	Classic		SEM	Flexed	ND	South					0			
110	Ind	Child	Classic	84	East RB	Flexed	Back	West		X			1			
111	Female	Adult	Classic	84	East RB	Flexed	Right	West					1		X	
112	Ind	Adol	Classic	84	East RB	ND	ND	ND		X	X		1			
114	Ind	Child	Classic	62	East RB	Flexed	Back	South		X			1			
115	Male	Adult	Classic		SEM	Semiflexed	Back	West					0		X	
116	Ind	Adol	Classic	89A	East RB	Semiflexed	Back	North					0			
117	Ind	Child	Trans	62	East RB	ND	Back	West	X				7	X		
118	Ind	Child	Classic	89B	East RB	Flexed	Back	East		X		X	0			
119	Female	Adult	Trans	89A	East RB	Semiflexed	Back	West					0			
120	Ind	Adol	Trans	89A	East RB	Semiflexed	Back	East					1			
121	Ind	Subadullt	Trans		SEM	Semiflexed	Back	West					1		X	
123	Female	Adult	Classic		SEM	Semiflexed	Back	West					0			
124	Ind	Child	Trans		E Plaza	Semiflexed	Back	East					0			
125	Male	Adult	Classic		SEM	Semiflexed	Back	West					0			
126	Ind	Adol	Classic	76	East RB	ND	ND	ND		X			0			
127	Male	Child	SF	86	SEM	Semiflexed	Sitting	West	X				0			
128	Ind	Infant	Classic	28	South RB	Semiflexed	Back	West	X	X			4		X	
129	Ind	Adult	Classic	28	South RB	Flexed	Back	East	X				0		X	
130	Female	Child	Classic	76	East RB	Semiflexed	Back	North		X			0			
131	Male	Adol	Classic	28	South RB	Flexed	Back	East		X			1		X	
132	Female	Adult	Classic	29	South RB	Flexed	Back	East					1		X	
133	Ind	Adol	Classic	29	South RB	Semiflexed	Back	West	X	X	X		3		X	
134	Ind	Child	Classic	29	South RB	ND	ND	ND					0			
135	Ind	Subadullt	Classic	28	South RB	Flexed	Right	North					2	X	X	
136	Ind	Child	Classic	28	South RB	Flexed	Sitting	North					2			
137	Ind	Infant	Classic	29	South RB	ND	ND	West					1	X		
138	Male	Adult	Classic	29	South RB	Flexed	Left	North					1			
139	Ind	Adult	Classic	29	South RB	Flexed	Back	South					1		X	
140	Female	OA	Classic	28	South RB	Semiflexed	Back	South					1			
141	Ind	Adol	Classic	28	South RB	Flexed	Back	North		X	X		1			
142	Ind	Child	Classic	28	South RB	Semiflexed	Back	South		X			0			
144	Female	Adult	Classic	29	South RB	Flexed	Back	North					1			
145	Ind	Child	Classic	28	South RB	Flexed	Back	West	X	X			1			

*Bds = Beads, Pen = Pendants, Bra = Braclet, Inl = Inlay, Ves = Vessel, Pal = Pallet, CB = Cobble Burial, Pnt = Point

TABLE 8.1 Nan Ranch Ruin Burial Data *continued*

Burial No.	Sex	Age	Temporal Location	Room No.	Spatial Location	Body Postion	Body Side	Direction	Bds*	Pen	Bra	Inl	Ves	Pal	CB	Pnt
146	Male	Adult	Classic	29	South RB	Flexed	Back	South			X		3		X	
147	Male	Adult	Classic	28	South RB	Flexed	Back	South					1		X	
148	Ind	Child	Classic	29	South RB	Flexed	Left	West					2			
149	Ind	Child	Classic	28	South RB	ND	ND	ND					1			
150	Male	Adult	Classic	28	South RB	Semiflexed	Back	North		X			1			
151	Female	OA	Classic	29	South RB	Flexed	Left	North					2		X	
153	Female	Adult	Classic	29	South RB	Flexed	Back	East					4		X	
154	Male	Adult	Classic	29	South RB	Flexed	Back	North					2		X	
155	Male	Adult	Classic	29	South RB	Flexed	Left	West					0			
156	Female	Adult	Classic	29	South RB	Flexed	Back	East					1			
157	Male	Adult	Classic	29	South RB	Semiflexed	Head	West					3			
158	Ind	Child	Classic	29	South RB	Flexed	Back	East	X	X	X		1			
159	Ind	Infant	Classic	29	South RB	ND	ND	ND					0			
160	Male	Adult	Classic		SEM	Semiflexed	Back	West		X			0		X	
161	Female	Adult	Classic	29	South RB	Flexed	Right	East		X			4		X	
162	Ind	Child	Classic	29	South RB	ND	ND	ND	X	X			0			
163	Ind	Adol	Classic	29	South RB	Flexed	Back	East		X			1		X	
164	Ind	Infant	Classic	29	South RB	Semiflexed	Back	West					0			
165	Female	Adult	Classic	29	South RB	Flexed	Back	North		X			1		X	
166	Ind	Child	Classic	29	South RB	ND	ND	ND	X				0			
167	Ind	Infant	Classic	29	South RB	Semiflexed	Back	West					0		X	
168	Ind	Adol	Trans	98	South RB	Flexed	Back	South		X			1			
169	Female	Adult	Trans	98	South RB	Semiflexed	Back	West					1			
170	Female	Adult	Classic	29	South RB	Semiflexed	Back	North					1			
171	Ind	Adol	Classic		SEM	Flexed	Back	NW					0		X	
172	Ind	Child	Classic	28	South RB	Flexed	Stomach	West					1		X	
173	Female	Adult	Classic	28	South RB	Flexed	Back	West					1		X	
174	Ind	Child	Classic	28	South RB	Flexed	ND	East	X			X	1			
175	Ind	Adult	Classic		SEM	Extended	ND	East					0			X
176	Ind	Child	Classic	29	South RB	Flexed	Back	South					0			
177	Ind	Child	Classic	28	South RB	ND	ND	North					1			
178	Male	Adult	Classic	29	South RB	Flexed	Back	North					1			
179	Female	Adult	Classic	29	South RB	Flexed	Back	East					2		X	
180	Ind	Infant	Classic	28	South RB	Semiflexed	Back	North					1			
181	Ind	Infant	3-Circle	99	SEM	Flexed	Sitting	South					0			
182	Ind	Infant	Classic	39	South RB	Flexed	Sitting	ND					0			
183	Ind	Child	Classic	29	South RB	Semiflexed	Back	North		X			2		X	
184	Male	Adult	Classic	28	South RB	Flexed	Back	East					1		X	
185	Female	OA	Classic	39	South RB	Flexed	Back	East					0			
186	Ind	Infant	Classic	94	South RB	Flexed	Back	South					1			
187	Ind	Child	Classic	29	South RB	ND	ND	West					0			
188	Male	Adult	Trans	98	South RB	Flexed	Back	North					1		X	
189	Male	Adult	Classic	39	South RB	Flexed	Back	South					X	0		
190	Ind	Infant	Classic	28	South RB	ND	ND	ND					0			

*Bds = Beads, Pen = Pendants, Bra = Bracelet, Inl = Inlay, Ves = Vessel, Pal = Pallet, CB = Cobble Burial, Pnt = Point

TABLE 8.1 Nan Ranch Ruin Burial Data *continued*

Burial No.	Sex	Age	Temporal Location	Room No.	Spatial Location	Body Postion	Body Side	Direction	Bds*	Pen	Bra	Inl	Ves	Pal	CB	Pnt
191	Ind	Infant	Trans	39	South RB	ND	ND	ND					0			
192	Ind	Child	Classic	94	South RB	Flexed	Sitting	East					1			
193	Ind	Child	Trans	98	South RB	Semiflexed	Left	West					0			
194	Ind	Infant	Trans	79	South RB	ND	ND	North					1			
195	Ind	Infant	Trans	104	South RB	Flexed	Right	South					2			
196	Ind	Child	Trans	104	South RB	ND	ND	East					1			
197	Ind	Infant	Trans	104	South RB	ND	ND	ND					1			
198	Female	Adult	Classic	29	South RB	Semiflexed	Back	South					5			
199	Ind	Adol	Classic	28	South RB	Flexed	Back	North					1			
200	Ind	Child	Trans	104	South RB	ND	ND	ND					2			
201	Ind	Child	Trans	104	South RB	Flexed	Back	East					1			
202	Ind	Infant	Trans	104	South RB	Flexed	ND	East				X	0			
203	Female	Adult	Classic	29	South RB	Flexed	Back	South					1		X	
204	Female	Adult	Trans	104	South RB	Flexed	Back	East					1			
205	Male	Adult	Trans	104	South RB	Flexed	Back	East					0			
206	Ind	Child	Classic	29	South RB	Semiflexed	Left	East					0			
207	Female	Adult	Trans	104	South RB	Flexed	Back	East				X	1			
208	Ind	Child	Trans	104	South RB	Flexed	Back	North					1			
209	Ind	Infant	3-Circle	95	SEM	Semiflexed	Back	NW					0			
210	Female	Adult	Trans	104	South RB	Flexed	Right	West					0			
211	Female	Adult	Classic	29	South RB	Semiflexed	Back	North					0			
212	Ind	Infant	Classic	29	South RB	Semiflexed	Back	South					0			
213	Ind	Infant	Trans	104	South RB	Flexed	Back	East					0			
214	Ind	Child	Trans	104	South RB	Flexed	ND	East					1			
218	Ind	Ind	Trans		E Plaza	Cremation	ND	N	X		X		6	X		
219	Ind	Adult	Classic	94	South RB	Flexed	Left	SE					0			
220	Ind	Child	Classic	94	South RB	Flexed	Right	West					0			
221	Ind	Infant	Classic	94	South RB	Semiflexed	Right	North					1			
222	Ind	Adult	Classic	94	South RB	Flexed	Back	West					0			
223	Ind	Adult	Trans	112	E Plaza	Flexed	Back	East					1			
224	Ind	Adult	Trans		E Plaza	Cremation	ND	ND	X	X			2			
225	Ind	Child	Trans		E Midden	ND	ND	ND					0			
226	Ind	Infant	Trans		E Midden	Flexed	Left	NW					0			
227	Ind	Adult	Trans		E Plaza	Cremation	ND	ND					2			
228	Male	Adult	Trans		E Plaza	ND	ND	West					0			
229	Ind	Adult	Trans		E Plaza	Cremation	ND	ND					7			
230	Ind	Adult	Classic		E Plaza	Cremation	ND	ND	X		X		5			
231	Ind	Adult	Trans		E Plaza	Cremation	ND	ND	X		X		0			X
232	Ind	Adult	Trans		E Plaza	Flexed	Back	West					0			
233	Ind	Ind	Classic		E Plaza	Cremation	ND	ND			X		0	X		X
234	Ind	Subadullt	Classic		E Plaza	Cremation	ND	ND	X				3			
235	Ind	Adult	Trans		E Plaza	Cremation	ND	ND					0			
236	Female	Adult	Trans		E Plaza	Cremation	ND	ND					7			
237	Ind	Adult	Classic		E Plaza	Cremation	ND	ND	X		X		6			

*Bds = Beads, Pen =Pendants, Bra = Braclet, Inl = Inlay, Ves = Vessel, Pal = Pallet, CB = Cobble Burial, Pnt = Point

TABLE 8.2. Burial Types by Phase

Body Position	Data	Temporal Location		Pithouse	SF	Trans	Grand Total
		3-Circle	Classic				
Cremation	Count	0	4	0	0	7	11
	Percent	0	36.36	0	0	63.64	100
Extended	Count	0	3	0	0	0	3
	Percent	0	100	0	0	0	100
Flexed	Count	3	95	2	0	18	118
	Percent	2.54	80.51	1.69	0	15.25	100
Semiflexed	Count	3	39	0	1	7	50
	Percent	6	78	0	2	14	100
Total count		6	141	2	1	32	182
Total percent		3.3	77.47	1.1	0.55	17.58	100

Temporal Location indicates phase: 3-Circle, Classic, SF (San Francisco), or Trans (Transitional) (Late Three Circle).

burials beneath floors (intramural) were easily assigned to rooms. Even in cases of superimposed rooms or floors, upper-floor burials usually penetrated the lower floors. Exceptions did occur, however, especially in room 29, where so many burial pits were excavated that the lower floors were mostly obliterated in certain areas. Not being able to trace the origins of pits in such cases made it impossible to assign a specific burial to a specific floor episode in the room, but a temporal assignment was often possible using relative depth of grave, degrees of leaching of grave fill, and ceramic microstyles. Other problematic examples occurred when extramural pithouse period burials were covered over by later surface architecture. We could not assign precise phase placement in such cases if ceramics were not included with the burial, but general placement was based on stratigraphic superposition, minimum age of ceramic sherds casually mixed in grave pit fill, and leaching of grave fill.

The majority of the in situ articulated inhumation burials were complete or relatively so, depending on degrees of preservation. Isolated human bones were encountered virtually everywhere we excavated due to prehistoric disturbances of underlying deposits that contained burials. Scattered human bones often marked relic hunter excavations as well. Prehistoric disturbance of burials was common, especially in extensively used areas such as the east plaza, and some examples suggest a disregard for previous burials. In room 29 at least three infant burials were totally destroyed in the excavation of the pit for burial 161. Some care obviously was displayed, however, in one exceptional case. In room 23A, burial 89 was cut in half by the interment of burial 88, and the disarticulated bones of burial 89 were placed at the feet of 88. The latter case was much less frequent than the former, however, and we saw no examples of where a pit feature or excavation for architecture was stopped because a burial had been encountered. The subfloor deposits in the southeast corner of room 29, for example, contained an assortment of disarticulated human remains and sherds from displaced mortuary vessels. Burials were also disturbed in room 89A by the excavation of adobe-mixing pots.

Some general comments can be made about Mimbres mortuary practices based on the information in Table 8.1. I will discuss some of these practices in regard to certain variables that show some changes through time. This general discussion of burial practices will be followed by a phase-by-phase overview that traces the evolution of the Classic Mimbres mortuary patterns back to the Three Circle phase.

Body position for 182 cases (cremation, extended, flexed, or semiflexed) is shown in Table 8.2. Certainly flexed (64.84 percent), where the arms and legs are flexed against the torso, and semiflexed (27.47 percent), where the knees are generally at right angles to the spine, were the traditional methods of positioning the dead regardless of time period. Only three extended burials were recorded. Two of these, burials 105 and 175, are anomalous.

TABLE 8.3. Body Position (All Burials)

| Body Side | Data | Temporal Location | | Pithouse | SF | Trans | Grand Total |
		3-Circle	Classic				
Back	Count	5	88	1	0	19	113
	Percent	4.42	77.88	0.88	0	16.81	100
Head	Count	0	1	0	0	0	1
	Percent	0	100	0	0	0	100
Left	Count	0	14	1	0	2	17
	Percent	0	82.35	5.88	0	11.76	10
ND	Count	0	1	0	0	0	1
	Percent	0	100	0	0	0	100
Right	Count	0	17	0	0	2	19
	Percent	0	89.47	0	0	10.53	100
Sitting	Count	1	5	0	1	0	7
	Percent	14.29	71.43	0	14.29	0	100
Stomach	Count	0	5	0	0	0	5
	Percent	0	100	0	0	0	100
Total count		6	131	2	1	23	163
Total percent		3.68	80.37	1.23	0.61	14.11	100

Temporal Location indicates phase: 3-Circle, Classic, SF (San Francisco), or Trans (Transitional) (Late Three Circle).

Burial 105 was laid out on the floor of room 84 before the room burned, and burial 175 was a cremation placed extended on a rack above the cremation pyre.

Nearly 70 percent of all burials were placed flexed or semiflexed on the back (Table 8.3). The remainder were placed on the right side (11.66 percent), on the left side (10.43 percent), or facedown (4.29 percent). One, burial 157, was placed headfirst in a narrow, deep pit.[27]

The direction was surprisingly uniform between the four cardinal directions, a factor probably dictated by the orientation of the wall next to where the burial was placed (Table 8.4). East was favored in 25.68 percent of the cases, whereas west was chosen for 24.4 percent of the burials. North (20.77 percent) and south (21.31 percent) were the next most common orientations. None of the intermediate orientations—northeast, southeast, northwest, or southwest—were well represented; northwest had the highest representation, at 3.83 percent.

The distribution of age groups by phase is shown in Table 8.5. This table shows that prior to the Late Three Circle phase transition, the numbers are terribly skewed, undoubtedly due to a number of factors, namely small sample size, mortuary practices, and preservation. The samples from the transitional and Classic phases, however, reflect the high rate of mortality among the very young. When the data are examined in regard to sexed adults, the distribution of males and females appears very balanced between the two (Table 8.6).

Although individual graves were not marked within the context of the room, plaza, or courtyard, most Classic period graves of adults and older subadults were marked beneath the surface by stone cairns. We can only speculate why this was done, but clearly it was a Classic period trait (Table 8.7). Since the practice of capping a burial with a cairn of stones parallels the time period of the corporate kivas, it may have been done to alert the excavators of later graves to the presence of one below. Or it may have simply been a practical matter of reinforcing the floor since the grave diggers knew that in time the grave would slump. Nevertheless, it is clearly a Classic period trait.

Placement and distribution of artifacts in graves undoubtedly carried important symbolic meanings about which we can only speculate. Mortuary associations for all

TABLE 8.4. Body Orientation by Phase

Direction	Data	Temporal Location 3-Circle	Classic	Pithouse	SF	Trans	Grand Total
East	Count	4	30	1	0	12	47
	Percent	8.51	63.83	2.13	0	25.53	100
NE	Count	0	1	1	0	0	2
	Percent	0	50	50	0	0	100
North	Count	1	33	0	0	4	38
	Percent	2.63	86.84	0	0	10.53	100
NW	Count	1	5	0	0	1	7
	Percent	14.29	71.43	0	0	14.29	100
SE	Count	0	2	0	0	0	2
	Percent	0	1	0	0	0	1
South	Count	1	35	0	0	3	39
	Percent	2.56	89.74	0	0	7.69	100
SW	Count	0	3	0	0	1	4
	Percent	0	75	0	0	25	100
West	Count	1	34	0	1	8	44
	Percent	2.27	77.27	0	2.27	18.18	100
Total count		8	143	2	1	29	183
Total percent		4.37	78.14	1.09	0.55	15.85	100

Temporal Location indicates phase: 3-Circle, Classic, SF (San Francisco), or Trans (Transitional) (Late Three Circle).

TABLE 8.5. Distribution of Age Categories by Phase

Age	Data	Temporal Location 3-Circle	Classic	Pithouse	SF	Trans	Grand Total
Adolescence	Count	0	13	0	0	2	15
	Percent	0	86.67	0	0	13.33	100
Adult	Count	2	67	2	0	18	89
	Percent	2.25	75.28	2.25	0	20.22	100
Child	Count	0	37	0	1	9	47
	Percent	0	78.72	0	2.13	19.15	100
Infant	Count	6	36	0	0	9	51
	Percent	11.76	70.59	0	0	17.65	100
Old adult	Count	0	7	0	0	3	10
	Percent	0	70	0	0	30	100
Subadult	Count	0	6	0	0	1	7
	Percent	0	85.71	0	0	14.29	100
Total count		8	166	2	1	42	219
Total percent		3.65	75.8	0.91	0.46	19.18	100

Temporal Location indicates phase: 3-Circle, Classic, SF (San Francisco), or Trans (Transitional) (Late Three Circle).
Age categories: infant, 0–1; child, 1–6; adolescent, 6–12; subadult, 12–20; adult, 20–50; old adult, 50+

TABLE 8.6. Distribution of Sexed Adults by Phase

| Sex | Data | Temporal Location | | Pithouse | SF | Trans | Grand Total |
		3-Circle	Classic				
Female	Count	2	29	1		7	39
	Percent	5.13	74.36	2.56		17.95	100
Male	Count	0	31	1		6	38
	Percent	0	81.58	2.63		15.79	100
Total count		2	60	2		13	77
Total percent		2.6	77.92	2.6		16.88	100

Temporal Location indicates phase: 3-Circle, Classic, SF (San Francisco), or Trans (Transitional) (Late Three Circle).

TABLE 8.7. Distribution of Rock Cairns Over Graves by Phase

| Age | Data | Temporal Location | | Pithouse | SF | Trans | Grand Total |
		3-Circle	Classic				
Adolescent	Count		6			0	6
	Percent		100			0	100
Adult	Count		37			1	38
	Percent		97.37			2.63	100
Child	Count		3			0	3
	Percent		100			0	100
Infant	Count		5			0	5
	Percent		100			0	100
Old adult	Count		4			0	4
	Percent		100			0	100
Subadult	Count		3			1	4
	Percent		75			25	100
Total count			58			2	60
Total percent			96.67			3.33	100

Temporal Location indicates phase: 3-Circle, Classic, SF (San Francisco), or Trans (Transitional) (Late Three Circle).
Age categories: infant, 0–1; child, 1–6; adolescent, 6–12; subadult, 12–20; adult, 20–50; old adult, 50+

phases at the NAN Ruin varied in quality and quantity and in time and space. Nonperishable items preserved in graves of various phases include pottery vessels, large sherds, jewelry items (stone, turquoise, and shell beads; stone, turquoise, and shell pendants; and *Glycymeris* shell bracelets), shells, inlayed objects, arrow points, a stone ax, stone palettes, sherd palettes, and painted stones. This listing does not include artifacts in cairns that covered graves. Among the items in cairns were manos, metates, an effigy stone mortar, a petroglyph on a recycled metate, and an occasional large sherd. Identified perishable items include traces of checker-weave mats and other textiles (probably used as shrouds), a woven sash, a G-string-like cordage apron, a coiled basket, and traces of a paho stick. The greatest variety of mortuary items occurred in the graves of children in the Three Circle, Late Three Circle, and Classic periods and with secondary cremations. A closer look at the variability in mortuary associations reveals some interesting clues to how Mimbres society may have been structured.

Fifty-five percent of all Classic period burials were associated with ceramics (Table 8.8); of these, 44 percent

TABLE 8.8. Number of Vessels per Burial by Phase

No. of Vessels per Burial	Data	Temporal Location 3-Circle	Classic	Pithouse	SF	Trans	Grand Total
0	Count	5	75	2	1	18	101
	Percent	4.95	74.26	1.98	0.99	17.82	100
1	Count	0	73	0	0	17	90
	Percent	0	81.11	0	0	18.89	100
2	Count	1	8	0	0	5	14
	Percent	7.14	57.14	0	0	35.71	100
3	Count	1	5	0	0	0	6
	Percent	16.67	83.33	0	0	0	100
4	Count	0	3	0	0	0	3
	Percent	0	100	0	0	0	100
5	Count	0	2	0	0	0	2
	Percent	0	100	0	0	0	100
6	Count	1	1	0	0	1	3
	Percent	33.33	33.33	0	0	33.33	100
7	Count	0	0	0	0	3	3
	Percent	0	0	0	0	100	100
Total count		8	167	2	1	44	222
Total percent		3.6	75.23	0.9	0.45	19.82	100

Temporal Location indicates phase: 3-Circle, Classic, SF (San Francisco), or Trans (Transitional) (Late Three Circle).
Age categories: infant, 0–1; child, 1–6; adolescent, 6–12; subadult, 12–20; adult, 20–50; old adult, 50+

had only one vessel associated with them. Multiple vessel associations accounted for 11 percent of Classic period burials. By contrast, 59 percent of Late Three Circle transition burials had single vessels, and 20 percent had multiple vessel associations. The latter percent is bolstered by the cremations, several of which had sherds from multiple vessels included. Table 8.8 shows the distribution of mortuary vessels by time. Only the Late Three Circle and Classic phases have samples sufficiently large to provide comparisons. Clearly the practice of including "killed" mortuary vessels, which accounts for the number of single-vessel inclusions, began in earnest during the pithouse to pueblo transition (Late Three Circle phase).

The pattern of distribution for jewelry among the burials is most interesting and was undoubtedly sex-linked. The jewelry per se is not striking so much as the kind of jewelry. *Glycymeris* shell bracelets, for example, were always associated with males in cases where sexing was possible (six out of six cases). By extension I assume all unsexed subadults with bracelets were males as well. Beads were also a male characteristic where sexing was possible (three out of three cases), but pendants were not. Pendants were associated with both adult males and females (five males and four females). Jewelry was not divided according to material class in Table 8.1, but I found that turquoise, like pendants, was mostly associated with males, though not exclusively so. Clearly something was going on with the symbolic and social significance of jewelry and the kind of jewelry in Mimbres burials. I assume that the material (e.g., shell and turquoise) had important symbolic significance and may have marked individual membership ascribed at birth or an initiation into one of several male sodalities. Given the fact that adornment with single *Glycymeris* shell bracelet among certain males, for example, was a Classic period trait, the formation of sodalities or fictional kin-based affiliations may have been a product of social reorganization associated with irrigation agriculture.

The burial sample from the San Francisco and Three Circle phases is small (one San Francisco, eight Three

Circle). The small sample is attributed to past cultural practices and to sampling. The assumed mobility and extramural placement of the dead during the earlier phases undoubtedly is a factor in the small sample. Also, artifacts associated with extramural burials are lacking, which would otherwise allow for a more accurate temporal placement. Assigning phase designation to extramural burials that were either not associated with diagnostic artifacts or otherwise not placed in sealed contexts that could be dated by other means was difficult prior to the Classic Mimbres phase and was based on relative stratigraphy and styles of sherds in the burial pit fill. With this caveat in mind, the changing patterns in the treatment of the dead are still readily apparent.

Prior to the San Francisco phase, burial was entirely extramural: no intramural burials were found, and extramural burials without ceramics could not confidently be assigned to any Late Pithouse period phase. An examination of the mortuary patterns for each phase demonstrates the qualitative changes that took place through time. These changes, summarized by phase below, reflect a restructuring in Mimbres society from a semimobile family-based organization to a fully sedentary corporate group organization.

Georgetown phase: No burials could confidently be assigned to the Georgetown phase component. Certain flexed extramural burials without mortuary associations such as burials 6 and 9, two pithouse period interments, were placed into the underlying paleosurface beneath Pithouse and Classic period deposits and probably represent some of the earliest of the burials encountered.

San Francisco phase: Here again, no extramural burials could confidently be assigned to the San Francisco phase, but one intramural burial was found in a San Francisco phase structure. Burial 127 in room 86 was an adult male placed in a sitting position along with an assemblage of associated items in a crypt excavated into the north wall of the pit structure. The crypt was sealed by constructing a cobble-adobe wall, which was plastered over. The burial was wrapped in a checker-weave mat; grave inclusion were a tubular stone pipe, a quartz crystal, a turtle plastron, two *Olivella* shell beads, and a biface (dart point preform, figure 3.10). More will be said of this burial later in the chapter. Burial 209, an infant placed in the floor of room 95, a San Francisco/early Three Circle phase structure, may belong to this phase; it is included in the Three Circle phase, however, in Tables 8.1 and 8.2.

8.3: Worked sherds associated with burial 86 at the NAN Ranch Ruin.

Three Circle phase: The mortuary patterns began to change in the Three Circle phase, with more frequent occurrence of intramural burials and associated artifacts. Nine burials were assigned to this phase. Modes of burial included flexed inhumations placed both intramurally and extramurally as well as one primary cremation. Flexed intramural inhumations were recorded in rooms 14 (burial 86) and 99 (burial 181) and in the southeast midden (burial 106). Semiflexed burials were recorded in rooms 14 (burial 93), 83A (burial 104), and 95 (burial 209). Female adult burials occurred in rooms 14 (burial 86) and 83A (104); infant burials were in rooms 14, 95, and 99 and the southeast midden (burials 106, 107, and 108). Burial 86 has been interpreted as the grave of a potter.[28]

Mortuary associations included smashed vessels (burials 86, 93, and 104), intact vessels (burial 86), worked sherds (burial 86), pot-polishing stones (burial 86), unfired Style I jars (burial 86), and inlayed and other adornment jewelry (burial 93). Worked sherds from burial 86 are shown in Figure 8.3. Burial 86 was wrapped in a checker-weave mat, and the associated objects listed above were placed in a coiled basket above the corpse. The unfired Style I jars (Figure 8.4) and lumps of white kaolin clay were around and beneath the burial. A broken Style I bowl containing red pigment was also placed beside the body (appendix I: Figure A.1F). In the fill immediately above the grave were sherds from a smashed Style I bowl (appendix I: Figure A.1E) and a small, complete Style I

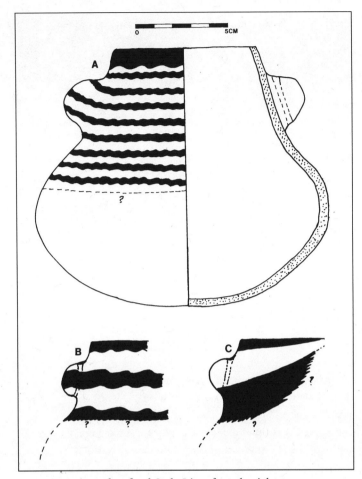

8.4: Drawing of unfired Style I jars from burial 86 at the NAN Ranch Ruin.

8.5: NAN Ranch Ruin burial 175 cremation pit after excavation.

seed jar (appendix I: Figure A.1G). Preservation of the textiles is attributed to constant moisture percolating through the deposits.

Burial 93 was an infant buried with an interesting assemblage of items. Ceramics included a Mimbres polished redware seed jar (appendix I: Figure A.1A), a small punctated mug (appendix I: Figure A.28G), and a plain brownware boat-shaped bowl with distal tabs (appendix I: Figure A.26E). Also included were a smashed palette, a shell pendant, a string of shell beads on the left wrist, two small turquoise pendants on the right wrist, and an inlayed object of turquoise and lead crystals. Room 14 was extraordinary in the NAN Three Circle phase community in regard to the number of burials and associated artifacts. Interestingly, this room underlay part of corporate kiva room 12 and may have been occupied by one of the founding lineages at the site, possibly ancestral to the lineage inhabiting the wealthy Cosgrove suite.

The only primary cremation at the site, burial 175, dates to the Three Circle phase. This too is an extraordinary burial both in terms of the way it was treated and the labor required in carrying out the ritual. The feature consisted of an elongated pit 1.66 m long and 53 cm wide, excavated 55 cm into the hardpan clay paleosurface (Figure 8.5). The fire baked the pit walls, preserving the digging stick marks. The pit had rounded ends and straight sides. A rack was constructed and supported by four posts set at each corner of the pit, on top of which was placed the corpse. Fuelwoods were stacked beneath the rack. The body of an adult male 30 to 39 years of age was placed extended on his back with the head to the east. No ceramics accompanied the burial, but a single corner-notched arrow point and two ears of corn were among the items recovered. Also, the charred remnants of a finely woven cotton(?) sash constructed of a close diagonal twinning, with a Z twist weft,[29] adorned the waist of the corpse, much like those seen on Mimbres Style III vessels. Archaeomagnetism samples collected from the pit walls yielded two clusters of dates: A.D. 710 to 775 or A.D. 840 to 900, and A.D. 700 to 920.[30] Since no ceramics were included with the body, we have no way of assessing which date is more correct. Regardless, the feature falls securely in the Three Circle phase.

In sum, the Three Circle phase marks a period of significant change in the rituals and beliefs in regard to the dead. Special treatment was accorded certain individuals and perhaps members of certain households. Although our sample is quite small, the trend appears to favor special treatment of females and children of certain families. Burials 86, 93, and 104 certainly were given special attention. These burials may well have initiated the practice of intramural burial at the site. Adult males were relegated to extramural placement and were not treated with special preparation or associations, the exceptions being burials 95 and 175.

Late Three Circle phase: The greatest variability in mortuary practices occurred during this phase. Mortuary practices include intramural inhumation, extramural inhumation, and extramural secondary cremation. The trend toward inhumation in the Three Circle phase becomes a dominant pattern in some households by the end of the Late Three Circle phase with the establishment of corporate cemeteries. Forty-three burials were assigned to this phase. Intramural burials account for 56 percent ($n = 24$) of the NAN Late Three Circle phase sample. Nine percent ($n = 4$) were placed in pithouse fill, and the remaining 35 percent ($n = 16$) were placed in various extramural locations, including the cremation cemetery. Intramural cemeteries were found in rooms 12, 89A, 98, and 104, and intramural burials were found beneath the floors of rooms 79 and 112. It was in the Late Three Circle phase that the ritual of placing a perforated inverted bowl (or in rare instances, a large sherd) over the head of the deceased began. Forty-four percent of the Late Three Circle phase burials had mortuary vessels over the head, and 53 percent ($n = 23$) had ceramics associated in some manner. The practice of placing a "killed" bowl over the head carries over into and throughout the Classic period. The manner of perforating the bowls mostly included percussion by knocking a hole from the inside or the outside with a sharp object; inside versus outside occurs in about equal proportions.

Late Three Circle phase extramural burials could be identified in several instances, based either on stratigraphy or associated ceramics. The fill of large kiva room 52 contained four burials dating to this phase (burials 51, 52, 53, and 60); another occurred beneath 75C, the grave of which cut into filled-in pithouse room 17 (burial 95), and in the east plaza burials 121 and 124 were buried in deposits dating to this phase. Other intramural inhumation burials without mortuary or stratigraphic association, such as 124, 228, and 232, probably date to this phase as well, since none had cairns covering the graves, a Classic period trait.

The cemetery for cremations established in the east plaza is a unique discovery for large Mimbres sites

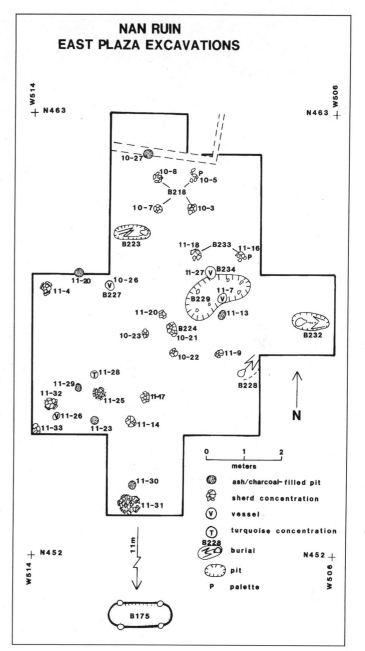

8.6: Plan of cremation cemetery in the east plaza at the NAN Ranch Ruin.

(Figure 8.6). Prior to the discovery of this cemetery, cremations were considered rare,[31] accounting for about 1 percent of Mimbres burials. I think their apparent rare occurrence is due to the subtle ways secondary cremations were marked, which led to them being missed by the imprecise techniques of the earlier excavators. For

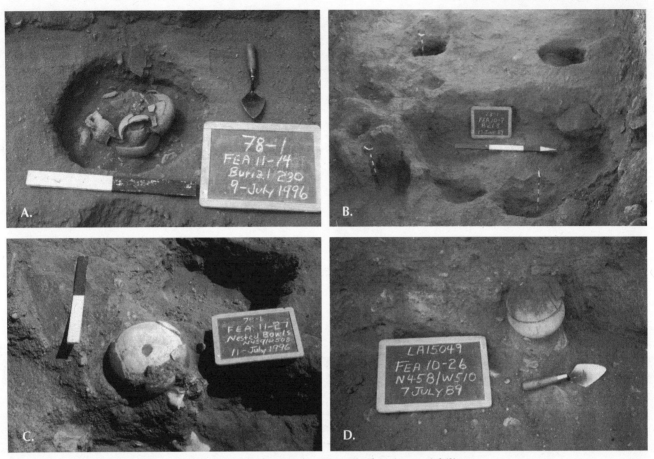

8.7. Four views of cremations at the NAN Ranch Ruin (A, B, C, D), showing variability.

that reason, I will take a closer look at the cremation cemetery at the NAN Ranch Ruin.

The cemetery was established in the Late Three Circle phase and continued to be used well into the Classic period. Twenty-three cremation features, most of which were associated with deposits of calcined human bone and represented at least 11 separate burials, were recorded. Prehistoric excavations for adobe-mixing pits, outdoor hearths, and pits disturbed an untold number as well. The middenlike deposit beneath the packed plaza surfaces contained scattered calcined bone fragments and sherds from fragmented cremation vessels, attesting to the extent to which this cemetery was used. At least six burials and seven cremation deposits date to the Late Three Circle phase, based on ceramics and other diagnostics such as corner-notched arrow points. A smooth continuum can be seen, however, in the ceramics present in the features showing use into the middle Classic period. Token deposits of calcined bone were placed in small pits capped with sherd concentrations (Figure 8.7A, B) or in ceramic vessels (Figure 8.7C, D). In the former cases, calcined bone was placed in the bottom of the pits, which ranged from 12 to 25 cm in diameter and 9 to 31 cm deep. The pits were then filled with an ashy matrix and usually capped with sherds from vessels that appear to have been subjected to cremation fires. Artifacts placed with cremations include vessels, sherds, shell fragments (*Pectan*), *Glycymeris* shell bracelet fragments, disk shell beads, *Nassarius* shell beads, turquoise beads, other stone beads, corn, smashed stone palettes, sherd palettes, pinch pot palettes, and obsidian arrow points.[32]

Some intriguing variability also exists among the pit features.[33] The calcined bones of burial 224 were mixed with burned *Pecten* shell fragments in a single pit capped with sherds from a Style II vessel (appendix: Figure 4H).

Calcined bones of burial 218 were placed in four pits about 80 cm apart, roughly in the four corners of a square aligned east-west and north-south. The pits were all capped with sherds (Figure 8.7B). Sherds from six vessels, four Style II (two restored vessels are shown in the appendix: Figure 4D, G), one Three Circle Neck Corrugated pitcher, and one Mimbres Fully Corrugated pitcher, were partly restored from the sherds mixed among the pits, leaving no question as to their contemporaneity. All of the vessels show evidence of intensive heat and some are warped, presumably from the cremation fire. Calcined bone burial 217 (Figure 8.7D) was placed in a Three Circle Neck Corrugated jar (appendix: Figure 28B) and capped with a Style II bowl (appendix: Figure 3I).

In sum, the establishment of corporate cemeteries for adults of both sexes, children, and infants in certain important households took place during the Late Three Circle phase, although the use of extramural space continued to be used for both adult males and females as well as children and infants. Another type of cemetery was created in the east plaza for the interment of secondary cremations. Unfortunately, we can only speculate as to the rules that dictated how a body was to be treated (buried in the flesh or cremated) and where the remains were to be buried. Interestingly, this area of the plaza was reserved for use as a cremation cemetery for well over a century, suggesting that it may have had some lineage connection.

Classic Mimbres phase: The late Three Circle phase trend toward intramural cemeteries became the dominant pattern in the Classic period. Fully 93 percent (156 of 168) of Classic period burials were intramural, with some 8 percent extramural, and of these approximately 2 percent ($n = 4$) were extramural cremations. These figures suggest that over 90 percent of the people who died at the NAN Ranch Ruin were probably members of residing families. Intramural cemeteries occurred in every habitation room that was occupied long enough for a death to occur. The more generations a room was used for habitation or as a corporate kiva, the more burials were interred beneath its floors. Habitation rooms converted into corporate kivas tended to have the larger cemeteries. Storage rooms attached to corporate kivas, such as rooms 42 and 60, contained burials, suggesting that any space contained within the private entrance of a corporate kiva could be used. In the latter examples, however, the burials were infants and children. Intramural corporate cemeteries contained anywhere from one to over 40 burials.

Placement of burials also followed a general pattern.

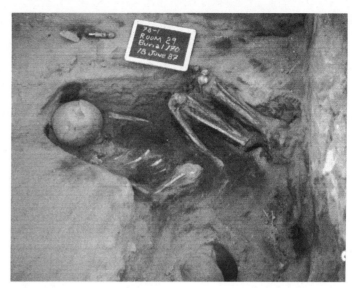

8.8: NAN Ranch Ruin burial 170 and mortuary vessel in situ.

Orientation trended along the axes of the walls, and initial burials were placed at the farthest distance from the hearth near a corner. As space in the cemetery began to fill, the location of the hearth may have been changed to continue the practice in such rooms as 28 and 29. Extramural inhumations consisted of isolated burials placed in courtyards, plazas, or middens, with a strong bias toward adult males. Except for the cremation area in the east plaza, no formal space was relegated for use as an extramural cemetery.

Evidence indicates that bodies were dressed prior to burial, a practice that probably dates back for some time, as burial 175, described above, suggests. Classic period burials 15, 88, 198, and 199 had traces of textiles, probably sashes or blankets. In each case, the type of textile weave was close diagonal twinning, Z twist weft.[34] The adult female in burial 15 was dressed in a cordage G-string and sash. Bodies were apparently wrapped in matting or blanket shrouds. Traces of desiccated matting were noted in earlier graves (burials 86 and 127), and fossil impressions of textiles were noted in Classic period graves (e.g., burials 46, 57, and 141), indicating that bodies were wrapped prior to burial. Differential preservation of perishable items allows us to consider only the presence or absence of them in these cases.

A mortuary bowl (or rarely, a large sherd) was placed over the face or head in 56 percent (92 of 167) of the Classic period burials (Figure 8.8). The bowls were perforated

8.9: Textile impressions on inside of mortuary bowl from NAN Ranch Ruin burial 141, showing that the placement of the bowl was over the shroud covering the body.

8.10: Stone cairn over burial 121 in room 41 at the NAN Ranch Ruin.

either from the inside or outside at or near the grave site and placed inverted over the head of the corpse; occasionally "kill" hole sherds were found in the grave fill, or, in the case of burial 123, placed at the foot of the grave. The vessel was apparently selected from a household assemblage based on observable use wear and placed on the wrapped corpse rather than beneath the shroud. Textile impressions in the interior of two mortuary vessels indicate they were placed exterior to the shroud (Figure 8.9), a finding supported by Bradfield at the Cameron Creek Ruin.[35] The placement of the hands over the mortuary bowl in burial 165, on the other hand, suggests either that the body was not wrapped or that the bowl was included beneath the shroud. An impression of a basket was found in place of a bowl in burial 26, suggesting that not all mortuary vessels were ceramic.

Adult graves measured approximately 90 to 100 cm long, 50 cm wide, and anywhere from 30 to 90 cm deep, usually depending on subfloor conditions. The size and depth of subadult graves was usually dictated by the size of the flexed corpse. Infants, for example, were placed in shallow oval pits just beneath the floors or surfaces, whereas larger children were placed in larger, deeper graves.

Cairns of cobbles or slabs covering adult and larger subadult graves regardless of where they were buried is a Classic period trait (Figure 8.10). This practice began at the very end of the Late Three Circle phase and became a predictable pattern in the Classic period. Only two (3 percent) of the cairn burials were Late Three Circle in age, contrasting to 58 (97 percent) in the Classic period. Cairns include stones from a variety of sources, cobbles, broken Sugarlump rhyolite slabs, and whole and broken metates and manos. Exceptions include burial 154, which had an inverted effigy stone bowl in the cairn (Figure 8.11A), and burial 151, which had a recycled metate with petroglyphs as a capstone (Figure 8.11B). When cairns were not used in the Classic period to cap a grave (burial 109, for example), stratigraphy often provided the means of dating. Graves without cairns originating from Classic period midden deposits were regarded as Classic in age.

Burial positions were also strongly patterned. Position information on 137 Classic period burials showed all but two to have been flexed or semiflexed. The exceptions include burial 105, an adult female left lying on her stomach on the floor of room 84 before the room burned, and burial 102, an infant in room 82. Burial 105 was the only case of a corpse being left on the floor. The Cosgroves mention two similar cases at the Swarts Ruin.[36] Seventy-five percent of Classic burials were placed on the back. Other flexed positions include on the right side (9 percent), left side (10 percent), sitting (4 percent), and stomach (2 percent). The two exceptions were burials 102 and 105, mentioned above, and burial 157, which, strangely, was placed semiflexed headfirst into a deep, narrow grave. Three nested vessels were placed upright beneath the head.

Flexed burials placed on the stomach are spatially clustered in the corporate household that included rooms 47, 49, and 50. Each of these room contained a flexed burial placed on the stomach. The only other flexed burials were burial 105 on the floor of room 84 and burial 172 in room 28. This unusual burial placement may have indicated lineage connections.

The secondary cremation cemetery in the east plaza, described above, continued to be used up through the middle Classic period. At least four secondary cremations and five possible cremation deposits date to the Classic period. Scattered calcined bones and Style III sherds from cremation vessels indicate that many more Classic period cremations occurred in the cemetery beyond those we could define. Token deposits of calcined bone placed in small pits capped with sherd concentrations continued (burials 233 and 237), with some variations. For example, remains were also placed in vessels (possibly burial 230 and certainly burial 234). Calcined bones of burial 230 may have been contained within a bilobed corrugated pitcher capped with a cluster of small vessels and sherds (appendix I: Figure A.29H). The calcined bones of burial 234 were placed in a Style III bowl (appendix I: Figure A.10I), along with four turquoise beads and one red coral bead. The bowl was sealed by an inverted Style III bowl (appendix I: Figure A.11F), which was "killed." This bowl was then sealed with yet another Style III bowl (appendix I: Figure A.7H). Finally the grave was capped with two rectangular rhyolite slabs. Contents of other secondary cremation deposits and probable cremation features include sherds or whole vessels, obsidian arrow points, corn, *Glycymeris* shell bracelets, a stone palette, stone beads, shell beads, and unworked turquoise. Ritual deposits found in the cremation cemetery include a cache of turquoise (raw and inlays) and inverted bowls without cremations that probably covered some perishable ritual cache. An additional cache, feature 7-47, of two matching bone pins

8.11: A. stone effigy mortar from cairn above burial 154; B. recycled metate with petroglyphs from burial 151. Both are from room 29 in the south room block at the NAN Ranch Ruin.

from the long bone of mule deer or elk, was recovered from a deep midden at the south end of the east plaza (see first two items on the left in Figure 11.9).

The absence of late Style III vessels in any of the cremation deposits suggests that use of this cemetery may not have lasted through the period. This does not seem to be the case with other methods of burial, however. Intramural cemeteries were used right up to and possibly even after abandonment. We have no convincing evidence of postabandonment uses except for in room 94, and even here the interments were placed in the floor before the room burned. In this case, the room itself may have been abandoned but not the lineage household.

Two burials, 12 and 76, were possibly Postclassic in age; both were buried near the surface of the rubble mound. Burial 12, a male, was in the ruins of room 40, placed tightly flexed in a near sitting position. Burial 78, a female, was intrusive in the ruins of room 64, a very late room attached to the north side of room 55. Neither burial was associated with surviving mortuary items and neither grave was capped with a stone cairn, so temporal phase placement is difficult to assess. Stratigraphically, however, these are arguably among the last burials to be interred at the site. Both burials have been included in the statistics for the Classic period, but both could be early Postclassic, possibly Black Mountain phase interments associated with a large Black Mountain phase pueblo 150 m north of the NAN Ranch Ruin.

Burials occur throughout the site,[37] and isolated human bones were encountered virtually everywhere we excavated. Treatment of the dead varied, and it is this variation that provides hints about the organization of and changes in Mimbres society. Obvious spatial clustering of intramural burials and secondary cremations occurred, in contrast to the apparent random distribution of extramural burials. Part of the clustering can be explained by changing patterns through time, as discussed above, with a trend away from extramural burial in the Late Three Circle phase during the restructuring of Mimbres society.

In the Classic period the vast majority of the dead were buried in family and corporate cemeteries; others, however, were placed in apparent random locations in civic rooms, plazas, courtyards, or midden areas, while still others were cremated and their remains placed in a designated public place in the east plaza. As noted earlier, intramural cemeteries were first established in the Late Three Circle phase. Intramural burials occurred in the Classic period in all investigated corporate kivas, in all habitation rooms except room 93, in all multiple-function rooms except room 16 (i.e., rooms whose function changed from habitation to storage or vice versa), in some storage rooms (e.g., rooms 42 and 60), in one granary (room 7), and in one civic room (room 39).

One of the first indicators of change, as noted above, was the intramural inclusion of adult females in the Three Circle phase, burials 86 and 104. Both burials contained multiple smashed vessels, and burial 86 had an array of pottery-making items. Burial 93, an infant with an assortment of jewelry, a stone palette, and three smashed vessels, perhaps began the trend of marking ascribed status to members of primary families.

The characteristic inverted "killed" bowl became the predominate nonperishable mortuary item in the Late Three Circle phase inhumations. Additional vessels, usually in the form of small pitchers or tecomate jars, were also included. The small jars may or may not have been smashed. Interestingly, jewelry items were rare in the NAN Ranch Ruin sample. One child was interred with a pendant (burial 202), and an adult male (burial 95) and an adolescent (burial 168) were adorned with *Glycymeris* shell bracelets.

Late Three Circle phase secondary cremations, however, were treated quite differently. An array of items apparently accompanied the body in the crematorium. The list might include any of the following: smashed bowls, jars, pitchers, shell beads, turquoise beads, stone beads, *Glycymeris* shell bracelets, stone palettes, sherd palettes, obsidian arrow points, chert arrow points, a painted stone, a paho stick, and burned corn. For secondary cremations placed in pits, burned shell artifacts were often mixed in with the token amounts of calcined bone, and other burned items such as palettes or palette fragments, arrow points, and corn were included in the ashy fill and capped with sherds from smashed crematory vessels. On the basis of the inventory size of included items, these cremations contained the most associated items at the site.

Classic period mortuary practices continued the patterns of association established in the Late Three Circle phase. Six out of 10 inhumations in corporate cemeteries were associated with at least one "killed" mortuary bowl. Males and females were accompanied with "killed" mortuary vessels, but the occurrence of multiple vessels accompanied predominately female burials, and most cases of multiple-vessel inclusion occurred in the south room block. As noted above, a strong pattern of placing a cairn at the top of the grave existed during the Classic period, especially for adults and larger subadults. Adornment jewelry (beaded necklaces, wristlets, anklets, pendants of turquoise, stone, and shell) occurred sparingly and is regarded as a male characteristic. All unequivocal instances of adornment jewelry on adults that could confidently be sexed occurred on males. Jewelry items were found with the graves of six adult females, but none of the jewelry items were in a position to suggest an item of adornment. In most cases, loose pieces of jewelry were recovered from the grave fill, either as an accidental inclusion or from graves disturbed by the interment of that individual. Burial 161 is an excellent example. At least three infant graves were destroyed by the excavation of the burial 161 grave; any one of these infants could have had adornment jewelry. *Glycymeris* shell bracelets on adults ($n = 6$) were found exclusively on males; also, unequivocal cases of adornment jewelry on adults involved males. Unsexed infants and children with *Glycymeris* bracelets and jewelry were very likely males as well. Occasionally loose jewelry items (a pendant, turquoise item, or shell bead) were recovered from the grave fill and are listed as associated in Table 8.1, for example, burial 130 in room 76, but these clearly should not be given the same weight in consideration as adornment items. The association of males with specific kinds of jewelry—*Glycymeris* shell bracelets, shell beads, turquoise, and red or black stone—might have identified these individuals as members of certain sodalities that crosscut lineages. The existence of such sodalities would have been advantageous for corporate groups in times when intensive labor was needed to maintain or repair irrigation networks. The exception to the association of jewelry items with sodalities may be the cremations.

Animal Burials

Animal burials are infrequently found in Mimbres sites, but if the NAN Ranch Ruin is typical, they were far more frequent than extant excavation reports suggest. Isolated occurrences of animal burials have been reported from the Cameron Creek, Swarts, Galaz, and Old Town ruins, most of them exotic parrots and macaws.[38] Two bird burials, for example, were reported from Cameron Creek. A macaw (*Ara macao*) was found with an adult male human burial in room 60 at that site, and a second animal burial, identified only as a parrot, was found by the entrance of pithouse 148. This parrot was covered by a plate-form vessel. A rabbit burial was found with a human infant at the Swarts Ruin, and the rabbit was covered with part of a ceramic bowl much like that in many human burials. The skeleton of a large bird was also found with a child burial (2-86) at Galaz; five turquoise beads accompanied the bird. Another macaw was recovered from the floor of kiva room 73 at Galaz, wrapped in strings of turquoise and shell beads, and a scarlet macaw was recovered from a structure wall at Old Town.

The largest assemblage of animal burials other than at the NAN Ranch Ruin is from the Wind Mountain site ($n = 24$), near Silver City, where a site was completely excavated. Wind Mountain burials include canids, birds, and a bear.[39] Eight canids, buried with 10 individuals, were the most common animal represented. The single bear burial, identified only as *Ursus* sp., is unique for the region. Among the bird burials were six turkeys in five burials, two golden eagles, a scarlet macaw, three hawks in two burials, and one mourning dove. The only animal burial with possible mortuary items was the macaw, which was associated with a mano with traces of mineral pigment. The temporal span of the Wind Mountain burials could be from the Three Circle phase through the Classic Mimbres period.

Twenty-three separate animal burials were recorded at the NAN Ranch Ruin. These include two canids (dogs), eight turkeys, five kestrals, five hawks, one eagle, one quail, and one jay. No exotic animals or birds are included in the sample, although macaws have been recovered from Mimbres sites.[40] Proveniences for each animal burial are listed in Table 8.9. The only burial with burial furniture was a turkey (*Meleagris gallopavo*), interred with a bird effigy pendant (Figure 11.13, p. 206, top right).

Burial location varied from plazas, both east and west, middens, and subfloor. Turkey burials were found beneath the floors of rooms 49, 54/61, 57, and 89A. Three turkey burials were also encountered in the southern end of the east plaza, and one was in the Classic midden between the east and west room blocks. Kestrals (*Falco* sp., probably *sparverius*) were found beneath the floors of rooms 8, 60, and 96 and in the southeast midden at the southern end of the east plaza. Hawks (*Buteo* sp.) were buried beneath the floors of room 82 and in the fill beneath room 109, in the midden at the southeast plaza, and in the Classic period midden between the east and west room blocks. The specimen in room 82 was covered with a single rhyolite slab (Figure 8.12, p. 161). A single jay (family Corvidae) was recovered from the southeast midden. A golden eagle (*Aquila chrysaetos*) was intrusive in the floor of room 83 and was stratigraphically dated to the Late Three Circle phase. Two dogs (*Canis* spp.) were among the animal burials; one was placed in the ruins of room 90 and the other in the southeast midden.

All animal burials at the NAN Ranch Ruin date to the

TABLE 8.9. Animal Burials at the NAN Ranch Ruin

Taxon	Context	Number	Age	Phase
cf. Kestrel	Room 8	1	Adult	Classic
Turkey	Room 57	1	Adult	Late Three Circle
Turkey	Room 54/61	1	Adult	Late Three Circle
cf. Kestrel	Room 60	1	Adult	Classic
Turkey	Room 49	1	Adult	Classic
Hawk	Midden a	1	Adult	Classic
Eagle	Room 83	1	Adult	Late Three Circle
Turkey	Midden	1	Juvenile	Classic
Hawk	Room 82	1	Adult	Classic
Turkey	Room 89A	1	Adult	Late Three Circle
Hawk	Midden	1	Adult	Classic
Jay	Southeast midden b	1	Juvenile	Classic
cf. Kestrel	Midden	1	Adult	Classic
cf. Kestrel	Southeast midden	1	Adult	Classic
Quail	Southeast midden	1	Adult	Classic
Turkey	Southeast midden	1	Adult	Classic
Turkey	Southeast midden	1	Adult	Classic
Turkey	Southeast midden	1	Adult	Classic
Hawk	Southeast midden	1	Adult	Classic
cf. Kestrel	Room 96	1	Adult	Classic
cf. Kestrel	Room 107	1	Adult	Classic
Canid	Southeast midden	1	Juvenile	Late Three Circle/Classic
Dog	Room 78/90	1	Juvenile	Classic

a Midden in east room block couryard above room 17 and between east and west room blocks (Figure p.2).
b Southeast midden is at the south end of the east plaza, overlying rooms 86 and 95 (Figure p.2).

Late Three Circle and Classic phases. The golden eagle and the turkeys in rooms 89A, 57, and 54/61 have been stratigraphically dated to the Late Three Circle phase. The remaining animal burials date to sometime in the Classic period.

Animals are not frequently interred in Mimbres sites and represent ritual disposal, as shown by the intentional burials and manner and inclusion of mortuary items. Two bird burials, one beneath the floor of room 82 and the other in the east plaza, were capped with slabs in much the same fashion as certain human burials in the Classic period. A turkey was buried beneath the floor of room 57 with a bird effigy amulet. One burial in the southeast midden contained two turkeys. The golden eagle, a kestrel, and three turkey burials lacked the cranium. Headless bird burials do occur among the assemblages of animal burials across the Southwest,[41] but since bird burials at the NAN Ruin were generally poorly preserved, often disturbed, missing elements were common. It is not possible to determine if the birds were decapitated prior to burial, although one method of killing birds used among Pueblo groups was wringing the necks.[42]

Totemic association with animals is very widespread worldwide, including among Native American groups. The reasons for ritual disposal of selected animals are unknown, but the behavior might pertain to totemic association of kin or corporate groups. Valli Powell[43] has shown that animal images on Mimbres Style III pottery are more frequent at some sites than others and identified fishes and birds as being the most commonly represented forms at the NAN Ranch Ruin. Birds shown on vessels that also appear in the burial assemblage include turkey, quail, and possibly hawk. The burial of birds might also relate to the uses made of their feathers as parts of costuming, wands, or pahos (prayer sticks). The ritual disposal of bird wings, probably used as fans in ceremonies or healing rituals, is not uncommon across the Southwest.[44]

Animal parts, especially the heads of deer, bison, and other large animals, are used as costuming among Southwestern Pueblo groups. Uses of deer head disguises are shown on Mimbres pottery. Bird heads may also have been used in ritual paraphernalia; this may account for the beheaded burials. The top part of a deer cranium with antlers was found on the floor of room 41. The item was either hung from a wall or on the floor at the time the room burned. Part of an articulated hind leg of an artiodactyl was found embedded in a Late Three Circle phase wall of room 110, perhaps part of a ritual offering. Also, a bobcat paw was found as part of the defacto floor assemblages in room 36.

Comparison of the Wind Mountain and NAN Ranch animal burial assemblages reveals some interesting similarities and differences. Forty-two percent of the Wind Mountain burials were canids, and birds made up 50 percent of the sample. In contrast, canids represented only 9 percent of the NAN sample, whereas birds represented 81 percent. Temporal bias in the two samples may account for the similarities and differences. Wind Mountain is primarily a Three Circle and Late Three Circle phase village, with a small Classic period component. The NAN Ranch Ruin has a relatively small Three Circle phase component, a relatively large Late Three Circle phase component, and a very large Classic component. Although the temporal placement of many Wind Mountain animal burials cannot be assessed simply because they lack diagnostic mortuary items, their distribution generally follows that of the extramural human burials. The temporal bias in the Wind Mountain sample is more likely toward the earlier components, whereas those at the NAN Ruin are

8.12: Bird burial beneath the floor of room 82 at the NAN Ranch Ruin.

clearly toward the Classic component. The point is that the high frequency of canids at Wind Mountain may reflect a higher participation in hunting, perhaps with the assistance of dogs. Bird burials at both sites may be due to a rise in the importance of corporate and public ceremonies in the Late Three Circle and Classic times and the uses of feathers and wings in ceremonial paraphernalia.

Summary

Were there "big men" in Mimbres society? If so, none were found at the NAN Ranch Ruin, and previous studies at other Mimbres sites failed to unequivocally identify high-status burials. This does not mean that status was not expressed in Mimbres mortuary practices, but evidence for vertical ranking has not been forthcoming. Burials such as 86, 104, 127, and 175 raise the issue of acquired status in the late San Francisco and Three Circle phase. Burial 86 was an adult female buried in the floor of room 14. Grave contents suggest that she was a Mimbres potter. Other burials containing notable assemblages include burial 127, an adult male placed in a sitting position in a specially prepared crypt dug into the north wall of pithouse 86. The crypt was walled up with cobble-adobe masonry. Crypt contents include a tubular cloudblower pipe, a quartz crystal, a turtle plastron, two *Olivella* shell beads, and two small biface projectile points, but unfortunately, no pottery. Burial 175, the primary cremation described above, received the special treatment of a public cremation that involved the excavation of the crematorium pit, gathering wood, and construction of the rack supporting the body. If importance is indicated by the amount of energy put forth in preparation and completion of the funerary process, then certainly the latter two burials would be suspect. No such special treatment was afforded burials in the Late Three Circle and Classic phases.

All of these burials stand out in some way. Burials 86 and 104, both females, were given intramural treatment, rare for Three Circle phase burials at the NAN Ranch Ruin. The assortment of artifacts associated with burial 127 suggests an assemblage of items that could be used in curing ceremonies (quartz crystal, cloudblower pipe, projectile points). This male may have been a shaman and an oracle. The makeshift cave in which he was placed was positioned in such a way that entry into the structure would allow visitation to the crypt. Note also that the entrance to room 86 was to the west; whether this has any bearing on the crypt is unknown but is perhaps something to consider.

The Late Pithouse period mortuary patterns suggest the possibility of a dialectic existing between the incipient emergence of more powerful male individuals based on personal achievement and the initial trend toward matri-centered households connected to prime agricultural lands. This is not to suggest males were elevated far above everyone else but that a trend in that direction may have been emerging in Three Circle phase semisedentary pithouse communities. This might indicate that the communities were held together by individuals recognized for their skills in crafts and leadership. The people who achieved such status in the community included both males and females whose roles were defined on the basis of sex (e.g., women making pots used in kiva ceremonies, men orchestrating healing ceremonies and leading task groups). These family clusters were unified through ceremonies and rituals carried out in the great kivas. If such a dialectic existed, the trend toward agricultural intensification decided the issue, and matri-centered lineage households won out. The Late Three Circle phase saw the establishment of these corporate households and cemeteries for certain families.

CHAPTER NINE

Bioarchaeology of the Mimbres People

Introduction

The success of any subsistence-oriented economic system is reflected in the overall health and physical development of its population. This evidence can be preserved in the skeletal record. Information derived from analysis of skeletal material can provide information on overall life expectancy and death rates, demographic makeup of the population, overall health and nutrition, stature, growth rates, and differential risks in the roles of males versus females. Skeletal analysis can also provide information on genetic affiliations.

Life in a pueblo community during the eleventh century was not easy by modern standards. The Mimbreños, however, were oblivious to the fact that better conditions may have been experienced by people living elsewhere. The Mimbres Valley and surrounding physical and social landscapes defined their world, a world in which they had learned to cope and survive as a population. Spending time in a pueblo room during cold nights and winter days with poor lighting and ventilation exposed each Mimbreño to smoke and an ideal environment for communicable diseases. These living conditions were also conducive to poor hygiene and exposed residents, especially children, to a variety of infections. We know, for example, that simple sores sometimes could lead to severe infections, if not worse, and that the chance of survival for a child was about fifty-fifty. In this section, I summarize the skeletal studies that have been done on the NAN Ranch Ruin population and what they reveal about the health and physical characteristics of the Mimbres.

Physical Characteristics

Males at the NAN Ranch Ruin had an average height of 162 cm, or 5 ft, 4 in. The average female stood 154.9 cm, or 5 ft, 1 in. These measurements are based on measurements taken from long bones. Neither males nor females were robust, although comparatively speaking, females were slightly more robust in the upper body than males. This contrast in robusticity was perhaps due to women's lifelong tasks of grinding plant foods and carrying weighty baskets. Males had slightly longer arms in relation to legs than did females.[1]

Facial features were highlighted by modifications created by occipital flattening. This flattening on the back of the skull was caused by confinement to cradle boards for long periods during infancy. Female noses were broad, whereas male noses were average to broad. Faces of males were larger, with more developed brow ridges.[2] We also observed that some adult women had slightly indented foreheads, caused, perhaps, from carrying over their lifetime burden baskets that were supported by tump lines across their foreheads.

Demography

The life expectancy of the Classic period population at the NAN Ruin was short compared to today's western standards but comparable to that of other ancient Pueblo populations and probably not very different from that in underdeveloped countries today. Information on life expectancy comes from a demographic study of the NAN Ranch Ruin skeletal sample by Suzanne Patrick.[3] Demographic archaeology, the study of human populations from archaeological contexts, seeks to learn the demographic trends of a population. Over a broad time span, these trends may include temporal trends of growth, decline, and density. Skewed age or sex numbers could flag areas of critical stress on a population, such as a high mortality rate for adult males due to warfare or an inordinately high mortality rate

Table 9.1. NAN Ruin Classic Phase, Abridged, Composite Life Table, Unsmoothed

	Dx	dx	lx	qx	Lx	Tx	ex
0–1	44	26.3457278	100	0.263457278	86.8271361	1959.450033	19.59450033
1–4.9	27	16.1666966	73.6542722	0.21949435	262.2836956	1872.622897	25.42449801
5–9.9	15	8.981498114	57.48757559	0.156233726	264.9841327	1610.339201	28.01195188
10–14.9	2.046	1.225076343	48.50607748	0.025256141	239.4676965	1345.355069	27.73580422
15–19.9	5.309	3.178851566	47.28100114	0.06723317	228.4578768	1105.887372	23.38967757
20–29.9	13.997	8.380935273	44.10214957	0.190034621	399.1168194	877.4294952	19.89539067
30–39.9	21.777	13.03933896	35.7212143	0.365030675	292.0154482	478.3126759	13.39015723
40–49.9	25.708	15.39309023	22.68187534	0.678651567	149.8533022	186.2972277	8.213484333
50+	12.173	7.288785103	7.288785103	1	36.44392551	36.44392551	5
	= 167.01	= 100					

NAN Ruin Classic Phase, Abridged, Composite Life Table, Smoothed

	Dx	Dx smoothed	dx	lx	qx	Lx	Tx	ex
0–1	44	44	26.16477864	100	0.261647786	86.91761068	1819.550739	18.19550739
1–4.9	27	28.66666667	17.04674972	73.83522136	0.230875582	261.247386	1732.633128	23.46621431
5–9.9	15	14.682	8.730710909	56.78847164	0.153740903	262.1155809	1471.385742	25.90993735
10–14.9	2.046	7.451666667	4.431163837	48.05776073	0.092204959	229.2108941	1209.270161	25.16284868
15–19.9	5.309	7.117333333	4.232351163	43.62659689	0.097013094	207.5521066	980.0592672	22.46471962
20–29.9	13.997	13.69433333	8.143390916	39.39424573	0.206715239	353.2255027	772.5071606	19.60964466
30–39.9	21.777	20.494	12.18684031	31.25085482	0.389968223	251.5743466	419.2816579	13.41664605
40–49.9	25.708	19.886	11.82529064	19.06401451	0.620293833	131.5136919	167.7073113	8.797061668
50+	12.173	12.173	7.238723872	7.238723872	1	36.19361936	36.19361936	5
	= 167.01	= 168.165	= 100					

TABLE 9.1 NAN Ruin Transitional Phase, Abridged, Composite Life Table, Unsmoothed

	Dx	dx	lx	qx	Lx	Tx	ex
0–1	12.376	28.12599427	100	0.281259943	85.93700286	1976.866961	19.76866961
1–4.9	5.626	12.78578246	71.87400573	0.177891608	261.924458	1890.929958	26.30895466
5–9.9	3	6.817871915	59.08822326	0.115384615	278.3964365	1629.0055	27.56903846
10–14.9	1.09	2.477160129	52.27035135	0.047391304	255.1588564	1350.609063	25.83891304
15–19.9	0	0	49.79319122	0	248.9659561	1095.450207	22
20–29.9	4.382	9.958638244	49.79319122	0.2	448.138721	846.4842507	17
30–39.9	8.764	19.91727649	39.83455297	0.5	298.7591473	398.3455297	10
40–49.9	8.764	19.91727649	19.91727649	1	99.58638244	99.58638244	5
50+	0	0	-7.10543E-15	0	-3.55271E-14	-3.55271E-14	5
	= 44.002	= 100					

NAN Ruin Transitional Phase, Abridged, Composite Life Table, Smoothed

	Dx	Dx smoothed	dx	lx	qx	Lx	Tx	ex
0–1	12.376	12.376	28.56175765	100	0.285617576	85.71912118	1681.322697	16.81322697
1–4.9	5.626	7.000666667	16.15637885	71.43824235	0.226158684	253.4402117	1595.603576	22.335426
5–9.9	3	3.238666667	7.474306111	55.2818635	0.135203585	257.7235522	1342.163364	24.27854777
10–14.9	1.09	1.363333333	3.146347468	47.80755739	0.065812763	231.1719183	1084.439812	22.683439
15–19.9	0	1.824	4.209489815	44.66120992	0.094253824	212.7823251	853.2678934	19.10534656
20–29.9	4.382	4.382	10.11293003	40.45172011	0.25	353.9525509	640.4855683	15.83333333
30–39.9	8.764	7.303333333	16.85488338	30.33879008	0.555555556	219.1134839	286.5330174	9.444444444
40–49.9	8.764	5.842666667	13.4839067	13.4839067	1	67.41953351	67.41953351	5
50+	0	0	0	-5.32907E-15	0	-2.66454E-14	-2.66454E-14	5
	= 44.002	= 43.33066667	= 100					

TABLE 9.2. Age and Sex Distribution of Classic Mimbres Phase Burials

Age Interval Totals	No.	% Males	No.	% Females	No.	% Unk Sex	No.	%
1. (0–.9)	–	–	–	–	47	27.3	47	27.3
2. (1–1.9)	–	–	–	–	30	17.4	30	17.5
3. (5–9.9)	–	–	–	–	16	9.3	16	9.30
4. (10–14.9)	–	–	–	–	2	1.2	2	1.10
5. (15–19.9)	2	1.2	2	1.2	–	–	4	2.30
6. (20–29.9)	6	3.5	7	4.1	–	–	13	7.60
7. (30–39.9)	13	7.5	7	4.1	–	–	20	11.6
8. (40–49.9)	14	–	10	5.8	–	–	24	14.0
9. (50+)	–	–	5	2.9	1	0.5	6	3.50
(20+)	3	1.7	2	1.2	3	1.7	8	4.70
(30+)	–	–	2	1.2	–	–	2	1.10
Totals	40	23.3	33	19.3	99	57.4	172	100

to famine and disease. The general makeup of the NAN Ruin population is indicated in age-sex ratios, numbers of surviving children, and overall life expectancy. These demographic patterns are compared to those in other extant skeletal samples in the Southwest to assess how successful the Mimbres culture was in providing for its population.

Patrick's sample included 172 individuals; here analysis was preceded by three assumptions: (1) the sample is random, (2) the biological assessments of age and sex are correct, and (3) the population was stable biologically and socially for the time period being investigated. The randomness of the sample cannot be proven, but it is probably as close to random as one might expect in an ancient population without historic records. One concern might be site sampling, but since large blocks of indoor and outdoor space and a variety of contexts were excavated, it is doubtful that a significant bias was introduced. Furthermore, all articulated burials were analyzed irrespective of preservation conditions. The fact that the NAN Ranch Ruin sample includes several intact household cemeteries that contained interments of all ages and both sexes helps to bolster the randomness argument. The weakness is in the unaffiliated and extramural burials, which are strongly biased toward adult males.

Information on mortality of the Late Three Circle and Classic populations at the NAN Ruin is presented in Table 9.1, in composite and abridged forms. The data from the two temporal populations are presented in a composite form since both populations include samples from an unknown number of generations. Age intervals are presented in abridged rather than single-year classes. Composite and abridged tables tend to smooth out fluctuations experienced by a population through time. The life tables provide information on the number dying (Dx), mortality rate (dx), survival rate (lx), probability of death (qx), number of years lived by persons between age intervals (Lx), total number of years lived after exact age x before all have died (Tx), and average future lifetime (ex). Age estimates for the life tables are presented in nine categories: birth to 1, 1 to 4.9, and continuing at five-year intervals to the age of 20 and in 10-year intervals thereafter.

Patrick focused only on Classic Mimbres phase burials since the samples of previous phases were too small for statistical analysis when divided on the basis of sex. In her sample of 172 individuals, 77 adults were over the age of 15 and 95 were juveniles (Table 9.2).[4] Age estimates in this sample are presented in 12 age categories: birth to 0–9, 1 to 4.9, and continuing at five-year intervals thereafter.

She ended with 50-plus years since it was simply not possible to estimate five-year intervals after age 50. Patrick compared the mortality rates between males and females where sex could be determined. Forty adults were identified as males, 33 as females, and 99 were unsexed, four of which were juveniles.

Age and sex determinations were based on current published standards for making such assessments as well as comparative collections of known chronological age. Criteria used to establish the age of juveniles were tooth calcification and eruption, the degree of epiphyseal union of long bones, and the length of long bones. Age determinations for adults were more problematic since rather than relying on developmental characteristics, one must rely primarily on degenerative changes. After eruption of the third molar and completion of epiphyseal unions in the late teens and early twenties, osteologists must assess adult age based on functional tooth wear, morphological characteristics of the pubic symphysis, relative degrees of obliteration of cranial sutures, general arthritic changes, and parietal thinning. A combination of traits rather than any single trait was used to estimate adult age.

Sex could only be determined with confidence for those individuals over the chronological age of 15. Beyond 15, Patrick felt that she could confidently assess age in 80 percent of cases using both metric and nonmetric criteria. Her confidence was improved when more than one criterion was available. The main nonmetric criteria included the relative width of the sciatic notch, features on the pubic symphysis, and relative robusticity. Patrick also measured the talus, calcaneus, femur, and tibia and used discriminate function values in assessing probability of sex. In some instances she encountered problems in the sex and age estimates because of poor preservation. Another potential source of error was use of a modern reference population for sex and age comparison. It is problematic to assume the reference population matured at the same rates as the archaeological population.

The third supposition Patrick applied in her calculations is the stable population theory, in which it is assumed that if birth and death rates remain constant over time, a characteristic age composition population results and the composition population remains in essence unchanged, barring changes in death rates and catastrophic interference (such as an inordinate loss of young males in warfare). Ideally, a stable population would be one that was both stable and stationary, with no in- or out-migration. Since these conditions are in essence met by the NAN Ranch Ruin sample, a dramatic change in health and nutrition is not anticipated for the Classic Mimbres period, to which most of the skeletal sample dates. Therefore, although we might assume the population was "stable" in a sense, the population is not assumed to be stationary. We have demonstrated the likelihood that some "outsiders" were buried within the village, and considerable social interaction took place both in and out of the NAN community. Despite the fact that the conditions for a stable and stationary population cannot be met, Patrick proceeded, rationalizing that although fluctuations may occur from year to year, they averaged out over the accumulated time represented by the sample. She treated the sample as a group of people theoretically born at the same time, who stayed in the same place, and followed them through successive years until they died. By treating the sample as a quasi-stable population, Patrick could calculate crude death rates and an age distribution profile that could be compared to similarly derived data from other extant skeletal samples.

Combining the information from the two studies by Patrick provides insight into the demographic characteristics of the NAN Ruin population in the Late Three Circle and Classic phases. Life tables show that infant mortality rates were high, especially at or shortly after birth, 26.35 percent, and 42.52 percent before children reached the age of five. During the primary childbearing years of 15 to 39.9, the mortality rate was expected to be slightly higher for females, but this was not the case: the highest mortality among females was in the 40 to 49-year range (14 percent). The heaviest male death rate came in the 30 to 49.9 bracket (81.5 percent) of adult male deaths. Life expectancy at birth was only 17.75 years, undoubtedly skewed by the high infant mortality rate. After reaching one year, the odds improved to 23.09 years; if one survived until five years of age, the chances were good that the individual would live to 30. The high mortality at birth is attributed to the stresses of births in such primitive conditions, whereas that at three may reflect the combined stresses of weaning and increased infection rates as children fended more for themselves. Mortality rates drop off sharply from eight to 18 years.[5]

The low mean skeletal age at death can be used as an indication of rising birth rate.[6] The high infant mortality rate may be an artifact of a higher birth rate. Patrick calculated the child/women ratio (CWR + N of children less than 5/N of women greater than 15 times 100). Her

TABLE 9.3. Child/Women Ratios

Period	Females +15	Children -5	Ratio
Classic	28	77	275
Late Three Circle	8	16	200

TABLE 9.4. Crude Mortality Rates

Site	Temporal Sample	Rate
NAN	Classic	59.38
	Late Three Circle	66.66
	All Phases	59.7
Grasshopper Ruin	Preabandonment	50.86
	Total Sample	70.57
Salmon Ruin		78.43
Point of the Pines		43.69
Turkey Creek		51
Chaco Canyon		37.72

sample included 24 Late Three Circle phase burials and 105 Classic examples. Her figures, shown in Table 9.3, suggest an increase in fertility in the Classic period, which may partly explain the population increase during this time. These findings, however, should be viewed with caution since the Late Three Circle phase sample may be skewed due to an under representation of infants and small children, who may have been placed in extramural contexts. Typically extramural burials are more poorly preserved and more subject to disturbances than those placed beneath floors.

Patrick also calculated the crude mortality rates for the NAN Ruin sample and compared the results to those from other Southwest Pueblo sites (Table 9.4). Crude mortality rates ($M = 1,000/x$, where x is the life expectancy at birth) are a useful comparative tool if the populations are stable and the samples are comparable. Although we cannot be confident that either of these conditions is met, the rate does provide a means of comparing the NAN Ruin population to others in the Southwest. Table 9.4 shows that the NAN Ranch Ruin sample is closer to those from the Grasshopper and Salmon ruins, probably because of better sampling strategies and less likelihood of artificially skewed samples.

Another measure of the relative success of a culture's ability to provide for its population is the comparative study of subadult growth rates. Marianne Marek[7] studied growth of the NAN Ruin Mimbres population. She examined 57 subadults with measurable long bones and dentition to determine the pattern of long bone growth. She defined subadult as any individual whose bones were still actively growing at the time of death, which included individuals from fetal to 18 or 20 years of age. Growth curves are determined by estimating the chronological age of each subadult, based on the sequence of tooth formation and eruption in North American Indian populations,[8] and measuring these individuals' long bones with unfused epiphyses. Marek measured the length of all measurable long bones (femur, tibia, fibula, humerus, radius, and ulna) and grouped them according to chronological age. Since sex assignment for subadults under 15 years is not reliable (distinguishing sex characteristics have not developed), growth rate was not examined by sex. Despite the fact that the NAN Ruin sample is considered small, Marek was able to provide some intriguing information. She compared the results with published data on long bone growth of prehistoric North American Indian populations from Indian Knoll (Kentucky), Grasshopper Pueblo (Arizona), and New Mexico pueblos and the prehistoric Arikara and Eskimos to determine if the samples differed.

Indian Knoll, Kentucky, is an Eastern Archaic site, and the skeletal sample represents a population of hunters and gatherers. Marek found that the samples were comparable up to about one year of age; after one year, the Indian Knoll long bone lengths exceeded the Mimbres lengths in each of the age categories except 15 years. Although the differences were not great, the samples suggest that the Indian Knoll people may have had a more balanced diet, since growth rates are largely determined by dietary patterns. Certainly the Indian Knoll population had more access to animal protein through hunting and fishing.

The Arikara were Caddoan-speaking Plains Indian farmers and bison hunters dating to the prehistoric period. Comparisons with the Arikara sample show almost identical results with the Indian Knoll sample; that is, up to one year, the samples are comparable, but after one year, the Arikara long bone lengths exceed those from the NAN Ranch sample. If bone lengths from Indian Knoll and the Arikara population were used to estimate ages for the NAN Ranch Ruin children, the ages for the latter would be underestimated. A probable reason for the healthier growth rate of the Arikara children is that they enjoyed a higher intake of animal protein after weaning, if bison were readily available to these populations, something that appears to have been denied the NAN Ranch Ruin children.

Contrasting with the Indian Knoll and Arikara findings, comparisons with Eskimo skeletal samples show long bone lengths for Eskimos to be shorter than those for the Mimbres. Although animal protein was not a problem for Eskimos, other environmental and genetic conditions may have been responsible for the shorter long bone means. The NAN Ruin sample bone lengths compare most closely with those from Grasshopper Pueblo, followed by other New Mexico pueblo samples, particularly from fetal to six years.

These findings suggest that growth rates for the children at the NAN Ranch Ruin were in keeping with those from other Southwestern Pueblo populations but were behind those of Plains village Indians and Eastern Archaic populations. Although it is not possible to determine why these differences exist, we can speculate that it was the lack of a balanced diet, especially a lack of animal protein, for the Southwestern Pueblo people, including the Mimbres. Given the environment and geographic locations, the Arikara and Indian Knoll populations probably fared better in this regard. Other environmental and physiological factors may explain the differences between the Pueblo people and the Eskimo populations.

Osteology and Intrasite Comparisons

Was the NAN Ruin population relatively homogenous in regard to meeting nutritional needs of respective families? Or were some families better off and so displayed better overall health and growth rates than others? Diane Young Holliday used osteological data to determine if certain lineage populations identified by cemetery association could be distinguished on the basis of diet, health, and size. The south room block exhibited slightly better architecture and contained more burials with multiple mortuary vessels than any other subgroup at the site. These differences suggest that the south room block may have housed the prime lineage in the village. If this was the ranking lineage and had access to the best agricultural lands, then the people residing in the south room block could have been better fed. Holliday hypothesized that if some lineage population was better fed than others, then these dietary differences might be reflected in differential susceptibility to illness and infection. She used the skeletal samples from the NAN Ranch Ruin to test this notion by comparing the south and east room block skeletal samples for bone composition (using trace element and stable isotope analysis), growth and development, frequencies of subadult anemia, dental health, skeletal evidence of infection, and trauma and degenerative changes. Although her data failed to show the south room block population as better fed, her findings provided some suggestions of behavioral variability within the NAN Ruin village.

To examine variability in diet, Holliday relied on trace element and stable isotope analysis. Unfortunately, her results were limited due to poor bone preservation but did provide some intriguing hints despite the small size of her sample ($n = 7$). Not surprisingly, carbon isotope analysis confirmed that the Classic Mimbres population relied heavily on maize. Her results also suggest that individuals buried in the middens may have exploited a wider range of resources and were not as dependent on maize. This finding supports previous interpretations that individuals buried in the middens were not affiliated with the lineages interred beneath the architecture. There is a caveat, however: the midden sample includes the only female and only early Classic phase burial in this small sample. Therefore we cannot rule out that the apparent difference between midden and room blocks may actually reflect factors of sex and/or time periods. Her evidence also suggests, based on low barium levels found in both the south and east room block populations, that the Mimbreños at the NAN Ranch Ruin pretreated maize with an alkaline or lime substance, a common practice of people with maize-dependent diets. Maize is very low in calcium, and this pretreatment increased the amount of available calcium.

Holliday also compared the room block samples for growth rates, adult size achieved, subadult anemia, infection, trauma, degenerative changes, and four dental disorders: enamel hypoplasias, caries, abscesses, and antemortem tooth loss. Overall, she found few differences between the two south and east room block samples, but the differences observed were intriguing. Her analysis of growth rates and body size revealed that adult males in the south room block had slightly larger bones than those in the east, but these differences are not statistically significant. Interestingly, Holliday found two statistically significant differences between the south and east room block females. The south room block females had more robust arms and, conversely, narrower tibia. Holliday cautions that these differences are difficult to interpret but could be either genetic or perhaps the result of different levels of use. For example, studies suggest that narrow, or platycnemic, tibias are the result of greater anterior-posterior strain, like that produced in climbing or running over uneven ground.

Holliday also compared the NAN Ruin room block samples for frequencies of bone marrow hyperplasia, or anemia, called porotic hyperostosis and cribra orbitalia, which results in spongy or coral-like appearance of the bone. Porotic hyperostosis typically occurs on the parietal, occipital, and frontal bones of the skull but may also occur on the sphenoid and temporal bones. Cribra orbitalia consists of porotic lesions within the eye orbits and is generally considered related to porotic hyperostosis. Cribra orbitalia was found in 35.9 percent of the 39 subadults examined. Ten of the 55 subadults (18.2 percent) exhibited porotic hyperostosis. Overall, the differences in frequencies of porotic hyperostosis and cribra orbitalia between the east and south room blocks were not significant. If one includes the more diffuse and smaller pitting noted on many parietals along with the more definitive evidence of porotic hyperostosis, however, the east room block group did fare worse (73.9 percent in the east room block compared to 39.3 percent in the south). The peak occurrence of both porotic hyperostosis and cribra orbitalia was in children between the ages of one and three years; again, those critical years of weaning. The children at the NAN Ranch Ruin were either not getting an adequate supply of iron in their diet, or, if they were, did not absorb sufficient iron due to diarrhea or other infections, or they were losing it through blood loss from parasites.

The NAN Ruin skeletal sample was also examined for evidence of infectious diseases that affect human bone. Most likely to have been present in the prehistoric Southwest were osteomyelitis, periostitis, tuberculosis, coccidioidomycosis, and possibility treponemal infections. Osteomyelitis is caused by a bacterial infection in the bone such as staphylococcal organisms. Periostitis, an inflammation of the membrane covering the bone, is symptomatic of a number of disorders, as well as trauma. Both tuberculosis and coccidioidomycosis result in the formation of osteolytic lesions, especially in the vertebrae. Treponematoses—yaws, inta, venereal syphilis, and endemic syphilis—are infections of spiral microorganisms called treponemes, and treponematoses usually indicate an advanced state of development of these diseases.

Holliday examined 140 individuals and found that 42.1 percent exhibited some evidence of infection, either active or healed, at the time of death. She found no difference in the frequency of infections between the adults in the east and south room blocks; subadults in the south room block showed a slightly higher frequency, but it was not statistically significant. The most common form of infection was healed lesions on the occipital bones: 44.8 percent of adults and 43.3 percent of subadults had active or healed scalp lesions at the time of death.

In sum, Holliday saw no significant difference in the incidence of infection among the people in the east and south room blocks or in the midden sample. The frequency of infections at the NAN Ruin appears much higher than that reported from any other Mimbres site, but Holliday cautions these figures can be adjusted on the

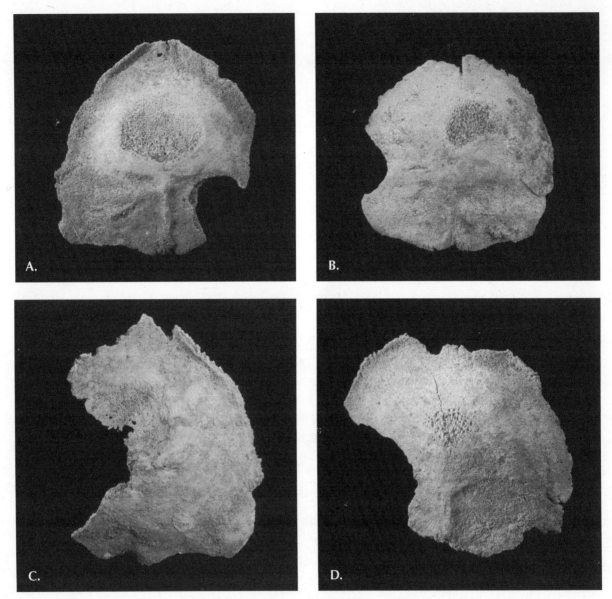

9.1: Examples of occipital lesions on infants from the NAN Ranch Ruin (photos courtesy of Diane Holliday).

basis of sample composition and skeletal completeness. When these adjustments are made, the figures for frequency of infection at the NAN Ruin are comparable to those from the Old Town Ruin and other reported Mimbres samples. Comparisons with other Southwestern pueblo samples, however, are difficult for a number of reasons, chief among them sample size, preservation, and differences in analytical methodologies. Overall, the frequency of infections for NAN Ranch Ruin population is comparable to that of other Southwestern populations, with the exception of Black Mesa in northeastern Arizona, where skeletal lesions appear to have been more frequent. Holliday found no definitive evidence of tuberculosis, treponemal infection, or coccidioidomycosis at the NAN Ranch. However, the poorly preserved remains of one adult, burial 58, suggest the possibility of the latter. Additionally, burial 1 may have been affected by coccidioidomycosis, although it was not indicated on the bones. The burial was encased in an adobe cast, naturally formed around the body. A few days after I broke through this cast

TABLE 9.5. Summary of Dental Disorders (% of population affected / % of teeth affected)

Sample	Caries		Periodontal Disease		Abscessing	
NAN Ruin	68%	14.8%	89%	53%	37%	3%
Swarts	48	–	41	–	19	–
Galaz	23	11	94	–	–	–
Cameron Creek	–	8	–	–	–	–
Average agricultural population	–	11.8	–	–	57	–

Source: After Olive 1989: Table 4.25; also incoporating data from Patterson 1984, Table 4.2, and Berry 1985.

and exposed the burial in 1978, I was diagnosed with this disease, and, according to the attending physician, I may have breathed ancient live spores of this malady.

All observable crania at the NAN Ranch exhibited occipital flattening to some degree, resulting from the use of a hard cradle board in infancy. One very interesting consequence of this practice observed by Holliday was that a surprising percentage of individuals had occipital lesions, or traces of diseased bone at the back of the head[9] (Figure 9.1). The location of each lesion just above the external occipital protuberance was very consistent. She also noted that no child over the age of one exhibited a lesion that would have been active at the time of death, but older children and adults exhibited evidence of healed lesions in this same area of the skull. The restricted location and ages of active and healed lesions suggested to Holliday that the pathology was related to the use of cradle boards. She suggests that the pressure and friction of an infant's head may have caused ischemic ulcers or bacterial infections such as impetigo or carbuncles.

Dental Health

The oral health and hygiene of the NAN Ruin skeletal sample were also examined, through an analysis of teeth. Teeth are usually the best-preserved part of a skeleton and are not subject to remodeling. They form a permanent record of developmental history and also preserve evidence of wear and trauma. Childhood stresses, oral health and hygiene, dietary habits, subsistence base, and use of teeth as tools can all be reflected in the tooth enamel. For these reasons, dental analysis provides valuable information on the quality of past lifeways. Also, genetic traits exhibited on teeth can provide information on population affinities.

Both Ben Olive and Holliday examined the oral health of the NAN Ruin sample, and Olive also examined morphological traits of the teeth. Olive's sample consisted of 27 individuals, 16 males and 11 females (Table 9.5). He recorded such dental disorders as periodontal disease, calculus, caries, trauma, and enamel hypoplasias and compared the frequencies of these dental disorders with those of other populations with similar subsistence lifeways. He discovered that males in the NAN Ruin sample had statistically significant higher frequencies of several types of disorders than did females, such as abscessing, calculus formation, and periodontal disease (such as alveolar resorption). Abscessing differences could either be an indication of slight differences in the diets of males versus females; differences in calculus formation could be due either to females using their teeth as tools, resulting in calculus removal, or to a differential intake of minerals. The higher rate of alveolar resorption in males may also be due to a higher incidence of calcerous deposits.

Olive's analysis showed that 14.8 percent of the teeth examined were affected by caries, which is above the average of 11.8 percent for an agricultural society in the Southwest. Abscesses occurred in 37 percent of the NAN Ruin individuals, which is considerably lower than the average rate of 56 percent for other prehistoric agricultural societies. Frequency of periodontal disease is high in the NAN Ruin sample (89 percent), which is consistent with that at Galaz (94 percent) but is much higher than that recorded for Swarts (41 percent). No figures are available for the frequency of periodontal disease in the average prehistoric agricultural population. Olive attributes differences in the frequency of dental disorders such as calculus formation between the two sexes to differences in diet. He suggests that males enjoyed a diet higher in certain minerals and vitamins.

Enamel hypoplasia lines and pits observable on tooth crowns are developmental defects that can be caused by stress, malnutrition, diarrhea diseases, and parasite infection during periods of tooth growth. Twenty-eight percent of the teeth examined exhibited traces of at least one hypoplasic pit or groove. This frequency was divided about equally among the males (50 percent), whereas 64 percent of the females were affected. Olive's findings showed that most hypoplasias formed in young children between the ages of two and four years old, the post-weaning period. This stands as independent verification of the other indicators of stress in this age group noted by both Patrick and Holliday and brackets the time when weaning usually occurs in subsistence-oriented cultures, with the change from a milk diet to a diet of solid foods. The prevalence of hypoplasias among two- to four-year-old children also correlates with the relatively high death rate for children in this age group, further suggesting that enamel hypoplasia in this population was probably related to periods of dietary stress experienced during weaning.

Olive concludes that the kinds and frequencies of dental disorders in the NAN Ranch Ruin sample are consistent with that of other prehistoric agricultural groups, although they are a bit higher compared to those of other Mimbres populations. The comparisons with other Mimbres populations, however, come with the caveat that the analyses were done by different people using different methodological criteria.

Holliday examined incidences of hypoplasias, caries, abscesses, and rates of antemortem losses. Her study included a larger sample but generally supported Olive's findings. She discovered, however, that the south room block females suffered significantly greater numbers of antemortem tooth loss than any other group within the NAN Ruin village. Conversely, the south room block males lost the fewest teeth. These findings are difficult to interpret, but perhaps the greater tooth loss was one downside for the south room block females for having greater longevity.

Genetic Affiliation

No DNA studies have been conducted on the NAN Ruin skeletal sample, but some information on genetic affiliation has been provided through the study of the teeth. Christy Turner II[10] examined the crown morphology of teeth from the NAN Ranch Ruin skeletal sample to determine if possible the epigenetic relationship of the NAN Ruin population to all other populations in the American Southwest and northern Mexico. Crown morphology is determined by growth and development largely regulated by polygenic inheritance, and crown trait frequencies better reflect ancient patterns because they are less susceptible to genetic and environmental shifts.

The NAN Ruin sample was compared to 23 other groups using 20 trait frequencies. The data were then subjected to multivariate statistical analysis. The results showed that the NAN Ranch Ruin population compared more closely to Casas Grandes (Paquimé) and other samples from northern Mexico than to other populations. This finding can be interpreted in several ways but could suggest that descendants of the NAN Ruin population resided in northern Chihuahua, not with the Western Pueblos or Hohokam.

Summary

In physical appearance, males averaged 162 cm, or 5 ft, 4 in, in stature, whereas females stood 154.9 cm, or 5 ft, 1 in. Collectively, the adult population was not robust, but comparatively, females were slightly more robust in the upper body than males. This telltale finding suggests a more laborious lifestyle for the women. Flattened heads resulted in wider skulls; noses were generally broad, slightly more so among women. Mouths were medium to wide, but faces were not prognathic.

The Classic Mimbres community at the NAN Ranch Ruin fared no better or worse than their Pueblo counterparts at Grasshopper, Arroyo Hondo, and other southwestern sites in regard to health and nutrition. Based on growth rates, however, they were not as well provisioned as Arikara Plains village farmers or the hunters and gathers of western Kentucky. This difference in growth rate can probably be attributed to the character of the Mimbres diet, which was heavy in starchy foods and low in animal protein. As a consequence, the population is characterized by relatively small long bones and high incidence of dental caries compared to the Plains and Eastern Archaic populations. Genetics could account for some of these differences, but a predominantly corn-based diet is probably a more likely cause.

There is a tantalizing hint of differences between groups within the NAN Ruin village. Although Holliday found only a few statistically significant differences, all were for south room block females. She found hints that the south room block women had slightly more robust arms and narrower tibias and suffered more ante-mortem tooth loss than other groups in the village. These differences are difficult to interpret, but the fact that the only statistically significant differences were for south room block females suggests that this group somehow was distinct from the rest of the village. Males buried in the middens perhaps enjoyed a more varied diet, suggesting that these people may not have been affiliated with the resident lineages. Single or unaffiliated males may have been more mobile in a matrilocal community and would have had access to a wider spectrum of foods. Olive also suggests that differences in dental disorders between males and females were the result of differences in diet and the intake of certain vitamins and minerals.

Living conditions undoubtedly contributed to health and hygiene problems as well. Although sedentary village life provided certain advantages in child rearing, it also created potentially favorable conditions for infectious diseases such as bacterial infections, diarrhea, and impetigo. The high mortality rate of children under five years and the presence of lesions attributed to confinement to cradle boards reflect poor hygienic conditions and nutritional stress associated with weaning.

The processes of sedentary lifeway and population increase in the Late Three Circle and Classic phases led to greater social differentiation within Mimbres society. As shown in previous chapters, social differentiation is apparent in architecture and mortuary patterns. Ceramic styles, the subject of the next chapter, also clearly point to social differentiation among the Mimbreños.

CHAPTER TEN
Mimbres Pottery

INTRODUCTION

Prehistoric southwestern cultures are known for outstanding creations in their material worlds. For example, the architecture of the Chaco Anasazi, as seen at Pueblo Bonito and Aztec; the cliff dwellings of the Mesa Verde Anasazi; the platform mounds and great houses of the Classic Hohokam of Arizona; and the great pueblo site of Paquime are identifying markers of these ancient cultures. For the ancient Mimbreños, it was not architecture, but pottery that set them apart from other ancient Pueblo cultures in the American Southwest and northern Mexico.

Archaeologists and art historians have paid much attention to the creativity and execution of Mimbres painted pottery designs, but the ancient Mimbreños were not the best ancient potters in the Southwest. Their pots are often lopsided and rarely symmetrical; some are thick, and others are thin. The clays used by the potters naturally fired to an uneven dark brown finish that had to be coated with a white kaolin clay slip before it could be painted. And when firing pots, the potters were not always able to control the oxygen and the paint was sometimes uneven. It was the use of this poorly formed brownware pottery as a canvass for expressing cultural myths and themes that identified the Mimbres among their contemporaries.

Mogollon pottery is characterized by a brownware paste composed of iron-rich clays heavily mixed with tempering agents composed of sand, crushed rock, mica, or a combination of the three. When fired, the natural oxidized colors of the clays prevailed, yielding hues varying from light tan, orange, brown, or black. From the Early Pithouse period through the Three Circle phase, Mogollon ceramic assemblages are remarkably consistent regardless of the region. This broad similarity is likely due to the relatively high residential mobility of the people, and pottery sherds left behind probably reflect their movements across the landscape and social sphere. Production of the white-slipped series, which began in the Three Circle phase with Three Circle Red-on-white and Style I Black-on-white, defined the Mimbres area within the broader Mogollon region. The more restricted geographic distribution of the white-slipped wares probably correlates with increases in population and decrease in residential mobility. Further decrease in residential mobility to a sedentary lifestyle is posited for the Late Three Circle and Classic Mimbres phases, when it is possible to recognize microstyles within Styles II and III produced in the Mimbres Valley.

All complete and nearly complete vessels recovered from the NAN Ranch Ruin excavations are illustrated in the appendix. The order of presentation roughly corresponds to the basic chronological sequence, beginning with redwares and proceeding with Mimbres Style I, II, and III Black-on-white and their respective microstyles. Plain and textured brownwares are presented last, again in approximate chronological order. Table 1 in appendix II provides provenience and metric information for each vessel.

POTTERY PRODUCTION

Pottery manufacture followed time-worn methods that are still used today by certain Pueblo potters.[1] In the following scenario it is assumed that the Mimbres followed similar methods. Ceramic production occurred in stages. The process began by obtaining clays from traditional local outcrops. The clays may have been used without further preparation and simply allowed to dry before mixing of temper and water. If the clay was granular and contained foreign particles, it may have been ground on metates and soaked. The dried clay was then mixed with a tempering agent consisting of ground volcanic rocks or tuft and sand. Size and composition of the temper varied depending on the kind of vessel being made. The paste of painted vessels had finer, smaller, and less angular temper, whereas corrugated jars generally had coarser paste, with more angular tempering particles.

Clays used in pottery manufacture at the NAN Ranch Ruin were quarried from Pleistocene river terrace deposits underlying the site. Clay-mining pits were found beneath the plazas and often showed digging stick marks. Trace element analysis has shown that the same clay used as building adobe was used to make pottery. Rock-tempering material presumably was obtained from traditional local sources, including river sands and crushed volcanic rocks. The purpose of the temper was to reduce cracking as the clay shrank during drying and firing and to reduce thermal shock during use.

Mimbres pottery is made by building up the body of the vessel using coiled ropes of clay. If painted images are true to form, the potter sat on the ground to do her work.[2] For painted pottery the coils, about 2 cm in diameter and 30 to 40 cm long, were welded together by pinching. The coiling began at the base by simply welding the coils together in a spiral as the sides were formed. Welded coils were evened out by scraping with a tool made of a bottle gourd sherd or a potsherd shaped for the purpose. In rare cases these coils were left unsmoothed and provide clear evidence for the method of construction (appendix I: Figure A.24G).[3]

The manufacture of corrugated jars followed a slightly different process. Coiling followed the same procedure, but the coils were only about half the diameter. The degree of smoothing also differed from that for the painted ware. The area below the shoulders of some jars was scraped and smoothed much like the bowls, but not polished. Coils above the shoulders were left unsmoothed on Three Circle Neck Corrugated jars and partially smoothed on Mimbres Partially Corrugated jars. On Mimbres Fully Corrugated jars the entire outer surface was covered with partially obliterated or smoothed corrugations.

Shaping was done entirely by hand; no use was made of a wheel or any turning device that created a centrifugal force. An exception may have been use of a large sherd to turn the vessel to finish the rim, especially for large jars. Vessels were scraped to an even thickness with sherd or gourd tools (Figures 8.3, 10.1) and rotated to achieve symmetry, but Mimbres bowls are rarely symmetrical. Greater symmetry was achieved with the jars regardless of whether they were painted or corrugated.

Once the vessel was shaped, it was put aside until the clay became leather hard. The vessel was set aside to dry before applying the white slip. Potters in many areas of the ancient Southwest, such as the Anasazi of the Colorado Plateau, customarily painted their designs directly on the paste, but the brown, iron-rich clays used by the Mimbres potters precluded this with the exception of Mogollon Red-on-brown. In order to achieve a black-on-white effect, Mimbres potters had to apply a white kaolin clay slip to the otherwise brown paste. The clays used fired to shades of brown and not white or gray. Since bowls were painted on the inside and jars on the outside, only these surfaces were slipped. Rarely were both sides of bowls slipped and painted.

Kaolin clays occur in several outcrops in the Black Range and Mimbres Mountains. It was not uncommon to find raw lumps of kaolin at the NAN Ruin, suggesting there was little restriction on obtaining the resource. The clay was applied as a wash to the surface to be painted with a skin or cloth, probably in several coats to obtain the desired finish. If applied too thin, the brown/gray color of the fabric might show through. The unslipped surface was often carelessly treated, as residual wash extended onto that surface just below the rim.

After the slip dried, the surfaces were burnished with a pebble-polishing stone (Figure 10.1). The purpose of burnishing was twofold: it brought the finest particles to the surface, giving a near polished appearance to the vessel, much like a mason would use a trowel to smooth the surface of freshly poured concrete, and it provided a smoother surface on which to apply the paint. The

10.1: Pot-polishing stones, sherd scrapers, and a sherd paint palette from the NAN Ranch Ruin.

potter painted the design using a paint that was probably made of a mixture of minerals laden with iron oxide and clay and yucca leaf brushes. Possible sources of the iron pigment were iron oxide or ochre nodules or nodules of magnetite. Paints were prepared in advance and stored as a dry paste. When needed, they were mixed with water, with interior surfaces of large sherds serving as paint palettes. Discarded sherd paint palettes are not uncommon in collections from the NAN Ruin (Figure 10.1).

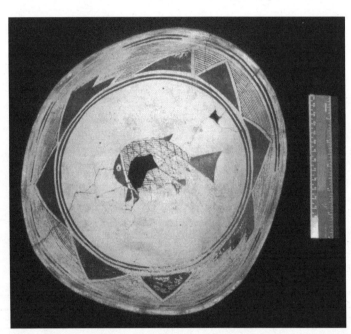

10.2: Warped Style III bowl with poorly applied paint.

The slips had to be sufficiently dried before the paint was applied. If the mixtures were not just right, the slip might not properly bond with the paste of the vessel (Figure 10.2). Paint was applied using a narrow yucca fiber brush, the width of which was determined by the width of the line to be painted. Occasionally a potter would burnish over the paint, perhaps to better ensure adherence to the slipped surface. Sometimes the painted designs were burnished before the paint was sufficiently dry and the paint became smeared (Figure 10.3A, B).

Crafts were taught to children when they were young, and girls most certainly learned how to make and decorate pottery during childhood. They most likely learned from immediate family members: mothers, older sisters, or aunts who resided in their extended family or lineage household. Although we do not know how the schooling was structured, the children clearly learned hands on. We recovered vessels that were poorly formed and crudely painted that must have been made by novices (appendix I: Figure A.21G–I). Virtually all large excavated collections of Mimbres pottery have poorly made and poorly painted examples, but these are rarely included in books of Mimbres pottery.[4] Exclusion of poorly painted and formed vessels showing the wide variability in production in publications of Mimbres painted pottery is unfortunate. It gives the impression that all Mimbres pottery is exquisitely painted, which is certainly not the case.

Designs followed set rules within each household, but the rules varied somewhat from one community to another and through time. Mimbres potters followed contemporary rules for basic style, but each potter

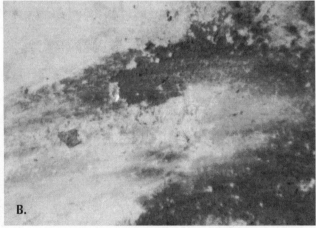

10.3: Two views of paint (A, B) on a Style III bowl smeared with a polishing stone; smearing indicates some vessels were polished after painting.

executed these rules applying her own interpretation. Archaeologists studying Mimbres pottery readily note the basic similarities within certain time periods as well as the differences when individual bowls are compared. There is a trend toward greater variability in overall designs through time, but this variability was expressed within certain parameters. Recognizing the broad rules and how they changed through time has allowed us to define a series of styles within the Mimbres painted pottery tradition.

Pottery firing was done in open kilns, probably much like those used historically by Pueblo women.[5] The ceramics were likely stacked in an open area and surrounded by wood fuel. To properly protect the paint from uneven firing and to achieve a black-on-white design, bowls were inverted to keep oxygen from reaching the painted surface. If a red-on-white color was desired, the bowl was placed upright. Jars were fired in a reduced atmosphere achieved by covering them with large sherds. Potters were quite successful in controlling jars against oxidation (appendix I: Figure A.25B) but much less so with bowls. Many bowls show the results of uneven firing.

Kiln fires varied from about 700 to 800 degrees C. Vessels that were unevenly heated or too hot during firing often warped due to poor-quality clays (appendix I: Figures A.13E, A.14D). Other pottery placed in kilns before it was properly dried would explode as moisture was converted into steam. So-called kiln wasters occurred, and examples can be recognized among the sherds, but we do not know how frequently this happened (Figure 10.4). It is not possible to identify sherds of a vessel that simply cracked in the kiln from sherds that came from a broken vessel.

Pottery making was traditionally done by women in Pueblo culture prior to the production of wares for commercial market, and the Mimbres were probably no different.[6] In fact, there is good reason to assume that potters were women, an assumption supported by the grave of a potter in Three Circle Phase pithouse room 14, described in chapters 3 and 6.

Presumably each Mimbres household could make its own pottery, although it is possible that some households did not and relied on relatives or reciprocal exchange to supply their needs. We assumed that pottery was made in each Mimbres village, but this assumption needed to be tested with petrographic and neutron activation analysis. Pottery production may have followed patterns

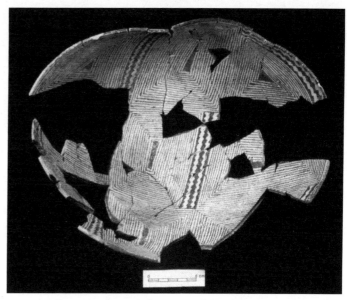

10.4: Badly warped vessel that is possibly a kiln waster from pit feature 11-13 from the east plaza at the NAN Ranch Ruin.

recorded historically among the Hopi and Zuni.[7] Each potter worked within a standard of rules or codes understood by other potters in Mimbres society. But if Mimbres potters, like most artisans, fell into two groups, one conservative and one progressive, we should expect stylistic lag and stylistic innovation. This would leave a trail of motifs through time reflecting both conventional and progressive styles, which is precisely what seems to occur in the Mimbres painted pottery tradition. The seemingly rapid stylistic evolution may be a reflection of competition between corporate groups involved in irrigation agriculture.

Classic Mimbres potters produced two separate categories of pottery: white-slipped painted vessels and corrugated vessels. This distinction involves both clays and temper, but the picture of production is a bit more complicated than that. To examine the issue of production, archaeologists have used methods that examine both clays and temper. Clay analysis involves technology of our nuclear age to help determine where the pottery was made. Potters using clays from different sources will unknowingly incorporate tiny amounts (in parts per million) of rare minerals. By comparing the clays from one locality to those of another, chemists working with archaeologists can establish a kind of fingerprint pattern for clays from a specific locality. This is accomplished by using instrumental neutron activation analysis (INAA), a method whereby samples taken from vessels and sherds are ground and placed into small capsule canisters to be irradiated in a nuclear reactor. The irradiation provides a means of identifying minute trace elements in parts per million. The signatures of elements in individual sherds and clays of known provenience were compared and statistically grouped in clusters based on similarities and differences of elements.[8] For example, if clay samples from the NAN Ranch Ruin are grouped with a cluster of sherds from the NAN Ruin and other sites based on similarities in trace elements, the vessels were likely made of clays from the same geological stratum as the NAN locality. The resolution of INAA analysis is only as good as the geological control of the sampled clays since the same clay stratum could outcrop at several nearby localities and potters from adjacent sites could use these same clays. Despite these caveats, INAA results do pinpoint distinct manufacturing loci within the Mimbres Valley, and one of these is the middle Mimbres Valley cluster at the NAN Ranch Ruin.

To demonstrate the usefulness of INAA analysis, samples of Mimbres Style III sherds from the NAN Ranch Ruin, Elk Ridge (in the upper part of the Mimbres Valley), and LA86736, near Three Rivers, New Mexico, were compared (Figure 10.5A). Sherds from Elk Ridge had not been tested before, and we wanted to know how they compared with sherds from sites in the middle and lower Mimbres Valley. We also included adobe clay samples from Elk Ridge for comparison since these clays were most likely gathered from local sources. Four clay groups were identified in the test, and sherds composing the clay groups were then examined for provenience. Group 1 clay samples consisted of adobe and sherds from Elk Ridge; group 2 were almost exclusively from the NAN Ruin with a small admixture of Elk Ridge sherds; group 3 is an unknown source, and the samples from group 4 were suspected to be from the upper Gila Valley, based on design characteristics. We furthered tested these clay groups with sherds from the Woodrow, Saige McFarland (both upper Gila Valley sites), and Galaz sites and data from the Ladder Ranch project.[9] These tests failed to identify the source for the group 3 clays, although the Ladder Ranch sherds were more likely to fall in that group than in any of the other three. The tests confirmed our assumption that group 4 clays were solidly upper Gila Valley since they matched the sherds from Saige McFarland and Woodrow. Overall, these INAA tests confirmed previous findings of multiple manufacturing areas for Mimbres Style III ceramics.[10] Virtually every large site sampled thus far has revealed a distinctive fingerprint but also that only about half of the painted vessels from any one site were made at the sites in which they were found.[11] Also, small sites may not have been involved in ceramic production. All of the painted sherds from NAN 15, a small 25- to 30-room site about 3 km from the NAN Ruin, for example, fell into large site clusters and did not show the unique clustering that would suggest local production. These findings indicate that Mimbres Style II and III ceramics were popular items of exchange between villages. The exchange apparently occurred more frequently between villages in close proximity, but exchange throughout the region was such that the extent of the Classic Mimbres interaction sphere can be measured by the geographic distribution of Style III sherds.

Temper gives the clay strength while the vessel is being made and durability when it is subjected to thermal shock in firing and subsequent use. Petrographic studies of Mimbres ceramics have shown that quartz and plagioclase were the most dominant minerals included, and temper in painted and many corrugated vessels was derived from volcanic rocks. One group of corrugated jars, however, was tempered with particles derived from plutonic rocks from an outcrop in the northern Cooke's Range. Vessels made with this temper occur at sites primarily in the southern part of the Mimbres Valley, such as the Old Town and NAN ruins, with a decrease in occurrence as one moves north. The only corrugated sherd from the NAN Ruin that has a plutonic rock temper was from a fully corrugated vessel. Temper size and shape also correlate with vessel categories. The temper in painted vessels and partially corrugated jars tends to have finer, more rounded particles composed of local sands derived from volcanic rocks or crushed volcanic rocks.[12] We wanted to know if the partially corrugated and fully corrugated jars were made from different clay sources since fully corrugated jars were identified among the vessels made with plutonic rock temper. An INAA analysis was conducted on jar sherds from the NAN Ranch Ruin, NAN 6 (McSherry Ruin), NAN 15, Old Town (LA1113), Lake Roberts Vista, and LA5841 (on Sapillo Creek, an eastern tributary of the upper Gila River); the latter two sites are in the Upper Gila drainage (Figure 10.5B, p. 180). The object of this test was to differentiate between the two technological styles of corrugated vessels, not so much to

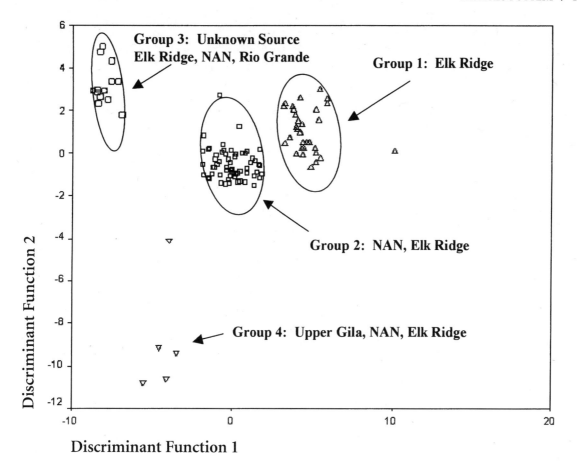

10.5A: Neutron activation analysis plots: neutron activation analysis results showing distribution of Mimbres Style III Black-on-white clusters, indicating multiple locations of manufacture. Samples are from NAN, Elk Ridge, and LA86736 (Rio Grande).

identify clay groups per se. Although the results were not as clear as in the Mimbres Style III study described above, the distinctions were statistically significant.[13] Partially corrugated vessels fell mostly into group 1 clays, fully corrugated sherds mostly into group 3 clays, and the Style III sherds included as background mostly into group 2. As one looks at the sources of the samples, the results suggest that fully corrugated jars were manufactured in two localities: one in the lower Mimbres Valley and the other in the upper Mimbres Valley or upper Gila Valley. Production of partially corrugated jars was more widespread, and these jars were identified among the middle Mimbres Valley clays. The results also suggest that these two technological styles of corrugated jars originated from different ceramic traditions.

Craft specialization often emerges in middle-range formative societies like the Pueblo societies in the Southwest.[14] Identifying evidence for ceramic craft specialization has been difficult, but some incipient form might be present in ceramic production as corporate groups arose. Burial 86, described above, certainly raises the possibility of craft specialization in the Three Circle phase, although there are other explanations for this unique burial other than that she was a craft specialist. The problem is: how does one distinguish the products of a skilled craftsman from those of a craft specialist?

One promising avenue to pursue in the issue of craft specialization is to examine paste constituents. We isolated one stylistic variant, Mimbres Style III Polychrome, to see if a common production area could be identified

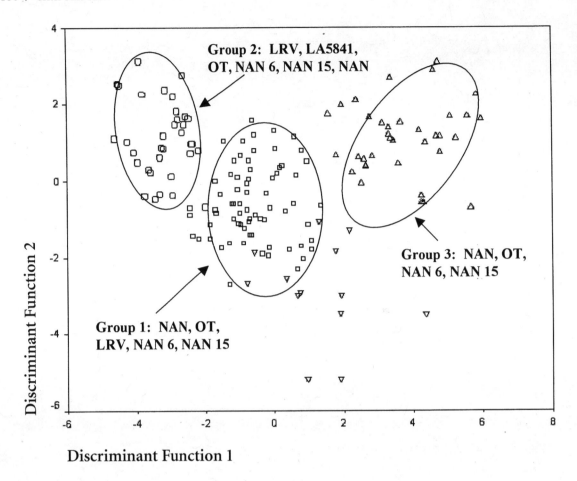

10.5B: Neutron activation analysis plots: neutron activation analysis of Mimbres Partially Corrugated, Mimbres Fully Corrugated, and Mimbres Style III Black-on-white clusters, indicating multiple clay sources of manufacture. Samples are from NAN, NAN 6 (McSherry Ruin), NAN 15, Lake Roberts Vista (LRV), and LA5841 (Ponderosa Ranch site). The Lake Roberts Vista and Ponderosa Ranch sites are in the upper Gila drainage.

through INAA analysis. Mimbres Polychrome vessels are among the most exquisitely painted examples of Style III, and the type was a likely candidate for a craft specialist's trademark. Samples of polychrome from the NAN Ranch Ruin, Old Town, Treasure Hill, and McSherry Ruin were examined and found to contain clays from at least two localities, one in the lower valley (Old Town) and the other in the middle valley (the NAN Ranch Ruin).[15] The production of Mimbres Polychrome appears to have been restricted to the larger towns but does not fit the pattern of craft specialization. Mimbres Polychrome, like other exquisitely painted vessels, was apparently the product of skilled craftsmen rather than craft specialists.

The observation made earlier about the distribution of similar but not identical designs and a lack of standardization within any one style or microstyle further indicates that a number of potters were involved in production. In other words, either no ceramic craft specialists existed or a lot of them did. Eventually archaeologists will probably be able to identify specific potters on the basis of INAA, petrographic, and design analysis. As noted earlier, clay and temper analysis has shown multiple manufacturing loci, suggesting that vessels were probably produced at each large Mimbres town.[16] Production of the prestigious Black-on-white and Polychrome pottery was very likely at the corporate level and may have been one of the material commodities used to promote the prestige of ritual knowledge held by primary corporate groups. Mimbres bowls rarely display identical designs, but close similarities exist, suggesting bowls were made by the same potter (appendix I: Figure A.16A, B). The chances of identifying the bowls by the same potter are very small because of the odds of sampling, and trace element analysis does not provide the scale of resolution at this time to confidently identify clusters to identify specific potters. Comparison of the distribution of naturalistic motifs supported with trace element analysis, however, has shown that certain motifs do indeed cluster at specific sites.[17] Birds and fish are the most commonly identified naturalistic motifs at the NAN Ruin and may identify the design preferences of resident lineages.

Identifying corporate households within large Mimbres settlements has provided a better context in which to understand ceramic production. My interpretation is that each corporate household had at least one competent potter, and very likely every adult female could produce functional pottery. Many potters spread among the towns, each following what they conceived of as the proper societal rules or codes for pottery design, and produced a myriad of design combinations within established parameters. The new evidence for microstylistic change combined with the results from INAA analyses has led to a better understanding of the production and distribution of Mimbres pottery.

The microstylistic changes suggest that a great deal of competition may have occurred between potters in the larger towns or between corporate groups. This is suggested by the frequent innovations and variations in the pottery within the broader rules of design. The adoption of negative design bands in the midst of a tradition of unframed Style II designs, the introduction of a square motif in the bottom of the vessel, adding one or more continuous lines to frame the bottom of the bands, subtle variations in framing lines, or patterns within framing lines were among the innovations that occurred; some were adopted as standard, others lasted perhaps a generation or less. Together, however, the changes demonstrate that a dialectic occurred in the population of potters between standardization and innovation.

Origins of sherds from Mimbres vessels recovered from desert Mogollon sites in the Tularosa Basin (e.g., Ojasen, Gobernadora, and North Hills in El Paso, on the west side of the Hueco Bolson) have been traced to the Mimbres Valley, 160 km to the west, by both petrographic and INAA analysis.[18] Pots from both the NAN and Old Town ruins[19] were among those represented in the Hueco Bolson samples, indicating that although many vessels never left the sites in which they were made, others were exchanged among the towns and between the settlements in the Mimbres Valley and beyond.

Mimbres Brownware Series

All Mimbres pottery, as mentioned earlier, is a brownware, meaning that the clays when fired turned an earthen reddish brown or gray. Within the brownwares, however, are four separate series, based on surface finish: unembellished plain brownware, red-slipped brownware, white-slipped brownware, and textured brownware.

Across the Mogollon region, unembellished plain ware has been lumped into one type, Alma Plain. Vessel forms mostly include hemispherical bowls, tecomate or neckless jars, and short neck jars (appendix I: Figures A.26E–I, A.27B–F). Exceptions such as ladles, boat-shaped bowls with tabs (appendix I: Figure A.26E), and pitchers occur, but these forms are rare. Using Alma Plain as a catchall category does not reflect the true situation. For example, within the Alma Plain type are sherds and vessels displaying thin, polished finishes similar to the finish of San Francisco Red but unslipped, sherds or vessels that are thick and have dull finishes, bowls with smudged interiors and exteriors, and variations between these extremes. Some of these variants, such as the polished plain brownware or certain vessel forms, may have chronological significance.

The earliest embellishment of the brownwares was the application of a red slip. Red-slipped brownwares first appear near the end of the Early Pithouse period.[20] Red-slipped wares are defined as brownware with a red slip applied to the exterior or interior surface. Jars are slipped on the exterior, and bowls may be either slipped on the interior or interior and exterior. Variation in color ranges from a near purple to a light orange.

One formal red-slipped type, San Francisco Red,[21] is distinguished by the highly polished, often dimpled dark red finish. The slip was burnished with a polished pebble to achieve a shiny polish. It is characteristically thin and well fired. One very diagnostic characteristic is the dimpling of the exterior surface, created when the potters deliberately left the welded coil surface uneven, only to be polished over. A variant of San Francisco Red, Mogollon Red-on-brown, is identical to San Francisco Red in all respects except that the interiors of the bowls have linear designs. San Francisco Red was never a popular type, accounting for only 1 to 2 percent of the sherds from the San Francisco phase deposits at the NAN Ruin. Only sherds of San Francisco Red and Mogollon Red-on-brown were recovered from the NAN Ruin excavations.

The popularity of red-slipped ware increased in the NAN samples, accounting for as much as 2 to over 8 percent of some sherd lots. By about A.D. 900, bowls and jars had noticeably thicker walls, with less emphasis on polishing the exterior. Some bowls are slipped only on the interior, whereas others are slipped both on the interior and exterior. The red slip on the later vessels was more mattelike compared to the polished San Francisco Red. The later red-filmed vessels are called simply Mimbres Red-slipped ware in this book. Vessel forms include neckless or tecomate jars (appendix I: Figure A.1A, B), hemispherical bowls (appendix I: Figure A.1C, D), necked jars, and possibly effigy vessels. The paste is the same as that of the unslipped brownwares made at this time. Strangely, red-slipped wares were no longer produced after about A.D. 1000. That red-slipped wares persisted through time up through the Late Three Circle phase, only to be abruptly abandoned, is an interesting problem. With the continuity of so many material and behavioral characteristics from the Late Three Circle through the Classic periods, it is difficult to understand why red-slipped pottery would cease to be made. A possible explanation is that the red-slipped vessels were somehow associated with the rituals conducted in great kivas. Aside from the fact that they both went out of vogue at about the same time, two additional findings may also associate redware with kiva rituals. One finding is a cache of 412 quartz crystals in a redware jar in the floor of kiva room 91 (appendix I: Figure A.1B), and the other is a redware bowl with burial 65 in the fill of great kiva room 52. Are these inclusions coincidental, or was red-slipped pottery deliberately selected? Plain redware may have been eventually replaced by oxidized red-on-white vessels. Iron-based mineral paint is responsible for the red (actually more of a burnt sienna) and black hues on Mimbres white-slipped pottery. The color depended on controlling the flow of oxygen. Perhaps vessels were deliberately fired to produce red designs to substitute for redware bowls in rituals and shrines.

Although some polished brownware bowls were embellished with red linear designs prior to about A.D. 750, an innovation occurred among certain Mimbres potters with the application of a white slip to the brownware paste. This innovation, which caught on slowly, started the white-slipped brownware tradition in Mimbres pottery. At first, the designs on these white-slipped vessels were much the same as before: broad linear designs in a four-quadrant field. Also, the method of firing, whereby the paint oxidized, resulting in the reddish hue, continued to be used with the earliest white-slipped Three Circle Red-on-white vessels. These vessels were only made for a couple of generations and represented a very small percent of all pottery produced at this time, probably no more than 5 percent, if that. The vessels may have been made for use in rituals or kiva ceremonies, which could account for the low production numbers.

Potters soon learned to fire the vessels to achieve a black-on-white effect by protecting the painted surface from oxygen, perhaps simply by turning them upside down in the open kiln. This technological change marked the beginning of the Mimbres Black-on-white tradition, in about A.D. 800 in the Late Three Circle phase, but again, only about 5 percent of all pottery at this time was slipped and painted.

Mimbres Black-on-white pottery has been divided into three major styles, based on changes in design through time: Styles I, II, and III[22] (see appendix). Within Styles II and III, additional substyles or microstyles have been defined.[23] This stylistic sequence is shown in Figure 10.6 and additional examples are illustrated in the appendix. These stylistic changes have proven to be important keys to dating periods of occupation at archaeological sites yielding Mimbres painted pottery.[24] Mimbres Style I was produced from about A.D. 800 to 900 and is distinguished by bold line designs executed in opposed or four-quadrant fields (appendix I: Figure A.1E–G). The designs are typically linear but may include interlocking motifs. A distinguishing motif is the presence of wavy lines as filler and hachure as the mode of depicting a curvilineal element or as the design itself. Designs extend to the rim and are not framed by rim bands.

Style II, which begins to appear in about A.D. 850 to 900, continues many of the characteristics of Style I and is distinguished by the use of fine lines as hachure in elements bordered by bold lines (appendix I: Figures A.1I, 2–5). The design fields on all early Style II vessels extend to the rim

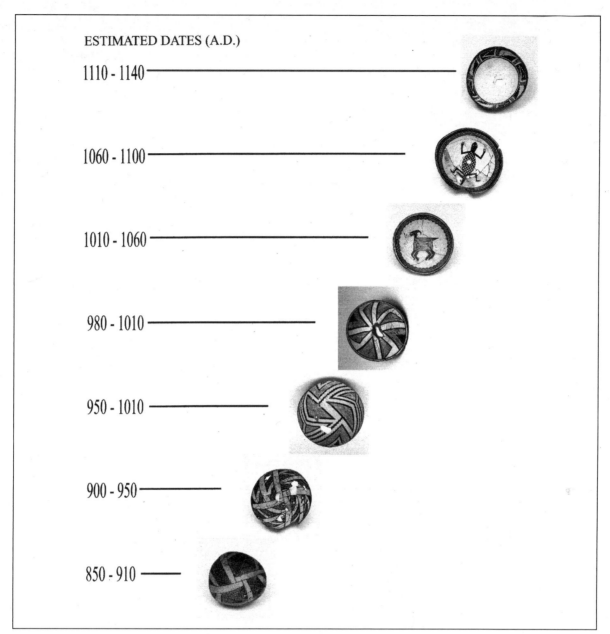

10.6: Mimbres Black-on-white stylistic sequence, arranged chronologically (illustration by Wayne Smith).

(appendix I: Figure A.1I, Figure A.2B, D), and this practice continued through most of the time period of production, which lasted from about A.D. 850 to about A.D. 1000 or 1010. Framing designs with bands or horizontal borders began in late Style II,[25] about A.D. 950 (e.g., appendix I: Figure A.3B, F–I). The first use of naturalistic (zoomorphic or anthropomorphic) motifs as part of design occurs in Style II (appendix I: Figure A.2E).

The evolution from Style II to Style III was subtle, and early Style III shows several carryover motifs from Style II. Early Style III, produced from approximately A.D. 1000 to 1050, includes three identifying motif combinations. One combination or carryover motif of Style II was the use of two- and four-quadrant fields (appendix I: Figure A.6), and designs extend to the rim in a small percentage of vessels (appendix I: Figures A.6A–F, A.7A–C). These vessels display fine-line hachure bordered by fine lines, which identifies them as Style III. Another combination is distinguished by the predominant use of framing bands around the rim. Subtle changes in these framing bands through time serve as key markers in identifying microstyles within Style III. Early Style III framing bands include a bold line above multiple fine lines encircling the rim on the inside of the bowl (appendix I: Figure A.7E–H). Sometimes this set of rim bands is followed by a geometric band, often negative painted (appendix I: Figure A.9A). Bands of fine lines may be closed off by a bottom line of pendant triangles (appendix I: Figure A.7E–I). Anthropomorphic and zoomorphic motifs appear in increasing numbers, with a notable emphasis on eyes (appendix I: Figures A.7E, G, H; A.8B, F, G). A third early Style III motif combination includes a rectangular or square in the bottom of the vessel (e.g., appendix I: Figures A.6A, B, D, I; A.10C, D, E). This bottom-framing motif is rarely seen in middle Style III and is replaced by a broad line circle (sometimes two lines) serving as the bottom framing line to a broad geometric design band (e.g., appendix I: Figure A.14G–I). Naturalistic motifs may be painted in the open space in the bottom or incorporated into the geometric band.

Middle Style III, from about A.D. 1050 to 1110, represents the height of production for Mimbres painted pottery. It is the best-represented substyle in all major collections. Designs fields are framed by bands of multiple fine lines, sometimes closed by one or more broad lines or by two or three broad lines (e.g., appendix I: Figure A.13A, D–I). The broad geometric bands framing the bowls are most often framed at the bottom by two broad line bands, leaving the bottom either plain or embellished by an anthropomorphic or zoomorphic motif, which has come to epitomize Mimbres painted pottery. With the exception of rim-framing lines, the designs on some pottery are composed entirely of anthropomorphic or zoomorphic figures or scenes depicting human actions.

One stylistic variant of middle Style III is the white-slipped bowl. These vessels are painted only around the top of the rim (as are all Mimbres painted bowls) but nowhere else (appendix I: Figures A.25H, I; A.26A).

Some Mimbres potters also experimented by adding another color of paint, a yellowish gold, to the black-and-white designs, creating a polychrome effect. Polychrome vessels are rare, accounting for less than 1 percent of all Classic period painted ware (appendix I: Figure A.22C, D). Despite their infrequent occurrence, the polychrome vessels as a group are among the most exquisitely painted examples of all.

Another Style III variant, the flare-rim bowl, was produced in middle Style III times and continued to be produced throughout the remainder of the Classic period. Flare-rim bowls, which also included polychrome variants, had different rules of design, albeit clearly within the Style III tradition (appendix I: Figures A.22E–I, A.23A–F).[26] Rim bands characteristically highlight the flared rim and were framed below, usually by two or three broad lines. Rim bands that extended beyond the flare and into the vessel body are infrequent. Naturalistic designs painted in the bottom of the bowls occur about 30 percent of the time. Flare-rim forms are also included among the polychrome vessels.

Sometime after A.D. 1110, the rules of design began to change for hemispherical bowls. The production of middle Style III may have continued or some vessels lasted to near the end, but a change occurred in rim treatment. Bands of multiple fine lines were replaced by a solid rim band starting at the lip and extending into the interior of the bowl (appendix I: Figures A.19A–I; A.20A—C; A.21E, F). In other examples, no band was used at all; instead, a solid geometric framing pattern became part of the design field itself (appendix I: Figures A.20D, E, F, I; A.21B). In other late Style III examples, design bands are suspended from a single narrow line (appendix I: Figure A.21D).

Mimbres Black-on-white jars generally follow the same stylistic rules as the bowls, but with much less variation. Style I and II jars are easily identifiable based on the basic design characteristics (appendix I: Figure A.5E, F, H). Style III jars follow much more conventional rules than do bowls. Jars are almost universally decorated by a broad design band placed around the upper part of the vessel, framed on the top and bottom by one or, less frequently, two broad lines (appendix I: Figures A.24H, I; A.25A–F). These rules apply equally to the duck-shaped human effigy jars (appendix I: Figures A.23G–I, A.24A). The lack of stylistic variability in Style III jars may be due to the fact that fewer were produced and their function as storage vessels resulted in longer use life. It is also possible that production of painted jars was more restricted than that for bowls.

Mimbres Style III tecomate or seed bowls are rare and represent only about 1 percent at most of the pottery made. These vessels show even less stylistic variation than do Style III jars (appendix I: Figure A.24F); furthermore, the contexts in which these vessels were found at the NAN Ruin suggest that they date primarily to the early and middle part of the Classic Mimbres period and ceased to be made in the latter part.

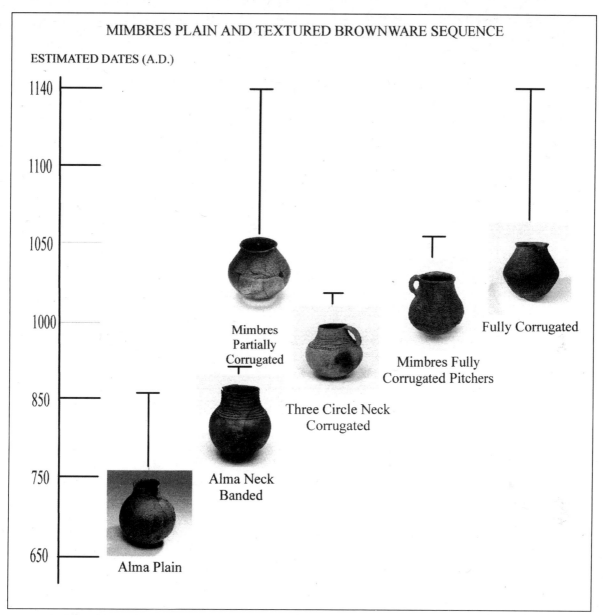

10.7: Mimbres plain and textured brownware sequence arranged chronologically (illustration by Wayne Smith).

The Mimbres Black-on-white pottery tradition came to an end shortly before A.D. 1140 in the Mimbres Valley and probably elsewhere outside the valley. The reason, discussed in more detail in chapter 12, was a total breakdown in the infrastructure and institutions associated with irrigation agriculture, such as corporate groups, calendar ceremonies, and feasts, all of which created the contexts for production and exchange of pottery in the first place.

Paralleling the development of Mimbres painted pottery was a tradition of textured brownware pottery that also underwent a series of subtle stylistic changes, albeit not as sensitive as with the painted wares. Figure 10.7 illustrates this brownware sequence as it occurred in the Mimbres Valley. Stylistic changes were more gradual in utility pottery compared to those for painted wares and are attributed to the different roles and contexts of use for ceramics in Classic Mimbres society. Vessels designed for cooking in a domestic setting, such as Mimbres corrugated wares, would have been less likely to carry stylistic messages. These vessels conform to a more functional style (cooking jars) than decorative style. The decorative styles of vessels used in public ceremonies and rituals, on the other hand, such as Mimbres painted bowls and jars, do convey coded messages. Mimbres corrugated wares were the predominate vessels used in cooking, whereas the painted wares were used primarily for serving.[27]

The textured brownware series, which perhaps began as early as A.D. 400, consists of vessels whose embellishments were added when the paste was wet. All pottery in the earliest pithouse villages, which preceded the pueblo towns, was plain. Jar forms included both neckless jars with in-curving rims and jars with straight necks. It was not until approximately A.D. 650 to 700 that the first embellishment of culinary pottery occurred in the from of neck banding on jars. Neck banding is created when the coils used to form the vessels are not completely smoothed over on the exterior surface around the neck of the vessel. Such vessels in the Mimbres area are known by the name Alma Neck Banded (appendix I: Figure A.27G, H). By A.D. 800, the individual bands had become much narrower and were left largely unsmoothed, resulting in a corrugated effect. The band field also covered more of the neck. This shift in neck decoration, identified by the type name Three Circle Neck Corrugated, occurs on jars. Jars may have appendages, tabs, or strap handles. Another characteristic of Three Circle Neck Corrugated is that the last corrugation was embellished by a series of punctations, or indentions (appendix I: Figure A.28A–C). During the A.D. 900s, the corrugations began to be smoothed slightly. The body below the shoulders was sometimes decorated with punctations on smaller vessels (appendix I: Figure A.28A, E). The rims of early Three Circle Neck Banded jars are straight, but they began to flare outward slightly by the mid-900s.

Part of the Three Circle Neck Banded series is a small group of vessels, usually mugs and pitchers, with incised, brushed, or punctated bodies. These vessels have traditionally been described in the Alma series (Alma Scored, Alma Roughened, etc.), but they clearly belong to the Three Circle Neck corrugated series and should not be regarded as separate types (appendix I: Figure A.28F, G). In this book they are regarded as variants of Three Circle Neck Corrugated. From the contexts in which these textured variants occur at the NAN Ruin (primarily in Late Three Circle phase features and deposits), lumping them into the Alma series misses an opportunity for more refined chronological placement.

By about A.D. 1000, or the early Classic Mimbres period, corrugations covered the upper one-third to one-half of the vessel. On these Mimbres Partially Corrugated jars, like the Three Circle Neck Corrugated jars, the bottom corrugation was tooled to set it apart. The corrugations were partially smoothed to varying degrees, and the remainder of the jars was lightly burnished (appendix I: Figure A.31A–I). Partially corrugated vessels are exclusively jars, of varying sizes from 8,000 cc to over 42,000 cc.[28]

Another type of corrugated vessel first appears in about A.D. 1000 or slightly before. This type is Mimbres Fully Corrugated. These vessels are corrugated over the entire exterior surface, beginning with a single coil at the bottom and continuing to just below the rim. The corrugations were also smoothed to varying degrees; some are almost obliterated (appendix I: Figures A.30, A.32A). The walls of fully corrugated jars tend to be thinner than those of partially corrugated vessels. The first fully corrugated vessels were small mugs and pitchers in the Late Three Circle/early Classic transition (appendix I: Figures A.28H, I; 29A–I). Pitchers and mugs last a couple of generations, and by A.D. 1060 or so, they were no longer produced. By A.D. 1000 or slightly thereafter, fully corrugated jars of varying sizes were made with a capacity of up to 21,000 cc.

Rims on both Classic Mimbres corrugated jar forms are out flaring. In overall proportion, the diameter of the body is slightly greater than the vessel height. The average neck diameter is nearly 18 cm, compared to 10 cm for painted jars.[29] These size differences suggest different functional roles for the two kinds of jars. The wider corrugated jar necks would provide easier accessibility to cooked or stored food, whereas the narrower-necked painted jars would be more suitable for water storage.

That two separate types of corrugated jars exist raises some interesting possibilities. Either certain villages were engaged in some form of craft specialization or groups of people included under the umbrella of Classic Mimbres society were, in fact, different groups. Domestic crafts and styles are among the more resilient material traditions since they derive from basic household use and are not displayed or shown publicly.[30] The two types of corrugated jars that represent domestic cooking ware do not change through the Classic phase despite the changes taking place in the painted pottery. Perhaps the two types were produced by people of different traditions, such as one group from the upper Gila and the other from the Mimbres Valley. Margaret Nelson has documented evidence of a population shift during the Classic period from the upper Gila to the Mimbres Valley[31]; might the two corrugated types be a product of such population mixing? If so, the traditions appear to have become well established.

Trade Pottery

Less than one half of 1 percent of the ceramics recovered from our excavations is from sources outside the Mimbres area. The origins of these trade vessels are from every direction and vary through time, but the most consistent sources are the Jornada area to the east and the Cibola area to the north. No full analysis has been made of intrusive ceramics at the NAN Ruin. But to provide some indication of regional interaction, I examined a random sample of 162 sherds drawn from ceramic lots throughout the site (Table 10.1, p. 189). This small sample is by no means representative of the entire site and was not temporally stratified. Nevertheless, the sample is indicative of the scale of regional interaction engaged in by the occupants of the site.

The preliminary study showed that El Paso brownware is the single most common trade pottery throughout the site's occupation sequence. El Paso ware from Three Circle and Late Three Circle phase deposits is plain, but a few vessels of El Paso Red-on-brown (Figure 10.8A–E) and early or Style I Polychrome (Figure 10.8F–M)[33] appear late in the Classic period. One complete vessel of El Paso Red-on-brown was recovered from room 74 (appendix I: Figure A.32D) associated with Mimbres Style III fully and partially corrugated vessels. The second most common source for trade pottery was the Cibola area to the north. Most (15 percent) is untyped. Red Mesa Black-on-white is represented by eight sherds (5 percent; Figure 10.9A–F) and one partially restorable vessel from Late Three Circle phase feature 11-4 in the east plaza (appendix I: Figure A.32F) associated with sherds of Mimbres Redware and El Paso Brown.[34] Puerco Black-on-white is the most frequent whiteware, with one pitcher (appendix I: Figure A.32G) and 17 sherds (10 percent) in the sample (Figure 10.9G–K). The pitcher was recovered from burial 135, associated with a late Style III bowl (appendix I: Figure A.16A). One untyped early whiteware bowl was recovered from great kiva room 52 (appendix I: Figure A.32E), and four sherds of this type were recovered from Three Circle phase

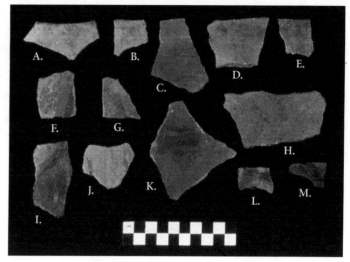

10.8: Trade wares: El Paso Brownwares. A–E, El Paso Bichrome; F–M, early or Style I El Paso Polychrome.

10.9: Trade wares: Cibola Whitewares. A–., Red Mesa Black-on-white; G–K, Puerco Black-on-white; I–N, unidentified early Cibola Whiteware; O, P, unidentified Cibola Whiteware.

midden deposits (Figure 10.9L–N). The third most common trade pottery, represented by 23 percent of the sherds, is a polished smudged brownware. These vessels are all bowls with smudged interiors and corrugated (10 percent), plain (9 percent), or punctated (3 percent) exteriors (Figure 10.10). One complete smudged bowl was recovered from the floor of room 42 (appendix I: Figure A.26D), and

188 / CHAPTER TEN

10.10: Trade wares: smudged brownwares.

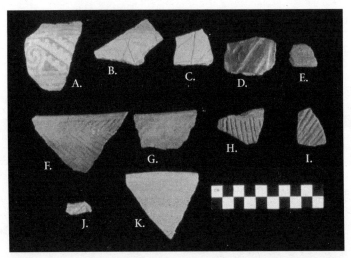

10.11: Trade wares: Hohokam, Playas, and Chihuahua wares. A, Sacaton Red-on-buff; B, C, untyped tooled red-on-brown; D, E, Chihuahua rubbed incised; F–I, Playas Red; J, Villa Ahumada Polychrome; K, unidentified Chihuahua orange ware.

unidentified Chihuahua orangeware (Figure 10.11K), a Villa Ahumada Polychrome (Figure 10.11J), and a large Convento Indented Corrugated jar from Chihuahua (appendix A: Figure A.32C). Also, nine sherds of locally made Playas Red (Figure 10.11F–I) were recovered. The Villa Ahumada Polychrome and Playas Red may have originated with the nearby Black Mountain phase site. Together this sample of trade ware indicates the direction and relative strength of interregional trade as represented by ceramics. On the basis of trade pottery, Mimbres regional interaction seemed to be equally strong with the Jornada area to the east and the Cibola area to the north. middle and late Style III is equally well represented in Jornada Doña Ana phase components.[35]

Discussion

The primary role of ceramics was for use as containers in cooking, serving, and storage. Embellishment of the otherwise plain pottery probably stemmed from its use in rituals and ceremonies to mark the sacredness of the occasion. The gradual increase in the frequency of painted ware through time may be related to expanding uses of vessels, the transformation of Mimbres society from high to low residential mobility, and the evolution of public ceremonies. Mimbres painted pottery defined the Mimbres as a separate group sharing a common ideology within the broader Mogollon and greater southwestern spheres.

In the early Three Circle phase, the white-slipped pottery was a very minor type in an otherwise brownware assemblage. The restricted production suggests it was primarily made for use in ritual or ceremonial occasions. The production of Style I increased over that of Three Circle Red-on-white, which probably reflects increased population and ritual activity and expanded roles for painted pottery, including its first use as a mortuary ware. Most domestic pottery remained plain and neck-corrugated ware. The roles of painted pottery continued to expand with Style II, as did production. Use contexts of pottery also expanded, including more frequent occurrences in burials and possibly as feasting ware and in exchange. By Classic Mimbres times, painted pottery had all but replaced plain wares, with the exception of domestic roles served by the corrugated wares. The increased popularity of painted pottery in the Late Three Circle and Classic Mimbres phases is directly tied to increases in population

another bowl with a punctated zigzag design on the exterior (appendix I: Figure A.32H, I) was recovered from burial 25 in room 41. The origin of these smudged bowls is likely the Reserve area, which is also the presumed source for the two Reserve Black-on–white sherds. In addition, two sherds of Sacaton Red-on-buff show interaction with the Hohokam region (Figure 10.11A). Chihuahua types include possibly a Convento Rubbed Incised (Figure 10.11D, E), untyped tooled redware (Figure 10.11B, C),

TABLE 10.1. Listing of Trade Wares in the NAN Ranch Ruin Collection by Type and Phase

Type	# Sherds	Percent	Vessels	Phase context
Untyped whiteware	20	12.3		Various
Untyped early B/W	4	2.4	1	Three Circle
Red Mesa B/W	8	5	1	Late Three Circle
Reserve B/W	2	0.1		Classic
Puerco B/W	17	10.5	1	Classic
El Paso Brown	18	11.1		Late Three Circle
El Paso R/Br	6	3.7	1	Late Classic
Early El Paso Polychrome	32	20		Late Classic
Smudged corrugated	17	10.5		Classic
Punctated smudged	6	3.8	1	Classic
Plain smudged	15	9.2	1	Classic
Sacaton Red-on-buff	2	1.2		Classic
Untyped tooled redware	2	1.2		Classic?
Victoria R/Br	1	0.6		Classic?
Playas Red	9	5.5		Late Classic/Postclassic
Untyped redware	1	0.6		Classic?
Villa Ahumada Poly	1	0.6		Postclassic?
Convento rubbed-indented	1	0.6		Classic?
Totals:	**162**	**100%**	**6**	

and more corporate groups involved in ritual activity, including ceremonies and feasts.

The context of production for the painted pottery and the roles served by the pottery were woven into the matrix of corporate group behavior and irrigation agriculture. When the irrigation systems failed and the power derived from corporate ceremonies and ancestor veneration dwindled, the reinforcing rituals and ceremonies were abandoned, and production of their associated material accouterments, including Mimbres Style III painted pottery, ceased. In other words, I firmly believe the production of Mimbres painted pottery was to reinforce the system of values and ceremonies sustaining the corporate networks that operated the irrigation systems. The pottery was produced in the context of the overall system of beliefs and values and not independent of it. Some have argued that Style III pottery continued to be produced as late as A.D. 1200,[36] a scenario based on murky archaeological findings. But this seems highly improbable when one looks more closely at the socioeconomic and ideological contexts of pottery making.

I also think the primary purpose of Mimbres painted pottery was for use in prestigious public events, such as ceremonies and feasts, orchestrated by various corporate groups. In other words, Style II and III pottery can be considered prestige items to display success and power.[37] Prestige items attract attention, create envy, and recruit surplus labor. Prestige may have been enhanced by giving the vessels away as part of gifts for exchange. The use history of any one vessel, which may have originated at the corporate or public event, moved through any number of functional and spatial contexts before disposal or breakage. The final context for most Mimbres vessels in collections was disposal in graves, but this was by no means the primary use. Mimbres bowls from burials display a wide range of use wear, indicating that most saw use in the domestic arena.

Previous studies on the function of Mimbres pottery sampled only mortuary vessels. Although the majority of the 250 complete and restorable vessels from the NAN Ranch Ruin also came from mortuary contexts, this sample accounts for only about one-fourth of 1 percent of the total number of ceramic specimens (approximately 100,000, including sherds) that I estimate were in our sample. Therefore, in order to gain a more complete understanding of the function of Mimbres pottery, we chose to sample the entire collection and to consider a broad range of contexts. A detailed analysis of the NAN Ranch Ruin ceramic collection was carried out by Robyn Lyle.[38] Lyle examined a sample of sherds from a Classic period midden and all vessels from domestic and mortuary contexts for patterns of use. We were interested in learning about household ceramic assemblages, but intact floor assemblages were rare at the site. So, we tried to approach the problem in another way. Lyle studied sherds from midden areas to compare the frequency of breakage of painted bowls to jar sherds to gain some idea of replacement rates. The assumption was breakage rates would provide some clues to the composition of a household assemblage. Although the ratio of bowls to jars was 3 to 1, Lyle correctly noted that with this approach, too many factors prevented the reconstruction of household assemblages, including household size and vessel longevity.

Lyle also compared domestic, mortuary, and midden assemblages to the burial assemblage to determine biases in the selection of mortuary vessels. Bowls dominated both burial and midden assemblages, but jars were more frequent in domestic assemblages. As noted previously, floor assemblages rarely were intact; abandonment of Mimbres structures was orderly and apparently structured to remove most of the usable items prior to burning or ritually terminating the structure. Cooking jars were the most common vessel forms left on floors, and rarely were bowls left behind. However, by demonstrating the high frequency of bowl breakage, she also showed that painted bowls were the most frequent vessel form produced in the Classic period. Since bowls are not specialized forms and provide unrestricted access, they can be used in a variety of ways, including in sacred, prestigious, or practical tasks. Use-wear and contextual analysis showed that bowls were used in food preparation, in serving, in storing (as jar lids), and as mortuary vessels.

As noted above, the majority of Classic Mimbres bowls in extant collections were recovered from mortuary contexts. Because of archaeological bias, some archaeologists assumed that the elaborately painted pottery was made for mortuary purposes.[39] Use as mortuary ware was restricted primarily to the Mimbres Valley and lake sites to the south, adjacent areas of the upper Gila, and high eastern flanks of the Black Range. Use as mortuary ware outside of these areas was extremely rare,[40] despite the fact that many Mimbres vessels were carried back to distant villages in the deserts of west Texas and northern Chihuahua.

A far different conclusion was reached when the mortuary pottery from the NAN Ranch Ruin was examined. This study revealed that wear from everyday uses was clearly evident in the bottoms of many bowls. Abrasion from scooping out foods or preparing foods wore away the painted designs and even the white slip. Nicks along the rim, soot from fires, and laced-up cracks all attest to the fact that many elaborately painted bowls were used for everyday food preparation and serving, among other things.[41] If the vessels were made for mortuary purposes, then the use-wear evidence creates a paradox. The mortuary ware interpretation proved to be incorrect when the overall contexts of discovery and detailed analysis of the vessels themselves were considered. Elaborately painted vessels were recovered on house floors, in storerooms, in outdoor areas, and as lids for jars. Unequivocally, the majority of bowls used in funeral ceremonies were taken from extant household assemblages. The placement of certain vessels in the graves was the last function served by these vessels. Why a certain bowl was taken is, of course, something we will never know, but the choice was almost certainly not random. In children's graves in the NAN community, a preference was found for small bowls with naturalistic motifs.

If Mimbres painted pottery was made as a prestige accouterment for use and display in reinforcing corporate and public ceremonies and rituals, then how did it become incorporated in household assemblages? The answer is that probably not all bowls made were used in ceremonies, perhaps due to flaws such as warping and misfiring, and some bowls were exchanged as gifts as part of the feasting behavior. Members of a village probably exchanged gifts more readily with those living in nearby or distant villages. Exchange was apparently frequent enough to supply outlier sites, such as NAN 15, with all of their pottery needs.

Archaeologists recover a large quantity of broken pottery in the trash-laden fill around the ruins of large Mimbres sites. Pottery vessels get broken through everyday use as well as in the firing process, and the more often a vessel type is used or produced, the more often it will be broken and its pieces thrown in the trash deposits. Some of the pottery used in sacred ceremonies may also have been broken at the termination of the ritual. Potsherds reveal traces of both naturalistic and geometric designs, attesting to the fact that there was no discernable discrimination as to which was used. In other words, although use wear is clearly evident on vessels, the breakage rates further indicate extensive domestic uses for the painted pottery.

The brownware jars, pitchers, and mugs were also used primarily for domestic purposes but were rarely included with burials. The exceptions generally occur in the Late Three Circle phase. Many of the corrugated jars bear traces of soot on the exterior surfaces, indicating their use in cooking directly over the fire. Large jars (appendix I: Figure A.31B, D) may have been used to cook large quantities of foods for feasts. Very large jars (appendix I: Figures A.31D—F, A.32C, D), perhaps were used for brewing a native corn beer similar to the *tesvino* of the Tarahumara of northern Mexico.[42]

The functions for painted jars, on the other hand, clearly were different from those of corrugated jars, although these functions overlapped. The painted jars are made from the same paste as are the bowls, are slightly different in proportion compared to the brownware jars, have smaller orifices, and have burnished exteriors. The burnishing, smaller orifice and finer paste make them more suitable for water jars and dry storage. Painted jars have been recovered, however, from subfloor caches holding dry storage, including one from the NAN Ruin that held desiccated squash.[43]

Both seed jars and effigy jars are rare in the Classic period: together they account for less than 1 percent of all vessels manufactured. The roles served by these vessels are obscured by the lack of functional contexts. Small jars with suspension holes, including the duck-shaped human effigy jars, may have been hung in special places, perhaps above shrines in kivas. More will be said of symbolism in chapter 12.

The vivid symbolism seen on Mimbres painted pottery has stimulated a considerable amount of literature from scholars and avocational archaeologists alike. Interpretations are often made from the perspective of the viewer's own culture, that is, from an outsider's perspective. No one really knows what was in the minds of the Mimbres potters when they painted the various geometric and naturalistic images. In other words, we will never get at the view from the insider's, or ancient Mimbres, perspective.

Meaning aside for the moment, archaeologists are interested in defining patterns, redundant styles, themes, or structure in the material record. When we relate the images on Mimbres pottery to those things we recognize, this is not to imply the ancient artisans were making the same kinds of relationships. For example, Mimbres potters frequently painted images of animal life of the Chihuahuan Desert and surrounding mountains to the north. Pronghorn, mountain sheep, deer, jackrabbits, lizards, snakes, turtles, birds, fish, and insects can all be seen painted with the signature cartoon style of the Mimbres artisans. Humans are depicted in action scenes doing many of the tasks of Mimbres daily life: hunting, weaving, making pottery, making arrows, or acting out a ceremony, or the paintings depicted anthropomorphic spirits. The Mimbres artists' depictions of human and animals were not always straightforward: creatures with a combination of human and animal features or a combination of animal features such as a bird body and a snake head (appendix I: Figure A.22C) or a ram's head and a turtle body with human legs (appendix I: Figure A.71) certainly suggest mythical creatures.

What was the meaning behind the images and scenes? Some view the action scenes as being accurate depictions of Mimbres hunting practices.[44] Pat Carr, among other scholars, recognizes characters or actors in myths common in Native American oral literature.[45] To be sure, a pictographic code existed among the Mimbreños that allowed the viewer familiar with the codes to recognize the characters and understand the themes depicted on the vessels. Archaeologists and art historians tend to ignore the geometric patterns, but the great variety in the individual motifs and the ways they are combined hint at some kind of abstract code as well. Such logographic images are not unique among the indigenous people of the Americas; indeed, it is precisely this kind of graphic code from which the written languages of Mesoamerican cultures such as the Maya evolved.

So why was so much emphasis placed on the painting of such elaborate pottery if it served primarily in domestic use? The answer to this question may lie in the social and ideological structure of Mimbres society; in other words, the way social distance was defined, the way large villages were connected through a network of canals and kinsmen, and the Mimbres worldview, which is discussed in chapter 12. As noted earlier, a great deal of pottery was exchanged among the larger villages, and indeed, the larger villages may very well have been supplying ceramics to a network of smaller outlier sites.

During the pithouse period the primary economic unit was the family. Precisely how the families were structured is unknown, but as in most indigenous American cultures, probably an extended family included male or female siblings and their children; in addition, the family unit may have included an older parent relative, an orphan, or other relatives. As noted in chapter 3, pithouses were often clustered around a common courtyard. Social interaction was mostly close and face-to-face. Social codes were encoded early and were understood by all family members as well as those in the social sphere immediately beyond the family, such as clans and kin-based totemic groups. Ceramics made during much of the pithouse period were mostly plain or textured and lacked elaboration that carried social messages; they served the basic functions of cooking, storage, and serving. The social interaction of these extended families was limited, and large social gatherings were probably unlikely or infrequent due to the fact that the Mimbres at this time were simply not capable of accumulating the large stores of food needed for such occasions.

Enlargements of the social groups and social networks occurred in the Late Three Circle and Classic Mimbres times. As the social spheres expanded via the elaboration of kin organizations such as clan, societies, or totem groups to include members scattered among the other larger villages and outliers, larger social gatherings during major calendar events predictably became more frequent and more institutionalized, especially with the accumulation of surplus food. Associated with these larger social gatherings were codes of identity and behavior carried by a mutual ideology. These codes were probably expressed in any number of ways, including tattooing, dress, and behavior and as symbols depicted on visual material culture items such as baskets and pottery used in ceremonies and feasts.[46]

People outside the Mimbres sphere may not have known the meanings of Mimbres codes and symbolism: they had their own cosmology and associated symbols. An institutionalized network of behaviors with associated codes and symbols, however, unified the people we call Mimbres in the Mimbres Valley and its tributaries into a common whole. The painted pottery expressed one aspect of these codes and symbols. Although people in the desert to the south and east and on the Colorado Plateau to the north knew the Mimbreños and interacted with them, they did not produce or copy Mimbres pottery.

The level of social integration for the pithouse dwelling desert groups south and east of the Mimbres Valley did not develop beyond that present in the Georgetown phase, and I seriously doubt that sufficient food surpluses were accumulated to attract large social gatherings among these desert people until long after the decline of the Classic Mimbres. In the meantime, many of these desert groups regularly visited Mimbres towns and carried away items such as Mimbres painted pottery and food as gifts or in exchange. Sherds of Mimbres Black-on-white are frequently found in contemporary pithouse villages from the San Simon area, northern Chihuahua, to the Tularosa Basin.[47] In the San Simon area, Mimbres painted pottery accounts for only about 2 percent of all sherds.[48] In the Tularosa Basin, it approaches 8 percent at some sites.[49]

Summary

Mimbres painted pottery has captivated western viewers for over a century. It has been used as the identifying marker for these ancient people. Yet despite the attention paid to and interest in the painted images and artistic tradition, the social and ideological contexts that nurtured the development of this tradition have never been satisfactorily addressed. Had it not been for the agricultural successes and the conditions that allowed for dense populations and integration of larger and larger social networks, Mimbres painted pottery would never have existed. Indeed, the plain and red-slipped brownwares of the pithouse period would have persisted. It was the development of an irrigation system that connected all of the towns along the river and the formation of corporate groups, or perhaps competing corporate groups, that provided the incentive to embellish the serving bowls and water jars with traditional motifs and scenes depicting daily and ritual life. When the corporate group organization dissipated during the early third of the twelfth century, so did the impetus to produce the painted pottery. The dynamics of social interaction and personal achievement were also responsible for the constant evolution or changes in ceramic styles. The public display of painted wares, gift giving or exchange, and aesthetic appeal all led to production of this ware beyond mere household needs. The distribution of Mimbres Style III pottery across the landscape not only maps out the Mimbres interaction sphere for archaeologists, but also reflects the extent to which the Mimbres and their neighbors sought the pottery. Technologically speaking, Mimbres brownwares are generally poorly made, with much softer fabrics than are customarily found in the Cibola area to the north. But aesthetically speaking, Mimbres pottery had no contemporary rivals. Although the painted pottery has been mostly recovered from mortuary contexts, it was by no means produced as a mortuary ware. The primary function of the black-on-white pottery was to publicly display graphic geometric and naturalistic images via feasts and ceremonies. Ceramic exchange occurred during these events, as shown by trace element analysis. Trace element analysis also suggests that painted vessels were being made in most large towns, probably the same towns that were hosting the ceremonies and feasts. When these occasions were over, the ceramics went the way of the participants and viewers, to be used in their homes for domestic cooking, serving, and storage. It was from these secondary domestic assemblages that mortuary vessels were drawn, thus placing them in a tertiary context. Extensive use wear on over 80 percent of mortuary vessels clearly documents their domestic uses.

The processes that distributed the painted pottery across the landscape were not the same as those for the utilitarian wares, especially the corrugated jars. These vessels were made in fewer locations but were readily exchanged among Mimbres villagers. The frequency of corrugated wares in sites occupied by Mimbres neighbors, however, is much lower than that of painted vessels.

CHAPTER ELEVEN
Technologies and Crafts

Introduction

The Mimbreños made and used tools, utensils, ornaments, and facilities to cope with daily life. A myriad of artifacts—those items altered or shaped by hand—are sprinkled through the deposits around, in, and beneath the NAN Ranch Ruin. These items were made of stone, bone, plant fibers, shell, clay, and wood. Broken, discarded, or lost tools and other items can be expected in the trash deposits and fill around a site that was occupied for several hundred years. Time has removed most perishable items from the archaeological record, however, leaving for study mostly the more durable items, such as those made of stone, bone, and clay.

A variety of tools were used by both men and women; some tools were probably used interchangeably, whereas others were more role specific, but no evidence suggests that any one tool was used exclusively by either men or women. Men, for example, may have made metates, but women mostly used them. The same can be said about the bow and arrow: men made and used them, but women probably were adept at using them as well. In terms of division of labor in everyday life, however, we can make certain assumptions about tool use and division of labor based on what we know about traditional Pueblo practices. Metates were traditionally women's tools, and bows and arrows were traditionally men's tools, for example. Mimbres art reflects these gender differences.

When tools are manufactured at the site, the residues and tools used in manufacture also occur in the trash and fill deposits. The presence or absence of such manufacturing debris can reveal important information on the uses of local versus foreign raw material and local production versus import of finished items. The physical context and association of items can be equally revealing: association relates to the relationship of one artifact with other artifacts or features. Artifacts found in what can be construed as a primary context, such as being left on a house floor or placed in a storage pit or burial, are especially informative. Artifacts recovered from construction fill or midden areas have been removed from their primary context of use. Such items do play a key role, however, in assessing chronological associations. A brief look at certain artifact classes other than pottery is presented in this chapter to illustrate some of the tools the Mimbreños used in their daily lives and what these tools may reveal about the Mimbreños. This is not a thorough inventory of Mimbres material culture; indeed, to present such an inventory would literally take several volumes. I emphasize certain artifact classes here for which primary context data are most revealing in terms of providing some insight into the organization and structure of Mimbres society.

Stone

The manufacture and use of certain classes of stone artifacts are well known, such as metates, or trough-shaped grinding slabs; manos, or handheld milling stones; and chipped stone projectile points. The uses of these tools survived well into historic times among the native peoples of northwestern Mexico and the Southwest. The uses of other artifacts—sometimes more abundant, such as chipped stone cobbles or flakes with damaged edges—are more uncertain. Tasks requiring tools for cutting, chopping, scraping, grinding, smoothing, battering, piercing, and sawing were accomplished by using resources immediately at hand.[1] Expediency, whereby the stone is selected, minimally altered to fit the need, used, and discarded, typifies Mimbres chipped stone tool technology.

A comprehensive study of the chipped stone tool assemblage at the NAN Ruin was conducted by John Dockall.[2] He approached the study with four basic goals in mind: (1) identify the raw materials used in stone tool manufacture; (2) identify all flaked stone tools; (3) identify and define strategies used to reduce the stone from a raw material state to finished form, based on a study of the chipping waste or debitage and finished tools; and (4) relate stone tools to stages of manufacture in a reduction trajectory to identify artifacts that were being made at the site as opposed to those imported in finished form.

In stone tool technology, chipped stone tools are made by removing individual flakes from a mass or core using some kind of hammer; tools take shape with the systematic removal of flakes, and the removal of each flake is a step in the manufacturing trajectory from raw material to finished tools. Mistakes will occur at any step along the way, and these mistakes fossilize the trajectory at that step. Lithic assemblages from residential sites typically contain many examples of such failures and when viewed together allow us to reconstruct not only the manufacturing trajectory but often the decision-making process. By altering the pattern of flake removal, for example, an artisan can change the trajectory, depending on the kind of tool he wishes to make. Furthermore, an analyst can determine if a tool class was made at a site by the presence or absence of the flakes and broken preforms and which trajectories were followed by the trail of failures along the way.

Special attention was given to the geological occurrence and physical properties of the utilized raw materials. Dockall conducted a site catchment study to examine the distribution of raw materials based on 1-km intervals. The catchment study took into consideration the geological formations and rock types in proximity to the site. From this information he was able to identify local and nonlocal stone resources and raw material types and procurement patterns. For example, the majority of stone artifacts were made of two locally occurring rock types, andesite/basalt and rhyolite. Andesite/basalt is ubiquitous in the gravels of the Mimbres River at the site, but rhyolite, although less common in the gravels, occurs in nearby outcrops. Rhyolite is found in various forms, some fine grained and suitable for flaked stone tool use, others coarse. A full range of reduction was evident at the site for the andesite/basalt group, but rhyolites were brought to the site in a partially reduced state. For example, NAN 57, a rhyolite quarry approximate 1 km from the site, showed evidence of direct procurement and initial reduction of a relatively fine-grained variety of this stone type.[3]

Technological studies and debitage analysis also showed that some raw material types were imported. Greenstone-grooved axes of uralitized diabase were brought to the site in finished form. This material outcrops some 17 km northwest of the site in the upper Mimbres Valley.[4] Other imported materials include tuff and latite slabs, especially those made of Sugarlump rhyolite, a material that can be extracted in large flat slabs. Sugarlump rhyolite outcrops about 8 km south of the NAN Ruin and could be quarried in slabs sufficiently large to cover doorways. Fine-grained cryptocrystalline cherts, chalcedony (a clear milky white cryptocrystalline rock), and obsidian (a volcanic glass) were also imported. Chert and chalcedony were primarily brought to the site in finished artifact form, although some core reduction is indicated by the presence of secondary debitage. Obsidian was imported in both nodular form and as finished projectile points. Known sources of NAN Ruin obsidian include Mule Creek, Ewe Canyon, and Antelope Wells,[5] all in southwestern New Mexico and 120 to 150 km from the NAN Ruin.

Reduction technology for the andesite/basalt and rhyolite was primarily handheld hard-hammer percussion. Cores were held in one hand or anchored on one's leg and struck with a fist-size stone hammer. Flakes and cores display prominent striking platforms and bulbs of force indicative of this technique. Small nodules of obsidian and chalcedony, however, were smashed using either hard-hammer or bipolar technology, whereby the nodule was placed on an anvil and smashed with another stone. This method provides virtually no control over the resulting debitage (flakes and spalls), and it is by luck or chance that a usable flake is produced that can be shaped into a small sharp-edge tool or projectile point. Flake and core analysis also showed that these reduction strategies were persistent and did not change through time. Tool analysis demonstrated the same thing: that core and flake tools did not change throughout the NAN sequence (from the Georgetown through Classic phases); the only changes occurred in the formal tool class of projectile points.

The geological abundance of raw materials in the immediate vicinity was reflected in the waste flakes or debitage. No significant changes were detected in the uses of coarse versus fine-grained material through time. This finding is in contrast to findings from other studies, which emphasized temporal differences in coarse and fine-grained materials,[6] attributing an increased proportion of coarse material to an increased dependence on processed plant foods.[7] The assumption was that the more durable coarse materials were more efficient for processing plant foods. The NAN Ruin analysis showed a different pattern. Coarse materials were always more abundant, but no relative change occurred in gross categories of coarse and fine materials from the Late Pithouse through the Classic periods. Dockall's study also showed that the areal distribution of raw materials was a more important influence on raw material variability than temporal changes. The rather dramatic shift in agriculture from the Three Circle to the Classic period was not reflected in the chipped stone assemblage as we expected, albeit with the possible exception of the introduction of the bow and arrow.

To define the functional range of artifacts in the expedient category requires more rigorous scientific study, based on use-wear patterns, residue analysis, replication experiments, and ethnographic analogy. These tools, however, were no less important in revealing the daily life of the Mimbres people than more easily identified items. Stone axes used to cut down a tree are easily recognized, but what about the tools used to strip the bark away or to shape a digging stick from a limb cut from the tree? Such tools have no formal shapes to aid in their easy recognition.

Flaked stone tools used in daily maintenance and subsistence activities at the NAN Ruin fall mostly in the nonformal (i.e., without a formal shape) category of expedient tools. These tools were made from andesite/basalt cobbles, rhyolite, chalcedony, and chert. Exotic stones, such as pieces of colorful chert obtained from distant outcrops in the desert to the south or obsidian obtained from distant source areas, were also used as small-cutting or piercing expedient tools. Expedient tools include cores or masses with just enough flakes removed to create a suitable cutting or chopping edge or flakes struck from cores and selected on the basis of a suitable cutting edge or edge angle. Others were selected merely on the basis of their fist size and mass and used as hammer stones. Tips for drills and flakes used for fine cutting were generally made of fine-grained rocks such as chert, chalcedony, or certain rhyolites. Rarely were the tools used long enough for wear to be manifested in the form of edge or surface damage, further indicating their expedient nature. When the task was completed, most of the tools were discarded, never to be used again.

Projectile Points

Over 350 chipped stone projectile points were recovered from the NAN Ruin excavations. This is the single most common chipped stone formal tool type. The collection includes both larger dart points and smaller arrow points. The larger dart points are associated with the use of the atlatl, or spear thrower and spear, a weapon that preceded the bow and arrow in all New World aboriginal cultures. The bow and arrow rapidly replaced the atlatl and spear when introduced by the time of the early Three Circle phase in the Mimbres region. Before then, projectile points were mostly expanding stem and corner-notched varieties of dart points, often variously grouped under the name types of San Pedro, Datil, and Chiricahua, and several unnamed varieties. With the introduction of the bow and arrow, however, a smaller stone tip was required and projectile points greatly diminished in size.

The bow and arrow was the weapon of choice by the time of the Three Circle phase; archaeological specimens recovered from dry caves in the area indicate arrows were probably tipped mostly with hardened wooden points,[8] although some were obviously tipped with chipped stone points. The arrow points were mostly made of chipped slivers smashed from obsidian pebbles (Figure 11.1A–O). Chert and chalcedony were other kinds of microcrystalline stones used to make arrowheads.

The deeply stratified deposits and contexts sealed by superimposed house floors provided an excellent opportunity to develop a temporal sequence of projectile points. Previous studies conducted with computer-assisted analysis of co-occurring attributes failed to demonstrate temporal changes in style.[9] Stratigraphic and chronological analyses of projectile points at the NAN Ruin clearly show changes among the formal point styles through time. Dockall has given formal type names to the arrow point forms; several of the dart point forms, however, have previously assigned named types, although no such distinctions are made here.

The atlatl-thrown spear was the principle weapon throughout prehistory and extending into the Georgetown and San Francisco phases. Dart points are larger and heavier than arrow points and are made from larger preforms that require reduction methods not required with the smaller arrow points. Dart point forms present in the early part of the Late Pithouse Period are shown in Figure 11.1P–AA. The earliest arrow points in the NAN

TECHNOLOGIES AND CRAFTS / 197

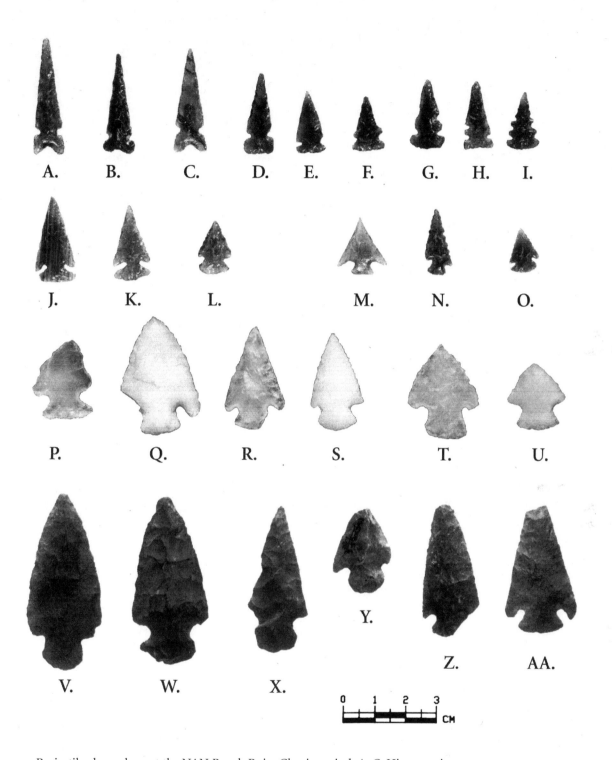

11.1: Projectile chronology at the NAN Ranch Ruin. Classic period: A–C, Hinton points; D–F, Swarts points; G–I, Cosgrove points; Late Pithouse period: J–O, Mimbres points; Early Pithouse period: P–AA, dart points.

sequence occur in the Three Circle phase and are delicate corner-notched Mimbres-type points (Figure 11.1J–O). Distribution of this type is solidly in the Three Circle and Late Three Circle phases; two specimens were recovered from possible San Francisco phase contexts, perhaps pushing the introduction of the bow back as early as the eighth century. By the end of the Late Three Circle phase, however, these forms are replaced by more triangular forms with parallel side notches that include Dockall's types Hinton, Swarts, and Cosgrove. Hinton points have parallel side notches and concave-to-indented bases (Figure 11.1A–C); Swarts points have parallel side notches but convex bases (Figure 11.1D–F). Cosgrove points have parallel side notches with usually straight or slightly convex bases but multiple notches along one edge (Figure 11.1G–I). Almost all of the parallel side-notched variants occur in the Classic period, if not exclusively so.

The distribution of the larger and heavier dart points includes all occupation phases, but most were recovered from Classic period contexts. Dart points date earlier than arrow points and were used to tip spears thrown with the aid of an atlatl. The distribution pattern might suggest to some that the atlatl and spear were used well into the Classic period or that these larger points were also used as arrow points. Neither interpretation is correct, for several reasons. First, as stated in the discussion above on manufacturing trajectories, no manufacturing waste, including broken preforms and discarded early stage failures, occurs in lithic assemblages from the Three Circle to Classic phases. Few aborted preforms are in the collection, and those that are generally fit the preform stages for small dart point forms shown in Figure 11.1. This finding indicates that many dart points were introduced into the local material assemblage as scavaged items. Second, the eclectic assemblage of temporally distinct dart point types ranges from Clovis to San Pedro. Clovis points are diagnostic for the first human occupants of the American Southwest, dating about 11,500 to 10,800 years before the present. San Pedro is a dart point type that occurs in the early agricultural and Early Pithouse period components in this part of the Southwest[10] (Figure 11.1U–Y) and was replaced by the corner-notched Mimbres-type arrow points. Some of the middle or late Archaic period types and early ceramic forms, including San Pedro, were likely collected by the Mimbreños from earlier sites scattered about the hillsides throughout the valley. Evidence of reuse and recycling into other tool forms that is seen on certain examples supports this contention. The tool shown in Figure 11.1W, for example, exhibits extensive wear and smoothing from handling. Third, further evidence that the use of the atlatl predates the Late Three Circle and Classic periods is the absence of this weapon system in Mimbres painted pottery. Depictions of the bow and arrow are frequent in Classic Mimbres pottery (appendix I: Figures A.19I, A.21E, A.F), and it is the only weapon system involving projectiles that was illustrated by the Mimbres themselves. Last, arrows hafted with the various arrow point types described above have been recovered in the Mimbres area, along with spear foreshafts with hafted versions of San Pedro and other late Archaic or early ceramic period types.[11]

None of the dart or arrow point types occur exclusively at the NAN Ruin or in the Mimbres Valley. These are all widespread forms that appear the same regardless of where they are found. The only major variance may be in raw material. Dart point types such as San Pedro vary widely in size and shape, owing largely to field retouching and reworking. Arrow points, on the other hand, are much more consistent in shape and size. The lack of regional style in projectile points compared to ceramics, for example, might be attributed in part to the mobility of males and the fixed residences of females in Mimbres Mogollon culture and society.

Metates and Manos

Metates were manufactured from rhyolite and basalt boulders gathered from the Mimbres River and selected on the basis of the medium or fine texture. They were roughly shaped by pecking away small bits with each strike of a hammer stone but gained the more traditional formal shape through use. Hammer stones used to make and maintain manos and metates were andesite/basalt cobbles collected from the same source. The repeated pounding eventually shaped the boulder; the metate preform had one approximately level face bordered on two sides by a ridge, with both ends were open (Figure 11.2 bottom).

Use of the metate required a grinding stone, pushed in a back and forth motion. The grinding stone, or mano, was preshaped to an elongated subrectangular form with one convex surface. Manos used in the Three Circle through Classic phases were long enough to be held by both hands (Figure 11.2 top); earlier-period manos were generally smaller, more oval in form, and generally the one-hand variety. Manos were also made of locally obtained andesite/basalts or rhyolites. Metate maintenance required the grinding surface worn smooth through use to be frequently roughened or pitted by pecking with a hammer stone; these metate pecking stones are among the most frequently identified stone tools in the collection. Vesicular basalt metates, however, did not require maintenance since grinding continually exposed new gas voids, which served the abrasive purposes.

Whole and fragmentary manos and fragmentary metates were scattered throughout the middens and rubble fill at the NAN Ruin. These items were used in the construction of cobble-adobe masonry and occasionally in hearth construction and were included among the stones in cairns over burials (Figures 8.10, 11.3). Their mundane uses suggest that once discarded as a mano or metate, the stones could be incorporated and used as any other stone in construction.

The evolution of metate forms has been correlated with the increased importance of corn in the diets of the ancient Mogollon people.[12] In the late Archaic period, prior to the incorporation of corn as a dietary mainstay, the grinding surfaces of metates were oval, basin shaped. As dry corn became incorporated as a dietary supplement, metate forms changed. By the Three Circle phase, metate shapes had changed to a trough type with one open end to facilitate the collection of the meal. As dry corn became more of a dietary mainstay in the Late Three Circle phase, metates evolved to a fully trough type open at both ends. The earliest trough metate was cached beneath the floor of Late Three Circle phase room 104. Paralleling this evolution in metate form are changes in manos, from oval one-hand varieties to elongated two-hand forms; the latter form predominates throughout the Late Three Circle and Classic times.

The distribution of whole metates across the site is very revealing in terms of how behaviors related to their use were organized. Each household evidently had at least one metate. Classic period metates occurred in habitation rooms (85, 94), on the ceiling (29, 46), in storage/granary rooms (108), in civic-ceremonial rooms (39), and in courtyards (16). In each case, they occurred singularly except for in room 39, the civic-ceremonial room. Here three were found in different parts of the room; none were together. Several manos were often found with metates, but this was not always the case. Three manos accompanied metates in room 94, and two were in proximity to metates in room 39. As noted elsewhere, both discarded

11.2: Manos (top) and metate (bottom).

metates and manos were frequently included among the stones in cairns placed above Classic period graves. We cannot dismiss the possibility, however, that these were merely incidental inclusions. Burial 1, for example, had two metate blanks, the cairn over burial 88 had a metate and four manos among the covering stones (Figure 11.3), and burial 151 had a petroglyph pecked into a recycled metate included in the cairn (Figure 8.11B).

Metate distribution within households in the Mimbres heartland is in marked contrast to that seen in the Anasazi and later mountain Mogollon, where mealing bins were commonplace. Mealing may have evolved as a woman's corollary to male kivas among the Anasazi during Pueblo II times,[13] but no such correlation can be made in the

200 / CHAPTER ELEVEN

11.3: Cairn over NAN Ranch Ruin burial 88, consisting of a metate and four manos.

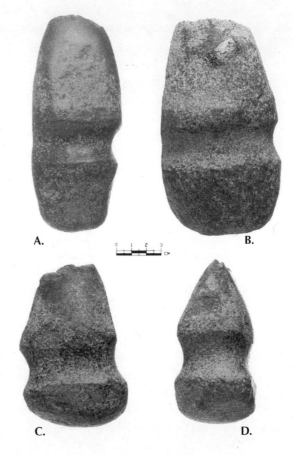

11.4: Three-quarter grooved greenstone axes.

Mimbres area. I suggested in chapter 6 that room 39 could have served a similar function, considering its unusual features and the presence of multiple metates, but it did not contain a mealing bin per se. Mealing bins were used by the mountain Mogollon after A.D. 1200 and could arguably be related to the Mogollon-Anasazi blend in that area during a time of Pueblo aggregation.

Grooved Axes

Three-quarter or full-grooved axes were only recovered from Classic period contexts. Axes were made of a uralitized diabase, a hard, dense, macrocrystalline igneous rock commonly called greenstone that outcrops in a tributary canyon of the Mimbres River about 17 km northwest of the NAN Ruin. These artifacts were prestige items apparently brought to the site in finished form (Figure 11.4). Evidence of their manufacture at the NAN Ruin is virtually nonexistent, despite the fact that rare cobbles of this material occur in ancient gravel deposits along the valley walls near the ruin. These axes, which were never numerous, were laboriously made by pecking and grinding this very dense stone. Occupants of the Galaz and Mattocks ruins had ready access to this material, and evidence of its exploitation at these sites is shown by the frequent occurrence of flakes from the manufacture of axes.

The greenstone axes were used, among other things, to acquire the timbers for room construction. Stumps of juniper used as the main support posts in room construction show signs of limbs being cut with stone axes. Since axes were associated with room construction, they may have been owned by and passed down through the lineage. This behavioral scenario may explain why an ax was found abandoned in virtually every residential unit excavated. Complete axes were recovered on the floors or fill of rooms 2, 29, 39 (2), 42, 62, 74, 79, and 85; one was recovered from beneath the floor of room 29. Axes were recovered from wall fall of rooms 39, 63, and 85, and another ax was recovered from courtyard 35.

The abandonment of these prestige items on the floors of rooms prior to terminating the rooms by burning and their inclusion as possible offerings in room construction, as suggested by the occurrence of axes in collapsed wall debris, is curious. It is also interesting that axes occur only in Classic period contexts, after the formation of corporate households. These patterns suggest that axes were considered part of the household and may have been "owned" by the lineage ancestors and matrilineal residents of the household (assuming the residential pattern was matrilineal).[14] Furthermore, both temporal and spatial contexts suggest that axes may have been one of the material correlates of corporate households and may have carried as much symbolic as functional importance.

Other Stone Artifacts

The collection of stone artifacts also includes items that were not used in technological roles, but in ritual activities. Such items as *tcamahias*, tubular stone pipes, palettes, and quartz crystals are among the more frequent items other than jewelry found at the NAN Ruin. Tcamahias were flat-bladed implements hafted on the ends of long sticks and used much like a spade (Figure 11.5). Tcamahias, often misidentified as hoes,[15] are thin, celtlike artifacts presumably used to tip digging sticks and in ritual performances. Most Mimbres tcamahias are chipped out of a tabular rhyolite procured in the Gila Wilderness, but one fragment (not shown) is a finely ground and polished specimen of a silicious banded mudstone from the Morrison Formation near the Four Corners area.[16] This specimen, recovered from general fill, is certainly an item of exchange from the Chaco region to the north.[17] Microscopic use-wear studies of the NAN specimens do not support their previously assumed use as hoes. Only two specimens were found in a primary context. One was on the floor of Late Three Circle phase kiva room 43[18] (Figure 11.5), and the other was on the floor of corporate kiva room 29. The remainder were recovered from general fill such as in loose rubble or midden contexts. As Florence Ellis shows,[19] the symbolic role of the tcamahia among the pueblos seems to have been the more important one, at least in historic times. The recovery of tcamahias in ritual contexts at the Mattocks site[20] and in Late Three Circle phase pit structure construction at the

11.5: Tcamahias.

11.6: Chipped stone knives.

Old Town Ruin[21] lends credence to this interpretation of their ritual function.

Most cutting and scraping were done with expedient cores and flakes obtained from local rhyolites or imported chalcedony and chert. These expedient tools were often discarded after only a few uses and represent the most common chipped stone artifacts in the lithic collection. Two unusual knives were recovered from the floor of

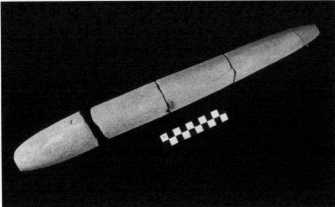

11.7: Tubular stone pipes.

11.8: Palettes and quartz crystals.

room 49. One is a much used biface of brown chert with a recurved blade (Figure 11.6). The blade edges are extensively dulled and damaged from use. The second specimen is even more unusual: it is a wide base-tanged knife of chalcedony (Figure 11.6). The distal end is not tapered but squared, and the sharp edge is finely retouched. Both knives may have been used for skinning and undoubtedly were curated items that saw considerable use.

Tubular pipes of stone and ceramic were among the items recovered from general refuse about the site (Figure 11.7). Only three specimens, all of stone, were recovered in primary context; two were in the fill of room 45,[22] the extraordinarily large Classic period room in the east room block, and one was associated with burial 127 in pithouse room 86. The role of the tubular pipe in rituals is well known in the American Southwest. Pipes were used in rituals and ceremonies to create smoke for purification and other cleansing or blessing ceremonies.

Palettes are another item that is much more common in the Hohokam area, but they also were found in both plain and decorated forms in Mimbres sites. They are usually of a slate or similar material that is relatively soft, including latite (Figure 11.8); some of the fragments are stained with pigments, suggesting their use in the preparation and use of paint. Complete or restorable specimens were mostly recovered from burial contexts, including both inhumations and cremations. For example, palettes occurred with Late Three Circle phase cremations dating from about A.D. 900 to 1000 (features 10-5/burial 218 and 11-16/burial 233). They also occurred in Three Circle and early Classic contexts (e.g., burials 93 and 117, respectively). One palette was recovered from the floor of Three Circle phase room 103.

Quartz crystals (Figure 11.8) must have held ritual power among the Mimbres. Although the occurrences of quartz were few, most crystals were recovered from special contexts. As described in chapter 4, a cache of 412 amethyst quartz crystals in a Mimbres Redware neckless jar was placed beneath the floor of room 91 in the approximate center of the room. Room 91 is a civic-ceremonial structure dating to the Late Three Circle phase.

Burial 127, an adult male placed in a crypt in the wall of pithouse room 86, contained a cluster of artifacts, including a tubular pipe and a quartz crystal. The items may have been part of a medicine kit associated with this burial. Another amethyst crystal was found in a posthole beneath room 8, possibly associated with room 5, and a single quartz crystal was recovered from the floor of room 39, a civic-ceremonial room dating to the Classic period.

Bone

Over 450 items were made of bone and antler, including tools as well as ornaments. Pointed bone implements, spatulate objects, gaming pieces, and rasps were among the items of modified bone (Figures 11.9–11). Over 200 specimens of pointed bone implements were recovered, the majority of which came from midden and fill deposits, but a number of specimens were recovered from floors. Most awls and pins were made of split long bones and the metapodial bone in the foot of artiodactyls (deer, antelope, mountain sheep), whereas ulnas and ribs of artiodactyls and even bones from smaller animal species, such as the metatarsal of a jackrabbit, were used for bone implements (Figure 11.9). Metapodial implements were made by variously modifying the bone to either leave an entire articular end or by splitting the metapodial to retain only half of an articular end or a long splinter was used. A number of complete metapodial specimens were recovered from room floors, including those of rooms 9, 12, 16, 18, 28, 29, 39, 50, 62, 63, 78, 94, 95, and 109. The only two complete ulna awls were found in room 16.

Ten bone implements were decorated; most were in the form of carved articular ends shaped into ram's heads or horns, incised or painted. Only one, the painted specimen from the floor of room 39, came from a primary context (Figure 11.10). Although often and perhaps incorrectly called awls, these tools probably served in a variety of functions, including weaving, sewing, quill work, basket work, shelling corn, pottery manufacture, head scratchers, and pins for robes. The forms have changed little through time, but the effigy items occur primarily, if not exclusively, in Classic period deposits.

The distribution of bone awls suggests that they were an integral part of the daily household tool assemblage. One possible role was as maize huskers in the shelling of corn. Implements called *tapiscadores,* which are often described as bone awls in the Southwest, are known to have been used in the process of husking and shelling corn in highland Guatemala.[23] One functional assemblage of artifacts recovered from the southeast corner of room 94 associates two bone awls with corn processing. A metate, three manos, and two bone awls composed the

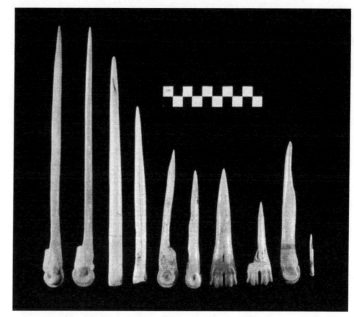

11.9: Bone awls and pins.

11.10: Decorated bone awls and pins.

assemblage. Another possible use for long bone awls or pins was as a hair ornament. The specimens with decorated ends may fall into this category, but none appeared in burials to suggest this use. Bone pins were used as hair ornaments in the mountain Mogollon groups that occupied the Grasshopper Pueblo.[24]

Another large class of bone artifacts is spatulate tools made from long bone shaft parts of large mammals, large mammal ribs, and modified jackrabbit innominates, or

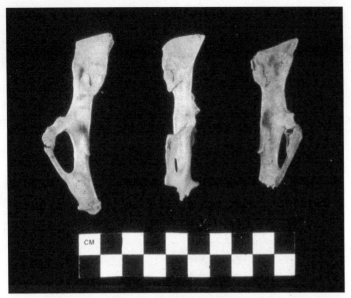

11.11: Spatulate tools of modified jackrabbit innominates.

11.12: Examples of textiles from the NAN Ranch Ruin.

analysis at the NAN Ranch site.[26] The majority of the modified jackrabbit innominates (approximately 100) came from floor structure and floor fill contexts; others were recovered from midden and fill deposits. Their uniform distribution and occurrence in fill and floor deposits suggest these items were part of workaday household tool kits, although their specific function remains a mystery. Temporal distribution shows that these tools were recovered mostly from Late Three Circle and Classic phase deposits; examples were found in the fill or floor of virtually every Classic period room excavated (Table 11.1, p. 206). Previous to the NAN faunal study, modified jackrabbit innominates were recognized only at Gran Quivira, a large Pueblo IV period site in east-central New Mexico. Since that time, however, these interesting artifacts have been recovered at the Old Town Ruin in the lower Mimbres Valley.

Fiber

Graphic images of decorated carrying baskets, mats, blankets, and garments are depicted on Mimbres Style III pottery, indicating that the Mimbreños had a rich basketry and textile tradition. Yet the Mimbres area is one of the poorest known in the American Southwest in regard to perishable industries. The conditions were not good for the preservation of fiber artifacts in this open-air archaeological site, although a small sample of desiccated or charred or fossil impressions of woven items was recovered. The sample is unique, however, in that it is the largest yet recovered from the Mimbres site and provides a glimpse of this class of material culture. These traces reinforce the graphic images left by the Mimbreños themselves on their painted pottery.

The fiber artifacts fall into two broad classes: basketry and textiles. Basketry is items manually woven without the aid of a frame or loom and includes baskets, mats, and nets. Textiles are woven with the aid of a frame or loom and include blankets, sashes, and garments.[27] Baskets are constructed by three methods: twinning, coiling, and plaiting. The technology of twinned baskets requires weaving elements or wefts around stationary elements or warps. Articles made with this technique include bags, mats, baskets, and sandals. Coiling is made by sewing or stitching flexible elements around a horizontal foundation of sticks, grass bundles, or whatever is the foundation choice. Basket containers are the predominate items

pelvis bones. Over 180 specimens of modified jackrabbit innominates were recovered, making them the most common form of modified bone found at the site[25] (Figure 11.11). The function of these tools is unknown, but they may have served as scraping implements or been used in shelling corn. Many show distinct smoothing and polish at the business end.

The jackrabbit innominates are unique tools not previously recognized in Mimbres material assemblages. They were discovered by Brian Shaffer during his faunal

TABLE 11.1. Distribution of Modified Jackrabbit Innominates by Room

Room/Pithouse	Frequency	Room/Pithouse	Frequency
11	2	55	7
12	1	56	2
14	1	57	2
15 a	3	59	1
25	3	60	8
28	3	64	1
29	1	65	3
35	4	74	3
37	1	78	4
39	5	81	1
43	1	82	3
45	7	83	4
18	1	84	2
46	7	94	2
47	1	109	4
50	14		

Source: After Shaffer 1991: Table 9.2. a Classic period midden fill overlying pithouse.

made by coiling. Plating involves the weaving of two elements over and under each other. Baskets, bags, mats, and sandals are among the items made by this technique. Textiles made on a frame or loom are constructed by simple plating. Variations in plating occur when different interlacing intervals are used.

The fiber sample from the NAN Ruin includes 63 fragmentary specimens plus a number of fossil impressions (Figure 11.12). The bulk of the collection was analyzed by James Adovasio, David Hyland, and Rhonda Andrews, and the discussion that follows is based largely on their analysis. They identified 15 twined textile fragments, 18 examples of coiled basketry, and 27 specimens of plaited basketry or textiles. An additional three examples of plaited basketry and several textile fossils have been added to their total. This is the largest extant collection of fiber artifacts from any Classic Mimbres site.

Only one structural type was found among the twinned specimens, consisting of a diagonal weave over paired warps. Both warps and wefts are single ply, Z spun cordage. All fragments came from burial contexts: 13 from burial 198 and one each from burials 15 and 199. The specimen from burial 15 is part of a garment worn around the waist, whereas those from burials 198 and 199 may be garments, blankets, and/or shrouds. Fossil impressions of finely woven blankets were also noted in Classic burials 46 and 141; these impressions were not included in the above analysis but provide further indication that burials were wrapped in mats or blankets prior to interment.

In contrast, three structural types were recognized among the coiled specimens and another three among the plaited specimens. One type, close coiling, bundle foundation, interlocking stitch, was used to fashion constricted-mouth storage vessels. One partially reconstructed container in room 95 measured about 8 cm at the mouth and 25 to 30 cm at the base. Another storage container fragment was recovered from room 74, and the third tightly woven example was recovered from Classic Mimbres midden deposits in an interior courtyard in the east room block.

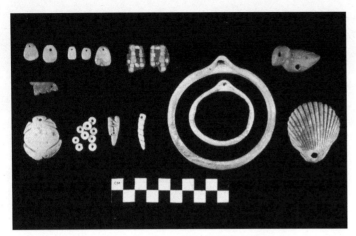

11.13: Examples of jewelry from the NAN Ranch Ruin.

A single basket or parching tray made by close coiling, whole rod foundation, noninterlocking stitch was interred with Three Circle phase burial 86 in room 14. The basket may have contained numerous artifacts associated with pottery making (polished pebbles, worked sherds). The third coiling technique, close coiling, two rod and bundle-bunched foundation, noninterlocking stitch, was used to construct shouldered, constricted-mouth bowls and globular bowls. Six fragments came from burial 86 and one from Classic Mimbres midden deposits in the east room block.

Thirty-one pieces of plaiting were recovered from the NAN Ranch Ruin excavations. Plaiting intervals varied from simple 1/1, 2/2, and 3/3. Contexts include domestic as well as mortuary, and the age of the plaiting extends from the San Francisco to the Classic phase. One piece of plaiting was part of a charred sandal from the floor of room 100; three came from burial contexts. Three Circle phase burial 86 in room 14 and cremation burial 175 contained pieces of plaiting; Classic Mimbres burial 88 in room 63 contained a trace of plaiting. The plaiting in burial 86 was part of a shroud mat encasing the body, whereas the latter two specimens were cloth items. The item with burial 175 was a sash adorning the waist; the textile with burial 88 may have been a cotton blanket. Plaiting was also recovered from a Three Circle phase pit containing burned shell corn (feature 11.24) and from Classic period rooms 11 and 74. The specimen from room 74 was a petate beneath a large jar.

Although the sample of fiber artifacts is small and highly fragmented, it provides a rare glimpse into the fiber industry of the Classic Mimbres. Graphic images of baskets, mats, and various articles of clothing are frequently depicted on Mimbres Style III pottery. The recovery of fragments of such material items as parching trays, bowls, jars, storage containers, sashes, garments, sandals, mats or petates, blankets and/or shrouds merely confirms that the pottery images depicted real things. The contexts of the samples also provide further information on mortuary behavior rarely reported for the Mimbres. Bradfield (1931) illustrates part of a shroud beneath a mortuary vessel at the Cameron Creek site, and the Cosgroves reported only two pieces of textiles from the Swarts Ruin: part of a twilled sandal and a coiled basket fragment. They too observed the fossil impression of a finely woven textile associated with a burial.

When the overall NAN Ruin fiber industry is placed into a regional and panregional perspective, it fits well with what is generally known for the Mogollon area and shows a blend of general southwestern and northern Mexican characteristics. Adovasio and Hyland attribute these characteristics to both the persistence of regional Archaic traditions and interregional interaction and suggest that the infusion of Mexican characteristics may have occurred with or following the introduction of ceramics into the region.

Ornaments and Jewelry

Broken or lost items of jewelry were found in the general fill throughout the excavations, especially in the fill adjacent to structures (Figure 11.13). A definitive study of the jewelry and its contexts was made by Maria Parks-Barrett.[28] Pieces of jewelry were also recovered from both the east and west plazas (perhaps lost during dances), on house floors, cached in room floors (a *Glycymeris* shell bracelet in room 28 and 412 quartz crystals in room 91), in the east plaza (turquoise), and associated with burials. The most frequent jewelry items are broken pieces of *Glycymeris* shell bracelets and *Pectan* shell fragments, especially in the east plaza, but effigy stone or shell pendants or beads, shell or stone beads, bone ornaments, turquoise pendants or beads, and rare copper crotals, or bells, were collected as well. Fragments of incomplete stone beads, pendants, and worked pieces of raw soapstone and turquoise indicate that some of the stone jewelry was made on the site. The shell, which included species from the Pacific Ocean, the Gulf of California, and possibly the Gulf of Mexico, was imported, probably in its modified form. In order of frequency, shell types include *Glycymeris* (361), *Nassarius* (182), *Pecten* (137), *Haliotis* (81), *Spondylus* (74), *Olivella* (34), *Conus* (5), coral (2), *Strombus* (2), *Turritella* (1), *Architectonicidae* (1), and *Columbella* (1).[29]

These lost or discarded items tell us about the range of materials used, forms of jewelry, technology, and patterns of style. Jewelry occurs in three primary contexts: as adornment jewelry in burials, cached in containers, or included as a mortuary or ritual offering. Prior to the NAN Ruin investigations, nothing was known about adornment jewelry except that it was found associated with some burials and not others. The distribution of mortuary jewelry from the NAN Ruin provides some interesting information on what kinds of jewelry were worn by whom. Jewelry was found in the form of pendants attached to the ears or worn around the necks of children, as bands of shell or shell and stone beads around the wrists or neck, as *Glycymeris* shell armbands, and as inlayed items, possibly worn around the neck. Classic Mimbres adults adorned with *Glycymeris* shell armbands and beads were all males in the NAN Ranch Ruin sample; none were found in an earlier context as adornment items. Children adorned with beads and bracelets at the time of burial were presumably males as well. Pendants were found as adornment on both males and females (Table 8.1). Cremation deposits dating from approximately A.D. 900 to 1050 also included fragments of burned *Glycymeris* shell bracelets, *Pectan* shells, *Nassarius* shell beads, and other shell items.[30] We could not determine if the jewelry adorned the body at cremation or was inclusions in the cremation pyre.

The context of adornment jewelry is one of the more powerful indicators of social marking among the ancient Mimbreños, perhaps equal to that of burial placement. If we assume that the society was matrilineal and practiced exogamous marriage (that is, taking a spouse from another village), then males would likely have been moving away from their community of birth. Their lineage or clan membership would not be immediately evident. One way of showing kin group identity may have been through dress, textile patterns, hair style or hair adornment, or adornment jewelry and the colors displayed in the jewelry (turquoise, shell, coral, red, black). Shell bracelets, red and black stone beads, and turquoise beads and pendants, for example, all occur independent of mortuary bowl association. Mortuary bowls, however, are restricted to indoor cemeteries in Classic Period times and, as argued here, are associated with those individuals having lineal connections. The independent occurrence of each of these items suggests that their presence as adornment jewelry may be marking certain individuals as members of a specific kin group or sodality.

Jewelry has been recovered in circumstances suggesting ritual placement rather than use as adornment or cache items. Four turquoise beads and one coral bead were included among the calcined bones of burial 234, placed in an early Mimbres Style III bowl. Neither of these items would have survived a cremation fire. Similarly, a cache of turquoise beads and pendants was found in the fill above room 113, presumably part of another cremation deposit that went undetected by the excavators. Another was placed in the fill of burial 130, a female, in room 76. A cache of 133 pieces of turquoise, including raw nodules as well as pieces of worked inlays, was recovered in the east plaza in the cremation cemetery area but not associated with a cremation. These occurrences clearly show that jewelry was not used merely as an embellishment of personal dress but was a class of material culture that was sex-linked and carried important symbolic meaning.

Three additional items of adornment worthy of mention are copper crotals, or bells. Three copper artifacts were recovered at the NAN Ruin. One bell was on the right wrist of burial 188, an adult male in room 98. This burial dates to Late Three Circle times. A complete copper crotal was recovered from the floor of late Classic room 47, and a damaged specimen came from the east plaza. The latter may have dropped off a dancer.

Summary

Material assemblages provide key sources of information about past cultures. It is largely on the basis of material assemblages that archaeologists are able to assess the approximate level of technological and social complexity. The approach taken here in examining the material culture of the ancient Mimbreños was to see what might be learned about their technology, how it was organized, and how it might relate to their subsistence and agricultural intensification or reveal information about their social organization. Analyses of the various classes of tools and related technologies of the ancient Mimbreños provide independent information that can be used to construct a model of Mimbres culture and society.

Stone tools provide information on Mimbres subsistence technologies and are dominated by artifacts associated with food processing, especially manos and metates, attesting to the relative importance of agriculture. Manufacture and maintenance of these tools required other tools, such as hammer stones or pecking stones, which also occur in relative abundance across the site. The distribution of manos and metates in a primary context suggests that food processing was not a collective enterprise, like that associated with the mealing bins of the Anasazi and mountain Mogollon, but rather was associated with individual households. Although we do not know precisely how the women so organized themselves, their organization differed from that of their peers in the Colorado Plateau.

Chipped stone technologies relate more to the mundane tasks that required expedient flake and core tools rather than to a concerted effort to produce hunting weapons. Arrow point manufacture did occur, but most arrow points were made of nonlocal imported raw materials, especially obsidian and chalcedony. But arrow point style is also revealing. Unlike the microstyles detected in the pottery, arrow point styles tend to be consistent across the Mimbres region. The most apparent is the Cosgrove type, the side-notched style with its multiple notches along one edge, a Classic Mimbres phase marker. The lack of variability in point styles across the region may be a reflection of the relative mobility of males in a matrilineal society, in contrast to the variability in ceramic designs and pastes, suggesting multiple nodes of production.

The primary contexts and site distribution of greenstone axes and jewelry may also indicate social divisions. Axes were abandoned on house floors, and broken or worn-out axes were often included in house wall construction. It is curious that axes, which require a great deal of labor to produce, would be left on house floors when almost everything else was removed at abandonment. One possible explanation is that the axes belonged to the house and by extension were the property of the matrilineage or ancestors and could not justifiably taken away at abandonment.

Certain material items, most tools of bone, for example, were merely part of each household's material assemblage and provide basic information on tools used in daily life. Awls, pins, and spatulate tools, although possibly made for specific tasks, probably had multiple uses. Because of their versatility and common occurrence, they do not provide information on social differences. The small spatulate tools made of jackrabbit pelvises, however, were a surprise, having gone unrecognized in previous faunal studies from Mimbres sites. In fact, with the exception of Gran Quivira, they have not been reported outside the Mimbres area. These mysterious little tools were the single most common form of modified bone in the collection and must have been part of each household's tool kit. Brian Shaffer and I have literally scratched our heads, searching for a function for these interesting items, and have found no corollary ethnographically. Maybe they were nothing more than spoons. If so, this might explain why the interior of serving bowls is often worn through the white slip.[31]

Only highly fragmentary and fossil textiles were recovered. This is the largest extant sample of Mimbres textiles from an open site and provides a valuable body of comparative information on the Mimbres textile industry. The range of vessels and items made of textiles include serving and storage containers, mats, shrouds, possibly blankets, sashes, and a sandal. Overall the NAN Ranch textile industry appears to be derived from northern Mexico, according to Adovasio and his associates, but shares many basic elements with the greater Southwest.

Another source of information on social organization is the distribution of adornment jewelry. Adornment jewelry was mostly restricted to certain males and certain children. The context of adornment jewelry is one of the more powerful indicators of social marking among the ancient Mimbreños, perhaps equal to that of burial placement. If we assume that the society was matrilineal and practiced exogamous marriage, then males would likely have been moving away from their community of birth. Their lineage or clan membership would not be immediately evident. One way of displaying kin group identity may have been through dress, textile patterns, hairstyle or hair adornment, or adornment jewelry and the colors displayed in the jewelry. Shell bracelets, red and black stone beads, and turquoise beads and pendants, for example, all occur independent of mortuary bowl association. Mortuary bowls, however, are restricted to indoor cemeteries in Classic period times and, as argued here, are associated with those individuals having lineal connections. The independent occurrence of each of these items suggests that their presence as adornment jewelry may be marking certain individuals as members of a specific kin group or sodality.

The display of items of a specific material class (shell, turquoise, red kaolin beads, etc.) may have been part of a code signaling social affiliation.

Finally, the various material classes provide strong evidence of distance procurement or exchange on several scales. Distance procurement simply means moving out of one's site catchment area into either resource zones shared by other communities or going to someone else's catchment area to acquire the desired material. Distance procurement would imply obtaining the materials directly, such as making a several-day journey to Mule Creek to obtain obsidian or making a day's trek down the valley to obtain latite. Quarry sites can be "owned" by the people on whose lands the resource occurs,[32] and the resource may be acquired simply by obtaining permission. Otherwise the material might be acquired through some form of reciprocal exchange. Hoarding valuable raw materials with the intent to exchange them for something of equal value doubtfully was part of the Mimbres economic system. Reciprocal exchange and reciprocal permission to acquire was more in keeping with the expected economic system of a middle-range society such as the Mimbres. Such reciprocal behavior would have been much more advantageous for cultures living on the brink of agricultural disaster.

Items obtained through distance procurement within the valley include Sugarlump rhyolite (latite) and other rhyolite slabs that do not occur in the immediate vicinity and cherts and chalcedony that are more prevalent in the lower reaches of the Mimbres Valley and on the Deming Plain. Local valley exchange is suggested by the procurement of complete greenstone axes and kaolin clay and red stone, soapstone, and possibly turquoise. Distant procurement outside the valley is indicated by the presence of obsidian nodules and artifacts of shell. Exchange outside the valley is certainly indicated for the procurement of all jewelry items made of shell. Much of this material ultimately came from the Hohokam area in a finished state through exchange. The same can be said of the copper artifacts: these were procured elsewhere, either from the Hohokam area or from neighbors to the south in northern Mexico.

CHAPTER TWELVE
Lost Ancestors or Oracles of Power

Introduction

Mimbreños expressed their beliefs and modeled their cosmology and perhaps even their social structure in the rich body of symbolism displayed in their material world. Mimbres symbolism expressed in architecture, on painted ceramics, and in mortuary patterns is especially unique, and together these forms of symbolism project a distinct cultural milieu that sets the Mimbres apart from all other cultural groups in the American Southwest and northern Mexico. Archaeologists tend to shy away from placing meaning on the symbolism because of the historical distance from modern Pueblo analogues and because meanings change. To understand such emic behavior requires one to be inside the culture itself. If the images and designs on the painted pottery held codes, they carried specific meaning only to those who could interpret the codes. The message, if any, a pottery motif or image was meant to convey is, of course, something we will never know. Any similarity to people in Mesoamerica or modern Pueblo people is apt to be more circumstantial than real, for these people were literally worlds apart in time, space, and cultural context. Since religious beliefs are among the most conservative of behaviors, the basic structure tends to endure despite substantive changes in the culture itself. An excellent example is the endurance of the basic structures of Christianity and Islam despite radical changes from the ancient world in which these religions were born to modern times. We can assume that modern Pueblo rituals and beliefs have some historical connection to prehistoric Pueblo and northern Mexican cultures, and therefore some underlying structural similarities could occur. How underlying beliefs are expressed on the surface in the material culture, however, may differ significantly, as will the people's explanations for these expressions. It is the surface expression of beliefs in the material record that archaeologists use to differentiate one ancient culture from another.

With these caveats in mind, I believe that given knowledge of the contexts in which symbolism is expressed, we would be remiss not to attempt some interpretation of its meaning. It is unrealistic to think that architectural changes, graphic designs on pottery, and placing mortuary bowls over the face of a body are beyond the limits of interpretation. If these facts stand alone, perhaps, yes, interpretation would be difficult. When placed in broader temporal, spatial, and cultural contexts, I think the symbolism can provide insight into Mimbres beliefs and cosmology, albeit not a complete understanding of the actual beliefs themselves. I will begin by briefly reviewing the contexts of this symbolism.

The changes from the community organization of pithouse times to that of the pueblo period were substantial, as noted in chapters 3 and 4. Architectural changes include a shift from extended entrances to ceiling hatchways, from circular to rectangular hearths, and of the location of hearths within rooms. Subsistence shifted in the Three Circle/Late Three Circle phase transition from mixed economy, in which agriculture was small scale and supplemental, to one in which it was large scale and the prime means of food production. Correlating with changes in subsistence economy were changes in storage behavior and the construction of formal granaries to protect the corn stored on the cob and other products of harvests. The shift to pueblo-style architecture correlates with the creation of enclosed corporate cemeteries with restricted access, the production of prestige black-on-white pottery embellished with iconography, and the expansion of interregional interaction networks to the people in the deserts to the south and east. These changes also reflect the reorganization of Mimbres society from what was probably the vestige of a family-based band organization of Archaic times to corporate lineages. The new organization was reinforced by rituals, feasts, and ceremonies whose primary emphasis was on bringing rain and ancestor veneration. These changes occurred throughout the Mimbres heartland and signaled a common reorganization in attitudes, values, and material expression of their worldview.

The basic material systems that characterized the Classic Mimbres culture—irrigation agriculture, architecture, mortuary customs, and Style III pottery—were clearly interconnected. Otherwise cobble-adobe pueblos and Style III pottery could have been produced no matter where the people went. A vestige of the mortuary behavior did linger for a short time in the Postclassic Black Mountain phase but eventually gave way to exclusively cremating the dead. None of these traditions were continued unchanged or transferred to other groups. I believe a common belief system connected the people to their ancestors, land, and water. This belief system is identified by the symbolism and stylistic themes on the pottery, which served as means of projecting and reinforcing corporate group identity and unity throughout the Mimbres community.[1] Unlike the spread of polychrome pottery and its associated ideology after A.D. 1250 in the Southwest,[2] the ideology that identified the Mimbres through their material expressions dissipated with the collapse of the system, about A.D. 1140. A number of lines of evidence in the Mimbres material record support the notion that the shift from pithouse to pueblo during the tenth century accompanied an expansion of the irrigation networks and a major change of emphasis in Mimbres symbolism and the way the symbols of the worldview were displayed as part of their religion.

Some understanding of how the Mimbres may have viewed their world can be gained by examining the general structure of Pueblo worldviews and using this to develop a generalized model or framework. The patterning in Mimbres material culture can then be considered within the context of such a structure. I am not suggesting that the Mimbres Valley people were direct ancestors to any of the Pueblos, but rather that they all shared historical roots in regard to their worldviews. In other words, the Mimbres were part of a larger group of cultures, extending from South America, Mesoamerica, northern Mexico, and the western United States, that shared a similar ideology. Similar motifs and icons expressed in material culture, however, may have far different meanings even though the underlying cosmology is similar.

Connections between Mesoamerican cosmology and Mimbres iconography have been suggested[3] or stated[4] by some scholars based on gross similarities between naturalistic motifs and writings and images from the Maya book *Popol Vuh*. As stated before, I think a shared cosmology exists across much of the Native American world that has deep historical roots. But to use Mesoamerican sources to interpret Mimbres iconography is at best a superficial and untestable exercise. We cannot hope to go to certain levels of interpretation because we simply lack the codes to communicate the meanings behind the symbols. Rabbits, for example, are a popular subject since they occur both in Maya and Mimbres iconography.[5] In Maya and other Mesoamerican cultures, rabbits may symbolize the moon. But animals, birds, and insects that dwell in the Mimbres habitat are commonly depicted in Mimbres iconography, including jackrabbits. In Huichol beliefs, deer are a metaphor for rain,[6] as are mountain sheep among the Shoshoni.[7] The iconic significance of jackrabbits may have been as a symbol for a fall harvest ceremony in which communal rabbit hunting played an integral part or as a symbol of a child's membership in a society. To assume that the meaning of rabbits or other Mimbres icons was drawn from Mesoamerican sources is to remove them completely from their contexts and interpret them outside the world within which they were produced.

In Native American cosmologies the boundaries of the physical world or territory are usually identified in the cardinal directions by natural features on the landscape, such as mountains or lakes. Within this space, the universe is seen as having multiple tiers, or layers.[8] Various layered pre-Newtonian universe schemes can be found among native cultures, and the numbers of layers may not always be the same.[9] For example, the tiered universe can be seen in the rock art of the Chihuahuan Desert[10] and among the Pueblo peoples,[11] Maya,[12] Huichol,[13] and Aztecs,[14] among others. This theme was expressed in various ways in the material world, and the layers usually included an Underworld, a Middleworld, and an Upperworld or Otherworld. The Underworld may have multiple layers of four or multiples of four. Indeed, this cosmological structure can be found in one form or another in belief systems worldwide, and a vestige is retained in the modern notions of heaven and hell. Although the latter duality is not found in Native American beliefs, Native American understanding of a layered universe and its boundaries in space is as much a part of the Native American natural world as morning and night.

The universe has seven directions: the four cardinal

directions mentioned above and zenith, nadir, and the intersection of all directions, the center. The center, or middle, of the cosmos is the sipapu, and the *axis mundi* through the center connects the various layers and is the path from one world to the next. Through this axis the dwellers of each world communicate through an open portal or hole. The Underworld is the world of the ancestors, the Middleworld is the world of the living, and the Otherworld is the world of the spirit beings. Many variations on these themes are found among the traditional beliefs of many native groups. One example is the Maya World Tree.[15] The scale on which this model of the cosmos can be re-created is infinite, a notion that has also been referred to as "symbolic resonance."[16] Such resonance may be reflected in the people's territory, a community, a household, an altar, or the arrangement of a burial.

Another characteristic of Native American beliefs is attention to detail, particularly to ritual, performance, and repetitive form or action. Since everything in the cosmos is knowable and therefore controllable, it is through control that harmony is achieved. Disharmony is a negative force and therefore must be avoided at all costs.[17] But within these strictures of detail, variability and substitutions are acceptable so long as certain prescriptions are followed. For example, in one instance at the NAN Ranch Ruin, a basket was substituted for a bowl as a mortuary vessel (burial 26).

Archaeologists have long known that native cosmologies and worldviews are expressed in behavior and material culture.[18] The vernacular architecture of the Mimbreños was built from resources obtained locally and within the region and probably conformed to their worldview. A major shift in house design from pithouse to pueblo could signal a change in either cosmology or the way their worldview was materially expressed. I suggest that the Mimbres house with the hatchway and associated features became symbolic of, or a metaphor for, the multilayered universe. An example of this characteristic in Native American cultures is the house of the Huichol in Jalisco and Nayarit, Mexico, which was built to replicate the cosmology of the people.[19] Farther afield is the close relationship between the Aztecs' concept of the universe and their architecture[20] and Maya architecture has been described as a human-made matrix complementary to the sacred landscape of the gods,[21] with pyramids re-creating mountains. The NAN Ranch Ruin community itself may have organized to conform to some kind of cosmic model, although we cannot define it on the basis of the room blocks and rooms that have been excavated or mapped. The general orientation for the architecture follows the cardinal directions, which seems to be the case for most large Classic period sites. If the vernacular architecture of the Mimbreños reflected the structure of their cosmology or worldview like that of the Huichol and Maya, how?

Ritual sites among mobile hunters and gatherers generally consist of places in the landscape such as springs, sheltered locations, and rock outcrops. Sedentary people create their sacred landscape within their architecture, as people do today with churches, synagogues, and mosques. The same pattern can be seen with the changing settlement patterns of the Mimbres when they settled down: they constructed their sacred landscape. Beginning in the Late Three Circle phase and continuing throughout the Classic period, habitation rooms with formal hearths apparently served dual purposes as family shrines and likely were constructed to conform to the cosmic model. When a cluster of habitation rooms developed in a single residential unit in the Classic period, one room was elevated to the next level above that of the other habitation rooms. These special rooms were embellished with a small, rectangular, slab-lined floor vault next to the rectangular hearth. Such rooms quite possibly were designated as the house of the dead or the ancestors. Rooms with floor vaults characteristically have higher numbers of burials beneath the floor than any other room in the suite. In other words, although any room could serve as one scale in which the cosmology was re-created, the rooms with the floor vaults represent another, albeit higher scale.

The Classic Mimbres did not have separate temples as did the Huichol of northwestern Mexico.[22] Use of rectangular great kivas in the Three Circle phase did not extend much into the Classic period, if at all. Rooms with floor vaults perhaps were the closest thing the Mimbres had to "temples." Nevertheless, I think the Mimbres re-created their sacred landscape of the layered universe in their vernacular architecture (Figure 12.1) much like the Western Pueblo people do with their subterranean kivas. In both the habitation rooms and those with floor vaults, the space above the floor in the room became the Middleworld, the world of the living; that space below the floor was the Underworld, the place of the dead. The Upperworld, the sky and the spirit world, was approached through the hatchway via the ladder. The hearth or the floor vault, depending on whether the room was a

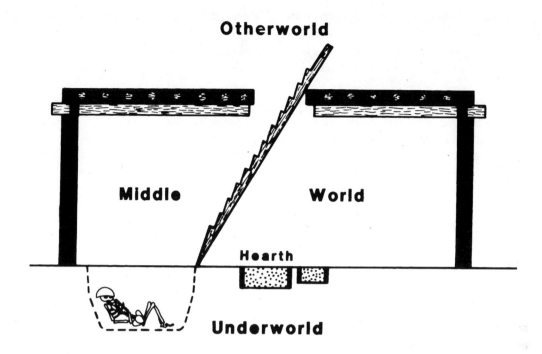

12.1: Proposed model of a Classic Mimbres kiva that re-creates their cosmology.

habitation room or a corporate kiva, was the portal, or sipapu, between the Middleworld and the Underworld, whereas the ceiling hatchway was the portal to the Upperworld. The ladder served as the axis mundi between the worlds. The rectangular hearth, vault, and ceiling hatchways represented the cardinal directions.

The ideology of the layered universe was expressed in the mortuary tradition as well. Placement of the dead in bounded cemeteries beneath the floor was to enter them into the Underworld realm of the dead. Perhaps more precisely, by burying the dead within the bounded space of the room, the room itself was re-created in the Underworld and was inhabited by the ancestors placed therein (Figure 8.8). Communication between the two worlds was facilitated by the hearth in habitation rooms, and the floor vault in corporate kivas served as the symbolic portal, or sipapu, of the emergence (Figure 5.7). The floor vault may also have served as a means of communicating with, and perhaps ritually feeding, the dead interred in the Underworld beneath the floor.

Barbara Moulard suggested that the layered universe was re-created in the mortuary ritual: the inverted bowl over the head of a corpse with the "kill" hole may have either served as a metaphor for the earth-sky dome[23] or symbolized the boundary to the Underworld. The idea that the sky was a solid dome that had to be pierced to get to the world beyond was widely held among native groups in America.[24] The "kill" hole in the inverted bowl may also have allowed the living to communicate with the dead and provided a portal through which the spirit of the dead could travel along the axis mundi between the Underworld and the Otherworld.

The practice of placing symbols for the passageway in the grave was widespread and varied among the groups in northern Mexico and the Southwest. The use of a "killed" mortuary vessel is just one possible method of symbolizing the emergence; placing a reed in the grave—as among the Tarahumara,[25] Huichol,[26] and Mayo[27]—is another. Among the pre-Classic Hohokam, Late Three Circle, and Classic Mimbres, cremation, reducing the body to ash, was one method of disposing of the dead. Ash is a widespread symbol for smoke, clouds, and ancestors, and cremating the dead may have been yet another way of admitting that person to the Otherworld as ash and smoke.

Although Moulard's theory seems plausible, yet another possible explanation exists for the burying of the dead beneath the floor of households and corporate kivas and placing a "killed" bowl over the face. Placement of burials beneath rooms with restricted access may have been to restrict access to the ancestors themselves. Presumably it was these individuals who held ritual knowledge and who therefore could have been consulted as oracles. The bowl may have served as a mask and the hole as the mouth through which communication and ritual feeding could occur. Ample ethnographic and archaeological evidence support this interpretation. In the great Mesoamerican city of Teotihuacán, for example, ancestors were placed in flexed positions and wrapped in bundles with carved masks placed over their faces. They were then placed in caves or crypts and consulted as oracles.[28] At the NAN Ruin, San Francisco phase burial 127, which was placed in a crypt, perhaps symbolic of a cave, could be a precedent for this kind of behavior, which had become well established by the Late Three Circle phase. It is appropriate to note that the practice of placing a bowl over the face of a burial is an almost exclusive characteristic of intramural burials. Classic period extramural burials at the NAN Ranch lack this feature; the one exception was burial 234, which was a cremation. Why did some burials have bowls and not others? Extramural burials were mostly unattached males who were probably not members of local corporate families and were therefore excluded from corporate cemeteries. Cremations may have been for members who died elsewhere, from unusual circumstances, or in some other way that excluded them from intramural interment. The fact that no cremations were found in any of the intramural cemeteries suggests some exclusionary rules applied. Burial 234 is exceptional in that it was a secondary cremation in the east plaza that was covered by a "killed" bowl. We can only guess why, but perhaps this individual was an important member of a local corporate group who died under circumstances that precluded intramural burial; because the person was important, he or she was buried with the "killed" bowl to facilitate communication anyway. The beads (three turquoise and one red coral) included among the calcined remains may relate to the individual's lineage or sodality membership.

Intramural burials were intramural because the dead were members of the lineage or corporate group, but within that larger group some may have held secret ritual knowledge by association regardless of age. Infants and children obviously were too young to grasp the meaning or significance of the knowledge, but in birth they automatically became members of the society that held such knowledge, and in death they became associated with or transformed into that society. When placed beneath the floor of the restricted access kiva, living members could consult with the ancestors through the floor vault portal. Through the ancestors, the living could claim legitimacy to the irrigated agricultural lands. The ritual of placing the vessel over the face transformed that individual into an ancestral spirit being. In ceremony, the ancestors could be personified by dancers wearing masks. I believe the behavior of masking an ancestor in this fashion is antecedent to the Katcina ceremonies and rain-making ceremonies of later Pueblo culture.

The idea that the Katcina ceremonies originated with the Mimbres is not new.[29] Graphic hints of Katcina and rain ceremonies began in the Late Three Circle phase with the emphasis on eyes and eye motifs and abstract motifs comparable to the Tlaloc-like images seen in Mimbres and Jornada rock art.[30] Eye motifs appear first in abstract geometric designs (appendix I: Figure A.2I) and in anthropomorphic and zoomorphic images. One notable petroglyph near the McSherry Ruin illustrates this point quite clearly (Figure 4.14, top). Interestingly, this particular site had a scatter of Mimbres Style II and Style III and Mimbres Corrugated pottery sherds on the slopes in front of the petroglyph, suggesting it was periodically provided with food offerings. Parallels in the eye motifs and other images seen in middle Mimbres Valley petroglyphs can be seen in late Style II and early Style III bowls (appendix I: Figures A.7E, A.G, A.12E).

Another means of projecting Mimbres religious themes, such as the layered universe, was in the rules of design followed in decorating pottery. Although one seldom finds two Mimbres bowls painted alike, the rules followed by the artists in exercising their individuality and creativity were precise, albeit not static. These precise rules, for example, were followed in executing the multiple fine lines and two or more broad lines framing the design fields at the rim, the one or two broad lines framing the center of the bowls, and the balance between solid and hatchure elements. The rules helped to define the style, and as the rules changed, so did the style. Variability in contemporaneous microstyles within Style III may therefore reflect various corporate traditions of potters within the valley. But it was the adherence to the underlying rules that created the unmistakable Mimbres Styles II and III pottery.

Patterned cultural behaviors such as the Mimbres mortuary tradition reveal much about how people structured their lives. There seems to be little doubt that the Mimbres cosmology and worldview were graphically expressed in both architecture and mortuary behavior.[31] Likewise, I would argue that the cosmology and worldview of the Mimbres was vividly displayed on their painted pottery, which projected themes, icons, metaphors, and many aspects of their rituals and ceremonialism.

Precise rules in design layout may also have been followed to communicate recognizable symbols or characters of important themes or myths. For instance, a connection may have existed between the designs and symbols painted on Mimbres pottery and earth, sky, and rain, and perhaps a connection between the living and the dead as well.[32] The structure of the design and various motifs, as mentioned in the previous chapter, displays elements of Mimbres mythology and cosmology. Although we will never know the precise meaning of the motifs and symbols or if the meaning was ever precise, a buzzard drying its wings and embellished with huge, Tlaloc-like eyes could easily have stood for rain (appendix I: Figure A.12E). The same design could also relate to an ancestor spirit associated with rain bringing, somewhat akin to the Western Pueblo Katcina ceremonies.[33]

Regardless of what the actual meanings were, the underlying themes seen in Mimbres painted pottery seem to relate to the layered universe and rain in one way or another. The framing of the vessel using parallel lines or design bands served to vertically separate the design fields within the bowl or on the jar. A fish or paired fish, red ants, lizards, toads, and other creatures that lived under the surface may have been metaphors or symbols relating to the various layers of the universe, creatures that were thought to dwell within, or perhaps relating to the ancestor or totems themselves. For instance, the Underworld may have been depicted by owls, bats, and other creatures of the night. Grotesque figures, composite figures, and wavy lines connecting motifs may depict spirits or transformations into the Otherworld. Scenes depicting daily life may have reflected the Middleworld or perhaps been metaphors for activities associated with specific corporate groups. Seasonal changes and calendar events may be shown as well. Frogs, insects that appear in the rainy season, a buzzard drying its wings, deer, and various abstract symbols possibly depicting clouds, rain, and lightning all may represent rain or the rainy season. The vessel shown in Figure A.18B in the appendix seems to depict a Mimbres potter's impression of a thunderstorm. Characters in myths, dancers, and other public ceremonies marking calendar events may have been ways of visually instructing other members of society on Mimbres traditions.

Or maybe we are trying to read too much into the graphic images and designs. They could just as well stand for totemic identities of various lineages or corporate groups or simply have been the fancy of the potter at the time she decided on the specific details of the design for that particular vessel. The painted pottery is rich in graphic symbolism and likely projected powerful messages for artisans and viewers alike. We can assume that these messages, codes, and themes served to reinforce Mimbres beliefs and values. We can speculate, as I have done here, on what those codes and symbols meant, but we will never known for sure.

Potters lived in each of the large Mimbres villages and probably in each corporate household. Neutron activation analysis has suggested that pottery was produced at each large Mimbres town.[34] Production of the prestige black-on-white and polychrome pottery was very likely at the extended household or corporate level and may have been one of the material commodities used to promote the prestige of ritual knowledge held by primary corporate groups. Mimbres bowls rarely display identical designs, but close similarities exist, suggesting that the bowls were made by the same potter (appendix I: Figure A.16A, B). It would be pure luck to have two or more bowls made by the same potter, chosen for mortuary use, and recovered by archaeologists. The chances of identifying the bowls of a similar potter are very small given the odds of sampling. At this time trace element analysis does not provide the scale of resolution to identify clusters within a general site area with confidence. A comparison of the distribution of naturalistic motifs, supported with trace element analysis, has shown that certain motifs do indeed cluster at specific sites.[35] As I said above, at the NAN Ranch Ruin birds and fish are the commonest identified naturalistic motifs.

Mimbres social and ideological patterns connected the people to the landscape in other ways as well. With the shift to agriculture as the primary subsistence mode in the A.D. 900s came a radical change in land-use strategies. Lands suitable for agriculture in the Southwest are far more limited than are lands that can be used to sustain hunters and gatherers, and therefore agricultural lands became highly valued, especially if surplus yields could be produced. The Mimbres River valley is notable for its large Mimbres ruins spaced 2 to 3 km (Figure 1.7). This spacing suggests that the irrigated lands were divided into territorial units, with kinship groups or extended households in each pueblo having the rights to its respective lands. Rights and claims to agricultural lands usually were handed down through the traditional lines of inheritance unless the land was abandoned.[36] Even then, landownership was retained and permission from the owner was probably necessary to reuse the plots. Kinship groups who claimed good farmlands may have justified their rights to lands through their ancestors.[37]

End of the Classic Period

So what brought about the demise of this rich, graphic tradition? Paul Minnis[38] has argued that the Mimbres overextended their uses of the agricultural lands and other resources and that failure in agriculture brought an end to the Classic Mimbres way of life. He and others have presumed this failure was brought about by years of below-normal rainfall beginning shortly after A.D. 1100. In all probability climate change was the culprit, but not in the way Minnis suggests. Recent findings along the Salt and Middle Gila rivers in Arizona document a period of severe channel entrenchment and widening that coincided with abrupt changes in Hohokam sequence. The authors of this study, Michael Waters and John Ravesloot, suggest this period of down cutting destabilized irrigation agriculture and interrupted cultural patterns.[39] Origins of the floodwaters include the Gila Wilderness, which also served as the headwaters of the Mimbres. The onset of this landscape change in the upper Gila may have led to early abandonment of Mimbres settlements along that stream. The landscape of the Mimbres River differs somewhat from that of the Gila, but the effects on irrigation networks may have been similar, causing eventual abandonment of the systems altogether.

Rooms were still being added to existing residential units at the NAN Ranch Ruin in the year A.D. 1109 to 1116, based on cutting dates from trees used in construction, but little building occurred after that time. Signs of abandonment, such as rooms going into ruin while an adjacent room was still used, were occurring, however, shortly after A.D. 1116. The last construction date represented in the tree-ring samples at the NAN Ranch Ruin was A.D. 1128 or shortly thereafter. This was for room 84, which was built on the ruins of an earlier room. An attached room, room 74, yielded a very late assemblage of pottery that included large vessels of Classic Mimbres, El Paso Bichrome, and Convento Indented Corrugated types (appendix I: Figures A.31D–F, A.32B–D). Final abandonment of the NAN Ranch Ruin probably occurred in about A.D. 1140.

The pattern of abandonment seen at the NAN Ranch Ruin was typical of that of other large Mimbres towns throughout the Mimbres area. Whether total abandonment of some sites such as the Old Town Ruin took place is debatable and difficult to prove one way or the other because of a lack of precise dating and substantial occupation on and near the Classic Mimbres ruin by people in the Mimbres Postclassic period.

Something caused the Classic Mimbres system to come apart, and I think it happened with a failure in the water management system. The failure was probably not site specific; more likely, it involved the network of towns along the river valley. Each town was dependent on the towns upstream for responsible water use and management. If something happened to disrupt this dependent network, then system failure was sure to occur. The blame may not have been merely social. If a connection was made between the ancestors and productivity of the land, the ancestors were probably held in high regard so long as the lands were producing surplus. If, however, the rains failed to come or episodes of serious floods interrupted irrigation systems, food production would have been affected. Such disharmony may have caused strained or severed relationships between the living and the ancestors. Once broken, the oracles lost their power, and all values related to ancestor veneration along with the material expressions of those values were no longer relevant. The power of corporate ceremonies and reinforcing symbols was weakened, and prestige painted pottery, one of the sources for reinforcing codes, ceased to be produced. Divorced from the land and ancestors, the Mimbres families abandoned their residences and moved elsewhere.

The Classic Mimbres, as they are archaeologically defined, are unlikely to have consisted of a single tribal or ethnic entity. Significant behavioral differences, as expressed in the mortuary customs and subtleties in ceramic design, distinguish the Mimbres in the Mimbres watershed from those in the upper Gila River area. Likewise, the Mimbres communities east of the Black Range, although clearly sharing many diagnostic traits of the Mimbres Valley folks, either may have constituted a separate group or have budded off and become a separate group after A.D. 1100 or so. There is some reason to suggest that the geographically separate groups went their own ways when the breakdown of the Classic Mimbres traditions occurred and many of the large towns in the Mimbres Valley were abandoned. This fragmentation may have been due to social conflicts that arose with the collapse of the networks responsible for managing the river's waters. The upper Gila Mimbres may have been absorbed into the Mimbres Valley populations or melted into the Reserve area, becoming part of later Mogollon groups in that area. The groups east of the Black Range may have integrated with other Rio Grande groups or mixed with displaced Cibola groups, whereas those in the middle and lower Mimbres Valley shifted their ranges southward. Some ventured into Mexico, eventually becoming part of the Casas Grandes sphere.

Some evidence suggests that although the old Classic towns were abandoned, periodic visitation occurred, probably to reinforce claims to the lands. Token Black Mountain phase activity has been noted at Swarts, Galaz, NAN Ranch, and Old Town, and interestingly, Black Mountain phase sites were established on or in immediate proximity to the Diesert, Galaz, Swarts, NAN Ranch, McSherry, Eby, Prewitt Ranch, and Old Town sites.

The Postclassic Mimbres world is not well known simply because of the lack of field research. After A.D. 1200 the region west of the Rio Grande and from the southern Mimbres Valley to northern Chihuahua and over to the Arizona border was sporadically inhabited by Mimbres descendants, who lived in aggregated adobe pueblos constructed of coursed adobe. Considerable variability appears in the overall patterning of material culture from one valley to the next, suggesting absence of a coherent or integrating religion among these communities, even with the rise of the Casas Grandes regional system. People in the short-term pueblo communities obtained their painted pottery from adjacent regions, such as the Cibola area to the north, the El Paso area to the east, the Salado area to the west, and Casas Grandes to the south. Playas Red, a culinary pottery used during both the Black Mountain and Cliff phases, was locally made. Ceramic assemblages, albeit with subregional variations, grossly tie these Postclassic Mimbres settlements to broader regional patterns, but architectural differences, such as the presence of ball courts in settlements to the south and west, suggests the ethnicity of the Casas Grandes/Mimbres/Salado world was complex.[40]

Conclusions

The Mimbres cultural tradition was born out of the Archaic tradition of the western deserts. By about 1500 B.C. the Archaic peoples of the Chihuahuan and Sonoran deserts obtained corn from their neighbors to the south in Mexico. Agriculture was the single most important ingredient that transformed the hunters and gathers into a middle-range corporate society. The process was slow and continuous, owing to a gradual population increase and changing subsistence strategies that reduced mobility and enhanced utilization of local wild and domestic plants. Early agricultural practices probably included dry farming, akchin irrigation, and possibly even pot irrigation. The transformation processes accelerated in the Three Circle phase with the initial construction of river irrigation networks that were fully in place by the Late Three Circle phase, from about A.D. 900 to 1110. The success of this strategy became evident with the reorganization of Mimbres households and society, construction of formal granaries, production of prestige pottery, establishment of restricted access cemeteries, and changes in ritual behavior.

The archaeological case for the rise and fall of the Classic Mimbres phenomenon has been presented in the preceding chapters. I have traced growth and change in the NAN Ranch Ruin community from the Late Pithouse period Georgetown and San Francisco phases through the Classic Mimbres period. These changes affected all aspects of Mimbres culture and society. Foremost among these changes was the shift from pithouses to surface pueblos. These changes, which went beyond architecture, underscore a fundamental reorganization that took place in Mimbres society and belief systems. The latter was necessarily brought about by organizational changes in the subsistence economy, technology, and political spheres to accommodate a growing population.

The rise and fall of the Classic Mimbres is well recorded in recent refinements of the chronology, but little effort has been made to explain how it all came to be and why it ended. A previous explanatory model claimed that the rise and fall of the Mimbres was a response to food stress from feeding a growing population and that the population exceeded the capacity of the technology and environment to sustain its peak. This model does not explain the development and demise of the material characteristics that identify the Mimbres in southwestern archaeology, which include surface pueblos, Mimbres painted pottery, and a unique mortuary tradition. In this chapter I present a model detailing the rise and fall of competitive corporate groups in Mimbres society, synthesized from information presented in previous chapters. This model incorporates information deduced from changes in Mimbres subsistence technologies, architecture, storage behavior, mortuary patterns, painted pottery, and symbolic behavior. I have argued that this transformation involved a societal reorganization around irrigation agriculture, which yielded food surpluses; successful implementation of irrigation agriculture led to the evolution of more tiers of social interaction in both the secular and nonsecular arenas. Expected correlates for these tiers of social interaction seen among the earlier pithouse people include decorated material items such as ceramics, textiles, production of prestige items, and evidence of feasting behavior. With the formation of corporate groups, lineage cemeteries, restricted access storage, and secret shrines would also be expected. All are arguably present in Mimbres material culture from approximately A.D. 950 to the early 1100s. This suggests that the Classic Mimbres social organization of the NAN Ranch Ruin community was structured around corporate groups defined along kinship lines. Although the integrity of each community was probably recognized, communities within the Mimbres River watershed were integrated through a segmentary lineage system based on exogamous marriage patterns. Precisely what form of political leadership emerged with these changes is unknown, but there is no indication that power was confined to a single individual or priestly class. More likely, leadership involved some form of management structured around corporate-based rituals. This does not preclude the possibility that powerful priests or lineages inhabited certain towns. Mimbres Valley communities closely shared a common religious order that left remarkably consistent patterns in mortuary practices and black-on-white pottery regardless of whether the settlement was at the lower end of the valley (e.g., Old Town), extreme upper end (e.g., Elk Ridge), or along a major tributary (e.g., Cameron Creek).

The Classic Mimbres phenomenon began with the shift from a residentially mobile mixed economy to a sedentary agriculturally dependent economy in the Three Circle phase (ca. A.D. 750–900). This shift began with the incorporation of new varieties of corn and likely initial experiments with irrigation agriculture. Irrigation networks probably became well established in the Late Three Circle phase (ca. A.D. 900–1000) with the formation of the corporate lineages, lineage cemeteries with restricted access, secret ceremonies, and all the associated material accouterments.

Late Pithouse period villages were probably composed of family groups, some clustered, others apparently single. Thin middens and lack of burials for the Georgetown and San Francisco phase components suggest these villages were not permanently occupied. They represent a continuation of the pattern of winter villages for a relatively mobile population that followed a mixed economy. This pattern extended back to the period of early agriculture prior to the Christian era in this part of the Southwest. Agriculture played a significant role in subsistence in the Late Pithouse period but was probably limited to individual extended family enterprises conducted on optimal subirrigated plots along the river or its spring-fed tributaries or on alluvial fans. Some degree of mobility is also suggested by the absence of formal granaries and the storage of shelled corn, behaviors characteristic of residentially mobile groups.

Family groups residing in larger communities were probably integrated via communal rituals and activities associated with great kivas. As populations increased, access to fertile lands was given prime importance as groups laid claim to prime irrigation plots. Residential space became fixed in the Three Circle phase (ca. A.D. 750–900), as suggested by long histories of rebuilding over the same location within the community, shown by the architectural history of the south room block. Some associated pit structures were probably arranged around courtyards, indicated by the findings at the Old Town and NAN Ranch ruins, and the establishment of lineal inheritance of the household is suggested in the Three Circle phase by the interment of important females in subfloor graves.

By the Late Three Circle phase (ca. A.D. 900–1010), this pattern began to change, and attention was paid to placing more labor in expanding productive lands by tapping into the river and diverting the waters to low-lying fields. This shift in subsistence technology is inferred based on such correlates as changes in residential architecture, storage patterns, and attitudes toward the treatment of the dead. Extended family structures became more clustered and centered around a core room, which also became the lineage cemetery. The formation of corporate linage groups is based on the emergence of such cemeteries and correlates with the demise of the great kiva, whose functions were largely taken over by secret corporate group ceremonies. Great kiva room 52 at the NAN Ranch Ruin was abandoned prior to the 900s, and the other great kiva room, 43, was apparently abandoned in the 900s.

Prime families—or, more likely, those who were there first—laid claim to residential space, as shown by a succession of construction episodes spanning three phases in the south room block at NAN Ranch. The Three Circle phase courtyard cluster beneath the south room block evolved into a grouping of early cobble-adobe pueblo-style structures with ceiling entrances. At first these appear to have been clusters of individual structures, but they evolved into aggregated room blocks in the Classic period. Among the Late Three Circle phase structures were primary households and formal granaries with restricted access. At least two varieties of corn, an eight-row variety and a 12 to 14 row variety, were now stored on the cob. Restricted access formal lineage cemeteries with people of both sexes and all ages were established beneath prime habitation rooms, as shown by room 104. The practice of placing a "killed" bowl over the face of the corpse began in the Late Three Circle phase. I interpret these Late Three Circle phase developments as evidence that corporate groups became fully established at this time, with their own lineal residences, granaries, cemeteries, and secret and public ceremonies as means of political control. These developments also correlate with the emergence of Mimbres water control features in the Rio de Arenas, and Mimbres Style II pottery was part of the material manifestation of these developments. Its production may have been part of the emergence of public ceremonies and ritual. Secret and public rituals are powerful methods of enlisting membership into corporate enterprises. These material patterns, seen developing in the Late Three Circle phase, continued into the Classic period, albeit with some elaboration.

Habitation rooms constructed in the Late Three Circle phase often became core rooms for some Classic period suites. This was especially the case with rooms 12 and 29. I suspect these were the residences of prime landholding families, particularly where the evolution of a suite can be traced to a core room such as the south room block. Contiguous room construction is a Classic period hallmark, and some individual suites demonstrably were occupied by related families. This interpretation is based on habitation rooms sharing long walls or examples of unique traits found only in one suite, such as burying a body facedown in a flexed position. Not until the Classic period, however, did corporate kivas become distinguished by associated features, such as underlying cemeteries, floor vaults, and, in individual cases, wall niches, benches, and wall shelves. I used the number of kivas present in the excavated part of the NAN Ranch Ruin to estimate the number of corporate households present in the community. There were at least six corporate kivas in the east and south room blocks combined and perhaps as many as 12 across the community during its peak population from A.D. 1060 to 1110. The ratio of corporate kivas to other rooms was about 1 to 8 at the NAN Ruin and is consistent with the ratio of rooms with floor vaults to rooms without floor vaults at Swarts; it is also consistent with the ratio of round kivas to rooms in Pueblo II and III Anasazi sites. Although some corporate kivas at the NAN Ranch Ruin were used for up to six generations, others were not: some were abandoned and relocated; others became established in the middle or late Classic period, perhaps due to occasional in-migration or budding off of social groups.

One can construct a model of the structure of the NAN Ranch Ruin community by recognizing the various tiers represented in Classic period architectural units. The organization begins with the household, composed of one habitation room with a formal hearth. These rooms rarely stood alone unless they were the first constructed. They usually occurred in combination with other habitation rooms sharing common granaries, large storage rooms, civic-ceremonial rooms, and a corporate kiva. This cluster of residential and common rooms formed the corporate households, the core residential unit for each large Mimbres site. Corporate households stood alone, as was the case with the south room block, or became aggregated with other corporate households, forming a large room block, as with the east room block at NAN Ranch and the north and south house at Swarts.

Corporate households were composed of six to 15 or so rooms, incorporating three to five or more individual habitation rooms. Corporate households can be identified at Swarts, Mattocks, the Wheaton-Smith Ruin, and NAN 15, where comparative data are available. Most sites in LaVerne Herrington's second-order to fourth-order sites in the Arenas Valley represent corporate households. In aggregated sites such as NAN Ranch, Swarts, and Mattocks, for example, corporate households apparently were not equal, judging from the architecture and mortuary goods. Certainly the south room block and the Cosgrove suite stand out at NAN Ranch in regard to high cemetery populations and relative wealth present in some graves. This suggests that some kind of hierarchical ranking existed among corporate groups. Given what we now know of the social organization and relative hierarchical ordering of such groups within Prehispanic and Western Pueblo society, some form of internal ranking can be expected.

The clustering of corporate households, whether standing separate, as at Mattocks and the south room block at NAN Ranch, or aggregated, as they were in the NAN east and west room blocks and the north and south houses at Swarts, formed the communities. Within each community, one plaza area was the focal point of public rituals and ceremonies. The "dance plaza" at Swarts and the east plaza at NAN Ranch contained features and other evidence to suggest extensive uses were made of these spaces for public rituals and ceremonies. Evidence from both Swarts and NAN Ranch also suggests that cremation cemeteries were established in these important plazas.

How the communities were organized in regard to leadership is unknown. As noted above, there is no indication that power was confined to a single individual or priestly class. No special or elaborate mortuary facilities or tombs exist at NAN Ranch. One possible exception is a very unusual burial at Old Town. More likely, leadership involved some form of management structured around corporate-based rituals. The internal leadership may have been structured around a ranking of corporate households and who held rights to the most important rituals and ceremonies. Nodes of civic or ceremonial leadership may have existed at different times or during different seasons. Externally, two Mimbres sites generally stand out in regard to size and evidence of social interaction, based on trace element analysis of pottery: Galaz in the middle Mimbres Valley and Old Town in the lower Mimbres Valley. Our main problem in assessing the relative political importance of these sites is that both have been all but destroyed, Galaz by commercial bulldozing and Old Town by a century of ambitious relic hunting. In comparison, however, NAN Ranch, with at least four known room blocks, was probably larger than Swarts and almost equal to Galaz in size.

Residential longevity at most large Mimbres towns can be traced back to at least the Three Circle phase, and residential continuity is evidenced in certain cemeteries. Some corporate cemeteries established in the Late Three Circle phase were used well into or throughout the Classic period. This longevity attests to the importance of maintaining group affiliation and genealogical connection to a fixed place (presumably both house and field). Restricted access to these cemeteries appears to have been of paramount importance, perhaps for reasons that I will explain later.

Studies of social organization based on mortuary patterns suggest that Mimbres society was matrilineal. This interpretation is strengthened by such patterns as adult females being restricted to intramural cemeteries and some adult males being buried outdoors without associated mortuary vessels. The extramural graves were very likely of people unattached to the corporate groups residing at the NAN Ranch community. The interpretation that the Mimbres society was matrilineal is also strengthened by other studies in the Southwest showing that matrilocal groups formed the foundation for polities based on corporate organization.

The zenith of Mimbres corporate group behavior was reached in the middle Classic period, approximately A.D. 1060 to 1110. Unusually warm climate conditions and favorable rainfall patterns provided optimal conditions for agriculture and expansion into slightly higher elevations during this time. It is probably a good bet that the Mimbres irrigation systems had matured by this time and were working to capacity.

Mimbres population had reached its peak during the middle Classic period as well. The largest number of rooms was occupied at the NAN Ranch Ruin from about A.D. 1060 to 1110. This is also when Mimbres Style III pottery production reached its peak and displays the greatest variability in motifs and motif combination within a relatively conservative stylistic framework. Ceramic studies have shown an increase in the size of jars from the Late Three Circle to Classic times. Some of these jars got really big in the Classic period, as did certain bowls, suggesting that progressively larger groups were being served. Studies have also shown the widespread distribution of Mimbres Style III pottery, extending well into the residentially mobile Doña Ana and San Simon assemblages through the processes of gift giving and exchange. If each corporate group held its own secret ceremonies and hosted public feasts, then some kinds of accompanying prestigious material accouterments would be expected. Style II and III ceramics are likely surviving candidates for prestige items used in public ceremonies, feasts, and gift giving.

If these were prestige items used to promote a particular corporate group, then variability in motifs might be explained within the context of corporate group behavior as projection of symbols identifying totemic affiliations and activities associated with the group's secret and public functions. Trace element studies using INAA have shown multiple production localities for Style II and III ceramics. Also, some intriguing evidence exists for site clustering in regard to certain naturalistic motifs, with birds and fish predominant at NAN Ranch. Additional INAA data were obtained on corrugated wares, specifically to test for paste differences between partially corrugated and fully corrugated jars. In the middle and lower Mimbres Valley, these jars factor out into two separate clusters of elements, suggesting that they are not only morphologically but technologically different. I have suggested that the two paste categories correlate with the two separate temper types identified in the middle and lower Mimbres Valley. To complicate the picture, however, fully corrugated jars in the upper Mimbres and Gila valleys were made of different clays. These findings suggest that at least two separate utility ware traditions are embedded within the milieu of potters producing Style III.

Secretness of corporate rituals is suggested by restricted access to corporate kivas and underlying cemeteries. The Late Three Circle phase shift in architecture to ceiling hatchways and subfloor cemeteries may symbolize a cosmic model of a layered universe incorporating the world of the living with the world of the dead. Placing dead ancestors beneath the floors of rooms occupied or used by lineage members legitimized corporate claims to agricultural lands. Moulard has suggested that the "killing" of a bowl symbolizes a passageway between separate spirit worlds and that the bowl is a metaphor for the sky dome. Alternatively, the function of the "killed" bowl may have been as a mask. In other words, not unlike highland Mexican versions of this theme, the mortuary practice of wrapping the flexed corpse and placing a mask over the face transformed the individual into a supernatural ancestor being and an oracle. The primary role of the oracle was to advise those who has access to the rooms of secret formulas, such as scheduling and orchestrating ceremonies for bringing rain. We will, of course, never know which, if any, of these interpretations are correct, but given the contexts of Katcina ceremonies and associated rituals in Puebloan belief systems, I think it is reasonable to assume that Mimbres mortuary behavior reflects something akin to Pueblo Katcina ceremonies. Secrecy of the information from the oracles was preserved by restricting access to the ancestor shrines. Restricted access to rituals also meant restricted access to information and ritual power. On this basis I suggest that competition existed between the corporate groups.

Something interrupted the corporate agricultural enterprises and tore apart the corporate infrastructure after A.D. 1100; presumably it was related to climate change since there is no evidence for social upheaval at this or any other time. Episodes of below-normal moisture and temperature beginning in the late eleventh century and continuing into the early twelfth century have been interpreted from tree-ring evidence. These episodes could have been associated with droughts and would not necessarily result in total failure of the system since one such episode apparently occurred from about A.D. 1025 to 1042. But heavy El Niño–like rains following a prolonged dry cycle could have had a drastic impact on the local environment in the form of severe channel cutting and erosion, as I argued in the previous chapter. The erosional episode interrupted irrigation systems and brought about the transition from Sedentary to Classic Hohokam. This well-documented climate phenomenon created by a severe dry spell was very widespread across the Southwest at this time. Since the headwaters of the Gila and Mimbres are in the same range, we would expect a correlation between the Gila and Mimbres in regard to channel trenching. In other words, failure in Mimbres agriculture, like the Hohokam interruption, was probably related to the effects of regional climate change, such as droughts followed by floods and channel erosion and down cutting. This idea is testable through future geoarchaeological studies of the Mimbres watershed.

The inability to immediately repair the irrigation systems probably resulted in the dissolution of the corporate groups, which were likely relatively weak to begin with. As food surpluses waned, the corporate groups broke up. Given the assumption that the real and spiritual worlds of the Mimbres were one and the same, I also think a breakdown or rejection may have occurred between the ancestor spirits and the living. This led to ritual burning of the corporate kivas, followed by abandonment of the corporate households and pueblos. And so went the ceremonies and feasts, the very social contexts that stimulated the production of Style III pottery, which was intricately tied to corporate group identify and behavior.

In conclusion, I have presented a model arguing that food surplus made the Mimbres phenomenon possible. The food surplus was the product of success implementation of irrigation agriculture, probably by the Late Three Circle phase. People come together when food is available or at times of food surplus; they disperse when food shortages occur. This pattern is well documented among hunters and gatherers and middle-range agricultural groups and even in modern times. The rise of irrigation agriculture and the formation of corporate groups to maintain and operate the irrigation systems gave rise to the Classic Mimbres phenomenon, which was probably some form of segmentary lineage system. Competition between corporate groups stimulated the move to corporate kivas to protect secret rites, converse with ancestor oracles, and engage in corporate initiation. The expected material correlates for food surplus, social responses to production, population aggregation, evidence for feasting, and production of prestige items were all in place by approximately A.D. 950 to 1110 in the Mimbres Valley. Among the material expressions of corporate group formation were kivas, restricted access corporate cemeteries, restricted access granaries, Style II and III pottery, and an emphasis on ancestor veneration, the vestige of which was probably the Katcina ceremonies.

Appendices

A.1: Mimbres Redware, Style I, and early Style II Black-on-white. A–D, Mimbres Redware; E–H, Mimbres Style I; I, early Style II.

APPENDIX I • POTTERY VESSELS FROM THE NAN RANCH RUIN / 225

A.2: Mimbres Style II Black-on-white.

A.3: Mimbres Style II Black-on-white.

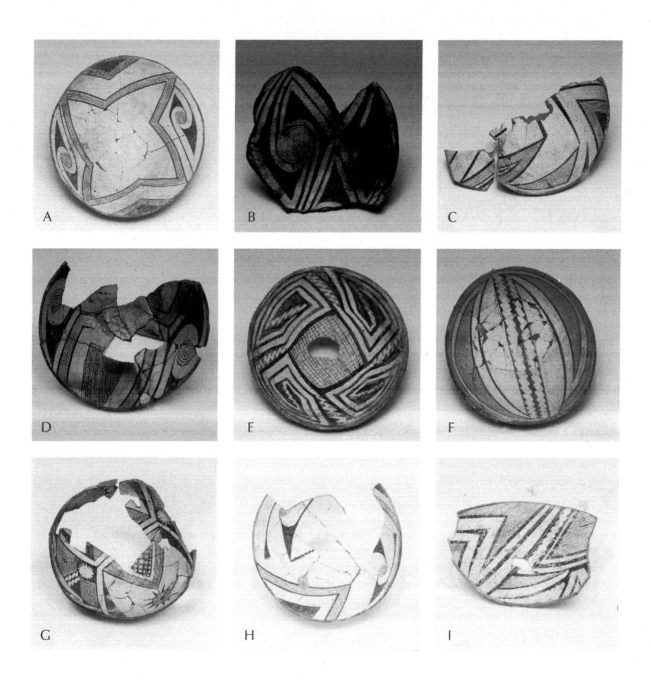

A.4: Mimbres Style II Black-on-white.

228 / APPENDIX I • POTTERY VESSELS FROM THE NAN RANCH RUIN

A.5: Mimbres Style II to III, Style II jars and Style II variant. A–D, Style II to III; E–H, Style II jars; I, Style II variant.

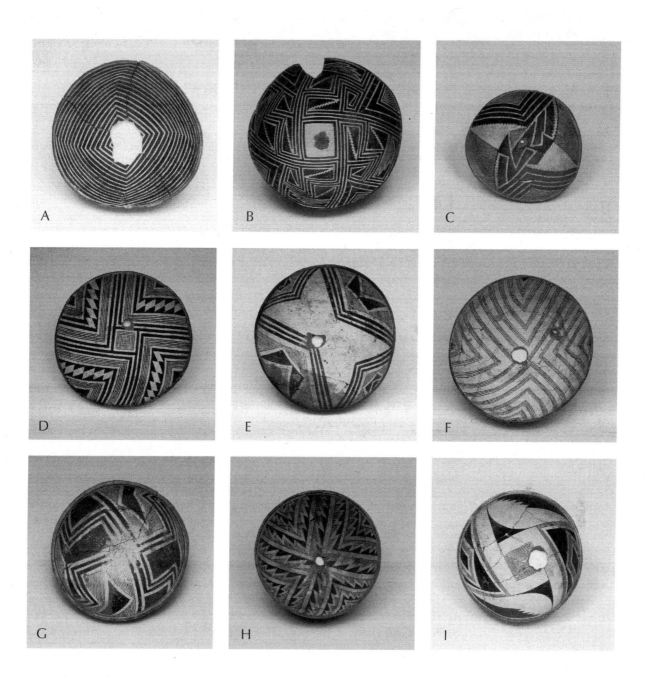

A.6: Mimbres Style II to III and early Style III bowls. A, Style II to III; B–I, early Style III.

230 / APPENDIX I • POTTERY VESSELS FROM THE NAN RANCH RUIN

A.7: Mimbres early Style III vessels; C, D are interior and exterior views of the same vessel.

A.8: Mimbres early Style III vessels; D, E, two views of the same vessel.

232 / APPENDIX 1 • POTTERY VESSELS FROM THE NAN RANCH RUIN

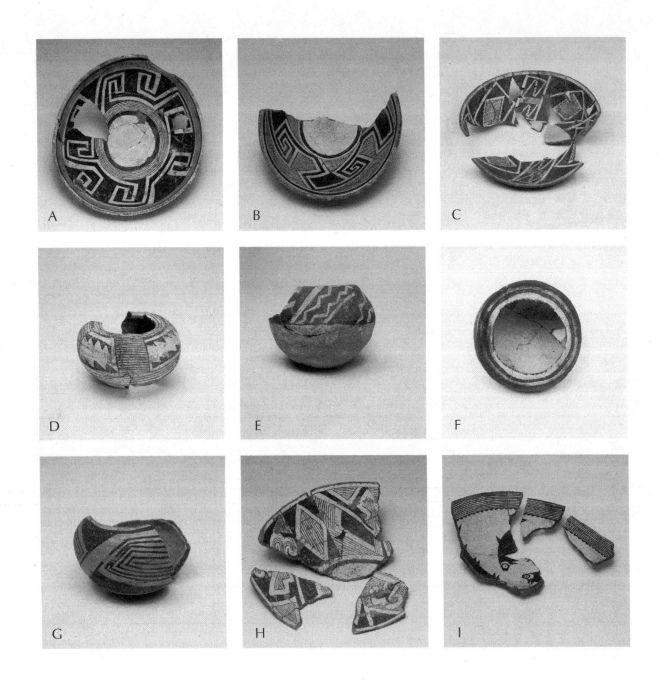

A.9: Mimbres early Style III bowls and seed jars. A–C, H, I, early Style III bowls; D–G, early Style III seed jars.

APPENDIX I • POTTERY VESSELS FROM THE NAN RANCH RUIN / 233

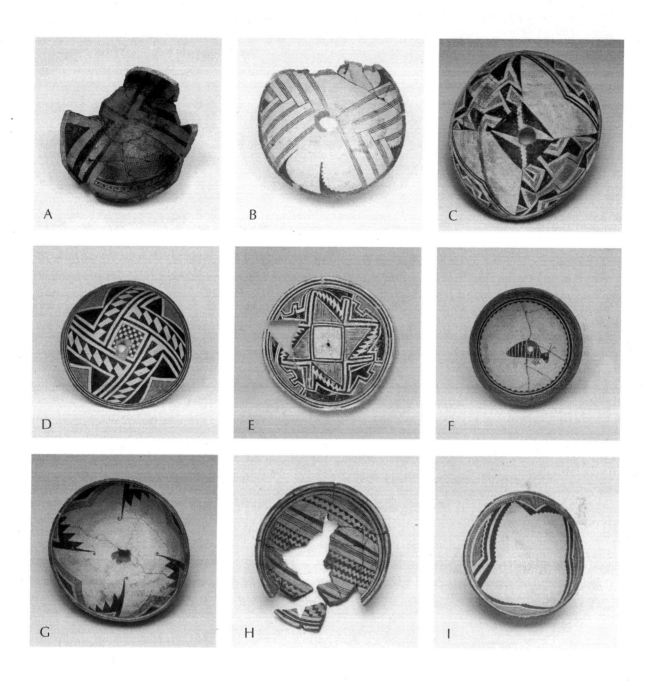

A.10: Mimbres early and middle Style III vessels. A, B, early Style III; C–I, middle Style III.

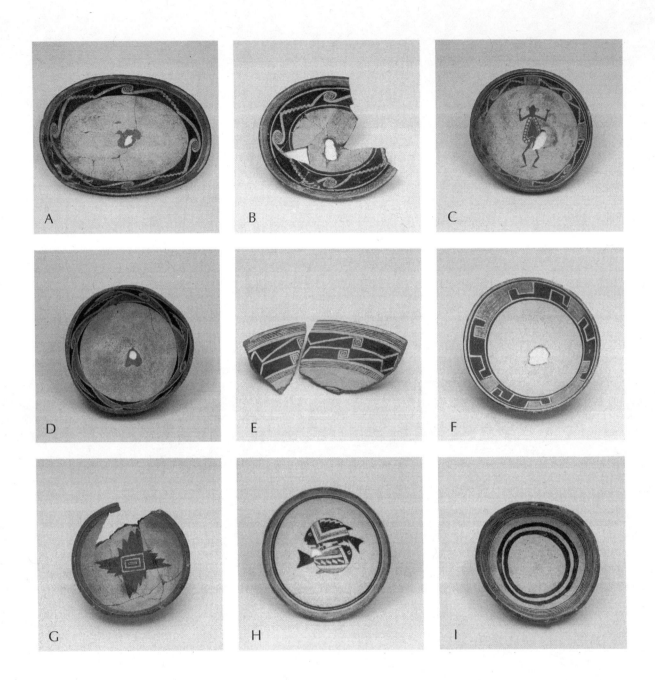

A.11: Mimbres middle Style III vessels.

APPENDIX I • POTTERY VESSELS FROM THE NAN RANCH RUIN / 235

A.12: Mimbres middle Style III vessels.

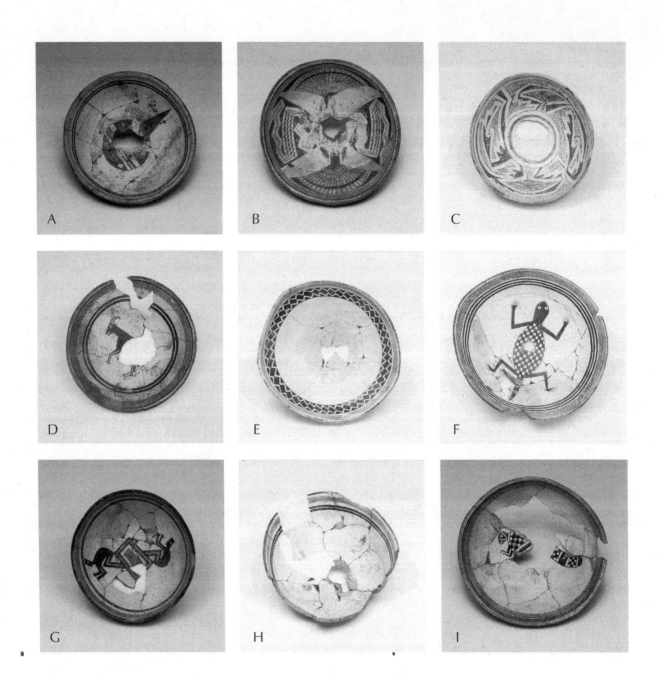

A.13: Mimbres middle Style III vessels.

APPENDIX I • POTTERY VESSELS FROM THE NAN RANCH RUIN / 237

A.14: Mimbres middle and middle-late Style III vessels. A–E, middle Style III; F–I, middle-late Style III.

238 / APPENDIX I • POTTERY VESSELS FROM THE NAN RANCH RUIN

A.15: Mimbres middle and middle-late Style III vessels; A–F, H, I, middle-late Style III; G, middle Style III.

A.16: Mimbres middle and middle-late Style III vessels. A–C, E–I, middle-late Style III; D, middle Style III.

240 / APPENDIX I • POTTERY VESSELS FROM THE NAN RANCH RUIN

A.17: Mimbres middle-late Style III vessels.

APPENDIX I • POTTERY VESSELS FROM THE NAN RANCH RUIN / 241

A.18: Mimbres middle-late Style III vessels. D–F are views of the same vessel; E is inside view, D, F are exterior views.

242 / APPENDIX I • POTTERY VESSELS FROM THE NAN RANCH RUIN

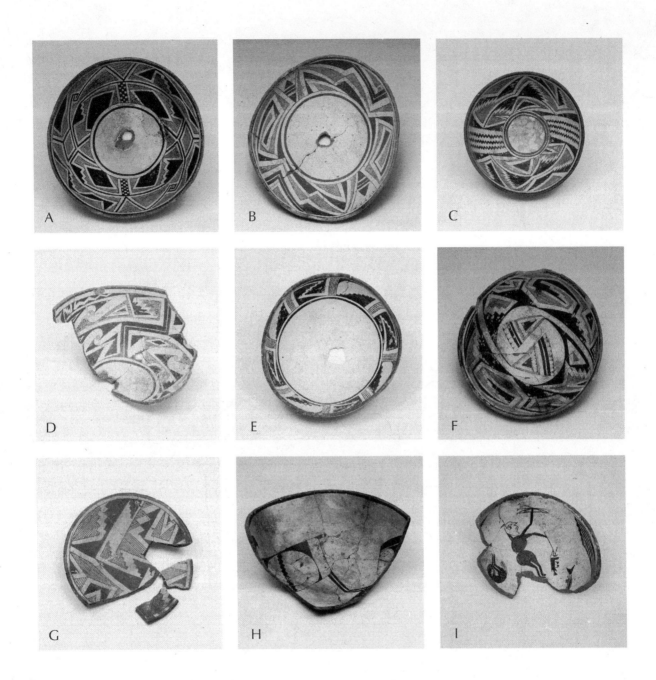

A.19: Mimbres late Style III. G is a plate.

APPENDIX I • POTTERY VESSELS FROM THE NAN RANCH RUIN / 243

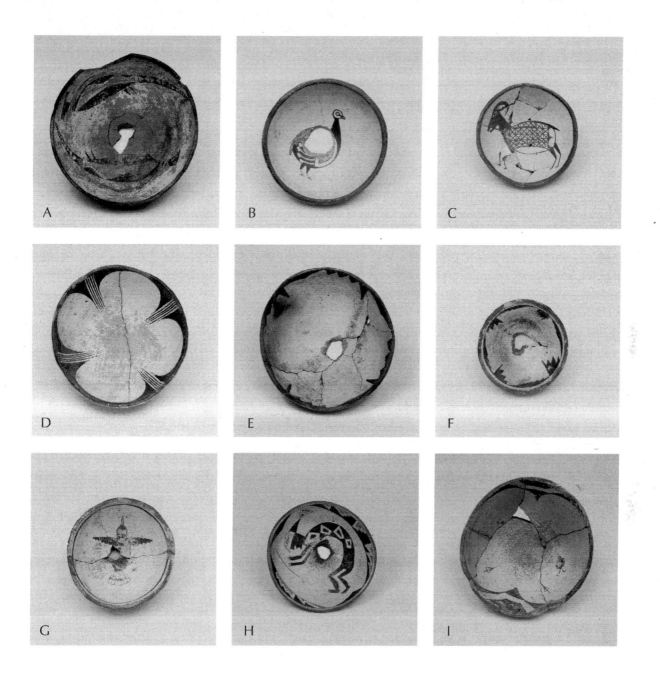

A.20: Mimbres late Style III.

244 / APPENDIX I • POTTERY VESSELS FROM THE NAN RANCH RUIN

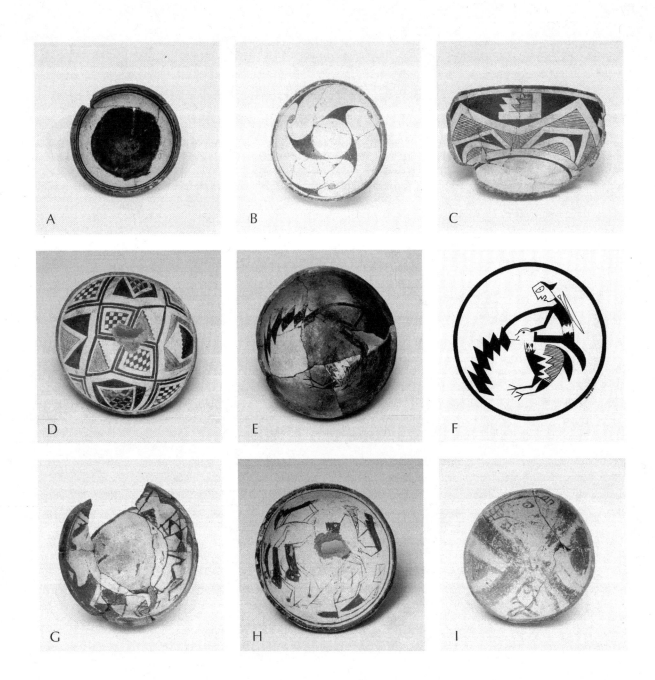

A.21: Mimbres late Style III. G–I illustrate vessels possibly decorated by novices.

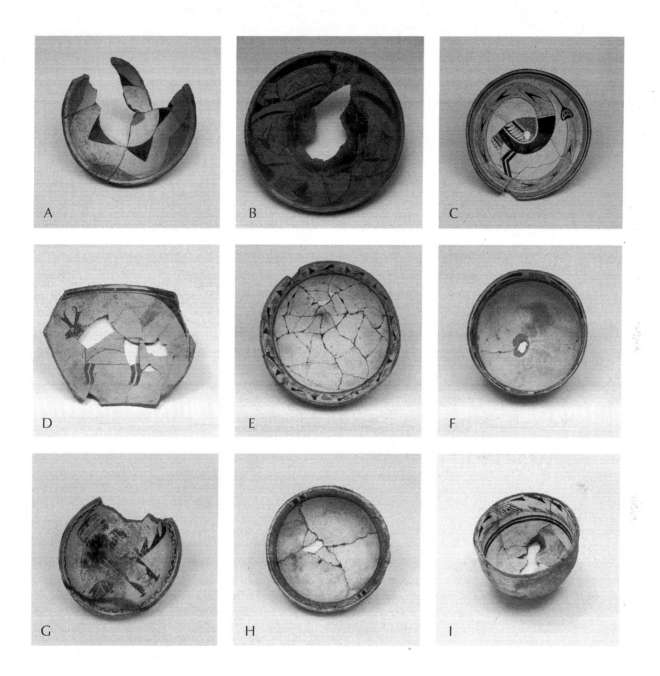

A.22: Mimbres late Style III, Style III Polychrome, and middle-late Style III flare-rim bowls. A, B, late Style III; C, D, Style III Polychrome; E–I, middle-late Style III flare-rim bowls.

A.23: Mimbres middle-late Style III flare-rim bowls and effigy jars. A–F, flare-rim bowls; G–I, effigy jars; profile of I shown in Figure A.24A.

APPENDIX I • POTTERY VESSELS FROM THE NAN RANCH RUIN / 247

A.24: Mimbres effigy vessels, Style III jars, and fully corrugated bowl. A, B, effigy jars (top view of A is shown in Figure A.23I); C, Style II fish effigy created from bowl sherd; D, F, Style III seed jars; E, miniature Style III jar; G, fully corrugated bowl; H–I, Style III jars.

248 / APPENDIX I • POTTERY VESSELS FROM THE NAN RANCH RUIN

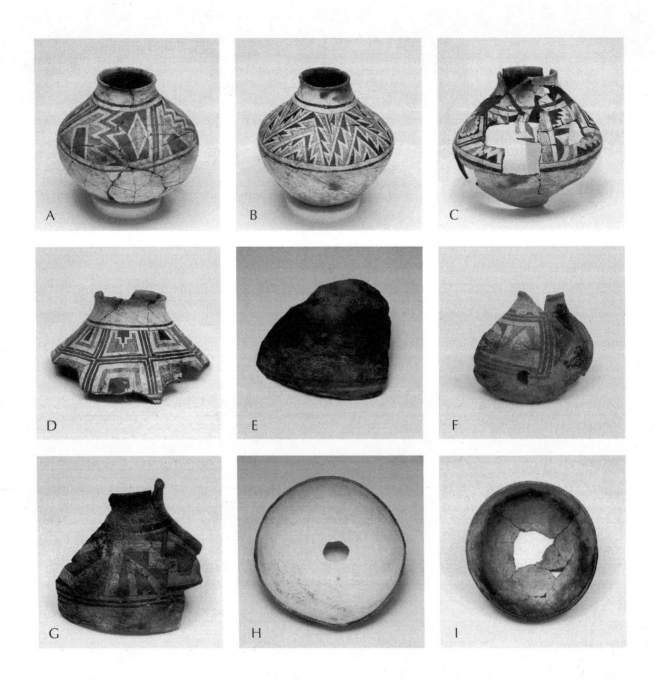

A.25: Style III jars, Mimbres Style III white-slipped bowls. A–G, Style III jars; H, I, Style III white-slipped bowls.

A.26: Mimbres Style III white-slipped vessels and Mimbres plain brownware vessels. A, Mimbres white-slipped bowl; B, Mimbres white-slipped seed jar; C, brownware pinch bowl; D, smudged brownware bowl; E, brownware oval bowl with tabs; F, brownware jar with suspension lugs; G, brownware seed jar modeled after bottle gourd; H, brownware mug; I, brownware jar.

A.27: Plain, neck-banded, and neck-corrugated vessels. A, polished smudged brownware jar; B–D, Alma plain jars; E, Alma Plain bowl; F, polished brownware seed jar; G, H, Alma Neck Banded; I, Three Circle Neck Corrugated pitcher.

A.28: Three Circle Neck Corrugated pitchers and jars, textured brownware mugs, and Mimbres fully corrugated mugs. A, B, D, E, Three Circle Neck Corrugated pitchers; C, Three Circle Neck Corrugated jar; F, G, textured brownware mugs; H, I, fully corrugated mugs.

A.29: Mimbres Fully Corrugated pitchers and mugs. A, D, and F are pitchers; B, C, E, and G–I are mugs.

APPENDIX I • POTTERY VESSELS FROM THE NAN RANCH RUIN / 253

A.30: Mimbres Fully Corrugated and plain vessels. A, fully corrugated mug; B–E, G–I, fully corrugated jars; F, plain brownware mug.

A.31: Mimbres partially corrugated vessels.

A.32: Mimbres Partially Corrugated, composite corrugated/plain, and trade vessels. A, partially corrugated jar; B, composite vessel with corrugated neck and plain bowl body; C, Convento Indented Corrugated jar; D, El Paso Red-on-brown jar; E, unidentified whiteware bowl; F, Red Mesa Black-on-white; G, Puerco Black-on-white pitcher; H, I, two views of smudged brownware bowl with punctated exterior design.

APPENDIX TABLE 1. Pottery Vessel Data

Lot Number	Figure	Type	Provenience	Age/Sex	Max. Dia.	Min. Dia.	Ht.
5-1110(14:B93)	1A	MR	Rm 14: B93	Infant	0.00	0.00	12.40
8-1072	1B	MR seed	Rm 91: SF45		11.40	5.20	10.40
9-608(29:B169)	1C	MR	Rm 29: B169	Adult female	27.90	27.20	12.60
4-925	1D	RW	Rm 52: B51	Adult male	13.80	13.40	6.40
5-1039(14:B86)	1E	I	Rm 14: B86, ves 2	Adult female	23.70	21.90	12.10
5-1057(14:B86)	1F	I	Rm 14: B86, ves 5	Adult female	13.60	12.90	8.70
5-1038(14:B86)	1G	I	Rm 14: B86	Adult female	0.00	0.00	8.60
3-500	1H	I	Rm 52		11.50	0.00	5.90
5-1364(14:B90)	1I	Early II	Rm 14		29.10	25.80	13.00
9-515(29:B168)	2A	II	Rm 29: B168, ves B	Adolescent	0.00	0.00	0.00
11-148	2B	LII	F11-15: B229	Adult crem	30.50	0.00	16.40
5-1863(17)	2C	EII	Rm 17		25.30	25.30	10.50
9-1373	2D	LII	Rm 104: B196	Child	23.70	23.60	10.40
4-1109	2E	II	Rm 57: B65	Infant	13.40	13.20	5.90
11-330(5)	2F	LII	F11-25: B236	Crem, SA/A, F?	7.84	0.00	0.00
11-330(2)	2G	LII	F11-25: B236	Crem, SA/A, F?	30.00	0.00	12.30
11-330(3)	2H	LII	F11-25: B236	Crem, SA/A, F?	19.60	19.00	10.30
11-330(1)	2I	LII	F11-25: B236	Crem, SA/A, F?	30.00	29.60	13.00
9-1297	3A	LII	Rm 104: B197	Infant	14.30	13.90	6.50
4-1073(12:B64)	3B	LII	Rm 12: B64	Adult male	35.00	34.40	15.70
9-1369	3C	LII	Rm 104: B200	Child	20.50	20.50	9.00
10-380	3D	II	10-7:B8	Adult crem	18.00	0.00	12.50
10-575	3E	LII	Rm 112: B223	Adult	22.50	0.00	15.50
9-1472	3F	LII	Rm 104: B204	Adult female	25.90	24.40	11.60
9-1486	3G	LII	Rm 104: B208	Child	17.60	16.40	7.20
9-1310	3H	LII	Rm 79: B194	Infant	21.20	20.20	11.20
10-978A	3I	LII	U13: B227A	Adult crem	14.00	14.00	6.80
5-1854(75:B95)	4A	LII	Rm 75: B95, ves 1	Adult male	27.20	26.50	12.60
6-539	4B	LII	Rm 83: B104	Adult female	28+	0.00	0.00
4-1115(12:B67)	4C	II	Rm 12: B67	Infant	27.90	27.90	14.20
10-986	4D	LII	F10-5, 10-8		20.00	0.00	8.00
4-1219(12:B70)	4E	LII	Rm 12: B70	Subadult Female	24.40	23.90	10.00
5-1855(75:B95)	4F	II	Rm 75: B95, ves 2	Adult male	24.40	22.20	11.50
10-985	4G	LII	U-9		25.50	0.00	12.50
10-777	4H	LII	F10-21	Crem	30.00	0.00	13.00
9-1471	4I	LII sherd	Rm 104: B201	Child	17.50	12.20	0.00
8-66	5A	II-III	U1: B121	Subadult	22.10	21.90	9.40
9-1279(29:B179B)	5B	II-III	Rm 29: B179, ves 2	Adult female	16.20	15.90	7.70
7-865	5C	II-III	Rm 89: B120	Adolescent	23.20	21.20	10.20
9-1609	5D	II-III	Rm 104: B207	Adult female	31.20	30.00	12.20

APPENDIX TABLE 1. Pottery Vessel Data *continued*

Lot Number	Figure	Type	Provenience	Age/Sex	Max. Dia.	Min. Dia.	Ht.
6-431	5E	II jar	Rm 83		19.00	7.80	20.00
7-752-7	5F	II jar	Rm 62: B117	Child	8.50	4.60	8.70
10-771	5G	II seed	U15: 10-20B		0.00	0.00	12.60
10-771	5H	II jar	U15: F10-20A		11.40	6.20	6.70
9-1536	5I	LII	Rm 104: 214	Child	21.10	2.00	8.30
9-1145(29:B188)	6A	II-III	Rm 29: B188	Adult male	23.90	22.80	9.30
4-669	6B	EIII	Rm 57: B48	Adult female	31.90	30.20	12.50
4-984(12:B54)	6C	EIII	Rm 12: B54	Child	23.20	21.40	8.40
7-752-1	6D	EIII	Rm 62: B117	Child	17.90	16.90	6.00
9-1352(29:B198A)	6E	EIII	Rm 29: B198	Adult female	22.40	22.00	8.70
2-558	6F	EIII	Rm 40: B13	Adult male	29.20	29.00	14.50
4-998(12:B57)	6G	EIII	Rm 12: B57	Adult female	18.80	18.20	8.40
2-661	6H	EIII	Rm 41: B20	Adult male	25.00	25.00	12.60
9-357(29:B165)	6I	EIII	Rm 29: B165	Adult male	22.10	21.40	10.30
11-85B	7A	EIII	F11-7		17.00	0.00	6.60
7-752-8	7B	EIII	Rm 62: B117	Child	0.00	0.00	0.00
11-318(2)	7C, D	EIII	11-32: B237	Crem, SA/A	9.70	9.70	4.00
9-1008(29:B178)	7E	EIII	Rm 29: B178	Adult male	18.00	17.80	7.50
9-1308(29:B157B)	7F	EIII	Rm 29: B157, ves B	Adult female	17.50	17.00	7.50
9-1309(29:B157C)	7G	EIII	Rm 29: B157, ves C	Adult female	16.80	16.40	6.20
11-310(1)	7H	EIII	11-27: B234	Crem, SA	21.50	0.00	7.70
9-513(29:B170)	7I	EIII	Rm 29: B170	Adult female	22.50	21.70	9.10
9-1299	8A	EIII	Rm 104: B195	Infant	16.80	15.80	7.00
11-85A	8B	EIII	F11-7		16.20	15.00	6.60
9-1307(29:B157A)	8C	EIII	Rm 29: B157, ves A	Adult female	30.90	29.60	12.90
11-250(1)	8D, E	EIII	F11-14: B230	Crem, SA/A	14.10	0.00	6.60
9-469	8F	EIII	U:16		26.40	0.00	10.10
11-250(3)	8G	EIII	F11-14: B230	Crem, SA/A	10.60	10.60	4.50
9-1278(29:B179A)	8H	EIII	Rm 29: B179, ves 1	Adult female	23.40	23.20	9.10
11-161	8I	EIII	F11-17		22.00	0.00	0.00
4-1073(12:B64)	9A	EIII	Rm 12: B64	Adult male	29.10	27.50	12.50
9-1358(29:B198B)	9B	EIII	Rm 29: B199	Adolescent	16.50	16.40	9.00
8-1449 (29:B146 & 158)	9C	EIII	Rm 29: B146 & 158	Child	24.00	24.00	8.50
11-14	9D	EIII seed	11-14:B230	Crem, Adult	11.20	5.50	7.00
Unk	9E	EIII seed	Unk		14.50	0.00	0.00
7-752-2	9F	EIII seed	Rm 62: B117	Child	11.60	7.20	7.50
7-752-2	9G	EIII seed	Rm 62: B117	Child	9.60	6.00	6.70
8-1538(29:B153)	9H	EIII	Rm 29: B153	Adult female	23.00	0.00	0.00
10-750	9I	EIII	F10-22		21.00	0.00	0.00

APPENDIX TABLE 1. Pottery Vessel Data *continued*

Lot Number	Figure	Type	Provenience	Age/Sex	Max. Dia.	Min. Dia.	Ht.
9-917(29:B183)	10A	EIII	Rm 29: B183	Child	19.00	19.00	10.70
9-867(28:B180)	10B	EIII	Rm 28: B180	Infant	20.80	20.60	9.20
4-1021(12:B62)	10C	MIII	Rm 12: B62	Adult male	30.10	27.20	13.30
9-1228(28:B173)	10D	EIII	Rm 28: B173	Adult female	23.70	22.80	0.00
4-1046(12:B58)	10E	MIII	Rm 12: B58	Adult female	25.30	24.60	9.60
9-218(29:B161A)	10F	EIII	Rm 29: B161, ves 1	Adult female	17.20	17.10	8.20
4-985(12:B55)	10G	MIII	Rm 12: B-55	Infant	19.90	18.40	9.90
11-318(1)	10H	EIII	11-32: B237	Crem, SA/A	17.00	0.00	6.00
11-312(3)	10I	EIII	11-27: B234	Crem, SA	19.00	18.20	9.00
1-614(2:B7)	11A	MIII	Rm 2: B7	Infant	22.20	15.30	5.20
9-820(29:B158)	11B	MIII	Rm 29: B158, fill	Child	23.00	17.50	6.00
AF8SF22-5	11C	MIII	Rm 9: B17	Infant	22.20	22.20	8.30
5-1867(11/22:B85)	11D	MIII	Rm 11/22: B85	Child	26.80	25.70	12.50
11-250(4)	11E	MIII	F11-14: B230	Crem, SA/A	0.00	0.00	22.00
11-311(2)	11F	MIII	11-27: B234	Cremation, SA	26.50	25.20	10.70
11-315	11G	MIII	F11-26		13.50	12.80	6.80
9-944(29:B183)	11H	MIII	Rm 29: B183	Child	21.70	21.60	10.00
3-406	11I	MIII	Rm 50: B34	Child	9.70	9.00	4.00
7-568	12A	MIII	Rm 62: B114	Child	13.70	13.40	6.00
8-1388(29:B137)	12B	MIII	Rm 29: B137	Infant	15.40	14.80	7.50
8-1150(28:B128)	12C	MIII	Rm 28: B128, ves 2	Child	15.40	14.60	6.50
11-318(3)	12D	MIII	11-32: B237	Crem, SA/A	24.00	0.00	0.00
8-1482(28:B147)	12E	MIII	Rm 28: B147	Adult male	25.50	25.40	11.70
11-331	12F	MIII	11-32: B237	Crem, SA/A	16.50	0.00	6.40
8-1558(29:B154)	12G	MIII	Rm 29: B154, ves 2	Adult male	18.20	17.70	9.70
A3F6-BH	12H	MIII	BHT		25.50	24.60	11.30
5-1388(22:B83)	12I	MIII	Rm 22: B83	Adult female	22.30	21.50	11.90
8-1507(29:B146)	13A	MIII	Rm 29: B146, ves 2	Adult male	19.90	19.50	8.20
5-266(18:B76)	13B	MIII	Rm 18: Unit 2, B76	Adult female	17.90	17.50	8.10
9-1089(28:B177)	13C	MIII	Rm 28: B177	Child	17.60	17.20	8.30
1-548	13D	MIII	Rm 31: B5	Child	17.20	17.20	5.20
9-1400(29:B203)	13E	MIII	Rm 29: B203	Adult female	25.00	23.20	10.30
9-992(28:B150)	13F	MIII	Rm 28: B150, fill	Adult male	25.40	22.80	9.20
2-838	13G	MIII	Rm 41: B27	Adult male	19.50	19.50	14.50
8-1294(29:B134)	13H	MIII	Rm 29: B161	Adult female	20.70	20.30	9.20
8-1517(29:B146)	13I	MIII	Rm 29: B146	Adult male	17.50	17.20	6.90
9-837(28:B136)	14A	MIII	Rm 28: B136, ves B	Child	20.40	19.60	9.30
3-345	14B	MIII	Rm 50		19.00	0.00	9.80
8-1272(28:B132)	14C	MIII	Rm 28: B132	Adult female	18.50	17.20	9.60
8-1268(28:B131)	14D	MIII	Rm 28: B131	Adult male	29.90	24.40	13.20

APPENDIX TABLE 1. Pottery Vessel Data *continued*

Lot Number	Figure	Type	Provenience	Age/Sex	Max. Dia.	Min. Dia.	Ht.
1-561(2:B6)	14E	MIII	Rm 2: B6	Adult male	18.10	18.10	8.00
8-1557(29:B154)	14F	MIII	Rm 29: B154, ves 1	Adult male	22.60	22.40	10.00
1-295	14G	MIII	Rm 30: Fl		38.50	35.90	14.50
7-441	14H	MIII	Rm 84: B110	Child	28.00	27.80	12.10
6-510	14I	MIII	Rm 67: B103	Adult male	32.20	31.40	13.40
8-1554(29:B153)	15A	MLIII	Rm 29: B153	Adult female	28.40	27.20	13.90
9-1523	15B	III	Rm 39		19.00	19.00	6.50
7-881	15C	ML III	U:22		21.10	0.00	9.50
8-1483(29:B148)	15D	MLIII	Rm 29: B148, ves 2	Child	12.90	12.60	5.50
2-704(8:B16)	15E	MLIII	Rm 8, B16	Adolescent	18.10	18.10	8.00
9-1091(29:B156)	15F	MLIII	Rm 29: B156	Adult female	21.50	20.90	9.20
4-1022(12:B59)	15G	EIII	Rm 12: B59	Adult	27.50	25.20	10.20
9-427	15H	MIII	Rm 94: SF2		20.20	19.20	9.00
7-614	15I	MLIII	Rm 84: B112	Adolescent	21.20	21.10	10.60
8-1295(28:B135)	16A	MLIII	Rm 28: B135	Subadult	22.90	20.90	9.60
3-389	16B	LIII	Rm 50: B34	Child	15.20	14.80	6.60
5-977(22:B82)	16C	MIII	Rm 22: B82	Adult male	27.70	26.40	12.50
5-99	16D	EIII	Rm 41: B 73	Adult female	29.80	28.20	16.60
10-2741	16E	MLIII	Rm 94: B221	Infant	20.00	20.00	10.00
8-733(29)	16F	MLIII	Rm 29		25.60	0.00	1.50
8-1463(29:B138)	16G	MLIII	Rm 29: B138	Adult male	30.00	30.00	15.70
5-1354(22:B91)	16H	MIII	Rm 22: B91	Adolescent	22.60	22.40	12.60
5-1338(22:B82)	16I	MIII	Rm 22: B82, ves 2	Adult male	24.50	22.60	12.20
8-1513(29:B151)	17A	MLIII	Rm 29: B151, ves 1	Adult female	27.00	26.30	13.40
8-1526(29:B139)	17B	MLIII	Rm 29: B139	Adult	27.10	25.80	12.60
8-1491(29:B146)	17C	MLIII	Rm 29: B146, ves 1	Adult male	29.00	28.70	12.60
3-593	17D	MLIII	Rm 50		28.00	26.50	14.70
8-1528(29:B144)	17E	MLIII	Rm 29: B144	Adult female	25.30	25.30	11.90
8-1421(29)	17F	MLIII	Rm 29: fill		22.70	22.00	11.90
4-414	17G	MLIII	Rm 49: B43	Adult female	26.00	24.60	11.20
2-878	17H	MLIII	Rm 41: B29	Adult	28.50	28.50	12.20
2-795	17I	MLIII	Rm 41: B21	Adult	29.00	29.00	12.40
8-1151(28:B128)	18A	MLIII	Rm 28: B128, ves 1	Child	22.60	21.30	10.40
2-760	18B	MLIII	Rm 41: B24	Child	26.00	26.00	12.00
8-1475(29:B148)	18C	MLIII	Rm 29: B148, ves 1	Child	21.60	20.10	9.90
7-440	18D, E, F	III	Rm 84: B111	Adult female	24.70	24.30	13.20
4-902	18G	MIII	Rm 59		26.00	0.00	0.00
4-558	18H	MLIII	Rm 49: B46	Adult female	25.40	23.80	12.50
D2(Rm 40: fill)	18I	MLIII	Rm 40: fill		15.80	0.00	6.90
5-1103	19A	LIII	Rm 63: B88	Adult male	29.70	29.20	12.60

APPENDIX TABLE 1. Pottery Vessel Data *continued*

Lot Number	Figure	Type	Provenience	Age/Sex	Max. Dia.	Min. Dia.	Ht.
8-1542(29:B151)	19B	LIII	Rm 20: B151, ves 2	Adult female	29.30	26.70	12.20
D1WF1(2)	19C	LIII	Rm 40: SF12-3		22.50	22.50	11.50
4-139	19D	LIII	Rm 49		24.00	0.00	12.00
9-236(29:B161C)	19E	LIII	Rm 29: B161, ves 3	Adult female	28.00	27.80	14.90
5-308	19F	LIII	Rm 65		24.70	23.80	11.40
4-706	19G	LIII	Rm 45		14.70	14.60	2.70
8-1234	19H	LIII	Rm 74: SF 52		29.00	0.00	13.50
D3F3SF6	19I	LIII	Rm 41: B19	Infant	13.70	0.00	6.80
4-296	20A	LIII	Rm 55: B39	Child	23.70	23.40	10.90
3-325	20B	LIII	Rm 47: B32	Child	18.90	18.20	8.40
3-341	20C	LIII	Rm 50: B33	Child	11.70	11.30	4.60
9-999	20D	LIII	Rm 94: B186		17.20	16.90	7.60
8-1543(28:B141)	20E	LIII	Rm 28: B141	Adolescent	16.10	15.50	7.40
8-1279(28:B128A)	20F	LIII	Rm 28: B128A, ves 4	Child	7.10	7.00	3.70
8-1278(28:B128B)	20G	LIII	Rm 28: B128, ves 3	Child	8.40	8.30	4.30
3-378	20H	LIII	Rm 47: B35	Infant	20.90	20.10	9.00
9-780	20I	LIII	Rm 39: SF49		10.80	10.80	6.50
2-481	21A	LIII	Rm 41: Q4-2		13.20	12.80	5.70
9-792(28:B136)	21B	LIII	Rm 28: B136, ves A	Child	13.50	12.80	6.00
2-263	21C	LIII	Rm 42		27.00	0.00	12.00
8-1410(28:B140)	21D	LIII	Rm 28: B140	Adult female	22.10	20.80	10.10
8-733(29)	21E, F	LIII	Rm 29		16.90	16.20	7.80
9-1545	21G	LIII	Rm 39		16.50	16.50	8.90
8-1293(29:B133)	21H	LIII	Rm 29: B133, ves 1	Child	15.70	15.40	6.50
9-226(29:161B)	21I	LIII	Rm 29: B161, ves 2	Adult female	12.80	12.40	4.70
9-1546(28:B174)	22A	LIII	Rm 28: B174	Child	0.00	0.00	6.00
4-676	22B	LIII	Rm 60: B45	Infant	21.40	21.10	9.60
9-1353(29:B199)	22C	Poly III	Rm 29: B199	Adolescent	25.90	24.90	9.20
4-577	22D	III poly	Rm 60		25+	0.00	0.00
8-325	22E	III flare	Rm 39: F86-35		25.90	25.60	13.40
1-777(3:B1)	22F	III flare	Rm 3: B1	Adult male	21.50	21.00	12.00
6-466	22G	III flare	Rm 84: SF1		14.20	13.20	7.30
9-172(29:B153)	22H	III flare	Rm 29: B153, ves 2	Adult female	14.70	14.50	6.70
9-652(28:B172)	22I	III flare	Rm 28: B172	Child	12.30	12.20	7.70
9-1009(28:B184)	23A, B	III flare	Rm 28: B184	Adult male	23.20	22.80	12.40
8-1415(29:F86-78)	23C	III flare	Rm 29		0.00	0.00	11.90
2-496(9:B15)	23D	III flare	Rm 9: B15	Adult female	27.70	27.70	13.50
4-559	23E	III flare	Rm 60		18.00	0.00	9.30
2-862	23F	III flare	Rm 41: B28	Adolescent	29.50	29.50	14.50
8-1518	23G, H	III effigy	29:B153	Adult female	12.60	4.00	11.70

APPENDIX TABLE 1. Pottery Vessel Data *continued*

Lot Number	Figure	Type	Provenience	Age/Sex	Max. Dia.	Min. Dia.	Ht.
10-373	23I, 24A	III effigy	108: SF14		12.00	0.00	11.20
8-1349(29:B133)	24, B	III	Rm 29: B133, ves 2	Adolescent	0.00	0.00	5.70
11-250(6)	24C	LII effigy	F11-14: B230	Crem, SA/A	10.50	0.00	2.00
8-471	24D	III seed	Rm 39: F86-42		25.00	8.10	0.00
8-1349(29:B133)	24E	III	Rm 29: B133, ves 3	Adolescent	0.00	0.00	6.30
CF1S3-2	24F	III seed	Rm 30 Floor		16.00	8.60	11.00
6-119	24G	MBrW	6-SF7		9.20	8.80	6.90
8-1178	24H	III jar	Rm 74: SF47		32.70	12.30	31.30
D1WF1(1)	24I	III	Rm 40: SF12-3		35.50	15.40	32.20
8-955(29:F86-66)	25A	III	Rm 29		13.10	13.00	28.40
4-486(2)	25B	III jar	Rm 60: SF1		29.60	10.80	28.00
8-1180	25C	III jar	Rm 74: SF 46		32.00	12.90	30.50
8-823	25D	III jar	Rm 74: SF13		0.00	11.90	0.00
9-996(29:B187)	25E	III	Rm 29: B187	Child	18.80	11.10	0.00
9-1524	25F	III jar	Rm 39		14.50	0.00	14.00
8-1574(29:B155)	25G	III	Rm 29: B155	Adult male	28.00	11.50	0.00
4-500	25H	III	Rm 57: B44	Infant	22.40	20.70	10.90
8-1477(28:B145)	25I	MIII	Rm 28: B145	Child	20.00	19.60	8.30
8-1497(28:B149)	26A	III	Rm 28: B149	Child	19.70	16.40	7.10
1-340	26B	III seed	Rm 30: SF2		0.00	0.00	12.50
11-318(4)	26C	BrW	11-32: B237	Crem, SA/A	8.80	7.50	3.60
2-52	26D	SBrW	Rm 42: F2		22.20	22.00	11.50
5-1110(14:B93)	26E	MBrW	Rm 14: B-93	Infant	18.40	10.70	7.00
4-486(3)	26F	BrW jar	Rm 60: SF1		10.00	2.60	10.00
7-752-6	26G	BrW seed	Rm 62: B117	Child	10.50	4.70	9.90
9-1294	26H	MbW mug	Rm 104: B195	Infant	8.10	6.00	8.60
9-516	26I	BrW	Rm 39: SF22		9.70	8.00	8.80
6-539	27A	PBrW	Rm 83: B104	Adult female	19.50	12.50	16.60
6-539	27B	BrW	Rm 83: B104	Adult female	20.40	9.40	20.90
9-1347	27C	AP	Rm 95: SF30		35.00	20.10	40.00
9-1345	27D	AP	Rm 95: SF28		30.45	0.00	25.64
5-1364	27E	MBrW	Rm 14		23.40	22.10	7.40
6-476	27F	BrW seed	Rm 82: B102	Infant	0.00	0.00	9.70
9-1475	27G	ANB	Rm 100: SF16		0.00	14.20	0.00
9-1344	27H	ANB	Rm 95: SF27		27.40	17.20	29.40
9-939(29:B163)	27I	TCNC	Rm 29: B163	Adolescent	8.50	8.20	14.90
11-330(4)	28A	TCNC	F11-25: B236	Crem, SA/A, F?	17.50	7.80	15.00
10-978B	28B	TCNC pitch	U13: B227B	Crem, Adult	15.80	8.00	13.40
5-1001(14)	28C	TCNC	Rm 14		0.00	0.00	23.50
8-623	28D	TCNC pitch	Rm 39: F86-44		22.00	13.00	23.00

APPENDIX TABLE 1. Pottery Vessel Data *continued*

Lot Number	Figure	Type	Provenience	Age/Sex	Max. Dia.	Min. Dia.	Ht.
9-514(29:B168)	28E	TCNC	Rm 29: B168, ves A	Adolescent	12.30	11.80	14.60
11-330(6)	28F	TCNC mug	F11-25: B236	Crem, SA/A, F?	9.00	7.80	7.80
5-1110(14:B93)	28G	MBrW	Rm 14: B93	Infant	6.10	5.90	7.00
7-752-4	28H	MFC mug	Rm 62: B117	Child	9.20	7.50	9.60
7-752-5	28I	MFC mug	Rm 62: B117	Child	12.70	9.60	12.40
8-1416(29)	29A	MFC	Rm 29: B139	Adult	0.00	0.00	13.00
9-1408(29:B198C)	29B	MFC	Rm 29: B198, ves C	Adult female	10.10	9.70	14.90
9-1408(29:B198C)	29C	MFC	Rm 29: B198. ves C	Adult female	7.50	7.30	5.40
7-282	29D	MFC	Rm 84		23.00	13.00	17.50
9-1408	29E	MFC mug	29:B198C	Adult female	7.50	7.30	9.40
11-318(5)	29F	MFC	11-32: B237	Cremation, SA/A	16.00	11.50	14.70
9-1408	29G	MFC mug	29:B198D	Adult female	14.50	10.10	14.90
11-250(5)	29H, I	MFC, mug	F11-14: B230	Crem, SA/A	14.00	6.00	16.00
7-782	30A	MFC mug	Rm 85: SF10		10.70	8.50	10.00
8-954	30B	MFC	Rm 74: SF3		49.50	28.30	52.60
2-D3	30C	MFC	41:SF25		22.40	38.10	37.30
3-1146	30D	MFG	Rm 47		26.00	15.00	20.00
9-872	30E	MFC	Rm 94: SF43		33.10	16.20	32.80
AT	30F	MBrW mug	Midden		11.60	8.40	12.00
2-806	30G	MFC	Rm 41: SF25		33.00	22.40	37.30
D2F2SF-1	30H	MFC	Rm 42		29.50	20.00	26.20
9-1522	30I	MFG	39:Floor		27.50	16.70	26.50
6-282	31A	MPC	B100:SF3	Adult male	23.50	19.50	0.00
CF3S2-18	31B	MPC	AM32		21.50	0.00	15.5+
D1F1SF2	31C	MPC	Rm 40		33.10	17.70	26.60
8-1172	31D	MPC	Rm 74: SF49		60.80	41.80	56.80
8-818	31E	MPC	Rm 74: SF12		54.00	38.00	58.50
8-1310	31F	MPC	74:SF12		36.00	0.00	45.00
4-486(1)	31G	MPC	Rm 60: SF1		34.80	21.10	32.30
5-1025(22:SF5)	31H	MPC	Rm 22		24.00	16.00	25.00
5-1025	31I	MPC	Rm 22:SF5		23.00	17.00	22.20
8-547	32A	MPC	Rm 39: F86-50		29.00	17.40	25.70
8-988	32B	MPC	Rm 74: SF19		29.70	6.70	21.50
8-957	32C	CIC	Rm 74: SF5		68.60	38.50	62.00
8-953	32D	EPRB	Rm 74: SF2		49.20	19.90	51.60
3-478	32E	IWW	Rm 52		23.00	22.00	10.90
11-68	32F	RMBW	F11-4		15.00	0.00	6.50
8-1337(28:B135)	32G	Puerco B/W	Rm 28: B135	Subadult	5.90	5.70	13.30
2-793	32H, I	ISBrW	Rm 41: B25	Adult male	29.90	29.30	12.80

Notes

PREFACE

1. C. B., Harriet, and Burton Cosgrove, Jr., carried out limited excavations at the NAN Ranch Ruin in 1926 during the course of their extensive excavations at the nearby Swarts Ruin (Cosgrove and Cosgrove 1932). Burt Jr. recalled that some digging had been carried out at the site prior to their excavations (personal communications with the author, December 1998).
2. The Mimbres Foundation, under the direction of Stephen LeBlanc, carried out extensive archaeological surveys of the Mimbres Valley and limited excavations in sites covering the entire Mimbres cultural sequence (Anyon and LeBlanc 1984; Blake et al. 1986; LeBlanc 1983; Nelson and LeBlanc 1986).
3. Creel 1989a; Sanchez 1996; Shafer 1992, 1995; Shafer and Brewington 1995; Shafer and Taylor 1986; Shafer and Drollinger 1998.

CHAPTER ONE

1. Fewkes 1916a, 1916b, 1923, 1924.
2. Lekson 1992:30.
3. Parham et al. 1983.
4. Trauger 1972.
5. Bailey 1913, 1931; Graybill 1975.
6. Bailey 1931; Findley et al. 1975.
7. Tagg 1996.
8. Turnbow 2000.
9. Brody 1977a:90; Creel 1995; LeBlanc 1983:117.
10. Lekson 1991; Stephen LeBlanc and Roger Anyon, personal communication 1998.
11. Nelson and Anyon 1996.
12. Shafer et al. 2001.
13. LeBlanc and Whalen 1980:271–316.
14. Nelson and Anyon 1996.
15. Lange and Riley 1970.

CHAPTER TWO

1. Lange and Riley 1970; Webster 1912.
2. Webster 1912.
3. Bradfield 1931; Cosgrove and Cosgrove 1932; Nesbitt 1931; Anyon and LeBlanc 1984:10–11.
4. Bradfield 1931; Cosgrove and Cosgrove 1932.
5. Cosgrove 1923.
6. Davis 1995.
7. Haury 1936a.
8. Graybill 1975.
9. Lekson 1990.
10. Lekson 1990; Nelson 1999:36, 37.
11. Blake et al. 1986; LeBlanc 1983; Anyon and LeBlanc 1984; Nelson and LeBlanc 1986.
12. Woolsey and McIntyre 1996.
13. Creel 1989b; Tidemann 2002.
14. Creel 1995, 1997.
15. Lekson 1990.
16. Nelson 1984, 1999; Hegmon et al. 1998.
17. Roth and Bettison 1992; Bettison 1997.
18. Lekson 1988; Nelson and Anyon 1996.
19. Shafer 1999.
20. Shafer et al. 1999.
21. LeBlanc 1985.
22. Lange and Riley 1970.
23. Lekson 1987.
24. Colonel Burt Cosgrove, Jr., personal communication January 1999.

CHAPTER THREE

1. Nelson 1999.
2. Mabry 1998; Turnbow 2000.
3. LeBlanc 1983: 37–40.
4. LeBlanc 1983: 37–40.
5. Anyon and LeBlanc 1984; Blake et al. 1986.
6. Diehl and Gilman 1996.
7. Griffen 1969.

8. LeBlanc 1983.
9. Mabry 1998; Turnbow 2000.
10. Anyon and LeBlanc 1984.
11. Turnbow 2000.
12. Turnbow 2000.
13. Blake et al. 1986.
14. Creel 1997; Lucas 1996.
15. Anyon and LeBlanc 1981.
16. Cosgrove 1947.
17. Kelly 1977.
18. Shafer 1985.
19. Fewkes 1891; LeBlanc 1997; Shafer 1999; for an alternative view, see Hegmon and Trevathan 1996.
20. J. Eghmy, personal communication 1988.
21. C. Stevenson, personal communication 1988.
22. Burden 2001.
23. See Burden 2001 for a full description of this possible great kiva.
24. Burden 2001.
25. George Burr, NSF–Arizona AMS Laboratory, Tucson, Arizona, personal communication 2002.
26. Anyon and LeBlanc 1981, 1984:132–141.
27. Di Peso 1974:106–110.
28. Haury 1936a; Anyon and LeBlanc 1984:31–90.
29. Young 1996.
30. Diehl 1996.
31. Brody et al. 1983:48–50.
32. Brody et al. 1983:50.
33. Brody et al. 1983:50.
34. Nelson 1999.
35. Renfrew 2001.
36. Lucas 1996.
37. Doelle et al. 1987; Rice 1987; Wilcox 1987.

CHAPTER FOUR

1. Wyckoff 1990.
2. Creel 1995.
3. Anyon and LeBlanc 1984:70–76.
4. Cosgrove and Cosgrove 1932:9–11.
5. Anyon 1980.
6. Anyon and LeBlanc 1984:49–53, 70–76.
7. Anyon and LeBlanc 1984:31–95.
8. Bradfield 1931.
9. Gilman 1987.
10. Kelly 1977; Hackenberg 1983.
11. r and +r are codes used by the Laboratory of Tree Ring Research at the University of Arizona. The symbol r means that less than a full section is present but the outermost ring is continuous around the available circumference, indicating a likely cutting date. The symbol +r indicates that one or more rings may be missing near the end of the ring series.
12. Burden 2001.
13. Eliade 1964; Schaefer and Furst 1996.
14. Burden 2001.
15. Creel 1989a.
16. Anyon and LeBlanc 1984:12.
17. Anyon and LeBlanc 1984:12.
18. Kidder et al. 1949.
19. Creel 1989a.
20. Bryan 1927a:333, 1927b:25, 28.
21. Woosley and McIntyre 1996:59.
22. Shafer and Judkins 1996.
23. Gould 1963; Hofman 1986; Underhill 1939:9, 136, 188.
24. Cosgrove and Cosgrove (1932:90) identify drawings of pottery vessels recovered from their 1926 excavations at a "nearby ruin," which was the NAN Ranch Ruin.
25. Brody et al. 1983:50–56.
26. Shafer and Brewington 1995.
27. Schaafsma 1994. I do not believe that the ancient Mimbreños were within the ritual sphere of Mexican cultures, but I do think that any similarities that may have existed had deep historical roots. In other words, they may very well have shared a very distant common ancestry.
28. Tidemann 2002.
29. Boyd 1998; Whitley 1998.

CHAPTER FIVE

1. Lekson 1999:164.
2. Blake et al. 1986.
3. Blake et al. 1986; LeBlanc 1983:152.
4. Lekson 1993.
5. Cameron 1999; Mindeleff 1981.
6. Shafer and Drollinger 1998.
7. Bruno 1988.
8. Bruno 1988.
9. Minnis 1981; Nelson 1999.

10. Bruno 1988.
11. Bruno 1988:70; Taylor 1981:9.
12. Room 74 was added to room 84, which has a construction date of A.D. 1128v; room 109 has a construction date of A.D. 1114.
13. Cosgrove and Cosgrove 1932:40.
14. Shafer et al. 1979.
15. Bradfield 1931:25.
16. Mindeleff 1891.
17. Burden 2001:175.
18. Morison 2000.
19. Shafer (1982) provides a description of Mimbres households. Identified household habitation rooms include rooms 3, 4, 5, 8, 9, 12, 16, 18, 22, 25, 28, 29, 30, 31, 37, 40, 41, 47, 48, 49, 50, 55, 62, 63B, 82, 84, 85, 93, and 94.
20. Lowell 1991.
21. Cameron 1999:50.
22. All burials are assigned to room 28A because it was not possible to determine on which floor the burial pits originated.
23. Shafer 1999; see also Rapaport 1982:29–30.
24. These two rooms meet all the criteria for corporate kivas except specific information on the presence of floor vaults. Room 9 was a large room whose hearth was destroyed by relic hunters. The hearth in room 49 was also mostly destroyed by a relic hunter's pit, so it was not possible to determine if a vault was present in either of these rooms.
25. Hill 1997.
26. Cameron Creek (Bradfield 1931), Mattocks (LeBlanc 1983), and Saige-McFarland (Lekson 1991).
27. McGuire and Schiffer 1983:40–41.
28. Moerman 1998:282–292.
29. Wall shelves were also reported at the Swarts and Treasure Hill sites by the Cosgroves (Cosgrove and Cosgrove 1932).
30. Cosgrove and Cosgrove 1932:18.
31. Ham 1989.
32. Shafer and Brewington 1995.
33. Shafer 1982.
34. The two intrusive vessels have the largest volume, 113.83 liters; the partially corrugated ollas average 42.4 liters and the fully corrugated jars 19.3 liters (Lyle 1996).
35. Turner and Lofgren 1966; Nelson and LeBlanc 1986.
36. Margaret Hinton, personal communication 1978.
37. Burden 2001:95–105.
38. Burden 2001:169, 170.
39. Mobley-Tanaka 1997.
40. Burden 2001:Figure 4.24.
41. Cosgrove and Cosgrove 1932:Figure 55a.
42. Cosgrove and Cosgrove 1932:14.
43. Shafer and Drollinger 1998.
44. Cosgrove and Cosgrove 1932:14.
45. Shafer and Drollinger 1998.
46. Di Peso 1956:142, 143; Hackenberg 1993; Hayden 1942, 1954:41–45, 405–407; Seymour 1988; Tuthill 1947:30.
47. Sobolik et al. 1997.
48. Lavold 1999, unpublished manuscript. The pollen concentration value of the pit fill was 22,469 per gram, whereas the pollen concentration of the floor was 8,650 per gram.
49. Beaglehole 1937.
50. Anyon and LeBlanc 1984; Bradfield 1931; Cosgrove and Cosgrove 1932:29; Creel and McKusick 1994; Woolsey and McIntyre 1996:281–286.
51. Ellis (1995) provides a historical background for the ditch and reservoir system. Stuck (1867) shows the ditch, and Bandelier mentions the reservoir on the Brockmann place (Lange and Riley 1970:182–183).
52. Ellis 1995. Ellis dated the ditch and reservoir, radiocarbon dating soil organic matter and carefully selecting samples from canal and reservoir fill.
53. Brody 1977a.
54. Creel 1997.

CHAPTER SIX

1. Wilshusen 1989.
2. Cameron 1999.
3. Doelle et al. 1987.
4. Cordell 1997:281–282.
5. Wilshusen 1989.
6. Dozier 1965, 1970.
7. Dozier 1965, 1970.
8. McAnany 1995:7–21; Howell and Kintigh 1996.

9. Lucas 1996.
10. Doelle et al. 1987; Rice 1987; Wilcox 1987.
11. Shafer 1995.
12. Herrington 1979:74, 76.
13. Darrell Creel, personal communication 1999.
14. Webster 1912:107.
15. Mobley-Tanaka 1997.
16. Lekson 1999.
17. Morris and Brooks 1987.
18. Crude death rate used (i.e., .0503 high or .036 low [taken from Story 1985]).
19. Cameron 1999:27–34.
20. Cameron 1999:53.
21. Cameron 1999:48.
22. Burden 2001.
23. Burden 2001:238–253.
24. Shafer 1986.
25. LeBlanc 1983; Ham 1989; Gilman 1990.
26. Eggan 1950; Cameron 1999; McGuire and Saitta 1997.
27. Ham 1989.
28. Peebles and Kus 1977.
29. Holliday 1996.
30. Cosgrove and Cosgrove 1932: Figure 76.
31. Hill 1997.
32. Herrington 1979.
33. Hill 1997.
34. Funk 1983.
35. LeBlanc 1977.

CHAPTER SEVEN

1. Minnis 1981.
2. Brown 1995; Howell and Kintigh 1996.
3. Eggan 1950:291–324.
4. Fritz 1994.
5. Hard and Roney 1998.
6. Turnbow 2000.
7. Minnis 1981.
8. Briffa and Osborn 2002; Creel 1997; Esper et al. 2002.
9. Nelson 1999; Ellis 1998.
10. Ellis 1998.
11. Diehl 1996.
12. Carolyn Rose, personal communication 2001.
13. Minnis 1981.
14. Diehl 1996.
15. LeBlanc 1983:117.
16. Lucas 1996:74.
17. Sayles 1945.
18. Shafer et al. 1999.
19. Brewington et al. 1995.
20. Bandelier 1892:357.
21. Herrington 1979.
22. Creel and Adams 1986; Creel 1990.
23. Ellis 1990, 1995, 1998.
24. Creel and Adams 1986; Creel 1990.
25. Ellis 1995.
26. Minnis 1981; Ellis 1998.
27. Shafer and Judkins 1996.
28. Herrington 1979:103–146.
29. Herrington 1979: 129–149.
30. Creel and Adams 1986; Creel 1990.
31. Creel 1990.
32. Ellis 1995, 1998:203–208.
33. Ellis 1995.
34. Bently 1993; Leach et al. 1993.
35. Minnis 1981, 1985.
36. Minnis 1981:169–175.
37. Carolyn Rose, personal communication 2001.
38. Minis 1981, 1985; Pendleton 1993; Lavold 1999.
39. Minnis 1984 in Anyon and LeBlanc 1984.
40. Minnis 1984; Pendleton 1993.
41. Shafer et al. 1989.
42. Young 1996.
43. Lavold 1999; Pendleton 1993.
44. Decker 1984.
45. Diehl 1996.
46. Lyle 1996.
47. Turner and Lofgren 1966; Shafer et al. 1999.
48. Anyon and LeBlanc 1984:169.
49. Whalen 1994; Shafer et al. 2001; Turner and Lofgren 1966.
50. Smith 1983:268–270, 1985; Lyle 1996.
51. Smith 1983, 1985.
52. Nelson 1981.
53. Di Peso 1974:vol. 6.
54. Lyle 1996; Turner and Lofgren 1966.
55. Minnis 1981.
56. Powell 1977.
57. Shaffer 1991.
58. Sanchez 1996.
59. Jett and Moyle 1986; see also Bettison et al. 1999.
60. Fewkes 1891.

61. Shaffer and Gardner 1995.
62. Bettinger and Eerkens 1999.
63. Cosgrove and Cosgrove 1932:Plate 50.
64. Ham 1989; Gilman 1990.
65. Geertz 1980:63–75.
66. Barth 1993:63–75; Geertz 1980:68–97.
67. Creel 1999.
68. Esper et al. 2002; Briffa and Osborn 2002.
69. Michael Waters and John Ravesloot, personal communication 2000.
70. Ely 1997; Hall 1990; Waters and Ravesloot 2001; Michael Waters, personal communication 2000.
71. Fitch 1996.
72. Ellis 1995; Herrington 1979; Creel and Adams 1986.
73. Blake et al. 1986.
74. Creel 1996.
75. Shaffer and Baker 2001.

CHAPTER EIGHT

1. Carr 1995.
2. Kidder 1977:290; Wormington 1961:158, 159.
3. Jernigan 1978:Figure 68.
4. Fewkes 1914; Webster 1912.
5. Cosgrove and Cosgrove 1932; Nesbitt 1931; Bradfield 1931.
6. Brody 1977a; LeBlanc and Whalen 1980.
7. Cosgrove and Cosgrove 1932:Figure 239.
8. Kidder 1977:290, 291; Wormington 1961:158, 159.
9. Anyon and LeBlanc 1984.
10. Shafer 1991e.
11. Gilman 1980.
12. Lyle 1996.
13. Gilman 1980.
14. Nelson 1999.
15. Anyon and LeBlanc 1984.
16. Hill 1997.
17. Woolsey and McIntyre 1996.
18. Ham 1989.
19. Peebles and Kus 1977.
20. Gilman 1990.
21. Hill 1997; Shafer 1990.
22. Nesbitt 1931.
23. Hill 1997.
24. Ellis 1968.
25. Moulard 1981; Shafer 1995.
26. Di Peso 1974; Thompson 1999.
27. Shafer 1991c: Figure 22.
28. Shafer 1985.
29. Adovasio et al. 1996.
30. Creel 1989a.
31. Creel 1989a.
32. Shafer and Judkins 1996; Parks-Barrett 2001.
33. Shafer 1990c; Shafer and Judkins 1996.
34. Adovasio et al. 1996.
35. Bradfield 1931:Plate IV.2.
36. Cosgrove and Cosgrove 1932:25.
37. Petrovich 2001:Figure 11.
38. Bradfield 1931:11; Cosgrove and Cosgrove 1932:29; Anyon and LeBlanc 184:201–202, 444, footnote 24; Creel and McKusick 1994; Woolsey and McIntyre 1996.
39. Woolsey and McIntyre 1996.
40. Creel and McKusick 1994.
41. Hill 2000.
42. Hill 2000.
43. Powell 2000.
44. Hill 2000.

CHAPTER NINE

1. Patrick 1988.
2. Patrick 1988.
3. Patrick 1988.
4. Patrick, 1995.
5. Marek 1990.
6. Sattenspiel and Harpending 1983.
7. Marek 1990.
8. Moorrees et al. 1963, Ubelaker 1984.
9. Holliday 1993.
10. Turner 1993, 1999.

CHAPTER TEN

1. Bunzel 1929; Guthe 1925; Chapman 1953.
2. Image on a Mimbres bowl in the Millicent Rogers Museum collection, Taos, New Mexico, shows a potter seated on the ground while forming a jar.
3. Cosgrove and Cosgrove 1932:Figure 81e.
4. Brody 1977a; Brody et al. 1983; Brody and Swentzell 1996.
5. Fewkes 1891; Bunzel 1929.
6. Hegmon and Trevathen 1996; LeBlanc 1997; Shaffer et al. 1997.
7. Brody 1977:115–120; Bunzell 1929; Fewkes 1891.

8. Gilman et al. 1994; James et al. 1996.
9. Hegmon et al. 1998.
10. Gilman et al. 1994.
11. Gilman et al. 1994; James et al. 1996; Powell 2000.
12. Lyle 1996:75.
13. Gottshall et al. 2002.
14. Mills 2000.
15. Brewington et al. 1996.
16. Gilman et al. 1994; James et al. 1996; Powell 2000.
17. Powell 2000.
18. Miller 1989, 1992; Miller and Batcho 1992; Shafer et al. 1999.
19. Shafer et al. 1999.
20. Anyon and LeBlanc 1984:22, 151.
21. Haury 1936b.
22. Brody et al. 1983.
23. Shafer and Brewington 1995.
24. Stokes 2000.
25. Shafer and Brewington 1995.
26. Fenner 1977.
27. Lyle 1996.
28. Lyle 1996.
29. Lyle 1996.
30. Brewington et al. 1995.
31. Nelson 1999.
32. Rugge 1978; Meinardus 1988.
33. Shafer et al. 2001.
34. Shafer and Judkins 1996.
35. Brewington and Shafer 1999.
36. Hegmon et al. 1998.
37. Hayden 1998.
38. Lyle 1996.
39. Brody 1977a:52.
40. Leach et al. 1997.
41. Lyle 1996.
42. Lumholtz 1900, 1902.
43. Shafer et al. 1979.
44. Shaffer and Gardner 1995.
45. Carr 1979.
46. Wobst 1977; Brewington et al. 1995.
47. Sayles 1945; Di Peso 1974; Miller 1989; Miller and Batcho 1992; Shafer et al. 1999.
48. Patricia Gilman, personal communication 2001.
49. Shafer et al. 1999.

CHAPTER ELEVEN

1. Dockall 1991.
2. Dockall 1991.
3. Dockall 1990.
4. Nelson 1981.
5. Schackley 1988.
6. Lekson 1990; Nelson 1981, 1984.
7. Nelson 1981, 1984.
8. Cosgrove 1947.
9. LeBlanc 1984:236–246; Nelson and LeBlanc 1986.
10. Haury 1936a; Turnbow 2000.
11. Cosgrove 1947.
12. Diehl 1996.
13. Schlanger 1996; Mobley-Tanaka 1997; Hegmon et al. 2000.
14. Peregrine 2001.
15. Ellis 1967; Judd 1954:282–283.
16. Shelley 1983.
17. Judd 1954:Figure 65.
18. Burden 2001:48.
19. Ellis 1967.
20. Nesbitt 1931; Lucas 1996.
21. Lucas 1996.
22. Burden 2001:Figure 4.24.
23. Hayden and Cannon 1984:83–88.
24. Reid and Whittlesey 1999.
25. Shaffer 1990.
26. Shaffer 1990.
27. Adovasio et al. 1996.
28. Parks-Barrett 2001.
29. Parks-Barrett 2001.
30. Shafer and Judkins 1996.
31. Lyle 1996; Shaffer 1990.
32. Hampton 1999:227, 244–248; Burton 1984; McBryde 1984; Shafer 1993.

CHAPTER TWELVE

1. Brody 1977a:213–215.
2. Crown and Bishop 1994.
3. Brody 1977a, 1977b.
4. Thompson 1999; Robins and Westmoreland 1991.
5. Shaffer 2000.
6. Boyd 1998.
7. Whitley 1998.

8. Boyd 1998; Ortiz 1972.
9. Ortiz 1972.
10. Boyd 1998.
11. Waters 1963; Tyler 1964:56.
12. Schele and Freidel 1990:64–95.
13. Zingg 1938.
14. Brundage 1979:7.
15. Freidel et al. 1993.
16. Fritz 1987.
17. Ortiz 1972:143.
18. McAnany 1998.
19. Zingg 1938:676.
20. Brundage 1979:4.
21. Schele and Freidel 1990:67.
22. Lumholtz 1902; Zingg 1938.
23. Moulard 1981:xviiii–xix.
24. Moulard 1981:xviii; Bunzel 1932a, 1932b.
25. Lumholtz 1902:384; Bennett and Zingg 1935:359.
26. Zingg 1938:155.
27. Beals 1943:53, 54.
28. Headrick 1998.
29. Schaafsma 1999.
30. Schaafsma 1999.
31. Brody 1977; Moulard 1981; McAnany 1998.
32. Brody 1977:212; Moulard 1981.
33. Hieb 1994; Adams 1994.
34. Gilman et al.; James et al. 1996; Powell 2000.
35. Powell 2000.
36. Titiev 1992.
37. McAnany 1998.
38. Minnis 1981, 1984.
39. Waters and Ravesloot 2001.
40. Fish and Fish 1999.

References Cited

Adams, E. C.
    1994 The Katsina Cult: A Western Pueblo Perspective. In *Kachinas in the Pueblo World*, edited by P. Schaafsma, pp. 35–46. University of New Mexico Press, Albuquerque.

Adovasio, J. M, D. C. Hyland, and R. L. Andrews
    1996 Perishable Industries from NAN Ranch Ruin, New Mexico: A Unique Window into Mimbreño Fiber Technology. Paper presented at the 61st Annual Meeting of the Society for American Archaeology, New Orleans.

Anyon, R.
    1980 The Late Pithouse Period. In *An Archaeological Synthesis of South-Central and Southwestern New Mexico*, edited by S. A. LeBlanc and M. E. Whalen, pp. 143–204. University of New Mexico, Office of Contract Archaeology, Albuquerque.

Anyon, R., and S. A. LeBlanc
    1981 Architectural Evolution of Mimbres-Mogollon Communal Structures. *Kiva* 45:253–277.
    1984 *The Galaz Ruin: A Prehistoric Mimbres Village in Southwestern New Mexico*. Maxwell Museum of Anthropology and University of New Mexico Press, Albuquerque.

Bailey, V.
    1913 Life Zones and Crop Zones of New Mexico. *United States Department of Agriculture, North American Fauna*. U.S. Government Printing Office, Washington, D.C., 35.
    1931 Mammals of New Mexico. *United States Department of Agriculture, North American Fauna*. U.S. Government Printing Office, Washington, D.C., 53.

Bandelier, A. F.
    1892 *Final Report of Investigations Among the Indians of the Southwestern States* Pt. II. Papers of the Institute of America Vol. IV. Cambridge, Mass.

Barth, F.
    1993 *Balinese Worlds*. University of Chicago Press.

Beaglehole, E.
    1937 *Notes on Hopi Economic Life*. Yale University Press, New Haven.

Beals, R. L.
    1943 The Aboriginal Culture of the Cahita Indians. *Ibero-Americana*, vol. 19. University of California Press, Berkeley, 1–86.

Bennett, W. C., and R. M. Zingg
    1935 *The Tarhumara, an Indian Tribe of Northern Mexico*. Rio Grande Press, Inc., Glorieta, New Mexico.

Bently, M. T.
    1993 Hot Well Village and Reservoir: A Preliminary Overview. *The Artifact* 31(2):1–32.

Berry, D. R.
    1985 Dental Attrition: Dental Paleopathology of Grasshopper Pueblo, Arizona. In *Health and Disease in the Prehistoric Southwest*, edited by C. F. Merbs and R. J. Miller. Arizona State University Anthropology Research Papers 34:253–275, Tempe.

Bettinger, R. L., and J. Eerkens
    1999 Point Typologies, Cultural Transmission, and the Spread of Bow-and-Arrow Technology in the Prehistoric Great Basin. *American Antiquity* 64(2):231–242.

Bettison, C. A.
    1997 *Analysis of Ceramics from Pithouses and Associated Structures at the Lake Roberts*

Vista Site, Gila National Forest, New Mexico. Final Submitted to Gila National Forrest, Supervisor's Office, Heritage Program by Western New Mexico University Museum, Silver City, New Mexico.

Bettison, C. A., R. Shook, R. Jennings, and D. Miller
- 1999 New Identification of Naturalistic Motifs on Mimbres Pottery. In *Sixty Years of Mogollon Archaeology: Papers from the Ninth Mogollon Conference, Silver City, New Mexico, 1996,* edited by S. M. Whittlesey, pp. 119–125. SRI Press, Tucson, Arizona.

Blake, M., S. A. LeBlanc, and P. E. Minnis
- 1986 Changing Settlement and Population in the Mimbres Valley, SW New Mexico. *Journal of Field Archaeology* 13:439–464.

Boyd, C. E.
- 1998 The Work of Art: Rock Art and Adaptation in the Lower Pecos, Texas Archaic. Unpublished Ph.D. dissertation, Department of Anthropology, Texas A&M University, College Station.

Bradfield, W.
- 1931 *Cameron Creek Village: A Site in the Mimbres Area in Grant County, New Mexico.* Monographs of the School of American Research No. 1, Santa Fe.

Brewington, R. L., J. E. Dockall, and H. J. Shafer
- 1995 *Archaeology of 41MX5: A Late Prehistoric Caddoan Hamlet in Morris County, Texas.* Reports of Investigations No. 1, Center for Environmental Archaeology, Texas A&M University, College Station.

Brewington, R. L., and H. J. Shafer
- 1999 The Ceramic Assemblage of Ojasen and Gobernadora. In *Archaeology of the Ojasen (41EP289) and Gobernadora (41EP321) Sites, El Paso County, Texas.* Texas Department of Transportation, Environmental Affairs Division, Archaeology Studies Program Report No. 13, Austin, and Center for Ecological Archaeology, Reports of Investigation No. 2, College Station.

Brewington, R. L., H. J. Shafer, and W. D. James
- 1995 Continuing Neutron Activation Analysis of Mimbres Ceramics: A Progress Report. Paper presented at the Ninth Jornada Mogollon Conference, El Paso, Texas.
- 1996 Production and Distribution of Mimbres Black-on-white Ceramics: Evidence from Instrumental Neutron Activation Analysis (INAA). Paper presented at the 62nd Annual Meeting of the Society for American Archaeology, Nashville.

Briffa, K. R., and T. J. Osborn
- 2002 Blowing Hot and Cold. *Science* 295:2227–2228.

Brody, J. J.
- 1977a *Mimbres Painted Pottery.* School of American Research, Santa Fe, and University of New Mexico Press, Albuquerque.
- 1977b Sidetracked on the Trail of a Mexican Connection. *American Indian Art* 2(4):2–31.

Brody, J. J., C. Scott, and S. A. LeBlanc
- 1983 *Mimbres Pottery: Ancient Art of the American Southwest.* Hudson Hills Press, New York.

Brody, J. J., and R. Swentzel
- 1996 *To Touch the Past: The Painted Pottery of the Mimbres People.* Hudson Hills Press, New York.

Brown, J. A.
- 1995 On Mortuary Analysis—with Special Reference to the Saxe-Binford Research Program. In *Regional Approaches to Mortuary Analysis,* edited by L. A. Beck, p. 3–26. Plenum Press, New York and London.

Brundage, B. C.
- 1979 *The Fifth Sun: Aztec Gods, Aztec World.* University of Texas Press, Austin.

Bruno, H.
- 1988 *Structural Timber and Wood Procurement at the NAN Ranch Ruin in Grant County, New Mexico.* Unpublished Master's thesis, Department of Anthropology, Texas A&M University, College Station.

Bryan, B.
- 1927a The Galaz Ruin in the Mimbres Valley. *El Palacio* 23:323–337.
- 1927b The Mimbres Expedition. *The Masterkey* 1:19–30.

Bunzel, R. L.
- 1929 *The Pueblo Potter: A Study of Creative Imagination in Primitive Art.* Columbia University Press, New York.

1932a *Introduction to Zuni Ceremonialism.* Bureau of American Ethnology Forty-Seventh Annual Report, Smithsonian Institution, Washington, D.C.

1932b *Zuni Katcinas.* Bureau of American Ethnology Forty-Seventh Annual Report, Smithsonian Institution, Washington, D.C.

Burden, D.
2001 *Reconstructing the Past: An Architectural Analysis of Communal Structures from the NAN Ranch Ruin (LA2465), Grant County, New Mexico.* Unpublished Master's thesis, Department of Anthropology, Texas A&M University, College Station.

Burton, J. E.
1984 Quarrying in a Tribal Society. *World Archaeology* 16(2):234–243. London.

Cameron, C. M.
1999 *Hopi Dwellings: Architecture at Orayvi.* University of Arizona Press, Tucson.

Carr, C.
1995 Mortuary Practices: Their Social, Philosophical-Religious, Circumstantial, and Physical Determinants. *Journal of Archaeological Method and Theory* 2(2):105–200.

Carr, P.
1979 *Mimbres Mythology.* Southwestern Studies, Monograph 56. Texas Western Press, University of Texas at El Paso, El Paso.

Chapman, K. M.
1953 *The Pottery of Santo Domingo Pueblo: A Detailed Study of Its Decoration.* School of American Research, University of New Mexico Press, Albuquerque.

Cordell, L.
1997 *Archaeology of the Southwest.* Academic Press, New York.

Cosgrove, C. B.
1923 Two Kivas at Treasure Hill. *El Palacio* 15(2):19–21.

1947 *Caves in the Upper Gila and Hueco Areas in New Mexico and Texas.* Papers of the Peabody Museum of American Archaeology and Ethnology Vol. 24, No. 2. Harvard University, Cambridge.

Cosgrove, H. S., and C. B. Cosgrove
1932 *The Swarts Ruin: A Typical Mimbres Site in Southwestern New Mexico.* Papers of the Peabody Museum of American Archaeology and Ethnology, Vol. 15, No. 1. Harvard University, Cambridge.

Creel, D.
1989a A Primary Cremation at the NAN Ranch Ruin, with Comparative Data on Other Cremations in the Mimbres Area, New Mexico. *Journal of Field Archaeology* 16:309–329.

1989b Anthropomorphic Rock Art Figures in the Middle Mimbres Valley, New Mexico. *Kiva* 55(1):71–86.

1990 Efforts to Date Water Control Features at Site NAN-20. In *Archaeology at the NAN Ranch Ruin, 1989 Season, Special Report 10,* edited by H. J. Shafer, pp. 136–138. Anthropology Laboratory, Department of Anthropology, Texas A&M University, College Station.

1995 Status Report on Excavations at Old Town Site (LA1113), Luna County, New Mexico, Summer 1994. Submitted to the U.S. Bureau of Land Management, New Mexico State Office. Texas Archeological Research Laboratory, University of Texas at Austin, Austin.

1996 Environmental Variation and Prehistoric Culture in the Mimbres Area. Paper presented at the 61st Annual Meeting of the Society for American Archaeology, New Orleans.

1997 *Status Report on Excavations at the Old Town Site (LA1113), Luna County, New Mexico, Summer 1996.* Submitted to the U.S. Bureau of Land Management, New Mexico State Office. Texas Archeological Research Laboratory, University of Texas, Austin.

1999 *Status Report on Excavations at the Old Town Site (LA1113), Luna County, New Mexico, Summer 1998.* Submitted to the U.S. Bureau of Land Management, New Mexico State Office. Texas Archeological Research Laboratory, University of Texas, Austin.

Creel, D., and B. Adams
　1986　Investigation of Water Control Features at NAN-20. In *The NAN Ranch Archaeology Project: 1985 Interim Report,* edited by H. J. Shafer, pp. 49–66. Special Report 7, Anthropology Laboratory, Department of Anthropology, Texas A&M University, College Station.

Creel, D., and C. McKusick
　1994　Prehistoric Macaws and Parrots in the Mimbres Area, New Mexico. *American Antiquity* 59(3):510–524.

Crown, P., and R. Bishop
　1994　*Ceramics and Ideology: Salado Polychrome Pottery.* University of New Mexico Press, Albuquerque.

Davis, C. O.
　1995　*Treasured Earth: Hattie Cosgrove's Mimbres Archaeology in the American Southwest.* Sanpete Publications and Old Pueblo Archaeology Center, Tucson, Arizona.

Decker, D.
　1984　Squash Seeds from NAN Ranch, New Mexico. Ms. on file, Department of Anthropology, Texas A&M University, College Station.

Diehl, M.
　1996　The Intensity of Maize Processing and Production in Upland Mogollon Pithouse Villages A.D. 200–1000. *American Antiquity* 61:102–115.

Diehl, M., and P. A. Gilman
　1996　Implications from the Designs of Different Southwestern Architectural Forms. In *Interpreting Southwestern Diversity: Underlying Principles and Overarching Patterns.* Arizona State University Anthropological Papers, Tempe.

Di Peso, C. C.
　1956　*The Upper Pima of San Cayetano Del Tumacacori.* Amerind Foundation Paper No. 7. Dragoon, Arizona.
　1974　*Casas Grandes: A Fallen Trading Center of the Gran Chichimeca.* 3 vols. Amerind Foundation Series No. 9. Amerind Foundation, Dragoon, and Northland Press, Flagstaff.

Dockall, J. E.
　1990　A Technological Analysis of rhyolite Quarry Debris from the NAN Ruin, New Mexico. In *Archaeology at the NAN Ranch Ruin: 1989 Season,* edited by H. J. Shafer, pp. 106–131. Special Report 10, Anthropology Laboratory, Department of Anthropology, Texas A&M University, College Station.
　1991　*Chipped Stone Technology at the NAN Ruin, Grant County, New Mexico.* Unpublished Master's thesis, Texas A&M University, College Station.

Doelle, W. H., F. W. Huntington, and H. D. Wallace
　1987　Rincon Phase Reorganization in the Tucson Basin. In *The Hohokam Village: Site Structure and Organization,* edited by D. E. Doyel, pp. 71–96. Southwestern and Rocky Mountain Division of the American Association for the Advancement of Science, Glenwood Springs, Colorado.

Dozier, E. P.
　1965　Southwestern Social Units and Archaeology. *American Antiquity* 31(1):38–47.
　1970　*The Pueblo Indians of North America.* Holt, Rinehart, and Winston, New York.

Eggan, F.
　1950　*Social Organization of the Western Pueblos.* University of Chicago Press.

Eliade, M.
　1964　*Shamanism: Archaic Techniques of Ecstasy.* Princeton University Press, Princeton, New Jersey.
　1987　Cosmology: An Overview. In *The Encyclopedia of Religion,* vol. 4, edited by M. Eliade, pp. 100–107. Macmillan Publishing Company, New York.

Ellis, F. H.
　1967　Use and Significance of the Tcamahia. *El Palacio* 74(1):35–43.
　1968　An Interpretation of Prehistoric Death Customs in Terms of Modern Southwestern Parallels. In *Collected Papers in Honor of Lyndon Lane Hargrave,* edited by Albert H. Schroeder, pp. 57–76. Papers of the Archaeological Society of New Mexico No. 1, Museum of New Mexico Press, Santa Fe.

Ellis, G. L.
- 1990 Geoarchaeological Excavations at LA15049. In *Archaeology at the NAN Ranch Ruin: 1989 Season,* edited by H. J. Shafer, 62–105. Special Report 10, Anthropology Laboratory, Department of Anthropology, Texas A&M University, College Station.
- 1995 An Interpretive Framework for Radiocarbon Dates from Soil Organic Matter from Prehistoric Water Control Features. In *Soil, Water, Biology, and Belief in Prehistoric and Traditional Southwestern Agriculture,* edited by H. Wolcott Toll, pp. 155–186. New Mexico Archaeological Council Special Publication No. 2, Albuquerque.
- 1998 *Epistemology and the Evaluation of Archaeological Theories: An Empiricist Approach, With a Case Study from the Mimbres Region of Southwestern New Mexico.* Unpublished Ph.D. dissertation, Department of Anthropology, Texas A&M University.

Ely, L. L.
- 1997 Response of Extreme Floods in the Southwestern United States to Climatic Variations in the Late Holocene. *Geomorphology* 19:175–201.

Esper, J., E. R. Cook, and F. J. Schweingruber
- 2002 Low-Frequency Signals in Long Tree-Ring Chronologies for Reconstructing Past Temperature Variability. *Science* 295:2250–2253.

Fenner, G. J.
- 1977 Flare-Rimmed Bowls: A Sub-type of Mimbres Classic Black-on-White? *Kiva* 43(2):129–141.

Fewkes, J. W.
- 1891 A Few Summer Ceremonials at Zuni Pueblo. *Journal of American Ethnology and Archaeology* 1:93–133.
- 1914 Archaeology of the Lower Mimbres Valley, New Mexico. *Smithsonian Miscellaneous Collections* 63(10):1–53. Washington, D.C.
- 1916a Animal Figures in Prehistoric Pottery from Mimbres Valley, New Mexico. *American Anthropologist* 18(4):535–545.
- 1916b Explorations and Field-Work of the Smithsonian Institution in 1915. *Smithsonian Miscellaneous Collections* 66(3):84–89. Washington, D.C.
- 1923 Designs on Prehistoric Pottery from the Mimbres Valley, New Mexico. *Smithsonian Miscellaneous Collections* 74(6):1–47. Washington, D.C.
- 1924 Additional Designs on Prehistoric Mimbres Pottery. *Smithsonian Miscellaneous Collections* 76(8):1–46. Washington, D.C.

Findley, J. S., A. H. Harris, D. E. Wilson, and C. Janes
- 1975 *Mammals of New Mexico.* University of New Mexico Press, Albuquerque.

Fish, P. R., and S. K. Fish
- 1999 Reflections on the Casas Grandes Regional Systems from the Northwestern Periphery. In *The Casas Grandes World,* edited by C. F. Schaafsma and C. L. Riley, pp. 27–42. University of Utah Press, Salt Lake City.

Fitch, M. A.
- 1996 *Late Quaternary Geomorphology and Geoarchaeology of a Segment of the Central Mimbres River Valley, Grant County, New Mexico.* Unpublished Master's thesis, Department of Geography, Texas A&M University, College Station.

Freidel, D., L. Schele, and J. Parker
- 1993 *Maya Cosmos: Three Thousand Years on the Shaman's Path.* William Morrow, New York.

Fritz, G. J.
- 1994 Are the First American Farmers Getting Younger? *Current Anthropology* 35(3):305–309.

Fritz, J. M.
- 1987 Chaco Canyon and Vijayanagara: Proposing Spatial Meaning in Two Societies. In *Mirror and Metapho,* edited by D. Ingersoll and G. Bronitsky, pp. 314–349. University Press of America, Lanham.

Funk, D. B.
- 1983 Investigations at Three Small Classic Mimbres Sites, Grant County, New Mexico. Unpublished Honors thesis, Texas A&M University, College Station.

Geertz, C.
- 1980 *Niagara: The Theatre State in Nineteenth-Century Bali.* Princeton University Press, Princeton, New Jersey.

Gilman, P. A.
- 1980 The Classic Mimbres. In *An Archaeological Synthesis of Southwestern and South-Central New Mexico,* edited by S. A. LeBlanc and M. E. Whalen, pp. 256–343. Office of Contract Archaeology, University of New Mexico, Albuquerque.
- 1987 Architecture as an Artifact: Pit Structures and Pueblos in the American Southwest. *American Antiquity* 52:538–564.
- 1990 Social Organization and Classic Period Burials in the SW United States. *Journal of Field Archaeology* 17:457–469.

Gilman, P. A., V. Canouts, and R. L. Bishop
- 1994 The Production and Distribution of Classic Mimbres Black-on-white Pottery. *American Antiquity* 59(4):695–709.

Gottshall, J. M., H. J. Shafer, and W. D. James
- 2002 Neutron Activation Analysis of Mimbres Corrugated Pottery from the NAN Ruin. Paper submitted to *Kiva.*

Gould, R. A.
- 1963 Aboriginal California Burial and Cremation Practices. *Reports of the University of California Archaeological Survey* 60:149–168.

Graybill, D. A.
- 1975 *Mimbres-Mogollon Adaptations in the Gila National Forest, Mimbres District, New Mexico.* Archaeological Report 9, U.S. Forest Service, Southwestern Region, Albuquerque.

Griffen, W. B.
- 1969 *Culture Change and Shifting Populations in Central Northern Mexico.* Anthropological Papers 13, University of Arizona. University of Arizona Press, Tucson.

Guthe, C. E.
- 1925 *Pueblo Pottery Making.* Publications of the Department of Archaeology, Phillips Academy, Andover, New Haven.

Hackenberg, R. A.
- 1983 Pima and Papago Ecological Adaptations. In *Handbook of North American Indians,* vol. 10, edited by Alfonso Oritz, pp. 161–177. Smithsonian Institution, Washington, D.C.

Hall, S. A.
- 1990 Channel Trenching and Climatic Change in the Southern U.S. Great Plains. *Geology* 18:342–345.

Ham, E. J.
- 1989 Analysis of the NAN Ruin (LA15049) Burial Patterns: An Examination of Mimbres Social Structure. Unpublished Master's thesis, Texas A&M University, College Station.

Hampton, O. W.
- 1999 *Culture of Stone: Sacred and Profane Uses of Stone among the Dani.* Texas A&M University Press, College Station.

Hard, R. J., and J. R. Roney
- 1998 A Massive Terraced Village Complex in Chihuahua, Mexico, 3000 Years Before Present. *Science* 279:1661–1664.

Haury, E.
- 1936a *The Mogollon Culture of Southwestern New Mexico.* Medallion Papers Vol. 20. Globe Pueblo, Globe, Arizona.
- 1936b *Some Southwestern Pottery Types.* Medallion Papers Vol. 19, Gila Pueblo, Globe, Arizona.

Hayden, B.
- 1998 Fabulous Feasts: A Prolegomenon to the Archaeological and Theoretical Importance of Feasting. Paper presented at the Society for American Archaeology Annual Meeting, Seattle.

Hayden, B., and A. Cannon
- 1984 *The Structure of Material Systems: Ethnoarchaeology in the Maya Highlands.* SAA Papers No. 3. Society for American Archaeology, Washington, D.C.

Hayden, J. D.
- 1942 Plaster Mixing Bowls. *American Antiquity* 7:405–407.
- 1954 *Excavations, 1940, at University Indian Ruin.* Southwestern Monuments Association Technical Series Vol. 54. Gila Pueblo, Globe, Arizona.

Headrick, A.
- 1998 The Street of the Dead ... It Really Was: Mortuary Bundles at Teotihuacán. *Ancient Mesoamerica,* 10(1):69–85.

Hegmon, M. M., S. G. Ortman, and
J. L. Mobley Tanaka
2000 Women, Men, and the Organization of Space. In *Women and Men in the Prehistoric Southwest,* edited by P. L. Crown, pp. 43–90. School of American Research Press, Santa Fe, and James Curry, Oxford.

Hegmon, M. M., and W. R. Trevathan
1996 Gender, Anatomical Knowledge, and Pottery Production: Implications of an Anatomically Unusual Birth Depicted on Mimbres Pottery from Southwestern New Mexico. *American Antiquity* 61:747–754.

Hegmon, M. M., M. C. Nelson, and S. Ruth
1998 Abandonment, Integration, and Social Change: Analysis of Pottery and Architecture from the Mimbres Region of the American Southwest. *American Anthropologist* 100:148–162.

Herrington, S. L. C.
1979 *Settlement Patterns and Water Control Systems of the Mimbres Classic Phase, Grant County, New Mexico.* Unpublished Ph.D. dissertation, Department of Anthropology, University of Texas, Austin.

Hieb, L. A.
1994 The Meaning of Katsina: Toward a Cultural Definition of "Person" in Hopi Religion. In *Kachinas in the Pueblo World,* edited by P. Schaafsma, pp. 23–34. University of New Mexico Press, Albuquerque.

Hill, E.
2000 The Contextual Analysis of Animal Interments and Ritual Practice in Southwestern North America. *Kiva* 65(4):361–398.

Hill, M. D.
1997 *Sociocultural Implications of Large Mimbres Sites: Architectural and Mortuary Behavior at Swarts Ruin, New Mexico.* Unpublished Master's thesis, Department of Anthropology, Texas A&M University, College Station.

Hofman, J. L.
1986 *Hunter-Gatherer Mortuary Variability: Toward an Explanatory Model.* Unpublished Ph.D. dissertation, University of Tennessee, Knoxville.

Holliday, D. Y.
1993 Occipital Lesions: A Possible Cost of Cradleboards. *American Journal of Physical Anthropology* 90:283–290.
1996 *Were Some More Equal? Diet and Health at the NAN Ranch Pueblo, Mimbres Valley, New Mexico.* Unpublished Ph.D. dissertation, University of Wisconsin, Madison.

Howell, T. L., and K. W. Kintigh
1996 Archaeological Identification of Kin Groups Using Mortuary and Biological Data: An Example from the American Southwest. *American Antiquity* 61(3):537–545.

James, W. D., R. L. Brewington, and H. J. Shafer
1996 Compositional Analysis of American Southwestern Ceramics by Neutron Activation Analysis. *Journal of Radioanalytical and Nuclear Chemistry* 192(1):109–116.

Jernigan, E. W.
1978 *Jewelry of the Prehistoric Southwest.* University of New Mexico Press, Albuquerque.

Jett, S. C., and P. B. Moyle
1986 The Exotic Origins of Fishes Depicted on Prehistoric Mimbres Pottery from New Mexico. *American Antiquity* 51:688–720.

Judd, Neil M.
1954 *The Material Culture of Pueblo Bonito.* Smithsonian Miscellaneous Collections Vol. 124 (whole volume). Smithsonian Institution, Washington, D.C.

Kelly, W. H.
1977 *Cocoa Ethnography.* Anthropological Papers of the University of Arizona No. 29. University of Arizona Press, Tucson.

Kidder, A. V.
1932 Introduction. In *The Swarts Ruin: A Typical Mimbres Site in Southwestern New Mexico,* H. S. Cosgrove and C. B. Cosgrove, pp. xv–xxiii. Papers of the Peabody Museum of American Archaeology and Ethnology Vol. 15, No. 1. Harvard University, Cambridge.
1977 *An Introduction to the Study of Southwestern Archaeology.* Yale University Press, New Haven.

Kidder, A. V., H. S. Cosgrove, and C. B. Cosgrove
    1949   The Pendleton Ruin: Hidalgo County, New Mexico. *Contributions to American Anthropology and History* No. 50. Carnegie Institution of Washington, Washington, D.C.

Lange, C. H., and C. L. Riley
    1970   *The Southwestern Journals of Adolph Bandelier, 1883–1884.* University of New Mexico Press, Albuquerque.

Lavold, L.
    1999   A Pollen Analysis at NAN Ranch Ruin. Manuscript on file in the Department of Anthropology, Texas A&M University, College Station.

Leach, J. D., F. A. Almarez, Brenda Buck, and Galen R. Burgett
    1993   The Hueco Mountain Reservoir: A Preliminary Assessment of an El Paso Phase Water Catchment Basin. *The Artifact* 31(2):33–47.

Leach, Jeff D., H. W. Clark, and J. A. Patterson
    1997   Evidence for Mimbres-Mogollon Mortuary Practices in the Desert Lowlands of Far West Texas. *Texas Journal of Science* 49(2):163–166.

LeBlanc, S. A.
    1977   The 1976 Field Season of the Mimbres Foundation in Southwestern New Mexico. *Journal of New World Archaeology* II(2):1–24.
    1983   *The Mimbres People.* Thames and Hudson, London.
    1984   The Structure of Projectile Point Form. *In The Galaz Ruin: A Prehistoric Mimbres Village in Southwestern New Mexico,* edited by R. Anyon and S. A. LeBlanc, pp. 236–246. Maxwell Museum of Anthropology and University of New Mexico Press, Albuquerque, New Mexico.
    1985   History and Environment in the Mimbres Valley. *Masterkey* 59(1):18–24.
    1997   "A Comment on Hegmon and Treathan's 'Gender, Anatomical Knowledge, and Pottery Production.'" *American Antiquity* 62:723–726.

LeBlanc, S. A., and M. E. Whalen
    1980   *An Archaeological Synthesis of Southwestern and South-Central New Mexico.* Office of Contract Archaeology, University of New Mexico, Albuquerque.

Lekson, S. H.
    1987   *Nana's Raid: Apache Warfare in Southern New Mexico, 1881.* Texas Western Press, El Paso.
    1988   Regional Systematics in the Later Prehistory of Southern New Mexico. In Fourth Jornada Mogollon Conference Collected Papers, edited by Meliha Duran and Karl Laumbach, pp. 1–37. Human Systems Research, Las Cruces, New Mexico.
    1990   *Mimbres Archaeology of the Upper Gila, New Mexico.* Anthropological Papers of the University of Arizona Vol. 53, Tucson.
    1992   *Archaeological Overview of Southwestern New Mexico.* Human Systems Research, Inc., Las Cruces.
    1993   Chaco, Hohokam, and Mimbres: The Southwest in the 11th and 12th Centuries. *Expedition* 35(1):44–52.
    1999   *The Chaco Meridian: Centers of Political Power in the Ancient Southwest.* Altamira Press, New York.

Lowell, J. C.
    1991   *Prehistoric Households at Turkey Creek Pueblo, Arizona.* Anthropological Papers of the University of Arizona Vol. 54, Tucson.

Lucas, J. R.
    1996   *Three Circle Phase Architecture at Old Town, a Prehistoric Mimbres Site in Luna County, Southwestern New Mexico.* Unpublished Master's thesis, University of Texas, Austin.

Lumholtz, C.
    1900   *Symbolism of the Huichol Indians.* Memoirs of the American Museum of Natural History, vol. 3. New York.
    1902   *Unknown Mexico: Explorations in the Sierra Madre and Other Regions, 1890–1898.* 2 vols. Charles Scribner & Sons, New York.

Lyle, R. P.
    1996   Functional Analysis of Mimbres Ceramics from the NAN Ruin (LA15049), Grant County, New Mexico. Unpublished Master's thesis, Department of Anthropology, Texas A&M University, College Station.

Mabry, J. B. (editor)
    1998   *Archaeological Investigations of Early Village Sites in the Middle Santa Cruz Valley: Part I, Analysis and Synthesis.* Anthropological Papers 19, Center for Desert Archaeology, Tucson.

McAnany, P. A.
- 1995 *Living with the Ancestors: Kinship and Kingship in Ancient Maya Society.* University of Texas Press, Austin.
- 1998 Ancestors and the Classic Maya Built Environment. In *Function and Meaning in Classic Maya Architecture,* symposium at Dumbarton Oaks, 7 and 8 October 1994, edited by Stephen D. Houston, pp. 271–298. Dumbarton Oaks Research Library and Collection, Washington, D.C.

McBryde, I.
- 1984 Kulin Greenstone Quarries: The Social Contexts of Production and Distribution of the Mt. William Site. *World Archaeology* 16(2):267–285.

McGuire, R. H., and D. J. Saitta
- 1997 Although They Have Petty Captains, They Obey Them Badly: The Dialectics of Prehispanic Western Pueblo Social Organization. *American Antiquity* 61(2):197–217.

McGuire, R. H., and M. D. Schiffer
- 1983 A Theory of Architectural Design. *Journal of Anthropological Archaeology* 2:277–303.

Marek, M.
- 1990 *Long Bone Growth of Mimbres Subadults from the NAN Ranch (LA15049), New Mexico.* Unpublished Master's thesis, Texas A&M University, College Station.

Meinardus, H.
- 1988 Petrographic Analysis of Mimbres Ceramics from the NAN Ranch Site: A Pilot Study. Ms. on file, Department of Anthropology, Texas A&M University, College Station.

Miller, M. R. III
- 1989 Archaeological Excavations at the Gobernadora and Ojasen Sites: Doña Ana Phase Settlement in the Western Hueco Bolson. El Paso, County, Texas. Report No. 673. Center for Archaeological Research, New Mexico State University, Las Cruces, New Mexico.

Miller, M. R. III, and D. Batcho
- 1992 Petrographic Analysis of Mimbres Whitewares and El Paso Bownwares. In *The Transitional Period in the Southern Jornada Mogollon: Archaeological Investigations in the North Hills Subdivision, Northeast El Paso, Texas,* pp. 222–268. Research Report No. 1. Batcho & Kauffman Associates, El Paso, Texas.

Mills, B. J.
- 2000 Alternative Models, Alternative Strategies: Leadership in the Prehispanic Southwest. In *Alternative Leadership Strategies in the Prehispanic Southwest,* edited by B. J. Mills, pp. 3–18. University of Arizona Press, Tucson.

Mindeleff, V.
- 1891 A Study of Pueblo Architecture: Tusayan and Cibola. In *Eighth Annual Report of the Bureau of Ethnology to the Secretary of the Smithsonian Institution 1886–1887,* edited by J. W. Powell, pp. 3–228. U.S. Government Printing Office, Washington, D.C.

Minnis, P. E.
- 1981 *Economic and Organizational Responses to Food Stress by Nonstratified Societies: An Example from Prehistoric New Mexico.* Ph.D. dissertation, University of Michigan, Ann Arbor. University Microfilms, Ann Arbor.
- 1985 *Social Adaptation to Food Stress: A Prehistoric Southwestern Example.* University of Chicago Press.

Mobley-Tanaka, J. L.
- 1997 Gender and Ritual Space During the Pithouse to Pueblo Transition: Subterranean Mealing Rooms in the North American Southwest. *American Antiquity* 62(3):437–448.

Moerman, D. E.
- 1998 *Native American Ethnobotany.* Timber Press, Portland, Oregon.

Moorrees, C. F. A., E. A. Fanning, and E. E. Hunt, Jr.
- 1963a Formation and Resorption of Three Deciduous Teeth in Children. *American Journal of Physical Anthropology* 21:205–213.
- 1963b Age Variation of Formation Stages for Ten Permanent Teeth. *Journal of Dental Research* 42:1450–1502.

Morison, M.
- 2000 The Turkeys of Elk Ridge. Paper presented at the 10th Mogollon Conference, Las Cruces.

Morris, D. H., and D. Brooks
- 1987 Cremations at the Marana Sites. In *Studies in the Hohokam Community of Marana,* edited by G. E. Rice, pp. 223–234. Office of Cultural Resource Management, Department of Anthropology Anthropological Field Studies Vol. 15, Arizona State University, Tempe.

Moulard, B.
- 1981 *Within the Underworld Sky: Mimbres Ceramic Art in Context.* Twelvetrees Press, Pasadena.

Nelson, B. A., and R. Anyon
- 1996 Fallow Valley: Asynchronous Occupations in Southwestern New Mexico. *Kiva* 61(3):275–294.

Nelson, B. A., and S. A. LeBlanc
- 1986 *Short-Term Sedentism in the American Southwest: The Mimbres Valley Salado.* Maxwell Museum of Anthropology, Albuquerque.

Nelson, M. C.
- 1981 *Chipped Stone Analysis in the Reconstruction of Prehistoric Subsistence Practices: An Example from Southwestern New Mexico.* Ph.D. dissertation, University of California. University Microfilms, Ann Arbor.
- 1984 Food Selection at Galaz: Inferences from Chipped Stone Analysis. In *The Galaz Ruin: A Prehistoric Mimbres Village in Southwestern New Mexico,* edited by R. Anyon and S. A. LeBlanc, pp. 225–236. Maxwell Museum of Anthropology and the University of New Mexico Press, Albuquerque.
- 1999 *Mimbres during the Twelfth Century.* University of Arizona Press, Tucson.

Nelson, M. C. (editor)
- 1984 Ladder Ranch Research Project: Report of the First Season. Technical Series of the Maxwell Museum of Anthropology Vol. 1. University of New Mexico Press, Albuquerque.

Nesbitt, P. H.
- 1931 *The Ancient Mimbreños, Based on Investigations at the Mattocks Ruin, Mimbres Valley, New Mexico.* Logan Museum Bulletin 4, Beloit College, Beloit, Wisconsin.

Olive, B. W.
- 1989 *The Oral Health and Dental Characteristics of a Mimbres Population from Southwest New Mexico.* Unpublished Master's thesis, Department of Anthropology, Texas A&M University, College Station.

Ortiz, A.
- 1972 Ritual Drama and the Pueblo World View. In *New Perspectives on the Pueblos,* edited by A. Ortiz, pp. 135–161. University of New Mexico Press, Albuquerque.

Parham, T. L., R. F. Paetzold, and C. E. Souders
- 1983 Soils Survey of Grant County, New Mexico: Central and Southern Parts. New Mexico State University Agricultural Experiment Station, U.S. Soil Conservation Service, Las Cruces.

Parks-Barrett, M. S.
- 2001 *Prehistoric Jewelry of the NAN Ranch Ruin (LA15049), Grant County, New Mexico.* Unpublished Master's thesis, Department of Anthropology, Texas A&M University, College Station.

Patrick, S. S.
- 1988 *Description and Demographic Analysis of a Mimbres Mogollon Population from LA15049 (NAN Ruin).* Unpublished Master's thesis, Department of Anthropology, Texas A&M University, College Station.

Patrick, S. S.
- 1995 Paleodemography of the NAN Ruin Population. Ms. on file, Department of Anthropology, Texas A&M University, College Station.

Peebles, C. S., and S. M. Kus
- 1977 Some Archaeological Correlates of Ranked Societies. *American Antiquity* 42:421–448.

Pendleton, M. W.
- 1993 *Late Holocene Paleoenvironment and Human Ecology in Southwestern New Mexico.* Unpublished Ph.D. dissertation, Department of Anthropology, Texas A&M University, College Station.

Peregrine, P. N.
- 2001 Matrilocality, Corporate Strategy, and the Organization of Production in the Chacoan World. *American Antiquity* 66(1):36–46.

Petrovich, S. N.
    2001 *Religious Determinants of the Spatial Aspects of Mortuary Behavior at the NAN Ranch Mimbres site.* Unpublished Master's thesis, University of Texas, Austin.

Powell, Susan
    1977 *Changes in Prehistoric Hunting Patterns Resulting from Agricultural Alternation of the Environment: A Case Study from the Mimbres River Area, New Mexico.* Unpublished Master's thesis, Department of Anthropology, University of California, Los Angeles.

Powell, V. S.
    1999 Iconography and Group Formation During the Late Pithouse and Classic Periods of the Mimbres Society, A.D. 970–1140. Unpublished Ph.D. dissertation, Department of Anthropology, University of Oklahoma, Norman.

Rapaport, A.
    1982 *The Meaning of the Built Environment: A Non-verbal Communication Approach.* Reprint, University of Arizona Press, Tucson, 1990.

Reid, J. J., and S. Whittlesey
    1999 *Grasshopper Pueblo: A Story of Archaeology and Ancient Life.* University of Arizona Press, Tucson.

Renfrew, C.
    2001 Symbol before Concept: Material Engagement and the Early Development of Society. In *Archaeological Theory Today,* edited by Ian Hodder, pp. 122–140. Polity Press, Malden, Massachusetts.

Rice, G. E.
    1987 La Ciudad: A Perspective on Hohokam Community Systems. In *The Hohokam Village: Site Structure and Organization,* edited by D. E. Doyel, pp. 127–158. Southwestern and Rocky Mountain Division of the American Association for the Advancement of Science, Glenwood Springs, Colorado.

Robbins, R. R., and R. B. Westmoreland
    1991 Astronomical Imagery and Numbers in Mimbres Pottery. *Astronomy Quarterly* 8:65–88.

Roth, B. J., and C. A. Bettison
    1992 A Preliminary Report of Excavations at the Lake Roberts Vista Site, May 18–June 19, 1992. Submitted to the U.S. Forest Service, Gila National Forest, September 11, 1992. Silver City, New Mexico.

Rugge, D.
    1978 *A Petrographic Study of Ceramics from the Mimbres Valley, New Mexico.* Unpublished senior thesis, University of California, Los Angeles.

Sanchez, J.
    1996 A Reevaluation of Mimbres Faunal Subsistence. *Kiva* 61(3):295–315.

Sattenspiel, L., and H. Harpending
    1983 Stable Populations and Skeletal Age. *American Antiquity* 8:489–498.

Sayles, E. B.
    1945 The San Simon Branch, Excavations at Cave Creek and in the San Simon Valley. I. Material Culture. Medallion Papers Vol. 34. Gila Pueblo, Globe, Arizona.

Schaafsma, Polly
    1994 Prehistoric Kachina Cult and Its Origins as Suggested by Southwestern Rock Art. In *Kachinas in the Pueblo World,* edited by P. Schaafsma, pp. 63–80. University of New Mexico Press, Albuquerque.
    1999 Tlalocs, Kachinas, Sacred Bundles, and Related Symbolism in the Southwest and Mesoamerica. In *The Casas Grandes World,* edited by Curtis F. Schaafsma and Carroll L. Riley, pp. 164–192. University of Utah Press, Salt Lake City.

Schaafsma, Polly (editor)
    1994 *Kachinas in the Pueblo World.* University of New Mexico Press, Albuquerque.

Schackley, M. S.
    1988 Sources of Archaeological Obsidian in the Southwest: An Archaeological, Petrological, and Geochemical Study. *American Antiquity* 53(4):752–772.

Schaefer, S. B., and P. T. Furst (editors)
    1996 *People of the Peyote: Huichol Indian History, Religion, and Survival.* University of New Mexico Press, Albuquerque.

Schele, L., and D. Freidel
- 1990 *A Forest of Kings: The Untold Story of the Ancient Maya.* William Morrow, New York.

Schlanger, S. H.
- 1996 Corn Grinding, Mealing Rooms, and Prehistoric Society in the American Southwest. Ms. on file, Museum of Indian Arts and Culture, Laboratory of Anthropology, Museum of New Mexico, Santa Fe.

Seymour, D. J.
- 1988 Extramural Pits and Other Features. In *The 1982–1984 Excavations at Las Colinas: The Mound 8 Precinct,* edited by David A. Gregory. Arizona State Museum Archaeological Series No. 162(3), Tucson.

Shafer, H. J.
- 1982 Classic Mimbres Phase Households and Room Use Patterns. *Kiva* 48:17–37.
- 1985 A Mimbres Potter's Grave: An Example of Mimbres Craft Specialization? *Bulletin of the Texas Archaeological Society* 56:185–200.
- 1986 *The NAN Ranch Archaeology Project: 1985 Interim Report.* Special Report 7, Anthropology Laboratory, Department of Anthropology, Texas A&M University, College Station.
- 1990a Archaeology at the NAN Ranch Ruin: 1984 Interim Report. *The Artifact* 29(1):5–27.
- 1990b Ten Years of Mimbres Archaeology. *The Artifact* 28(4):1–4.
- 1990c *Archaeology at the NAN Ranch Ruin, 1989 Season.* Special Report 10, Anthropology Laboratory, Department of Anthropology, Texas A&M University, College Station.
- 1991a Archaeology at the NAN Ruin (LA15049): 1985 Interim Report. *The Artifact* 29(1):1–29.
- 1991b Archaeology at the NAN Ruin: 1986 Interim Report. *The Artifact* 29(2):1–42.
- 1991c Archaeology at the NAN Ruin: 1987 Interim Report. *The Artifact* 29(3):1–43.
- 1991d Classic Mimbres Architectural and Mortuary Patterning at the NAN Ranch Ruin, Southwestern New Mexico. In *Mogollon V,* edited by P. H. Beckett, pp. 34–39. COAS Publishing Co., Las Cruces.
- 1991e The Swarts Ruin Revisited: An Assessment of the 1920s Excavation and Data Potential. *The Artifact* 29(1):31–41.
- 1992 Archaeology at the NAN Ruin: 1989 Season. *The Artifact* 29(4):23–47.
- 1993 Research Potential of Prehistoric Quarry Sites. In *Archaeological Site Testing and Evaluation on the Henson Mountain Helicopter Range AWSS Project Areas, Fort Hood, Texas,* D. L. Carlson, general editor, pp. 45–60. United States Army Fort Hood Archaeological Management Series Research Report No. 26, Fort Hood.
- 1995 Architecture and Symbolism in Transitional Pueblo Development in the Mimbres Valley, SW New Mexico. *Journal of Field Archaeology* 22(1):23–47.
- 1999 The Mimbres Classic and Postclassic: A Case for Discontinuity. In *The Casas Grandes World,* edited by C. F. Schaafsma and C. L. Riley, pp. 121–133. University of Utah Press, Salt Lake City.
- 2000 The Classic Mimbres Phenomenon and Some New Interpretations. In *Sixty Years of Mogollon Archaeology: Papers from the Ninth Mogollon Conference, Silver City, New Mexico, 1966,* edited by S. M. Whittlesey, pp. 95–106. SIR Press, Tucson.

Shafer, H. J., and R. L. Brewington
- 1995 Microstylistic Changes in Mimbres Black-on-White Pottery: Examples from the NAN Ruin, Grant County, New Mexico. *Kiva* 64(3):5–29.

Shafer, H. J., and H. Drollinger
- 1998 Classic Mimbres Adobe-Lined Pits, Plazas, and Courtyards at the NAN Ruin, Grant County, New Mexico. *Kiva* 63(4):379–399.

Shafer, H. J., and C. K. Judkins
- 1996 Archaeology at the NAN Ruin: 1996 Season. *The Artifact* 34(3&4):1–62.

Shafer, Harry J., and Anna J. Taylor
- 1986 Mimbres Mogollon Architectural Dynamics and Ceramic Style Change. *Journal of Field Archaeology* 13(1):43–68.

Shafer, H. J., J. E. Dockall, and R. L. Brewington
1999 *Archaeology of the Ojasen (41EP289) and Gobernadora (41EP321) Sites, El Paso County, Texas.* Texas Department of Transportation, Environmental Affairs Division, Archaeology Studies Program Report No. 13, Austin, and Center for Ecological Archaeology, Reports of Investigation No. 2, College Station.

Shafer, H. J., S. Judjahn, W. D. James, D. G. Robinson, and R. P. Lyle
2001 Ceramic Analysis and Interpretation. In *The El Paso Loop 375 Archaeological Project: Phase II Testing and Phase III Mitigation,* edited by J. P. Dering, H. J. Shafer, and R. P. Lyle, pp. 311–360. Texas Department of Transportation Environmental Affairs Division, Archaeological Studies Program Report No. 28, Austin, and Center for Ecological Archaeology, Reports of Investigation No. 3, College Station.

Shafer, H. J., M. Marek, and K. J. Reinhard
1989 A Mimbres Burial with Associated Colon Remains from the NAN Ranch Ruin, New Mexico. *Journal of Field Archaeology* 16:17–30.

Shafer, H. J., A. J. Taylor, and S. J. Usrey
1979 *Archaeological Investigations at the NAN (Hinton) Ranch Ruin, Grant County, New Mexico.* Special Series No. 3, Anthropology Laboratory, Texas A&M University, College Station.

Shaffer, B. S.
1990 The Modified Rabbit Pelvis of the Mimbres: A Preliminary Description of a New Tool Type. *The Artifact* 28(2):7–14.
1991 *The Economic Importance of Vertebrate Faunal Remains from the NAN Ruin (LA15049), A Classic Mimbres Site, Grant County, New Mexico.* Unpublished Master's thesis, Department of Anthropology, Texas A&M University.
2000 Sexual Division of Labor in the Prehistoric Puebloan Southwest as Portrayed by Mimbres Potters. In *Sixty Years of Mogollon Archaeology: Papers from the Ninth Mogollon Conference, Silver City, New Mexico, 1966,* edited by S. M. Whittlesey, pp. 113–118. SIR Press, Tucson.

Shaffer, B. S., and B. Baker
2001 Diachronic Fauna Frequencies in the Mimbres Valley Relative to Horticulture: A Case Study from the NAN Ruin with Theoretical Considerations. Paper submitted to *Kiva.*

Shaffer, B. S., and K. M. Gardner
1995 The Rabbit Drive Through Time: Analysis of the North American Ethnographic and Prehistoric Evidence. *Utah Archaeology* 8:13–25.

Shaffer, B. S., K. M. Gardner, and H. J. Shafer
1997 An Unusual Birth Depicted in Mimbres Pottery: Not Cracked Up to What It Is Supposed to Be. *American Antiquity* 62:727–732.

Shelley, P.
1983 *Lithic Specialization at Salmon Ruin, San Juan County, New Mexico.* Ph.D. dissertation, Department of Anthropology, Washington State University, Pullman.

Smith, M. F., Jr.
1983 *The Study of Ceramic Function from Artifact Size and Shape.* Ph.D. dissertation, Department of Anthropology, University of Oregon.
1985 Toward an Economic Interpretation of Ceramics: Relating Vessel Size and Shape to Use. In *Decoding Prehistoric Ceramics,* edited by B. A. Nelson, pp. 254–309. Southern Illinois University Press, Carbondale.

Sobolik, K. D., L. S. Zimmerman, and B. M. Guilfoyl
1997 Indoor Versus Outdoor Firepit Usage: A Case Study from the Mimbres. *Kiva* 62:283–300.

Stokes, R. J.
2000 Mimbres Pottery Microseriation: Determining Subsurface Room Locations from Surface Ceramic Collections. In *Sixty Years of Mogollon Archaeology: Papers from the Ninth Mogollon Conference, Silver City, New Mexico, 1966,* edited by S. M. Whittlesey, pp. 135–143. SIR Press, Tucson.

Story, R.
1985 An Estimation of Mortality in Pre-Colombian Urban Populations. *American Anthropologist* 8:519–535.

Stuck, I.
    1867   Field Notes of the Subdivision of Township 19S. Range 10W. Of the Principal Meridian in the Territory of New Mexico. Microfiche volume R52, Township 19S Range 10W. Public Room, Bureau of Land Management, Santa Fe.

Tagg, M. D.
    1996   Early Cultigens from Fresnal Shelter, Southeastern New Mexico. *American Antiquity* 61(20):311–324.

Taylor, M.
    1981   *Wood in Archaeology.* Shire Publications, Aylesbury, Great Britain.

Thompson, M.
    1999   Knife-wing: A Prominent Mesoamerican, Mimbres, and Pueblo Icon. In *Sixty Years of Mogollon Archaeology: Papers from the Ninth Mogollon Conference,* Silver City, New Mexico, 1996, edited by S. M. Whittlesey, pp. 145–150. SRI Press, Tucson.

Tidemann, K.
    2002   *Mimbres Rock Art: A Graphic Legacy of Cultural Expression.* Unpublished Master's thesis, Texas A&M University, College Station.

Titiev, M.
    1992   *Old Oraibi: A Study of the Hopi Indians of Third Mesa.* University of New Mexico Press, Albuquerque.

Trauger, F. D.
    1972   *Water Resources and General Geology of Grant County, New Mexico.* Hydrologic Report 2, New Mexico State Bureau of Mines and Mineral Resources. Socorro, New Mexico.

Turnbow, C.
    2000   Early Agricultural Settlements in the Big Burrow Mountains, New Mexico. Paper presented at the Mogollon Conference, Las Cruces.

Turner, C. G. III
    1993   Southwest Indians: Prehistory through Dentition. *National Geographic Society Research & Exploration* 9(1):32–53.
    1999   The Dentition of Casas Grandes with Suggestions on Epigenetic Relationships among Mexican and Southwestern U.S. Populations. In *The Casas Grandes World,* edited by C. F. Schaafsma and C. L. Riley, pp. 229–233. University of Utah Press, Salt Lake City.

Turner, C. G. III, and L. Lofgren
    1966   Household Size of Prehistoric Western Pueblo Indians. *Southwestern Journal of Anthropology* 22:117–132.

Tuthill, C.
    1947   *The Tres Alamos Site in the San Pedro River, Southeastern Arizona.* Amerind Foundation Paper No. 4. Dragoon, Arizona.

Tyler, H. A.
    1964   *Pueblo Gods and Myths.* University of Oklahoma Press, Norman.

Ubelaker, D. H.
    1984   *Human Skeletal Remains: Excavation, Analysis, Interpretation.* Manuals on Archaeology. Taraxacum, Washington, D.C.

Underhill, R. M.
    1939   Social Organization of the Papago Indians. In *Columbia University Contributions to Anthropology,* vol. 30, Columbia University Press, New York.

Walker, P. L.
    1985   Anemia Among Prehistoric Indians of the American Southwest. In *Health and Disease in the Prehistoric Southwest,* edited by C. F. Merbs and R. J. Miller, pp. 139–164. Anthropological Research Papers No. 34. Arizona State University, Tempe.

Waters, F.
    1963   *Book of the Hopi: The First Revelation of the Hopi's Historical and Religious World View of Life.* Penguin Books, Harmondsworth, U.K.

Waters. M. R., and J. C. Ravesloot
    2001   Landscape Change and the Cultural Evolution of the Hohokam Along the Middle Gila River and Other River Valleys in South-Central Arizona. *American Antiquity* 66:285–299.

Webster, C. L.
    1912   Archaeological and Ethnological Researches in Southwestern New Mexico. *Archaeological Bulletin* 3(4):101–115.

Whalen, M. E.
- 1994 *Turquoise Ridge and Late Prehistoric Residential Mobility in the Desert Mogollon Region.* University of Utah Press Anthropological Papers No. 118. Salt Lake City.

Whitley, D. S.
- 1998 Finding Rain in the Desert: Rock Art and Landscape in Far Western North America. In the *Archaeology of Rock Art,* edited by C. Chippindale and P. S. C. Tacon. Cambridge University Press, Cambridge.

Wilcox, D.
- 1987 New Models of Social Structure at the Pal Parado Site. In *The Hohokam Village: Site Structure and Organization,* edited by D. E. Doyel, pp. 71–96. Southwestern and Rocky Mountain Division of the American Association for the Advancement of Science, Glenwood Springs, Colorado.

Wilshusen, R. H.
- 1989 Unstuffing the Estufa: Ritual Floor Features in Anasazi Pit Structures and Pueblo Kivas. In *The Architecture of Social Integration in Prehistoric Pueblos,* edited by W. D. Lipe and M. Hegmon, pp. 89–111. Occasional Paper No. 1. Crow Canyon Archaeological Center, Cortez.

Wobst, M.
- 1977 Stylistic Behavior and Information Exchange. In *For the Director: Research Essays in Honor of James B. Griffen,* edited by C. E. Cleland, pp. 317–342. Anthropological Papers No. 61. Museum of Anthropology, University of Michigan, Ann Arbor.

Woolsey, A. I., and A. J. McIntyre
- 1996 *Mimbres Mogollon Archaeology: Charles C. Di Peso's Excavations at Wind Mountain.* University of New Mexico Press, Albuquerque.

Wormington, H. M.
- 1961 *Prehistoric Indians of the Southwest.* Denver Museum of Natural History, Denver.

Wyckoff, L.
- 1990 *Designs and Factions: Politics, Religion, and Ceramics on the Hopi Third Mesa.* University of New Mexico Press, Albuquerque.

Young, L. C.
- 1996 Pits, Rooms, Baskets, Pots: Storage Among Southwestern Farmers. In *Interpreting Southwestern Diversity: Underlying Principles and Overarching Patterns,* edited by P. R. Fish and J. J. Reid, pp. 201–210. Arizona State Anthropological Research Papers No. 48. Arizona State University, Tempe.

Zingg, R. M.
- 1938 *The Huichols: Primitive Artists.* G. E. Stechert and Co., New York.

Index

Pages with illustrative material or tables are indicated by **bold type**.

Acequia Seca site, 14
adobe, 56, 65, 75, 77, 81, 82, 116, 122; mixing pit for, **56**, **71**; puddled, 43, 46, 84
Adovasio, James, 205, 206, 208
aggregated multihousehold units, 88, 98–107
agricultural dependence, 40
agricultural intensification, 110, 111, 112, 113, 162, 207
agricultural system, collapse of, 110
agriculture in Southwest, evolution of Mimbres agriculture, 111; origins of, 111
air vents, 44, 62, 73, 77, 79, 94
akchin agriculture, 111, 217
altars, 33, 38, 49, 76
Amerind Foundation, 13, 14
Anasazi tradition, xiii, 4, 5, 11, **13**, 56, 70, 80, 112, 199; burials in trash mounds, 95; and graded metates, 123; pueblos of, 95
andesite/basalt, 195, 196, 199
Andrews, Rhonda, 205
Anyon, Roger, 51, 138, 139
Apaches, 10, 17
archaeomagnetic dating, **19**, 33, 34, 47, 91, 152
Archaic period, 5, 22, 25
architectural chronology, 91
architecture, xiii, xvi, 55; changes in, xiii, 40, 41; and community structure, 88; and erosion, 96; pithouse, 22; rooms with civic and ceremonial roles, 35; and signs of deterioration, 8; symbolism expressed in, 210, 215; "Transitional period", 43
Arikara people, 168, 172

arrow points, 149, 154, 196, **197**, 198, 208; corner-notched, 129, 152, 154
Arroyo Hondo, 172
artifacts, 79; and chronological associations, 194; fiber, 204–6; shell, 112
artiodactyls, 203; exploitation of, **128**
ash deposits, 29, 49, 80
atlatls, 6, 23, 38, 196, 198
awls, 67, 80, 123, 203, **203**
axes, 75, 76, 80, 123, 149, 196, 200–1, **200**, 208
Aztecs, 212

Baca ruins, 57
Baker, Barry, 134
Bali, 131
Bandelier, Adolph, 10, 11, 16–17, 86, 112, 116
basketry, 204–5
Beaglehole, Ernest, 85
beans, 6, 22, 24, 40, 118
Beaugard site, 126
Beloit College, 11
benches, 76, 77, **78**, 78, 105
Bettison, Cynthia, 15
bins, 59, 70; mealing, 95, 199–200; metate, 123
bioarchaeology, 163–73
Black Mesa, 170
Black Mountain phase, 117, 132
bones, 146, 154, 155, 158, 169; as raw material for tools, 203–4, 208
bowls, mortuary, 208; size of, 124, **125**; use of, 190
bows and arrows, 38, 129, 194, 196, 198
Bradfield, W., 136, 156, 206
Brockmann, John, 11, 16, 94

Brody, J. J., 38
Burden, Damon, 33, 49, 78
burials, 32, 45, 46, 74, 75, 120, 135–62; age and sex distribution, **165**; of animals, 43, 86, 98, 135, 159–61, **160, 161**; artifacts associated with, **30**, 30; beneath floors, 7, 8, 11, 29, 32, 37, 38, 46–47, 50, 63–64, 65, 68, 69, 72, 76, 80, 89, 92, 140; body orientation by phase, **148**; body positions, 6, 146, **147**, 156; Circle Three phase pattern, 50; in Classic Mimbres phase, 155–59; comparison of animal assemblages at Wind Mountain and NAN Ranch Ruin, 161; data on, **141–45**; direction of bodies, 147; distribution of age categories by phase, **148**; distribution of rock cairns over graves, **149**; distribution of sexed adults by phase, **149**; extramural, 37; and "killed" mortuary vessels, 150; in Late Three Circle phase, 153–55; number of vessels per burial by phase, **150**; outdoor, 30, 38, 50; per hearth type, **70**; in plazas and courtyards, 89; spatial analysis of, 139; in Three Circle phase, 151–53; types by phase, **146**; in upper Gila Valley compared to Mimbres Valley, 138
burnishing, 175, 176
Burro Mountains, 111

cairns, 64, 85, 138–39, **149**, 156, **200**; discarded metates and manos in, 199; stone, 147, **156**
Cameron, Catherine, 96
Cameron Creek Ruin, 21, 35, 42, 43, 70, 109, 112, 136, 139, 156, 159, 206
Camp Mimbres, 116
canals, 86, 113, 116
Canyon de Chelly, 5
Carr, Pat, 191
Casas Grandes culture, 36, 124, 172, 217
ceiling construction, 80
cemeteries, xiii, 7, 10, 52, 70, 132; bounded, 52, 131; indoor, 50; lineage, 50, 52, 89, 93, 95, 98, 110, 131, 140, 155; and residential space, 89; and spatial clustering, 140; subfloor, 40, 69, 70, 91. *See also* cremation cemeteries
ceramics. *See* pottery
ceremonial space, 26, 39
ceremonies, 132, 134, 162, 185, 193, 215; as attractor of outside people, 131, 189; importance of, 40; need for prestige items at, 220; and production of Style III pottery, 124, 221; use of pipes in, 202
Cerro Juanaquena site, 111
Chaco Canyon, 5, 56, 95
chalcedony, 4, 195, 201
channel erosion, 132, 221
check dams, 113, **113**

Cheno-Ams, 85, 116, 134; pollen counts from, 120
chert, 195, 196, 201
Chihuahuan Desert, 3, 4, 5, 25, 125, 191, 211
child/woman ratios, **167**
chronometric dating, 33
Cibola people, 5, 187, 188
civic-ceremonial rooms, 98
civic-communal rooms, 89
Classic Mimbres phase, 40, 47, 50, 51; aboveground construction in, 29; functional change for rooms in, 64; mortuary practices in, 155–59
clays, 175; analysis of, 177, 180
Cliff Palace, 70
climate change, 221
cloudblower pipes, **30**, 80
Clovis culture, 5
Clovis spear point, **5**
cobble-adobe, 43, 65, 91
cobbles, 65, 79, 81; tools made from, 196
coccidioidomycosis, 169, 170
Cochise, 10
Cocopa people, 52
Colorado Plateau, 5
community structure, four tiers of, 88–109
Convento phase, 36
Cooke's Peak, 4, 10, 16
Cooke's Range, 16, 178
coppicing, 57
coprolite, 120, 121
corn, 6, 7, 22, 24, 25, 37, 40, 68, 85, 110, 111, 118, 123, 152, 154, 157, 219; beer made from, 191; burned, 47, 48, 51, 76, 119, 121, 158, 206; and evolution of metates, 199; maiz de ocho variety, 37, 112; and mobility patterns, 125; new varieties of, 113, 218; roasting of, 85; shelling of, 203–4; stored, 121; storing shelled vs. on the cob, 122
corn pollen, 85
corporate extended family households, 88, 219; clustering of, 220
corporate kivas, 66, 71, 72, 99, **102**, 131, 140, 219; with attached storerooms, 75; distribution of, **99**; east-west orientation of, 95; and individual attributes, 69; and religious activities, 70, 78; subfloor storage pits in, 64; and venting problem, 74
Cosgrove, C. B., xiii, **xvi**, 12, 17, **17**, 51
Cosgrove family, 45, 46, 56, 72, 94, 98, 107, 206; Swarts Ruin burial location map, 136
Cosgrove, Harriet, 12, 17

Cosgrove, Hattie, 140
Cosgrove Jr., Burt, xiii, **xvi**, 12, 17, **17**
Cosgrove suite, 140, 152
cottontail, exploitation of, **128**
courtyard clusters, **31**, 39
courtyards, 82, 83
cradle boards, 171
craft specialization, 179
crawlways, 69, 74, 75, 89, 93, 99, 101, 105
Creel, Darrell, 14–15, 27, 87, 112, 132
cremation, 7, 8, 9, 10, 37, 50, 52, 83, 138, 202, 213; artifacts associated with, 51; four views of, **154**; in main plaza, 89; secondary, 86, 155, 214
cremation cemeteries, 34, 37, 39, 40, 49, 50, 51, 153, 157, 220; plan of, **153**
cremation pit, **152**
crystals, 49, **50**, 151
cultivars, 125–26

dart points, 25, 129, 196–98
dating challenges, 35, 113
dating methods, 91
deflector stones, 28, 33, 36, 43
Delk Ruin, 109; plan of, **108**
Deming Plain, 2, 4, 16, 57, 209
dendrochronology, 47, 91
dental disorders, **171**
dental health, 171–72
Di Peso, Charles, 13
diseases, infectious, 169
ditches, irrigation, 20, 114, 117; map of, **117**
Dockall, John, 195, 196, 198
Doña Ana phase, 15, 112, 117
doors and doorways, 62, **63**
Dozier, E. P., 89
drying racks, 81

earth ovens, 85
Earthwatch, xiv, xix
east room block, 126
Eby site, 136, 217
El Paso phase, 117
Elk Ridge, 178
Ellis, Florence, 140, 201
Ellis, Lain, 86, 112, 116
Emory (Lieutenant), 15
entrances, two types of, 44
Eskimos, 168

excavations, 11; at Lake Roberts Vista site, 15; at NAN Ranch Ruin, 14, 27; at Old Town Ruin, 27; of Saige-McFarland site, 13; of Treasure Hill, 12; at Wind Mountain, 13–14; of Y-Bar site, 24

faunal exploitation, 126
feasting, 124, 129, 131, 132, 134, 185, 193, 220, 221
Fewkes, Jesse, 2, 11, 14, 17, 135, 136, 139; burial drawing by, **136**
fiber, 204–6
fiesta pots, 124
fish, bones of, 126; as images on pottery, 129
Fitting, James, 13, 15
floor assemblages, 37, 44, 75, 76
floor vaults, 62, 70, 71, 101, 140, 212
floors, 48, 69; adobe, 76, 80; and ash deposits, 29, 49; features of, **102**; sunken, **42**, 43, 44
folklore, 40
food, changes in processing facilities, 112; as power, 110; production of, 109; surpluses of, 110, 113, 134, 192, 218, 222
Forest Home, 6, 111
Fort Bayard, 10
Fort Cummings, 10
Fort Webster, 10
Fort West, 10
fossil pollen, 115–16, 117

Galaz Ruin, 21, 35, 42, 43, 51, 109, 123, 126, 136, 139, 172, 178, 200, 220; mortuary patterns at, 138
Gavilan Canyon, 14, 17, 112, 113, 114, 120; main ditch of irrigation system, **115**, **116**
Gavilan Canyon, Battle of, 10
genetic affiliation, 172
Georgetown phase, 7, 13, 21, 27, 30, 40; and burials, 151; consumption of maize during, 122
Geronimo, 10
Gila Wilderness, 2, 13, 57, 132, 201, 216
Gilman, Patricia, 139
Glycymeris shell bracelets, 51, 64, 149, 150, 154, 157, 159, 206, 207
gophers, exploitation of, **128**
Gran Quivira, 204
granaries, 44, 48, 64, 65, 68, 75, 76, 85, 89, 93, 94, 98, 112, 121, 132; identification of, 122; surface, 47
Grasshopper area, 56, 167, 168, 172
Grasshopper Pueblo, 203
graves, artifacts in, 147, 149

Graybill, Donald, 13
Guatemala, 203

habitation rooms, 66, 70, 89, 95; artifacts found in, 66–67; features of, 69; and hearths, 65; size of, 66; subfloor storage pits in, 64
Ham, Elizabeth, 105, 139
Harris Village, 13, 35
Harvard University, 12
hatchways, ceiling, 41–42, **44**, 44, 48, 62, **64**, 66, 76, 94, 133; as metaphor for layered universe, 212
Haury, Emil, xiv, 13
Hawikkuh, excavation of, 12
hearths, 37, 44, 46, 65, **70**, 70, 75, 77, 78, 79, 89, 93, 133, 134; and adobe-lined pits, 84; changes in design and location of, 43; compartmentalized, 101; construction of, **59**; and domestic function, 45; kinds of, 36, 43, 59; sizes of, 59; slab-lined, **44**
Hegmon, Michelle, 15
Herrington, LaVerne, 109, 112, 113, 114, 219
Hill, Mara, 107, 139, 140
Hinton, Margaret, xiii, xix
Hodge, F. W., 12
Hohokam tradition, xiii, 4, 5, 8, 11, **13**, 39, 52, 172, 188, 202; and adobe-mixing pits, 84; and channel erosion, 132
Holliday, Diane, 105, 168–71, 172
Holloway, Richard, 116
Hopi Indians, 140, 177; architecture of, 96
Hot Springs site, 35
Hueco Bolson site, 181
Huichol people, 54, 212
hunting, 25, 38, 126–29
Hyland, David, 205, 206

iconography, 211
Indian Knoll, Kentucky, 168
inheritance, changes in rules of, 22
instrumental neutron activation analysis (INAA), 177, **179**, 181, 215, 221
iron (in diet), 169
irrigation agriculture, xiii, xvi, 5, 7, 16, 55, 110, 131, 134, 185, 189, 222; destabilization of, 216; labor requirements for, 88; and reorganization of Mimbres social groups, 22; societal reorganization around, 218

jackrabbit innominates, 203–4, **204**; distribution by room, **205**

jackrabbits, 4, 38, 129, 191, 203; exploitation of, **128**
jar size, 124
jewelry, 4, 38, 49, 109, 135, 139, 150, 158, **206**, 206–7, 208
Jornada people, 5, 15, 117, 119, 187, 188
Jornada phase, 117, 188
juniper trees, 4, 57, 72, 73; pollen from, 121, 122; stumps of, 200; support posts made from, 80

Katcina ceremonies, 214, 221
Katcina worship, 131
Kidder, A. V., 12, 51, 55, 56
"killed" bowls, 7, 9, 50, 80, 86, **137**, 153, 158, 213, 219, 221; popular ideas for purpose of hole in, 140; rain-bringing rituals, 131
kilns, 177
kinship groups, redefinition and reorganization of, 22
kivas, 9, 14–15, 49, 64, 131, 191; great kiva at NAN Ranch Ruin, 33, 47; great kiva at Y-Bar site, 23; key-shaped, 95; painted lines in, **35**; proposed model of, **213**; rituals and redware, 182. *See also* corporate kivas
knives, chipped stone, **201**, 201–2
Kus, Susan M., 105, 139

Ladder Ranch project, 15, 178
ladder rests, 62, **63**, 66, **70**, 72, 104
Lake Roberts Vista site, 35, 178, **180**; excavation of, 15
Lampbright Draw, 112, 113
land rights, 9
LeBlanc site, 51
LeBlanc, Steven, xiv, 13, 138, 139
Lekson, Steve, 15
lineage households, 88–89, 90–98, 101, 109, 123, 158
lineage ranking, 105
lineage rights, 88
Lyle, Robyn, 190

maize, 169
Mangas Colorado, 10
manos, 67, 112, 122–23, 149, 156, 194, 198–200, **199**, **200**, 203, 207–8
Marek, Marianne, 167–68
matrilineal corporate groups, 140
Mattocks site, 8, 21, 70, 109, 126, 129, 136, 139, 200, 201, 219, 220
Maya World Tree, 212
McAnally site, 22
McIntyre, A. J., 138

McSherry Ruin, 57, 70, 136, 178, **180**, 180, 214, 217
Mesa Verde, 5, 70
metates, 67, 80, 112, 122–23, 149, 156, **157**, 174, 194, 198–200, **199**, **200**, 203, 207, 208
Mexico, xiv, 2, 5, 36, 52, 53, 111, 191, 194, 208, 212, 217
microseriation, 139
Mimbres, origin of word, 1
Mimbres archaeology, commercial destruction of, 13; contemporary study compared to earlier studies, xiv; history of, 11–20; use of new tools, xiv
Mimbres art, market for, 11
Mimbres ecology, xiv
Mimbres Foundation, xiii, xiv, 13, 14, 22, 55, 118, 120, 126, 129, 133, 134, 139; model of Mimbres subsistence, 111
Mimbres Mountains, 2
Mimbres River, 16, **17**, 30, 57, 112, 114; landscape of, 216
Mimbres Salado people, 52
Mimbres society, abandonment of towns, 217; belief in layered universe, 140, 211; bioarchaeology of, 163–73; change from mobile to sedentary villages, xvi; contemporary uses of designs and motifs from, 1; death rates, 166; decorative pottery of, 1, 12; diet of, 117–25, 168, 171, 172, 199; effect of irrigation agriculture upon, 22; egalitarianism of, 105; and family, 192; interaction with Salado culture, 10; lack of exchange of ceramics with Anasazi, 5; landscape degradation as factor in collapse of, 13; physical characteristics, 163; popular misconception of poor architecture in, 56; reorganization of, 55, 110; restructuring of, 151; significance of pottery, 174; social fabric different from Anasazis, 56; social hierarchy, 105; worldview and cosmology, xvi, 140, 210, 212, 215
Mimbres towns, **9**
Mimbres Valley, **3**, 14, 163, 178, 181, 209; flora and fauna of, 4; geographical and geological description of, 2–4; mineral resources of, 3–4; population changes in, xiv
Minnis, Paul, 118, 126, 131, 133, 216
Mitchell site, 126
mobility, 37
Mogollon Plateau, 2
Mogollon tradition, xiii, 4, 11, **13**, 56, 112
Mogollon Village, 13
Montezuma site, 126
mortality rates, **167**, 167
mortar, stone effigy, **157**
mortuary customs, xvi, 64, 86, 104, 135–62; 215; changing, 50; myths about, 135; and subsistence, 135

motifs, 191, 210, 220, 221; anthropomorphic, 38, 183, 184, 214; clustering at specific sites, 181, 215; eye, 214; and mythology, 215; naturalistic, 183, 190; square, 181; zoomorphic, 38, 183, 184, 214
Moulard, Barbara, 213, 221
multilineage communities, 109
mythology, 40, 191

NAN 6, 14
NAN 15, 8, 14, 109, 178, **180**, 190, 219; plan of, **108**
NAN 20, 115
NAN 37, 115
NAN 57, 195
NAN Ranch Ruin, 15–16, 21, 129, 180, 181; aerial view of, xiv; animal burials at, **160**; animal species recovered from, **127**; and Black Mountain phase sites, 217; burial data, 141–45; composite life tables, **164**; condition in June 1978, **16**; dating techniques used at, 18–20; demographic characteristics, 166; excavations by Cosgroves at, 13, 17; excavations from 1978 through 1989, 14; first pithouses at, 27; history of investigations, 16–20; importance of investigations at, xiii; infant mortality, 166; and instrumental neutron activation analysis, 178; life expectancy, 163, 166; naming of, xiii; pithouse rooms at, 27; pithouse villages at, 26; plants from, 119; projectile points from, **197**; rise and decline of Mimbres culture at, xiv; room data, 60–61; site maps, xv, **98**; south room block, 55, 89; trade wares list from, **189**; transitional structures, **41**; vaults, **70**. See also burials; habitation rooms; *rooms by number*; south room block; storage rooms
Nana (Apache chief), 10, 16–17; subfloor pits, 63
neck banding technique, 30
Nelson, Margaret, 15, 38, 187
Nelson, Nels, 11
Nesbitt, Paul H., 136, 139
"new archaeology", xiv
North House, 140

obsidian, 4, 195
obsidian hydration dating, 19, **20**, 33, 91
obsidian points, 51
occipital lesions, **170**
Old Town Ruin, 2, 14, 21, 35, 39, 42, 57, 94, 109, 129, 132, 136, 159, 170, 178, 180, 181, 204, 216, 220; clustering of rooms at, 91; pithouse courtyard cluster at, 26; pithouse structure at, **14**; and tcamahias, 201; Three Circle phase pithouses at, 27

292 / INDEX

Olive, Ben, 171, 172, 173
oracles, 214, 221
Osborne, E. D., 2, 11, 14
overpopulation, 111

paho sticks (prayer sticks), 51, 158, 161
palettes, 202, **202**
Parks-Barrett, Maria, 206
Patrick, Suzanne, 163, 165–67, 172
Peabody Museum of Archaeology and Ethnology, 11, 12, 17
Peebles, Christopher S., 105, 139
Pendleton Ruin, 51
petates, 76
petroglyphic analysis, 177, 178, 181
petroglyphs, 40, 53, 149, 156, **157**, 199, 214
Pima sites, and adobe-mixing pits, 84
pins, 203, **203**, 208
pipes, tubular stone, 151, 201, 202, **202**
pit containers, 122
pithouse communities, 21–39; and agricultural subsistence, 22; changes in location of, 22
pithouse to pueblo transition, 210, 212; forms of change during, 40
pithouse villages, 5–6, **26**, 91; archaeological indications of, 23; first, 22; great kivas as common structure in, 35; number of structures in, 25; size in San Francisco phase, 28
pithouses, **14**; architectural changes in, 7; architectural characteristics, 22; clustering of, 31; domicile, 28, 32; entryways of, 24; facing central courtyard, 27; movement out of, completed, 8; as precursor to pueblos, 21; round, 21, 25; schematic profile of, **21**, **42**; seasonal, short-term use, 22, 24; shapes during San Francisco phase, 28; uses for, 28
pits, adobe-lined extramural, 84; for adobe mixing, 83, **83**, 98; burial, 120; quarry, 98; roasting, 85, **85**, 98, 120; storage, 64, 120; uses for, 84
plants, dietary and ritual use of, 120
plazas, 26, 82, 83; dual role for, 84
pollen, 85; analysis of, 120–21; background, 120; distribution of, 119–20. *See also* fossil pollen
Ponderosa Ranch site, 35, **180**
Popal Vuh, 211
population, estimates of, **8**, 55; increases in, 22, 133, 174, 188; and overpopulation, 111; peak, 132; shifting, 15, 38, 109, 187
population growth, 7, 23, 25, 55

population pressures, 13
porches, 81
postholes, 28, 29, 35–36, 43, 44, 45, 48, 49, 69, **71**, 77, 78
posts, 57, 76, 79
potholes, 105
pot-polishing stones, **175**
potters, 121, 215; Hohokam, 38; Mimbres, 123; and pottery design, 176, 181; and use of Hohokam designs, 112; women, 32, 177
pottery, 11, 28, 174–93; association with food production, 123; and bottle gourd model, 7; breakage, 190; and composition of clays, 174; and dating, 32; design layouts, 38; effigy jars, 191; elaborateness of, 38; embellishments of, 186; end of Mimbres Black-on-white pottery tradition, 185; fish images on, 129; and microstyles, 91, 92, 93, 95, 101, 140, 146, 174, 181, 182, 184, 214; Mimbres scenes depicting subsistence pursuits on, **130**; painted, 28, 38, 40, 134, 138, 140, 188; as prestige items, 189, 190; production of, 174–81; reconstructed vessel forms, **24**; and signs of deterioration, 8; and symbolism, 38–39, 140; trade, 187–88; use of naturalistic and geometric designs, 2, 8, 191, 193; use-wear studies, 139; varied uses of, 123; and women, 32, 177. *See also* "killed" bowls; vessels
pottery, by type, Alma Neck Banded, 186, **250**; Alma Neck Banded jar, 29, 30, **185**; Alma Plain, 138, 181, **185**, **250**; Alma Plain jar, 29; Alma Scored, 186; black-on-white, 1–2, 4, 7; brownware, 6; Chihuahua indented corrugated jar, 76; Chihuahua orangeware, 188, **188**; Chihuahua polychromes, 10; Chihuahua rubber incised, **188**; Cibola Whitewares, **187**; Convento Corrugated jar, 124; Convento Indented Corrugated, 216, **255**; Convento Indented Corrugated jar, 188; Convento Rubber Incised, 188; El Paso Bichrome, **187**, 216; El Paso Bichrome jars, 76; El Paso Brown, 53, 187; El Paso Brownware, 187, **187**; El Paso Polychrome, 9, 10, **187**; El Paso Red-on-brown, 124, 187, **255**; with flared rims, 186; Fully Corrugated, **185**, **251**–**54**; Fully Corrugated Pitchers, **185**; Gila Polychrome, 10; hemispherical bowls, 182, 184; Jornada Brownware, 112; Mimbres Black-on-white jars, 184; Mimbres Black-on-white, three major styles of, 182; Mimbres Boldface, 12, 38; Mimbres Boldface Black-on-white, 52; Mimbres Brownware bowls, **249**; Mimbres Brownware jars, **249**; Mimbres Brownware pinch bowls, **249**; Mimbres Brownware series, 181–87; Mimbres Classic Black-on-white, 12; Mimbres Classic bowls, 51; Mimbres Corrugated, 214; Mimbres early Style II, **224**; Mimbres early Style II Black-on-white, 32;

Mimbres early Style II bowls, 32; Mimbres early Style III bowls, **232**; Mimbres early Style III seed jars, **232**; Mimbres early Style III vessels, **230–31, 233**; Mimbres Fully Corrugated, 186; Mimbres Fully Corrugated bowls, **247**; Mimbres Fully Corrugated jars, 76; Mimbres late Style III, **243–45**; Mimbres middle-late Style III, **242**; Mimbres middle-late Style III effigy jars, **246**; Mimbres middle-late Style III flare-rim bowls, **245–46**; Mimbres middle-late Style III vessels, **237–41**; Mimbres middle Style III Black-on-white, 68; Mimbres middle Style III vessels, **233–39**; Mimbres miniature effigy jars, **247**; Mimbres miniature Style III jars, **247**; Mimbres Partially Corrugated, **185, 255**; Mimbres Partially Corrugated jars, 75, 76; Mimbres plain brownware, 52; Mimbres plain brownware vessels, **249**; Mimbres polished redware seed jar, 152; Mimbres Red-filmed seed jar, 49; Mimbres Red-slipped brownware, 52, 53, 181; Mimbres Red-slipped ware, 182; Mimbres Redware, 35, 52, 187, **224**; Mimbres Redware bowls, 50, 53; Mimbres Redware jar, **50**; Mimbres Style I, 32, 35, 38, 49, 182, **224**; Mimbres Style I Black-on-white, 174; Mimbres Style I bowls, 32, 33, 151; Mimbres Style I bowls (smashed), 151; Mimbres Style I jars, 32; Mimbres Style I jars (unfired), 151, **152**; Mimbres Style I seed jars, 32, 151–52; Mimbres Style II, 8, 35, 49, 53, 72, 178, 182–84, 214; Mimbres Style II Black-on-white, 42, 43, 48, 52, **225–27**; Mimbres Style II bowls, 46, 50; Mimbres Style II fish effigy created from bowl sherd, **247**; Mimbres Style II jars, 43, **228**; Mimbres Style II to III, **228, 229**; Mimbres Style II variant, **228**; Mimbres Style II vessels, 92, 98, 129, 154; Mimbres Style III, 15, 46, 49, 53, 72, 74, 97, 101, 112, 114, 115, 178, 184, 214; Mimbres Style III Black-on-white, 69, 179, **180**; Mimbres Style III Black-on-white jars, 75, 76; Mimbres Style III bowls, 53, 67, 68, 74, 76, 101, 122, 157, **176**, **229**; Mimbres Style III flare-rim bowls, 75, 79, 184; Mimbres Style III jars, 64, 74, 122, **247, 248**; Mimbres Style III lid bowls, 64; Mimbres Style III plates, 80; Mimbres Style III Polychrome, 179, **245**; Mimbres Style III seed bowls, 184; Mimbres Style III seed jars, 67, **247**; Mimbres Style III vessels, 98, 129; Mimbres Style III white-slipped bowls, **248, 249**; Mimbres Style III white-slipped seed jars, **249**; Mogollon Red-on-brown, 28, 29, 38, 175, 182; Mogollon Red-on-brown jar covers, 51; necked jars, 182; neckless or tecomate jars, 182; plain brownware boat-shaped bowls, 152; plain brownware bowls, 32; plain narrow-necked jars, 75; plain/textured and slip/painted, 124; plainware bottles, 75; Playas Red, 9, 10, **188**, 188, 217; Puerco Black-on-white, 187, **187**, **255**; punctated mugs, 152; Ramos Polychrome, 9; Red Mesa Black-on-white, 53, 187, **187, 255**; Sacaton Red-on-buff, 53, **188**, 188; Salado Red, 10; San Francisco Red, 30, 53, 138, 181; seed jars, 191; smudged brownwares, 188; St. Johns Polychrome, 9; textured brownware, 181; Three Circle Neck Corrugated, 43, 52, **185, 250–51**; Three Circle Neck Corrugated jars, 32, 33, 186; Three Circle Neck Corrugated pitcher, 155; Three Circle Red-on-white, 29, 38, 174, 182; Three Circle Red-on-white tecomate jars, 29; Tucson Polychrome, 10; unembellished plain brownware, 181; Villa Ahumada Polychrome, 9, **188**, 188; white-slipped brownware, 181; whiteware bowls, 33

Powell, Valli, 161

prestige items, 189, 190, 200, 201, 220–21

Prewitt Ranch site, 57, 217

projectile points, 23, 196–98

pueblo communities, and agricultural subsistence, 22

Puebloan Tradition, 11

pueblos, 210; architectural characteristics, 22; building and abandoning, 10; preceded by pithouses, 21; weathering of, 56

quartz crystals, 202, 206

radiocarbon dating, 19, 20, 113, 114, 115, 116, 118

rain bringing, 130, 215

rainfall patterns, **133**

ramadas, 81

ramps, 44

ram's horn tenon, 80, **80**

Ravesloot, John, 132, 216

reciprocity, 110

relic hunters, 12, 14, 17, 69, 76, 98, 101, 140, 146

religion, 9

Reserve Filet Rim, 9

reservoirs, 86, 114, 116; map of, **117**

residences, xiii

rhyolite, 4, 199, 201

rhyolite slabs. *See* Sugarlump rhyolite slabs

Rio Arenas Valley, 109

Rio de Arenas, 112, 113, 219

rituals, 162, 182, 202, 215, 220

roads, 15

rock art, **53**, 214; dating of, 53

roofs, 45

room 1, 105

room 2, 200

room 3, 105

room 4, 105

room 5, 105, 202

room 7 (granary), **75**, 76, 105, 122, 158

room 8, 62, 84, 85, 105, 107, 159, 202; floor plan of, **104**

room 9, 62, 69, **104**, 105, **106**, 107, 203; as communal room, 76; floor plan of, **106**

room 10, 67, **104**, 105, 107

room 11, 64, 107, 206

room 12, 36, 37, 41, 45, 50, 59, 62, 66, 67, **70**, 71, 72, 74, 78, 83, 84, 98, 152, 153, 203; floor plan, **71**; hearth in, **59**; schematic profile, **71**; wall shelves in, **72**

room 13, 41, 43

room 14, 31, 32, 37, 51, 121, 151, 152, 162, 177, 205, 206

room 15, 31

room 16, 62, 107, 158, 199, 203; schematic profile of, **66**

room 17, 31, 36, 153

room 18, 80, 107, 203

room 22, 64, **67**, 67, 107; floor plan, **68**; as habitation room, 67

room 23, 67, 107

room 23A, 64, 146

room 23B, 41

room 24, 82, 107

room 25, 64, 67, 84, 107; schematic profile of, **66**; wall fall in, **58**

room 25A, 62, 83

room 25B, 82, 83; walled bin in, **66**

room 26, 67, 105

room 28, 62, 64, 67, 68, 69, 90, 93, 94, 95, 96, 97, 155, 156, 203, 206; floor plan, **69**; as habitation room, 67, 68–69

room 28B, 68

room 29 (corporate kiva), 59, 62, 64, 66, 68, 69, 71, 74, 75, 79, 80, 90, 92, 93, 94, 95, 96, 97, 123, 146, 155; and axes, 200; floor plan of, **73**; hearth and floor vault in, **59**; metapodial specimen recovered in, 203; and metates, 199; polychrome vessel in, 107; and tcamahias, 201

room 29A, 72, 73

room 29B, 73, 74

room 32, 62

room 35, schematic profile of, **66**

room 36, 161

room 37, 59, 82, 107

room 39, 58, 59, 62, 75, **78**, 81, 84, 92, 94, 95, 96, 123, 158, 200, 202; and axes, 200; floor plan, **79**; metapodial specimen recovered in, 203; schematic profile of, **46**; and women's ritual activities, 80

room 40, 47, 62, 99, 105, 121; cache found beneath floor, 122; with interior vertical support posts, **58**

room 41, 59, 62, 66, 69, 75, 80, 84, 95, 98, 99, **100**, 100, 161, 188; seeds from, **122**; and subfloor pits with large jars, 122

room 42, 58, 59, 62, 75, 99, **100**, 122, 155, 158, 187, 200; floor plan of, **74**

room 43, 33, 36, 37, 41, 42, 48, 201, 219

room 45, 100, 202; double-wall construction in, 80; floor plan of, **81**

room 46, 47, 105, 123, 199; and subfloor pits with large jars, **64**, 122

room 47, 47, 62, 67, 82, 98, 101, **103**, 107, 157, 207; ceiling hatchway fall in, **64**

room 48, 34, 47, 62, 80, 98, 99, 100, 105, 107, 122

room 49, 62, 69, 98, 101, **103**, 107, 157, 159, 201

room 50, 62, 82, 98, 101, **103**, 107, 157, 203

room 51 (granary), 41, 43, **47**, 47, 107, 119, 122

room 52 (great kiva), 33, 37, 47, 48, 50, 122, 153, 182, 187, 219; and accelerator mass spectrometer dating, **35**; floor plan and overhead view of, **34**

room 54, 62, 76, 101, **103**, 159, 160

room 55, 59, 62, 66, 69, 75, 81, 82, 95, 98, 101, **102**, 158; overhead view of, **57**

room 56, 98, 101, **102**

room 57, 41, 43, 45, 50, 159, 160

room 58 (communal), 41, 43, 45, 62, 64, 67, 69, 76, **78**, 78, 98, 99, 105

room 59, 72, 78, 82

room 60, 62, 75, 82, 95, 98, 101, **102**, 155, 158, 159

room 61, 41, 43, 45, 159, 160

room 62, 51, 59, 66, 69, 98, **101**, 101, 200, 203

room 63, 62, 64, 67, 107, 200, 203, 206

room 63A, 75

room 63B, 62

room 64, 158

room 65, 82

room 67, 107

room 71 (round pit), **36**, 36

room 74, 216

room 74 (communal room), 59, 76, 77, 84, 100, 124, 187, 200, 205, 206

room 75, 64, 67; schematic profile of, **66**

room 75A (granary), **75**, 76

room 75B, 64, 76

room 75C, 64, 153

room 76 (granary), 48, 76, 98, 119, 122, 159, 207

room 76A, 41, 43
room 76B, 43, 45, 47, 76
room 78, 58, 59, 75, 79, 203
room 79, 62, 75, 95, 153, 200; schematic profile of, **46**
room 79A, 62, 72, 75, 76, 122
room 79B, 41, 43, 45, 92, 93, 94, 95
room 80, 41, 43, 45
room 80A, 62
room 81, 76, 107
room 82, 41, 43, 45, 82, 84, 107, 156, 159, 160
room 83, 31, 32, 41, 42, 83, 159; floor plan of, **33**
room 83A, 42, 151
room 83B, 31, 32, 36, 37, 42
room 84, 59, 62, 76, 89, **101**, 156, 216
room 84A, 43, 100, 107
room 84B, 101
room 85, **101**, 101, 123, 199, 200
room 86, 29–30, 31, 36, 37, 151, 202; artifacts from, **30**; floor plan of, **30**
room 88, 84
room 89, 48, 50, 98; plan of, **45**
room 89A, 48, 146, 153, 159, 160
room 89B, 41, 43, 45, 48
room 90, 59, 62, 79
room 91, 41, 43, 48, 83, 107, 182, 202, 206; ash deposits in, **49**; floor and subfloor map of, **49**; overhead view of, **48**
room 92, 81, 89, **90**, 107
room 93, 81, 89, **90**, 158
room 94, 62, 67, 94, 95, 96, 97, 123, 157, 199, 203
room 95, **27**, 28, 29, 31, 36, 121, 151, 203, 205; floor plan of, **29**
room 96, 159
room 97, **27**, 41, 43, 45
room 98, 41, 43, 45, 92, 93, 95, 153, 207
room 99, **27**, 37, 41, 43, 151
room 100, **27**, 28, 206
room 101, 41, 43, 92, 93; schematic profile of, **46**
room 102, 31, 32, 33, 36, 91; overhead view of, **33**; schematic profile of, **46**
room 103, 31, 36, 91, 202
room 104, 41, 43, 45, 91, 92, 93, 95, 123, 153, 199, 219; schematic profile of, **46**
room 105, **27**, 28
room 106, 91, 93, 94, 123
room 108, 62, 199
room 108A, 76, 94

room 108B, 31, 36, 91
room 109 (storage), 31, 59, 76, 78, 84, 85, 92, 94, 159, 203
room 110, 161
room 111, 94
room 112, 41, 43, 153
room 113, 31, 36, 37, 207
room 115, 36, 41, 43, 92
room 116, 31, 36, 37, 41, 42, 91, 92
room 117, 36, 37
rooms, changes in function, 44, 64, **65**; civic-ceremonial, 44, 48; determining function of, 59; domestic, 44; with floor vaults, **98**; profile of sunken floor, **42**; schematic profile of, **46**; use life of, 96
Roth, Barbara, 15

Saige-McFarland site, 15, 21, 70, 109, 178; excavation of, 13
Salado culture, 10
Salmon ruins, 167
San Francisco phase, 7, 13, 21, 29–30, 35, 40; and burials, 151; consumption of maize during, 122
Sanchez, Julie, 126, 129, 134
Sapillo Creek Ruin, 178
Schaafsma, Polly, 53
School of American Research, 11, 12
sedentism, short-term, 10
Shaffer, Brian, 126, 129, 134, 204, 208
shamans, 25–26, 162
sherd paint palette, **175**
sherd scrapers, **175**
sherds, 49, 53, 67, 74, 76, 80, 85, 112, 149, 158, 178; in grave pit fill, 146, 151, 155; Mimbres Style III, 115; worked, 151, **151**
shrines, 53, 70, 72, 74, 182, 191; lineage, 7
single-family households, 88, 89
sipapus, 33, 49, 70, 212
slips, 176; red slips, 181, 182; white slips, 182
Smithsonian Institution, 2
social differentiation, 105, 139, 173
social grouping, 27
social interaction, 220
social organization, 88–109; matrilineal, 107, 220
social unity, 88
sodalities, 150, 159, 207, 208, 214
sotol stalks, 24
southeast midden area, **90**

south room block, 31, **55**, **93**, 129, 140, 168, 172, 173, 219; burials in, 95; construction sequence, **93**; death rate, 97; deaths per year, 96; faunal remains in, 126; importance of, 89; inferred number of generations, 97; plan of, **91**; thickness of walls, 90

Southwest Museum of Los Angeles, 11, 51, 138

space, domestic use of plaza, 84; exterior, 82; outdoor, 82; ritual, 130; roof, 82

squash, 6, 22, 24, 25, 40, 64, 111, 118

squash seeds, **122**

stone tools, 194–204

storage rooms, 75–76, 78; east-west orientation of, 95; subfloor storage pits in, 64

stratigraphy, 92, 95, 105, 113, 139, 151, 156; burial, 93, 153

strip mining, 13

subfloor caches, 64, 120; seeds from, **122**

subfloor pits, 37, 75

subfloors, features of, **102**; reinforced, 122

Sugarlump rhyolite slabs, 57, **57**, 59, 82, 92, 159, 196, 209; in cairns, 156; framing air vents with, 62; framing hearths with, 65; used as ceiling, 80; used as door, 73, 195; used as grave cappings, 157; used as subfloor pit covering, 122; used in shrine, 72

Superordinate/Subordinate Dimensional model, 139

Swarts Ruin, 21, 35, 43, 70, 98, 107, 109, 138, 139, 157, 172, 217, 219; animal burials at, 11, 159; clustering of corporate households at, 220; Cosgroves' description of mortuary practices at, 136; "dance plaza" at, 84; excavation of, **12**, 17, 56; and matrilineal corporate groups, 140; south house at, **137**; wall shelves at, 72

sweat baths, 49

symbolic resonance, 212

symbolism, 38, 40, 134, 140, 191–92, 207, 210, 211

tapiscadores, 203

tcamahias, 201, **201**

tecomates, 24

Teotihuacán, 214

Terminal Classic period, 8

terraces, stone-faced, 113

Texas A&M University, xiv, xvi, xix, 14, 17

textiles, 28, **204**, 204–6, 208; impressions of, **156**

Thompson site, 22

Three Circle phase, 7, 13, 21, 27, 29–30, 34, 35, 40–54, 121; aboveground construction in, 29; absence of formal granaries in, 37; architectural variability in, 36; and beginning of irrigation agriculture, 112; burials in, 151; changes in mortuary behavior in, 37; changes in symbolism during, 38; consumption of maize during, 122; pithouse structure from, **14**; significant changes in rituals and beliefs regarding the dead, 152; and village structure, 31

TJ Ruin, 94

"Tlaloc" eye motif, 53

tools, 194

towns, intercommunity network of, 88

transitional rooms, 91

trash, 95

Treasure Hill Ruin, 12, 72, 94

tree-ring dating, **18**, 34, 47, 65, 69, 76, 78, 80, 93, 95, 96, 97, 101, 133, 216; use of codes in, 264n. 11

tschamahia, 74

turkey pens, 65

Turner II, Christy, 172

ubiquity indices, 118

universe, layered, 211, 214, 215, 221; seven directions of, 211–12

University of Colorado, 11

University of Minnesota, 11, 51, 138

University of New Mexico, 13

vegetation, 57

vessels, **177**; ceramic, **2**; effigy, 182; intact, 151; mortuary, 64, 86, 138, 139, 140, 153, 190, 193, 206; process of making, 175; size and volume of, 123; smashed, 151, 158; use of, 124. *See also* pottery; pottery, by type

Victorio, 10

villages and social organization, 88

wall bases, 58

wall construction, 57, 82, 91

wall niches, 73, **73**, 74, 79

walls, 90; cobble-adobe, 43, 55, 58, 65, 82, 91; single and double coursed, 72; and wall-bonding patterns, 93

water control methods, 112–13; map showing, 114

water management system, failure of, 216–17
Waters, Michael, 132, 216
Webster, Clement, 11, 17, 94, 116, 135, 136, 139; burial drawing by, **136**
West Fork Ruin, 112
Wheaton Smith Ruin, 109, 219
Wind Mountain site, 51, 119; excavation at, 13–14; mortuary patterns at, 138
witchcraft, 52
women, as potters, 32, 177; and ritual activities, 80; and ritual space, 95; and use of metates, 194
Wood Canyon, 6, 111

Woodrow site, 178
woods for construction, 57, 134
Woolsey, A. I, 138
Wunder, Virginia, 17, 76

Y-Bar NAN Ranch site, 11, 14, 23–25; excavation of, 24; semisedentary lifestyle of inhabitants at, 24; site map, **23**

Zuni Indians, 177
Zuni Pueblo, 129